UNSTOPPABLE

Also by William B. Friedricks

Henry E. Huntington and the Creation of Southern California

Covering Iowa: The History of the Des Moines Register and Tribune Company, 1849-1985

In for the Long Haul: The Life of John Ruan

Investing in Iowa: The Life and Times of F.M. Hubbell

The Real Deal: The Life of Bill Knapp

Constructing a Legacy: The Weitz Company and the Family Who Built It

A Great State Fair: The Blue Ribbon Foundation and the Revival of the Iowa State Fair

With great respect *Roxanne Conlin*

UNSTOPPABLE
The Nine Lives of Roxanne Barton Conlin

WILLIAM B. FRIEDRICKS

bpc

ISBN-13: 978-1-950790-02-9
Library of Congress Control Number: 2020905931
Business Publications Corporation Inc., Des Moines, IA

Business Publications Corporation Inc.
The Depot at Fourth
100 4th Street
Des Moines, Iowa 50309
(515) 288-3336

CONTENTS

Foreword by Bonnie Campbell | vii
Acknowledgments | xi

INTRODUCTION: ON A MISSION | 3

ONE | 8
A Rocky Beginning

TWO | 28
Raising Her Consciousness

THREE | 42
Change Agent

FOUR | 69
Trailblazer

FIVE | 83
Exploratory Effort

SIX | 93
A Run for Governor

SEVEN | 119
Bouncing Back

EIGHT | 149
Hear Me Roar

NINE | 175
Taking on Icons

TEN | 212
Changing Pace

ELEVEN | 229
Ever the Advocate

CONCLUSION: NINE LIVES | 247

A Note on Sources | 253
Notes | 259
Index | 313

Photographs appear following pages 110 and 202

FOREWORD

Even before I moved to Iowa, I knew a few things about Roxanne Conlin. Her name and reputation as a political activist within the Iowa Democratic Party were well known around the Senate office of former Iowa governor and then-senator, Harold Hughes, where I was lucky enough to be working.

In February of 1974, my future husband, Ed Campbell, and I were moving to Iowa to work in a Democratic primary campaign for governor and later for the Senate campaign of former senator John Culver. As Ed and I were driving across Interstate 80 on what must have been the coldest, windiest day in all of recorded human history, I was fervently hoping that my decision to leave the Washington, DC, area where I had lived for nine years was a good one and that I would enjoy working in a campaign, a new experience for me.

That same year, 1974, Roxanne was on the campaign trail, too. She was leading the Iowa effort to ratify the Equal Rights Amendment to the U.S. Constitution, along with Mary Louise Smith, a well-known and well-regarded Republican. Soon after arriving in Iowa, I had the great pleasure of meeting Roxanne and seeing her in action firsthand. The opportunity to observe Roxanne at dozens (maybe hundreds) of political events and to get to know her personally, quite literally, changed my life. She became a dear friend, and, as any friend of Roxanne would tell you, her friendships are special and very important to her.

I thought I knew a lot about Roxanne's life, and, I did. After all, she has been a public figure for most of her life. But, after reading Roxanne's biography, I realized that, yes, I do know much about her life, both through our personal friendship and media coverage of her, but I never knew it all or put it all together. Very few people accomplish so much against such formidable odds and make it all look easy.

Roxanne Conlin is one amazing woman.

She is brilliant. She is nice. She is compassionate. She is a remarkably talented fighter for justice for individuals and whole classes of people being treated unfairly. She genuinely cares for others (humans and animals, especially kitties). She is generous of spirit and in her financial support for good causes. She is a wife, a mother, a sister, a grandmother, a friend to many, and the list goes on.

And, she is funny . . . very funny.

I have always loved Roxanne's sense of humor. After reading her life's story, I realized that humor is the thread that runs through her life and has made it possible for her to navigate a chaotic childhood, marry and raise a wonderful family to which she is fiercely devoted, become one of our nation's most distinguished lawyers, and be friends and mentors to so many. As she was leaving the U.S. attorney's position to which she was appointed by former President Jimmy Carter, Roxanne quipped: "U.S. attorneys serve at the pleasure of the President, and I did not please Ronald Reagan, but he didn't please me either."

My kind of humor – a little self-deprecating and right on target.

Often Roxanne uses her wonderful humor to show her friendship. I have two stories that I cherish.

When Roxanne ran for governor in 1982, she was in a three-way Democratic primary. One of her opponents was Ed Campbell, my (now-deceased) husband. On many occasions, I would represent Ed at events he was unable to attend and give my pitch for why he would be our party's best nominee. Roxanne, with a twinkle in her eye and affection in her voice, would introduce me and tell the Democrats in attendance that she didn't know for sure but did suspect that I would vote for her in the upcoming primary. Of course, I didn't, but, immediately after Roxanne's impressive victory in the primary, I contacted her campaign and happily volunteered until I started law school in the fall. Ed passed away in 2010 after surviving metastatic lung cancer for twenty-seven years; Roxanne was always there to comfort and console and, as is often the case, offer medical advice.

More recently, I received a call from Roxanne chastising me because I had failed to tell her that I was dating someone. Well, in my own defense, she was deeply immersed in one of her huge legal cases and it didn't seem to be a good time to just get together and chat. Our phone conversation started something like this: "How could you not share with me that you are seeing someone? Why did I have to hear this from other people? Tell me all about him so that I can check him out." Of course, this was Roxanne's humorous way of telling me that she was happy for me and wanting to get together so that we could get caught up with each other's lives. In May, 2018, I married that man, Mark Hamilton, whom I had known since we worked together in Senator Hughes's office in 1973. The good news is that Roxanne apparently approved of Mark and she and Jim attended our wedding.

That leads to my, and just about everyone else's, favorite story about Roxanne. She and Jim decided to get married after knowing each other for two days and they have been married for fifty-six years. I think that fact alone captures what I admire most about her, and Jim, for that matter.

But there is so much to admire about Roxanne Conlin. Her many outstanding qualities, including her decisiveness, dedication, passionate approach to everything she does and ability to persevere with grace and humor have propelled her forward and, as a result, have advanced our society. This captivating book is a compelling reminder of Roxanne's vast professional and personal contributions – a story of vision, determination and courage that inspires us all.

—by Bonnie Campbell

Acknowledgments

Like many others in Iowa, I was well aware of Roxanne Barton Conlin; I had followed her multifaceted career through the media since I moved to the state in 1988. I did not meet her until 2012, however, and then only briefly, when I interviewed her for my biography of real estate developer and philanthropist Bill Knapp. Meanwhile, I had gotten to know her sister-in-law, Judy Conlin, because we had served together on several committees. It was Judy who suggested I consider this project. I was immediately interested, and she put me in touch with Roxanne. After several conversations and nearly three years of research and writing, this book is the result.

Many people helped make this possible. Deb Palmer, Roxanne's legal secretary, and Angie Meyer, Roxanne's legal assistant, cheerfully answered my many questions and went through the firm's records for me. Roxanne's son, J.B., was invaluable. He sat for several interviews, dug up family information, suggested important people I should contact, and located photographs for me. I also appreciate the many others who provided me with information through interviews and telephone conversations or who opened their personal papers to me. I could not have written this book without their willingness to share their memories and recollections. A complete list of these individuals appears toward the end of the book.

Des Moines journalist Walt Shotwell started a biography of Roxanne in 2006 but abandoned the project the following year. Roxanne gave me copies of Shotwell's research notes and rough drafts of a couple of chapters that I found useful. Librarians and archivists were also generous with their knowledge and time. Special thanks to Claudia Frazer and Katherine Lincoln of Drake University's Archives and Collections, Kären Mason and Janet Weaver of the Iowa Women's Archives at the University of Iowa Libraries, Liz Grimsbo at Simpson College, and various reference librarians at Des Moines's Central Library.

Daryl Sasser, Linda Sinclair, and Levi Lefebure were especially accommodating in giving a little extra to help run the Iowa History Center while I focused on this book.

Once again, I was happy to work with the team at Business Publications Corporation. Suzanna de Baca oversaw the project, and Emily Schultz guided the manuscript through the publication process. This time around, I was particularly fortunate to have Holly Carver do the copyediting. A top-notch editor, Holly meticulously reviewed the manuscript, caught careless mistakes and silly typos, and made this a much better book.

I've been lucky to have had the unwavering support of my family. My daughters, Sarah and Emily, can't remember a time when I wasn't talking about my research and writing, and now son-in-law Kyle Essley patiently endures these conversations as well. I'm sure all three consider Roxanne a close friend by now. Jerry Crawford, my father-in-law, often personally knew the subjects of my books and enjoyed discussing them with me. Unfortunately, he did not live to see this one completed. I will miss his constant words of encouragement.

My biggest fan has always been my father. At the age of ninety-one, he moved here from southern California this past fall, and I was looking forward to seeing him regularly. Tragically, he died unexpectedly just three weeks after arriving in Iowa. I miss you, Dad. Thank you for all you've done for me.

My wife, Jackie Crawford, deserves my deepest gratitude and love. As usual, she nurtured me through this project with her generosity of spirit, patience, and understanding. And as always, she read and reread several drafts of the manuscript. Her critical questions and keen comments undoubtedly improved the narrative.

UNSTOPPABLE

Introduction: On a Mission

Elvis Presley, the pop star a young Roxanne Barton Conlin adored, became such a sensation that he did not require a last name. He was just Elvis. And so it was with Roxanne. "She's one of those people in this town who doesn't have a last name," wrote a longtime Iowa political commentator about Des Moines. "You just say 'Roxanne' and everyone knows who you're talking about."[1]

That was not always the case. Early in her career, Roxanne realized that people often did not hear her. As a female attorney, even well into the 1980s, she was usually the lone woman in a roomful of men, and when she spoke up her ideas were ignored, even when she presented them in her often booming voice. However, if a man offered the same ideas a moment later, they were regularly received as novel and interesting. Roxanne soon tired of this and decided that if colleagues did not hear her, she would be sure they saw her. One day in a meeting, when as usual she was the only woman, she stood up before she spoke. With all eyes focused on her, she addressed her colleagues. It worked, and Roxanne has been heard ever since.[2]

Passionately standing up for herself and for those around her was something Roxanne learned early in life. An alcoholic and abusive father dominated the Barton household. The oldest child, Roxanne stood up to her father, often intervening in violent situations to protect her mother, her brother, and her four sisters. This difficult home life gave her compassion for others, especially the most vulnerable and disadvantaged. Given this compassion and her boundless self-assurance, Roxanne grew up believing she could make a real difference. In the 1960 presidential campaign, for instance, the idealistic teenager put John Kennedy bumper stickers on cars and knocked on doors to encourage people to vote for him. When he won the election, Roxanne was certain she had put him in the White House.[3]

These attributes set her on a lifelong path of activism, where Roxanne fought against inequality and intolerance. It began when the socially aware fourteen-year-old joined the local chapter of the National Association for the Advancement of Colored People. She then became involved in the Polk County Young Democrats and has remained active in the party over the course of her life.

Roxanne was also driven to make money so she could escape the desperate straits she and her family experienced because of her father's inability to hold a job. Good advice convinced her to become a lawyer, which provided her the means to attain a growing number of her goals. Still in high school, she added a new aspiration to her list: Roxanne began telling people that she planned to be the governor of Iowa. From there, she could stand up for all Iowans while pushing the state in a more progressive direction. Most must have discounted this as the pipe dream of a naive youngster. It was no such thing for Roxanne. She did not have an exact timetable for her objective, but it remained prominent in her thinking.

Gifted intellectually, Roxanne breezed through school, and because she was often bored in class, she was a smart aleck. "I now cringe at how insufferable I must have been," she recalled. She qualified for a special program at sixteen and left high school at seventeen before graduating to start college. Soon out of the house and on her own, the goal-oriented Roxanne continued rushing through her life, finishing her undergraduate courses and law school by the time she was twenty-one.[4]

In the midst of this, she met her match. Jim Conlin walked into her life one evening and never left. He was the first man Roxanne did not intimidate, and he showed no signs of wanting her to back away from her feminist positions. She hurried here in romance as well, and the two were married fifteen days after their first encounter.

Being young and only one of the few women at Drake University's Law School, Roxanne knew discrimination firsthand. Law professors did not call on her in class, and she had trouble landing her first job in the field, even though fellow students remembered her as being among the brightest in her class. In rejecting Roxanne, one law firm explained, "We are not going to hire you because our clients will not take advice from a woman."[5]

She persevered. After brief stints at a couple of different jobs in law, Roxanne landed a job as an assistant state attorney general, starting on a part-time basis because she had two small children at home. Here she was able to exercise her passion for the underdog by heading the department's new civil rights division. Attorney General Richard Turner found her to be "a very fine lawyer" who was "dedicated to her job" and worked "hard." Colleagues would later agree with and expand on these comments. Brad Beaman, who clerked for Roxanne and is now a Des Moines attorney, captured the sentiments of many: "She's smarter than anyone, she outworks anyone, and she has more compassion than anyone."[6]

At the attorney general's office, Roxanne became a leading figure in the Iowa women's movement when she founded and then headed the Iowa Women's Political Caucus, the state chapter of the National Women's Political Caucus. The bipartisan organization fought for the rights of women and strove to increase their political participation and representation. It quickly became the largest and most influential women's group in the state. Through it, Roxanne worked to make Iowa laws on rape, inheritance, and welfare more favorable to women. For Linda Hanson, a young feminist at the time, Roxanne "loomed larger than life. We needed a revolution, and we had one with Roxanne."[7]

Her job and her efforts at the IWPC garnered Roxanne a lot of attention in the press. This continued with her pathbreaking achievement when she became the first of two women appointed as a U.S. attorney in 1977.

Meanwhile, there was a growing amount of talk that Roxanne would seek public office. In 1981, she moved to fulfill her dream of being governor and began to explore the possibility by traveling and speaking around the state. She officially threw her hat into the ring in 1982. Her campaign—which seemed more like a movement than a campaign—generated a great deal of excitement among Iowa women. A spring poll had her leading all Democratic and Republican candidates for governor. When she won the primary, it looked like she had the momentum to become Iowa's first female governor. But a major misstep put Roxanne on the defensive and derailed her campaign. Republican Terry Branstad shot ahead in the polls and stayed there. He defeated Roxanne in November and went on to become the nation's longest-serving governor.

The loss was devastating. Roxanne had long believed she was destined to be governor, and she had no Plan B. After months in the doldrums, she had her eureka moment when she realized that plaintiff law was what she was meant to do. It was here that she would have her greatest impact in an already impactful life. Roxanne represented those who had been injured, particularly in the areas of discrimination, employment, sexual harassment and assault, civil rights, medical malpractice, personal injury, and premises and product liability. And she represented her clients with a tenacity second to none.

"Roxanne was on a mission when she was handling a case. She had a great ability to know if people were lying or telling the truth, and because she believed her clients were wronged, she went to the end of the earth seeking justice for them," recalled Andrew Smith, one of her former clerks. Pushed by this zeal, Roxanne read all the documents for her cases, and aided by her exceptional memory, she typically knew and recalled the facts better than her opposing counsel did. If her cases went to trial, she had another edge. Roxanne was adept at reducing complex issues to understandable components. Then the consummate storyteller could weave her material into compelling narratives, most often swaying juries in her clients' favor.[8]

Her career has been marked with a number of big cases. Roxanne led the way in advancing the law in a number of areas, especially sexual discrimination, sexual harassment, employment discrimination, and premises liability by winning precedent-setting decisions in court. She also stood up to large interests on behalf of her clients—including such entities as Eastman Kodak, Iowa Beef Processors, asbestos manufacturers

Manville Corporation and Keene Corporation, United Parcel Service, Iowa State University, the University of Iowa, municipalities, police departments, hospitals, doctors, and the state of Iowa. The case that made the biggest splash may have been her $255 million class action settlement against Microsoft, but that paled in comparison to the nearly $15 billion settlement she helped engineer against Volkswagen for its emissions cheating scandal.

Roxanne's peers soon recognized her as a rising star. She moved rapidly through the ranks of the Association of Trial Lawyers of America, becoming its first female president in 1992. Three years later, she was inducted into the Inner Circle of Advocates, an invitation-only group of the one hundred top plaintiff attorneys in the country. Admitted attorneys had to have tried at least fifty cases and won at least one million-dollar award.

While Roxanne was locally recognized for her legal skills and the dozens of million-dollar or higher verdicts she has won, central Iowans were also well aware of her passion for animals, especially cats. This led her to become an important volunteer for the Animal Rescue League of Iowa, fostering hundreds of rescue kittens before they were old enough for adoption. Her passion spilled over to her law office, where a couple of rescue cats roamed, and until very recently Roxanne raised foster kittens there.

Of course, Roxanne's story is not devoid of struggles, mistakes, defeats, and humiliations—one of the most public being her drunk driving arrest. Nevertheless, like a prizefighter, Roxanne gets back up after each blow and keeps on battling. She lives up to the nickname her family gave her: Rocky.

Roxanne is a fighter, and standing up for those injured by others is part of her essence. After a huge victory where Roxanne's unwavering pursuit of justice was on full display, a fellow lawyer gave her a pair of purple boxing shorts with the phrase "Killer Conlin" inscribed across the back. "Suing bad guys is my specialty," Roxanne once observed, and as she has done for decades, she continues taking them on and bringing them down.[9]

ONE

———

A Rocky Beginning

Appearances gave a false impression of Roxanne Barton's early life. In the 1950s, her family seemed to be one of the millions across the country enjoying the American dream. Like the rest of their generation, her parents, Marion William "Bill" Barton and his wartime bride, Alice Bernice Madden, were raised during the Great Depression and came of age during the global conflict. They were now ready to put these troubled times behind them and ride the wave of postwar prosperity sweeping the nation.

The new economic abundance had been set off by pent-up demands and increased savings from the war years, the baby boom, and advances in technology and productivity. Median income rose by 70 percent over the 1950s, increasing from $3,300 to $5,620, and the economic surge threw open the doors to a rapidly expanding middle class. The transformation pushed commentators to see the decade as "the happiest, most stable, most rational period the western world has ever known since 1914."[1]

At the center of this brave new world were single-family homes, which rose rapidly in newly created neighborhoods. Here young nuclear families held sway, and the American dream unfolded as breadwinner husbands donned business suits and headed off to work, while their wives oversaw the household and raised the children. Growing disposable income and revolving credit cards fueled a consumption-oriented frenzy as parents filled their homes with the latest gadgets and appliances and their garages with at least one automobile. Family was celebrated, togetherness was cherished, community and church were held in high esteem, and summer vacations, often road trips in the family car, became standard fare of the good life.[2]

Hollywood glorified this American dream with a number of popular television sitcoms portraying, as David Halberstam wrote, "a wonderfully antiseptic world of idealized homes, in an idealized, unflawed America."[3] Programs such as *The Adventures of Ozzie and Harriet, Father Knows Best,* and *Leave It to Beaver* depicted idyllic family life, where cheerful, wise, white Anglo-Saxon, Protestant parents raised well-scrubbed, well-behaved children. Serious problems did not exist in this altered reality.

Like many children growing up in the 1950s, Roxanne, the Bartons' oldest, was fascinated with television and watched these family-based sitcoms as well as other popular programs such as *Make Room for Daddy.* She was especially struck by the fact that Danny Thomas called his television daughter princess. Roxanne often fantasized that her father would do the same to her, but he never did.[4]

Roxanne was soon aware of another disconnect. From the outside, the Bartons looked like a model middle-class family, similar to those portrayed on television. But there was a dark and growing secret inside the household. Bill was an alcoholic who eventually became violent at home. His attacks first focused on Alice, but later he battered Roxanne, her brother, Raymond, and her sister Rebecca as well. By the late 1950s, the family was in a downward spiral. Bill began having trouble at work, his drinking increased, and his behavior grew more erratic. The physical abuse escalated, and money was short.

As her American dream turned into a nightmare, Roxanne survived, even thrived, developing a resilience and a determination that carried her forward. Actively involved in helping care for her younger siblings and then trying to protect them and her mother from her father, she found solace in school, where the precocious youngster was an outstanding student. Initially, she thought acting would be her ticket to stability, money, and success, but fortuitous advice from a nun led her to choose the law. Roxanne escaped her dysfunctional home in 1961, when the seventeen-year-old went to college, and she moved into her own apartment the following year. Her break was complete when she married two years later.

Roxanne's parents' story began four decades earlier in east central South Dakota. Before making their way to the Great Plains, ancestors on her mother's side had originally come to the country from Ireland in 1848 during the infamous potato famine, while those on her father's side can be traced back to eighteenth-century South Carolina, most likely migrating from the British Isles. Her father was born in July 1923, the eldest child of Ray and Charlotte Grant Barton. Bill and his sister, Charlotte, were raised on the family's general-purpose farm just outside Cavour, a South Dakota town of 250 people in Beadle County, nine miles east of Huron, the county seat. Stern and hardworking, Ray and Grant somehow eked out a living on three hundred acres during the agricultural depression that befell the countryside, largely caused by overproduction from the increased demands of World War I.[5]

Things got no better in the 1930s, when the nation was engulfed by the Great Depression. Matters grew worse for South Dakota farmers, whose crops were devastated by drought, dust storms, and grasshopper infestations. These problems only exacerbated his family's hardscrabble life, and not surprisingly Bill evidently did not plan to stay on the farm. A very intelligent child, he excelled in school and was skipped ahead a grade, graduating from high school in 1940 just before he turned seventeen. He attended Huron College that fall. Sometime over the next couple of years, the handsome 6-foot college student met pretty and petite Alice Madden.[6]

Alice's family had troubles of their own. She was born in July 1924, the seventh and last child of William and Elizabeth "Bess" Madden. Sadly, the oldest child and only son, William, died in infancy; even worse, several months before Alice was born, her father was killed in a car accident. Strong and capable, her mother went to work to support the family. She initially took small jobs and continued her late husband's insurance business, then became the deputy treasurer of Beadle County.

She went on to serve two terms as the county's treasurer, and according to family lore she was the only Republican elected to office in Beadle County during Franklin Roosevelt's 1932 Democratic presidential landslide.[7]

A friendly and talkative child, Alice loved singing, and she and a friend often went to the Huron radio station to sing on the air. She graduated from Huron High School in 1942, took some classes at Northwest College of Commerce—a Huron business college—and landed a job with Armour and Company in town. At some point, the fun-loving, articulate, and musically talented Bill Barton caught her eye, and the two began dating. In February 1943, Bill was drafted into the army and sent to Fort Snelling, Minnesota. Private Barton returned for a visit that June before heading to the University of South Dakota in Vermillion, 180 miles to the southeast, where because of his intelligence he had been selected for the elite Army Specialized Training Program in engineering.[8]

It was very likely during this visit that Bill and Alice, as did so many other servicemen and their girlfriends, decided to get married before his deployment overseas. The two were wed on September 6, 1943, at St. Michael's Catholic Church in Huron, then went on a short honeymoon to Lake Kampeska, ninety miles to the northeast. Bill then headed back to Vermillion, while Alice returned home to live with her mother in Huron.[9]

That fall, Alice became aware that she was pregnant. Several months later, in February 1944, she traveled to Vermillion to spend a few weeks with Bill. When he completed his engineering coursework in March, the army was in the process of dissolving its Specialized Training Program because of manpower shortages, and it dispersed members to general ground force units. Bill was sent to Fort Leonard Wood, Missouri, to join the 97th Infantry Division, and Alice went back to Huron. He returned home on a twelve-day furlough in May but was back at the base when Roxanne Elizabeth Barton was born on June 30, 1944. Bill would see her for the first time in August during a furlough from Camp San Luis Obispo, California, where his division had been sent for amphibious training under the auspices of the navy and the Marine Corps in preparation for action in the Pacific.[10]

Just before the 97th was ready to head toward Japan, plans changed. The German offensive through Belgium's Ardennes Forest that December, the Battle of the Bulge, resulted in a high number of casualties, and additional American troops were needed for the final advance on Germany. The 97th was one of the units tapped for European action. The Trident Division, as it was also called, arrived in La Havre in March 1945. It crossed into Germany at the end of the month and engaged in one of the last major offensives of the war, the Battle of Ruhr Pocket, which involved more than 800,000 American and German soldiers. Here Bill served with the headquarters battery, artillery division. After operations in the Ruhr were completed toward the end of April, the 97th invaded Czechoslovakia; the division was near the town of Pilsen when the war in Europe ended in May.[11]

Bill had been promoted to private first class after the campaign, and when the Trident Division came home in June, the troops were given a thirty-day furlough. Bill must have returned home to see his wife and toddler before heading to Fort Bragg, North Carolina, where his division was being readied for the invasion of Japan. Before it shipped out, the United States dropped atomic bombs on Hiroshima and Nagasaki, and the war ended when the Japanese surrendered on August 15, 1945. The 97th still went to Japan, arriving toward the end of September, but it went as part of an occupying force, not an invading one. Bill was in Japan five months before his three-year service stint ended; he was discharged from Fort Leavenworth, Kansas, and was back in Huron in February 1946.[12]

The trauma of war complicated Bill's reentry into civilian life, and his family believed he came home a different man. Like so many others, Bill had dealt with the stress of war by drinking and gambling, and while he did not continue betting stateside, he did continue to drink heavily. According to Alice's sister Eleanor Cleary, Bill had had a wild side before his military service, including a tendency to drink too much. The war aggravated his drinking, and going forward his alcoholism only heightened his naturally short temper, leading to violence against his wife and some of his children. Tragically, such postwar behavior was more widespread than had been assumed. Historian Michael C. C. Adams explained: "We have been slow to document much of this damage done by the war, partly because families hushed it up and partly because, for years, alcoholism and wife beating were tolerated, even material for comedians."[13]

Once home, Bill faced two adjustments. The first was married life—he and Alice had never really lived together. The second was fatherhood. These issues were not unique to the Bartons: a growing number of couples who had married hastily during the war divorced. Marriage rates had soared after the Selective Service and Training Act—the draft—passed in 1940, then after Pearl Harbor the following year. Some wed thinking they might die in the conflict, some were impatient to marry no matter what, and some hoped to enjoy spousal benefits if their loved ones were killed. Shortly, however, many saw their marriages as mistakes and remedied the problem through divorce—the divorce rate more than doubled between 1941 and 1946. Bill and Alice stayed together, but one incident suggests that the two were already having trouble. Sometime in late 1946 or early 1947, Roxanne remembered riding in the back seat of the family's Chevrolet sedan. Her parents were in the midst of a heated argument in the front when Bill hit Alice. Roxanne screamed and cried, and her father turned around and slapped her into submission. Memories are murky here, but such physical abuse seemed to be only sporadic in these early years.[14]

Learning to be a father was equally challenging for Bill. As he noted in a few short pages he penned about Roxanne, she had been raised for nearly two years exclusively in the company of women, largely her grandmother and "doting aunts," while Alice was working and he was away. He described the awkward situation: "We were both profoundly frightened of each other and I'm sure, equally uncomfortable in each other's presence."[15]

Getting acquainted with Roxanne and reacquainted with Alice largely took place in Vermillion, where the family had moved that summer of 1946. Here Bill attended the University of South Dakota on the G.I. Bill, which offered millions of veterans tuition and living expenses for up to four years of college or vocational training, a year of unemployment benefits, and low-interest mortgages and small business loans.[16]

The family took up residence in University Park, near the present Al Neuharth Media Center on the west side of campus, an area developed to house married veterans returning to school and their families in small trailers provided by the Federal Housing Administration. Although the cramped quarters must have been frustrating for her parents, the trailer park was a veritable playground for the adventurous Roxanne. She was soon running around with two little boys, and together they were, according to her parents, "the terrors of the neighborhood." They played, they screamed, and they fought with others to the point that her father decided he should teach her to box to protect herself. Roxanne thoroughly enjoyed her time roughhousing with these playmates. Early on she realized that "being a girl was not a favored status in society," so she refused to wear dresses.[17]

Roxanne's father remembered her as an especially bright and curious child with "a fertile imagination." She kept a menagerie of imaginary pets—circus animals—under the family trailer and became "incensed if mom or dad, neighbors or playmates could not or would not recognize these animals as she brought them out." On a whim her father, who was taking an educational psychology class that included a unit on I.Q. testing, decided to give his three-year-old daughter the intelligence test. After Roxanne did extremely well on the sequencing questions, Bill administered the last portion of the test, asking her to express her ideas or thoughts in sentences and then counting the words. Children her age, he recalled, were supposed to be able to put together sentences of six to ten words. Bill stopped counting after Roxanne strung together a number of complex sentences, each with twenty or more words.[18]

When Bill reported back to the class that Roxanne had scored incredibly high on the I.Q. test he gave her, putting her well over the 130-point threshold for superior intelligence, his professor suggested that the results were most likely inaccurate because the test had been given by a biased father. Two students volunteered to reevaluate Roxanne, and to the amazement of all their results put her I.Q. even higher than her father had estimated. While it is difficult to judge the validity of these tests, Roxanne was obviously highly intelligent. For her, the results were significant because, she noted, "I was always treated as though I was really, really smart, and I certainly tried to live up to everyone's expectations."[19]

Such treatment over the years added to Roxanne's already blossoming poise and self-confidence, but another event in Vermillion also played a significant role in her development. One day, after she came home crying about being mistreated by one of the boys in the neighborhood, Bill told her that she was as strong and as capable as any boy and that she should stand up for herself. She did, taking a plastic toy sand shovel and hitting her tormentor on the head and shoulders. Little boys no longer bothered her, but much more important was the fact that these were the first of many words of encouragement Bill gave Roxanne over the years, explaining that she was capable of anything and that the strict gender roles of the period need not keep her from aspiring to do anything.[20]

The Bartons remained in Vermillion through 1948. Bill graduated with a degree in business that spring. While there, he had also gone through the Reserve Officers' Training Corps program and was commissioned as an officer in the United States Army Reserve, where he met his part-time duty obligation over the next eight years. Shortly before the Bartons left Vermillion in early 1949, after Bill took a job in West Point, Nebraska, eighty-three miles to the south, there had been an addition to the family. Raymond was born in November, and Roxanne's days of being the center of her parents' attention ended. Like many only children who lose that favored status when a sibling is born, Roxanne was not happy about her new brother, and she acted out. As an infant, Ray slept in a dresser drawer, and several times while he was napping Roxanne shut the drawer. Sometime later, she pushed him down some stairs. Fortunately, Ray was unhurt, and Roxanne finally accepted her brother, reasoning that there was nothing she could do about him.[21]

It is unclear what lured Bill to West Point, but the family was there only a few months. That fall, the Bartons moved to Sioux City in the northwestern portion of Iowa, where Bill took a job as an engineer with W. A. Klinger Company, a construction firm. Here the family put down roots, and four more children were born over the next five years: Rebecca "Becky" in 1950, the twins Rhoda and Rhonda in 1952, and Regina "Gina" in 1955.[22]

It was here in Sioux City that the Bartons came closest to the Hollywood version of the ideal family. Roxanne's sister Becky saw their time in northwest Iowa as "the good years." Bill was satisfied with his job and kept his drinking in check. Although he was a stern taskmaster who had extremely high expectations for his children, Roxanne observed, he was also "charming and charismatic." Alice was caring and kind but was constantly busy around the home, as there were always children in diapers. Importantly, while in Sioux City Bill did not abuse any of the children, and if he hit Alice here, it was rarely.[23]

Roxanne started kindergarten at Hunt Elementary School that fall of 1949, shortly after the family arrived in the city. She could already read and write, which put her well ahead of her fellow students. This made her popular with her teacher, who soon had Roxanne reading to her classmates. The five-year-old loved school, but her father felt she was not being challenged enough, and the following year he and Alice moved Roxanne to the Catholic school associated with the family's church, St. Ambrose Cathedral.[24]

Bill was not Catholic, but when he married Alice he agreed that their children would be raised in the Catholic Church. A Methodist, although not devout, he did not convert to Catholicism or attend church with the rest of the family, but he believed the church offered education superior to the public schools and thought Roxanne and then the other children would be better served by parochial schools.[25]

Roxanne flourished in school, but after the twins were born in the fall of 1952, it became clear that a three-room apartment was not big enough for a growing family. Bill was doing well at work—much of his time was spent designing grain elevators and storage facilities—and in 1953 he and Alice therefore took another step toward the American dream by purchasing their own home. With the aid of the G.I. Bill's home loan program, the Bartons bought a new three-bedroom ranch house on Floyd Avenue in the residential neighborhood of Leeds, northeast of downtown. Unfortunately for Roxanne, this required her to change schools, and she spent the last half of third grade in public school at Hawthorne Elementary. Almost immediately, her intelligence and apparently flippant attitude led to a run-in with her new teacher.[26]

Always curious, Roxanne had taken an interest in her father's slide rule, a mechanical calculator often used by engineers and scientists. He taught her how to use it, and the gifted youngster soon mastered elementary calculations on it. Shortly after arriving at Hawthorne, while her teacher was explaining double-digit multiplication to the class, Roxanne raced through the worksheet using her slide rule instead of performing the task on her own. The frustrated teacher sent her home, only to have Roxanne's mother march down to the school to defend her daughter. But her stay at the school was brief; Bill and Alice returned her to Catholic school for fourth grade, when Roxanne attended St. Michael's Catholic School.[27]

In many ways, Roxanne's life looked similar to that of numerous middle-class children of the era. In the mid-1950s, the family joined millions of other Americans when they purchased their first television, and they gathered around their small set nightly to watch their favorite shows. They also enjoyed Bill's piano playing, especially during the holidays when, accompanied by their father, they sang Christmas carols. But this Norman Rockwell image could be deceptive, and Alice and the children understood when not to join Bill at the piano. "We could always tell the mood he was in by the way he was playing," said Roxanne's sister Becky. "If it was a softer song, it was okay to be around him, but if he was pounding the keys, we knew to stay away from him."[28]

The family also had the opportunity to fly with Bill from time to time. He had gotten his pilot's license, probably at the behest of his firm, which owned a plane that made it easier for him to travel to job construction sites. Roxanne loved to fly with her father, even though he tried to scare her with barrel rolls and steep dives, and she would eventually go on to get her pilot's license. Flying seemed the lone exception to the family's middle-class lifestyle. Like many others, the Bartons took regular summer vacations, most often driving to South Dakota, where they spent time on Bill's parents' farm. Roxanne relished her time on the farm, and it was probably here that she developed her love of animals. She was also especially close to her grandmother Grant, and the strong woman would become something of a role model for her. Other road trips for the Bartons included an excursion to Mount Rushmore and the Black

Hills and a long drive to Atlanta, Georgia, with all eight family members jammed into a standard sedan to visit Alice's sister Irene, her husband, and six children.[29]

At home, Roxanne loved riding her bicycle through the community. She was actually trying to ride home from St. Michael's on June 8, 1953, when the Floyd River flooded Leeds and she was stopped by a bartender, who happened to work at the bar where her father drank, because of the high water. She stayed with him upstairs for a few hours until someone in a rowboat took her up the street and reunited her with her parents, who had not been contacted and feared she might have drowned. Beyond this misadventure, she and her best friend Patty Barr played on the swing set in the Bartons' backyard, roller-skated in her family's basement, slept over at each other's houses, and enjoyed free movies in the neighborhood park on summer evenings.[30]

Another ritual soon developed around the family's dinner table. Probably fueled by Bill's love of books and his obsessive belief in the importance of education, he began requiring his children to practice new vocabulary words around the table and read aloud from classic novels. Perhaps these sessions encouraged Roxanne's interest in the outside world and her own love of reading.[31]

Roxanne's first awareness of larger issues came with the Korean War, which began in June 1950. She followed the war, particularly on the radio since her family did not yet own a television set. She was concerned for America's troops and became especially worried that her father, as an army reservist, would be called to active duty and sent to war. As the war dragged on, she lost some interest in it, but she became angry in July 1953 when no one told her it ended. Missing that key event led the exceptional nine-year-old to read the newspaper daily to stay up to date on current events.[32]

About this same time, Roxanne discovered the Leeds branch of the Sioux City Public Library. The small, stately library had been built with funds from Andrew Carnegie in 1917. One summer, Roxanne decided she would read all the books it held. This was of course ridiculously ambitious, but according to her friend Patty Barr "she read all the time, was a very fast reader, and retained absolutely everything she read; she must have had a photographic mind." Roxanne made it through a good chunk of the collection before leaving the city, but her father took some books, like Dostoyevsky's *Crime and Punishment*, away from her because he thought them too difficult for the youngster.[33]

In fourth grade, when Roxanne was back in Catholic school at St. Michael's, she almost immediately met Judy Beller, and the two became nearly inseparable. Her friend remembered: "Roxanne had it all; she had ambition, she had brains—oh my Lord was she smart—she was cute, she was funny, and everybody liked her." The nuns at St. Michael's liked her, too. Because Roxanne was so far ahead of the other students, her teachers often had her help struggling classmates. It was about this time that Roxanne's goals changed. Earlier she had aspired to be a cowgirl or, interestingly, a piano player or a pilot like her father. While at St. Michael's, she became interested in singing and dancing and became convinced that she wanted to be a singer, a dancer, or an actor. She was Gretel in the play "Hansel and Gretel," and she and Judy Beller performed a dance on *Canyon Kid's Kid Corner*, a children's television program that aired on Sioux City's KCAU-TV.[34]

Roxanne's Catholic education was again interrupted in sixth grade, when her teacher, Sister Mary Damien, a young nun new to the classroom, decided to grade on effort rather than performance. Even though the eleven-year-old did not have to work very hard to receive perfect scores on all her assignments, nevertheless she brought home a report card filled with Cs. Roxanne's mother intervened, but she could not persuade the nun to change her approach, and Alice ultimately pulled her daughter from the school at the end of the year. Roxanne began seventh grade in the fall of 1956 at Leeds Junior Senior High School.[35]

That spring, Roxanne had taken advantage of an opportunity that would have made her the envy of millions of young girls across the country: she went to see Elvis Presley. The twenty-one-year-old rock and roller had just released his single "Heartbreak Hotel" that January, and in March his first album, *Elvis Presley*, came out. Over the course of that year, Elvis made more than 110 tour stops, and to Roxanne's delight he performed in Sioux City's Municipal Auditorium in May. Just shy of twelve, Roxanne along with several thousand screaming fans was enthralled by his electric songs and gyrating hips. She would remain a lifelong Elvis fan.[36]

Meanwhile, Roxanne gradually began taking on more responsibilities at home. She became more and more of a helpmate to her mother, especially after the twins were born in 1952. She was of such great assistance in bathing and caring for the babies, in fact, that the following year her mother stopped hiring babysitters, and whenever she or she and Bill went out nine-year-old Roxanne would be left in charge of her four and then five younger siblings.[37]

Right around Gina's birth in 1955, Bill started having trouble. He began complaining that the managers at Klinger did not know what they were doing, and he began to drink more. By all accounts he was very smart, but this sometimes got in the way of his job when he felt the need to tell his bosses what they were doing wrong. It is not clear whether this happened at Klinger or whether Bill was fired or quit, but by 1956 he was working at Younglove, a rival construction firm in Sioux City. He lasted there only a year, and in early 1957 the family pulled up stakes and moved across the state to Clinton, 350 miles to the southeast on the Mississippi River, where Bill had taken a job with Pillsbury Mills.[38]

Although she did not want to leave her friends in Sioux City, Roxanne had shuttled between schools enough to making her amenable to change, and she easily adjusted to Clinton Junior High, where she was so far ahead of her seventh grade classmates that she was given advanced, supplementary classes. The following year, she was back in Catholic school, St. Mary's Elementary. Intelligent and outgoing, with big brown eyes and a ready smile, Roxanne took her new school by storm. She was elected class president and captain of the cheerleading squad, spent time with her first boyfriend, a talented piano-playing classmate named Tommy Joe Mooney, and topped it off by winning the *Clinton Herald*'s county spelling bee. Interestingly, she had been eliminated in an early round for her spelling of "gaily." Self-assured as always, Roxanne challenged the ruling and was proved correct. Three hours later, she won the contest with her spelling of "vicissitudes."[39]

The following fall, Roxanne went to Mount St. Clare Academy, a select all-girls Catholic high school, on a scholarship. Her passion for drama and the stage was met here when she starred in the school's production of Molière's "The Imaginary Invalid." And her parents indulged their daughter's interest in performance that year, driving her to Chicago to audition for the *Ted Mack and the Original Amateur Hour* television show. She breezed through the first few audition rounds but failed to make it onto the program. Nonetheless, Roxanne remembers her time at St. Mary's and Mount St. Clare as "really fun years," but her fond memories did not carry over to the family's general experience in Clinton.[40]

Unlike Roxanne, Bill did not handle change well. He was unhappy with his job, drank more often, and took out his frustrations on Alice, yelling at her frequently and now beating her often. The children were constantly scared and did their best to stay out of his way. One night, during an especially vicious attack on her mother, Roxanne ran to the house next door and roused the neighbor. He and the thirteen-year-old hurried to the Barton home, where Bill greeted them at the door and claimed the incident was a figment of his daughter's imagination, explaining that she must have had a nightmare. Thin though the story was, the neighbor bought it and left. But the interruption stopped the violence for the night, and Roxanne took that as a victory.[41]

By early 1959, it was clear that Bill's position at Pillsbury was not working out, and the Bartons moved two hundred miles west to Des Moines. Bill found a job as a supervisor at Hot Spot Detector, a firm that manufactured temperature monitors for grain elevators and mills. The family settled into a small rental west of downtown at 1349 Forty-Third Street, although they would buy a two-story, four-bedroom home thirteen blocks to the east of it that summer. Roxanne was enrolled in St. Joseph Academy, an all-girls Catholic high school, while her school-age siblings went to St. Augustin Catholic School. An outsider once again, Roxanne adapted quickly to her new home. She plunged into school, made friends, began working a variety of part-time jobs, and was soon dating, all the while helping care for her younger siblings.[42]

When she arrived at St. Joseph's, Roxanne was academically far ahead of her ninth grade classmates. Over the years, a number of her teachers had suggested that she be skipped ahead a grade or two, but her parents (especially her father, because of the poor experience he had had being advanced a grade in school) did not agree. This meant that Roxanne generally was given work above her grade level; at Mount St. Clare, she had taken junior and senior courses. She was put in similar classes at St. Joseph's. In fact, in her sophomore year, school administrators looked to Roxanne to take over a world history class when the instructor became very ill, and she taught her peers for half a semester.[43]

Roxanne's interest in singing and drama continued, and she starred in two of the school's annual stage productions, including "Meet Me in St. Louis." She still envisioned performing as her future, and she took part in the Bill Riley Talent Search competition. As a sophomore, she was hoping to head to southern California that coming summer, where she could study acting in a special program at the Pasadena Playhouse while living with an aunt. The plan did not materialize because the family did not have enough money to send her; however, also that year, Roxanne's homeroom teacher suggested an alternative future for the tenth grader. Sister Mary Katrine Johnson saw great potential in the teenager and urged her to focus on more serious pursuits. She recommended that Roxanne combine her dramatic gifts with her superior intellect and become an attorney. The suggestion would alter Roxanne's life.[44]

Outside of school, Roxanne was a whirlwind of activity. She and her new friends, especially best friend Sara Quinn, spent a lot of time together at slumber parties, and they drove about town—more specifically, they scooped the loop by repeatedly driving around downtown on Grand Avenue and Locust Street on Friday and Saturday nights—while chatting and flirting with other teenagers. And as part of their youthful rebellion, they took up smoking. Roxanne also dated a lot, usually going out with older boys, often from Dowling Catholic High School. She frequently had dates every Friday and Saturday night, and much to her mother's consternation she sometimes had two or three dates on the same night.[45]

But she also remained busy around the house. She continued to help her mother with the younger children, who, according to youngest sister Gina, saw her as "a second mother." At the same time, Roxanne managed to squeeze in part-time work, getting her first job downtown as a waiter at the Katz Drug Store lunch counter at fourteen, although because she was not old enough to work outside the home she had to lie about her age. She left Katz shortly for a much more convenient job as a soda jerk at Reppert's Pharmacy at Thirty-Fifth Street and Ingersoll Avenue, just a few blocks away from her home. These responsibilities separated Roxanne from many her age. In the words of her friend Sara, "Roxanne could be a teenager, and she did go out with us sometimes, but she was working and doing the mother thing. It was clear her life was totally different than ours."[46]

Over the next few years, Roxanne would have a number of part-time jobs. She worked as a dance instructor at an Arthur Murray studio, assembled mailers for *Look* magazine's subscription department, cared for children at Tiny Tots Day Care Center, and under the auspices of the Jan Lamont Modeling Agency modeled clothing at Feldman's, a women's clothing store. She demonstrated products at Dahl's Foods on Ingersoll Avenue and was hired to jump out of a box at a man's eightieth birthday party.[47]

Initially, Roxanne gave all the money she made to her family. As she remembered: "Nothing I did cost any money. On dates, the boys paid. I didn't buy very many clothes. At St. Joseph's I had a uniform, but I never had a new one; all the uniforms were hand me downs from other girls, and when I went out on a date, I wore jeans." Her contribution was welcome because her father was not making enough at Hot Spot to support the large clan. But her home situation had become much worse. The move had not worked out as Bill had hoped. He was not happy with his job or his bosses, and as his drinking increased, so did his violence. He beat Alice with growing regularity, and he also began attacking the three oldest children, Roxanne, Ray, and Becky.[48]

During one of Bill's rages, Roxanne again intervened. She de-escalated a dangerous situation by rushing her mother to the basement and placing her seven-year-old sisters in front of the basement door, correctly believing that her father would not harm the twins and would calm down before he could get to Alice. Although Roxanne succeeded in protecting her mother this time, many times she could not.[49]

Roxanne remained a target of her father's abuse over the next two years. She finally took decisive action one evening in 1960. The incident began in the Barton living room. Bill had come home drunk, got in an argument with Alice, and starting hitting her. All the children except Roxanne sought refuge upstairs on the second floor. When Alice got away from Bill and ran into the dining room, Roxanne stepped in between her parents. Bill threw her up against the wall, held her there by the throat, and hit her in the face. Roxanne fought back, which infuriated him, and he finally let her go. He left the house and went to a liquor store. While he was gone, Roxanne called the police. They arrived quickly, and when Bill returned they decided that the situation was serious, and they arrested him.[50]

The following day, Bill appeared in court. The municipal judge, Luther Glanton, Jr., who would go on to become Iowa's first African American district judge in 1976, ordered him out of the Barton home and had officers escort him there to pick up some clothes. Bill moved to the downtown YMCA. He returned home a few weeks later, promising to change, and at first the beatings ceased. The significance of Glanton's action stayed with Roxanne, who was convinced that the judge's decision to remove Bill from the house had saved her life. Decades later at a social event, she had the opportunity to remind him of the incident and thank him.[51]

Bill would soon lose his job at Hot Spot, and although he would find work as a salesman at Doherty Construction and later Central Bearing, there were significant stretches of unemployment between these positions, and at one point he drove a taxi. He was embarrassed by this, though, and Ray remembered that he hid his cap in a briefcase when he went off to the taxicab depot. He dealt with his difficulties by drinking and again took his frustrations out at home by beating Alice, Ray, and Becky. After the arrest, however, Bill never hit Roxanne again.[52]

Bill's job woes forced Alice to take jobs outside the home. She worked the night shift as a nurse's aide at Mercy Hospital, then managed the twenty-four-hour coffee shop at the Hotel Fort Des Moines and later the Kirkwood Hotel. She also worked for a while at Barbara's Bake Shoppe several blocks away from their home at Twenty-Eighth Street and Ingersoll Avenue. Times were now tough. Food was sometimes short, and the Bartons almost lost their home, but they pulled through, assisted in part by the older children. Ray, who had a *Des Moines Register* paper route, and Becky, who cleaned for Monsignor Gerald Walker, began contributing their earnings to the family cause just as Roxanne was already doing. Roxanne even bought the family a used car—a white Nash Rambler—in the late 1950s. The church provided support as well. When it became clear that the Bartons could no longer afford school tuition, Monsignor Walker paid for Roxanne's schooling, while her younger siblings received full scholarships to continue at St. Augustin's.[53]

Despite these distractions and problems, Roxanne remained a top student at St. Joseph's. Early in her junior year, she learned of a special Drake University program that admitted exceptional high school students without a diploma. Her parents had a change of heart and supported her skipping ahead a year. Admission required applicants to pass the college entrance exams and have a letter of recommendation from their principal. Roxanne sailed through the tests, but her principal, Sister Mary Denis Gregory, refused to support her application, believing the sixteen-year-old too immature. As she had done years earlier, Alice again headed to the school to confront the nun. This time she prevailed, convincing Sister Mary Denis to back her daughter's application, although the nun predicted that Roxanne would flunk out of college and said she would not be permitted back at St. Joseph's. This proved to be just the motivation Roxanne needed, and in August 1961, without graduating from high school, she started at Drake.[54]

Roxanne lived at home during her first year in college, but she moved out sometime during her second, taking a one-room apartment with a shared bath just south of campus at 3101 Cottage Grove Avenue. She continued holding several part-time jobs, generally working more than forty hours a week, and her course load was heavy, nineteen to twenty-one hours per semester, but she maintained close to a 4.0 grade point average. Remarkably, she had enough credits to be a college senior after just two years, but she was already looking ahead when she noticed another special Drake program.[55]

Top students could enroll in law school and combine their senior-year studies with their first year of law school. "I was always in a hurry," Roxanne recalled, "I was goal oriented. I wanted money. I didn't like being poor." Not surprisingly, she met all the requirements, and after she passed the necessary tests Martin Tollefson, dean of the law school, admitted her.[56]

She started law school in the fall of 1963, while her family left Des Moines for Omaha, where Bill had taken another job. Roxanne maintained her frenetic pace of work and school while still finding time to date. All seemed to be going according to plan: she finished her combined first year of law school and last year of college as a top student, graduating Phi Beta Kappa with an undergraduate degree in psychology.[57]

But midway through that spring semester, in March, Roxanne's life took an unexpected turn. On Friday evening, March 6, 1964, she was working her job as a coffee shop waiter at the Holiday Inn South when she met Jim Conlin. A native of Fort Dodge, a small city ninety-five miles northwest of Des Moines, Jim and best friend Tom Groff were returning from Arizona for the funeral of Groff's father in Dubuque. They stopped at the Greenwood Lounge, a longtime watering hole on Ingersoll Avenue, to meet Marty Dunn, a high school friend from their days at Wentworth Military Academy in Missouri. Dunn was then a second-year law student at Drake, and he told Jim that he should meet his "bright and beautiful" classmate Roxanne.[58]

Jim got in his car and headed right over to the Holiday Inn coffee shop. He spotted Roxanne and asked the host to seat him in her section. When she came over to take his order, Jim explained that Dunn had suggested they go out. She was immediately "charmed" with Jim, who she thought was "tall, dark, and handsome, with beautiful eyes." They talked throughout the evening, and he ended up staying until the restaurant closed. The two agreed to go out the following night, but Jim went over to Roxanne's apartment midafternoon, and they picked up their conversation where they had left off. The talk turned serious when they began to discuss the future, and within twenty-four hours of meeting they decided to marry, "one of the few impulsive things I've ever done in my life," Roxanne remembered.[59]

For Roxanne, it was love at first sight, but that was not the reason she married him. She explained, "He was an unusual man. Nothing about my being in law school distressed him. I was always testing people at the time about how they viewed women. We talked about roles. He didn't flinch when I told him, 'You have to understand I do not cook, I do not clean, I do not wash, and I do not iron. And I never will. He said, OK, fine.'"[60]

They got their marriage license that Monday, planning to wed the next Saturday. On Wednesday, the day the announcement ran in the newspaper, Roxanne received a call from the man she was supposed to date on Thursday evening, who observed correctly that he guessed their plans were off. Roxanne's parents, of course, tried to talk their daughter out of what they saw as a rash move. Jim, they argued, was older, had been married before, had a five-year-old daughter, and, as he admitted when he and Roxanne went to Omaha to discuss their plans, had no real job prospects.[61]

"He didn't look like a good bet from an objective standpoint," Roxanne noted, and he "didn't look like ideal husband material to my parents, but he did to me." Her parents' objections to the union were shared by her good friend Sara Quinn as well, but their protests only succeeded in delaying the couple's plans for a week. Nineteen-year-old Roxanne and twenty-three-year-old Jim married on Saturday, March 21, in an unceremonious wedding officiated by Justice of the Peace George Hahn in his dingy back office in West Des Moines. Sara Quinn stood up for Roxanne, Tom Groff for Jim. Roxanne's brother, Ray, was the only other person there.[62]

The wedding capped a tumultuous beginning for Roxanne. She had been forced to grow up fast with a difficult and ultimately violent father. In the end, adversity made her stronger and more independent, just the traits a young woman who wanted to have it all needed at a time when women were not supposed to aspire to balance married life with a career in the male-dominated legal profession.

Two

—

Raising Her Consciousness

Drake Law School was not exactly what Roxanne had imagined. Like law schools around the country, it was a male bastion with only a handful of women in its ranks. Her initial efforts to fit in by being one of the boys failed miserably, and Roxanne soon realized that "I didn't have a niche. I didn't have a way to belong." Sexism was pervasive in such institutions. As she recalled, "There was a very strong sense communicated to me—'You do not belong here. You are taking the place in this law school that ought to be occupied by a man.'" Ultimately, "it was a very solitary and very radicalizing experience for me."[1]

Her embrace of feminism was further informed by the trailblazing work of Betty Friedan and the difficulties Roxanne faced in the workplace. Home life with an abusive father fed her growing social conscience and empathy for others, strengthening her devotion to social justice, progressive causes, and Democratic Party politics. The varied activities that supported these issues influenced her budding legal career even as Roxanne negotiated her first years of marriage and parenthood. Although buried in the minutiae of daily life as an attorney, activist, wife, and mother, she was ultimately trying to answer the very basic question other women were asking at the time: "Could I really have it all?"

When Roxanne began law school in the fall of 1963, it was immediately clear that she differed from the majority of her classmates. Her signature red hair, which she began dyeing at fourteen, and her sharp mind had distinguished her in the classroom since her early teens, but now she was conspicuous for other reasons. Women had begun to break into the law school ranks, but nationally they made up only 4.2 percent of the entering class of 1963–64. At Drake the percentage of women in Roxanne's graduating class was higher, sitting at just under 10 percent, but that meant that she was one of only three females out of a total of thirty-one students.[2]

Unfortunately for Roxanne, the other two women in her class—Anna Marie Schinkle and JoAnn Shirley—were in very different stages of their lives. Both were married with older children, and both were attending law school with second careers in mind. Roxanne could not relate to these women and instead tried to connect with her male peers. But here she was hampered by gender.

Law schools of the time were very much boys' clubs. Besides the fact that the students were overwhelmingly male, faculties and administrations were heavily dominated by men as well. At Drake's law school, for example, there were no female instructors or administrators. Female law students were at best oddities and were frequently treated as second-class citizens. Roxanne remembered that the two other two female students were not taken seriously. It was generally thought, she recalled, that "they were going back to law school so that they would have something to talk about to their husbands. But I did not have a husband, and therefore, I had no reason to be there."[3]

Scholars Susan Martin and Nancy Jurik found discrimination of female law students of the period pervasive, explaining, "Both faculty and men students made the educational environment inhospitable to women. While all students were subject to ridicule, particularly if they did not provide the right response when called on in class, women were rarely called on, and on such occasions, they were subjected to questions designed to embarrass them (e.g., being asked to explain the details of rape cases) or were humiliated by such comments as 'better go back to the kitchen' if they stumbled in recitation."[4]

Fellow law student Gary Ordway was aware of informal rather than overt bias against women. "Guys studied together in the library, and when it closed, those who lived close to campus went out for drinks at Peggy's [a longtime favorite tavern for Drake students]. They socialized together and got to know each other. And when honors were to be bestowed or leadership positions opened up, guys selected those they knew and trusted." Such male networks took shape early on, but the three female students were not among them.[5]

Inclusion here was that much more difficult for Roxanne because she was still a teenager. She began law school at nineteen, at least two years younger than her youngest classmates, and her life experience differed from most of her classmates. Likewise, because she worked several part-time jobs, she had almost no time for a social life. At one point, she "worked at the Holiday Inn South as a waitress from 5 to 10 p.m., babysat until 3 in the morning, and then had a job at the Tiny Tots [Day Care] Center at 6 in the morning." Fortunately, according to her sister Rhoda, Roxanne never needed much sleep, but this demanding schedule meant that she could study only in snippets and typically only on her own.[6]

Thus, albeit not by choice, Roxanne was a loner in law school and did not have the benefit of belonging to study groups or bouncing ideas off her peers. But that did not hold her back. Classmate Larry Van Werden once overheard Professor Herbert Myers talking to a colleague and expressing awe over Roxanne's ability to recite complex cases verbatim. Gary Ordway, meanwhile, was always impressed by the fact that Roxanne "understood the big picture, when the rest of us were just trying to learn the law."[7]

But there were additional hurdles as well. Like a number of others in her class, after her March 1964 wedding Roxanne was also adjusting to married life. The newlyweds initially moved into a small duplex just north of University Avenue at 1205 Twenty-Third Street, several blocks east of Drake. Jim—Roxanne always called him James as a reaction to his nickname, Chick—had just started working at American Republic Insurance, but the position required a lot of travel, and he soon quit. He then began what became a string of short-term jobs, including night manager at the Hotel Fort Des Moines, maître d' at Johnny and Kay's, a renowned restaurant on Des Moines's south side, and various positions selling everything from garbage disposals to awnings.[8]

With Jim moving from job to job, Roxanne thought he should go back to school to get his degree. He had attended several colleges socially, he once explained, most recently Arizona State University, and was very bright, but he was dyslexic, which made reading and studying extremely difficult for him. This and a wild streak meant that he overindulged in the fun side of college life, and he ended up dropping out of every institution he attended. Jim once joked, "My social schedule was too burdensome to keep up with the scholastic demands." But Roxanne now convinced him to give it one more try, and while he continued working, he enrolled part time at Simpson College, twelve miles south of Des Moines in Indianola, in the summer of 1964. Jim took courses at Simpson through the following spring, but he was not getting much out of them and again dropped out. A year later, however, he found his vocation when he began selling real estate for Cooper Homes.[9]

Shortly after they married, looking for ways to supplement their meager income, Roxanne and Jim landed on an idea that satisfied Roxanne's love of animals. They would rescue poodles, one of her favorite breeds, nurse them back to health, and sell them to good homes. The couple began accumulating poodles, soon housing a dozen dogs in their tiny duplex. Unfortunately, the plan went awry. They gave the dogs away instead of selling them; even worse, the large number of animals they had led to their eviction in the fall of 1964. They bought a two-bedroom ranch-style home on the city's south side at 1610 Carrie Avenue, several blocks south and east of the Wakonda Club.[10]

On Carrie Avenue, Roxanne became better acquainted with Carmela "Cookie" Brown, who lived across the street; the two had initially met through Democratic politics. Their budding friendship led Roxanne to take up cooking, something neither did. Before they married, when she and Jim had talked about marital roles, Roxanne had made it clear that she did not cook and never would, but now she thought that learning some basics would be a good idea, and she signed Brown and herself up for a cooking class at Des Moines Technical High School on Grand Avenue. Called Food Basics for the Bride, the class was actually designed for young women who were about to be married. The two struggled in the course until the final project, which really threw Roxanne. Each student was to make an item for a Thanksgiving meal, and the instructor assigned Roxanne dinner rolls. While mixing the ingredients in a bowl, she accidentally flung the contents across the room. The teacher was furious, and neither Roxanne nor Cookie was allowed to participate in the final project.[11]

The two did receive certificates for the course, but Cookie never picked up cooking, and in her words "Roxanne kind of learned to cook." Jim, however, had a different opinion. After recounting his wife's many accomplishments in a 1974 interview, he noted that she was a terrible cook.[12]

On the job front, Roxanne had dropped a couple of her part-time efforts, replacing them with work for the Iowa Legislative Services Agency, which provided research and analysis to state senators and representatives and assisted them in drafting legislation. She left that position at the beginning of 1965, when she received a clerkship at Davis, Huebner, Johnson and Burt, a highly regarded general practice law firm in Des Moines, located downtown in the Fleming Building at Sixth Avenue and Walnut Street. But a few months into the job Roxanne became pregnant, and in an odd coincidence two of the three legal secretaries at the firm, Patty Huston and Judy Howard, became pregnant as well.[13]

Once again, Roxanne faced discrimination because of her sex: she was fired for being pregnant. Interestingly, Huston and Howard were not fired—they remained at the firm because they were secretaries, traditionally acceptable roles for women. Roxanne, on the other hand, was trying to break into the male-dominated ranks of attorneys, and at the time there was little willingness to deal with pregnancy among law clerks or associates.[14]

Luckily, Roxanne found another job in the legal world, this time at the attorney general's office, but her pregnancy soon caused problems for her at Drake as well. Dean Maurice Kirk was willing to accept a few women in law school, but having a pregnant one among his students was too much to abide. Scholarships had paid for Roxanne's education, and in an effort to push her out of the program, Kirk took the funds away late in the summer of 1965, just before her final year of law school began. Roxanne rushed to Ralph Flowerree, the director of Drake's financial aid and student employment office, who had helped her as an undergraduate. She explained her situation and her dire need for assistance. The sympathetic Flowerree arranged a National Defense Student Loan—a low-interest college loan program for students begun during the Cold War in the late 1950s, after the Soviets launched *Sputnik*—for her on the spot.[15]

But this solved only part of the Conlins' financial woes. Jim had brought nearly $15,000 of debt into the marriage, and without other funds available the couple was in real trouble. The two tried everything—they even pawned Roxanne's wedding ring—but as she recalled, "We had no more way to pay the money back than the man in the moon." Finally, they went to First Federal State Bank just down the street from Drake at Twenty-Fourth Street and University Avenue and visited with banker George Montgomery, who agreed to loan them $2,300 without any collateral.[16]

Together, Flowerree and Montgomery saved the day for the Conlins. "They are both my heroes," Roxanne explained. "We couldn't have eaten without the faith Montgomery had in us, and without Flowerree, the dean . . . would have been successful in his effort to get rid of me."[17]

Roxanne remained in law school and graduated, but it was a difficult year. Generally petite, she gained so much weight during her pregnancy that she could not fit in a standard desk, which had a table-arm designed to wrap around the front of the seated person. Worse, Roxanne recalled, she was largely ignored in class, and instructors stopped calling on her during her pregnancy "for fear of upsetting me and causing me to go into labor." Drake operated under the fairly standard academic calendar of the time, which meant that the fall semester ended in early January, immediately followed by finals. Roxanne gave birth to daughter Jackie on January 2, 1966, and final exams began a little over a week later. She worried about passing and studied for finals in the hospital "as hard as I ever studied." She "did fine" on her exams.[18]

In the midst of all this stress and change, Roxanne read Betty Friedan's pathbreaking 1963 book, *The Feminine Mystique*. Friedan challenged the idea that all women found fulfillment by taking up their roles as wives and mothers. Instead, she argued, society sold this idealized life to women through the education system, the media, and advertising, which pushed them into becoming homemakers. She concluded by suggesting that the feminine mystique held many women back, preventing them from developing their identities and finding personal fulfillment.

The widely read and discussed book was largely credited with launching the second-wave feminist movement, and three years later Friedan was one of the founders of the National Organization for Women. For Roxanne, it was like a light bulb went on: "I realized I was a feminist and always had been. Like so many other women I was relieved that there was a name for my unshakable belief that women were equal and entitled to equal rights." She soon became an ardent and vocal advocate for women's rights.[19]

But many were not yet ready for feminism, and her first speech on the subject did not go well. The talk grew out of a conversation Roxanne had at her bridge club with Mary Lou King in 1968, when King invited the young attorney to talk to her Sunday school class about women's issues. Roxanne readily agreed and soon spoke to a group of roughly thirty people about the basic inequalities in society, arguing that women should have the same legal rights as men. To her surprise, the crowd was immediately "offended" and "angry with me." "They ridiculed some of what I said," and "I was lucky I didn't get stoned on the spot" for espousing equal rights between the sexes.[20]

Her nascent association with the women's movement grew out of Roxanne's personal experience and her crusading spirit, which had already involved her in Democratic politics and the fight for civil rights. As with many young people of the era, Roxanne's first association with politics came with John Kennedy's bid for the White House. She was captivated by the dashing young candidate and, along with her classmates and instructors at St. Joseph Academy, thrilled by the possibility of a Catholic president. She volunteered for the Kennedy campaign and "put bumper stickers on cars at Merle Hay Mall whether the drivers really wanted them or not." On election day, the sixteen-year-old headed up the Polk County Democratic Party babysitting pool, which sent sitters to people's houses so they could go vote. When he won, Roxanne often said, "I thought my work had put Kennedy over the top."[21]

From there, Roxanne joined the Polk County Young Democrats, where she became acquainted with other young activists such as Cookie Brown, Tom Whitney, Dan Johnston, and Jerry Crawford. She moved up the group's ladder rapidly and in 1963, she defeated Ronn Pepper for its presidency, even though as a local KIOA disk jockey he plugged his candidacy on his radio program. While serving as its president in 1964, she increased the group's membership by more than 50 percent, bumping it up from 440 to over 700. She was also elected vice-president of the Iowa Young Democrats in 1964, and she served as its national committeewoman for the following two years.[22]

While Roxanne was in leadership roles with the Iowa Young Democrats, the group passed a number of liberal resolutions, including a call for the United States to recognize the People's Republic of China and abolish the House Un-American Activities Committee, loyalty oaths, and right-to-work laws. The Young Democrats also went on the record as condemning the Gulf of Tonkin Resolution—the 1964 congressional act that essentially gave Lyndon Johnson a blank check to carry out the war in Vietnam—and Roxanne soon became active in the mounting antiwar movement. She participated in peace demonstrations and marches through the early 1970s, when the United States finally pulled out of Vietnam.[23]

Roxanne also remained committed to boots on the ground campaigning. She volunteered for Harold Hughes's successful gubernatorial run in 1962 as well as his two reelection efforts and then his U.S. Senate victory in 1968, doing whatever was necessary around the state to ensure his victories. In 1964, she became a delegate to the Iowa State Democratic Convention and would remain so through 1974. Over that period, she served on the platform committee and the rules and bylaws committee. And if that were not enough, she was a precinct committeewoman, representing

Democratic voters in her precinct at the Polk County Democratic Party level from 1966 through 1972.[24]

Roxanne played important roles in two additional campaigns. In 1964, she supported prominent trial lawyer Lawrence "Larry" Scalise for attorney general. From Carlisle, a small town just south of Des Moines, Scalise had served as assistant Polk County attorney and as the first director of the Iowa Liquor Control Commission, and he had been the Democratic nominee for attorney general in 1962. Roxanne worked hard on his behalf in the primary and turned out the vote for him in a narrow victory over Des Moines attorney Don Wilson, who had been the Democratic candidate for attorney general in 1958 and 1960. She continued working for his successful campaign over Republican W. N. "Bill" Bump in November. Scalise must have been impressed with Roxanne's organizational skills and intelligence, for after she was fired during her pregnancy in 1965, he hired her in the attorney general's office.[25]

At the same time, Roxanne had undertaken a much more ambitious political task: she managed Willie Stevenson Glanton's campaign for the Iowa General Assembly. The wife of Luther Glanton, Jr., the municipal judge before whom Roxanne's father stood when she had him arrested in 1960, Glanton was a pathbreaker in her own right. She was born in Arkansas and received her college education in Tennessee before attending law school in Washington, D.C. After marrying and moving to Des Moines, she became only the second African American woman admitted to the Iowa State Bar Association in 1953. Three years later, she became the first African American woman to become an assistant county attorney in Polk County. Glanton was active in the Democratic Party, the League of Women Voters, and the National Association for the Advancement of Colored People.[26]

It was at the Des Moines chapter of the NAACP that Roxanne first met Willie Glanton in the early 1960s. Her initial ties to the organization began when Roxanne was introduced to the group by African American jazz musicians Irene Myles and Ernest "Speck" Redd, whom she had joined onstage as a singer a few times in downtown Des Moines clubs. This affiliation with the NAACP broadened and developed Roxanne's views on basic rights for all. Her insights solidified during her part-time work with many disadvantaged African American children at Evelyn Davis's Tiny Tots Day Care, the first such center in Des Moines's inner city, and they matured while she was in law school. Classmate Gary Ordway remembered Roxanne's ardent advocacy for civil rights and found her analysis of discrimination and the need for equality both sophisticated and heartfelt. The evolution of her thinking on these subjects was clearly influenced by Glanton's progressive ideas and activism. Roxanne soon saw her as a mentor, and the two developed a close friendship, which naturally spilled over into Democratic politics.[27]

In March 1964, Glanton announced her candidacy for the Iowa House of Representatives, and she selected Roxanne to head her campaign after the nineteen-year-old volunteered for the job. Glanton had been won over by Roxanne's passion, intelligence, and take-charge attitude, remembering her as an "attractive, alive, and vibrant" young person full of ideas. [28]

Glanton called for greater state aid to education, abolition of the death penalty, and expanded rights for African Americans. She acknowledged that her race was a factor in the election, but she said, "I would hope the substance of what I've had to say would take care of that." Roxanne organized, she networked, and she got Glanton supporters out to the polls. It worked. In the primary, Glanton came in second among the thirty-three Polk County Democrats seeking eleven nomination spots for the general election, which these candidates swept, winning all eleven House seats. She became the first African American woman elected to the Iowa General Assembly. A thrilled Roxanne recalled, "Neither of us had a clue what we were doing, but we won anyway."[29]

Glanton stayed in the statehouse one term but then returned to her private legal practice, where she continued advocating for equality in the realm of both civil rights and women's rights. Later she worked at the U.S. Small Business Administration and served on many church and community boards. She became a role model for Roxanne, and the two remained good friends until Glanton's death in 2017.[30]

Despite all these activities and responsibilities, Roxanne finished law school, graduating second in her class of 1966, although as fellow student

Larry Van Werden said, "She was probably our top student, although her attendance was less than stellar. She could get through with a lot of absences because she was that much smarter than the rest of us." With the end of law school in sight, Roxanne and her classmates started applying for jobs, but Drake officials would not let her participate in on-campus job interviews because of her pregnancy. As she struggled in her quest for a job, she kept thinking about another female law school graduate who was able to find work only as a legal secretary. Determined to avoid a similar fate, Roxanne assiduously avoided learning how to type, figuring that would take her out of the running for such positions.[31]

Richard Brinkman of Des Moines-based Dial Finance wanted to hire her as a corporate counsel and even upped his offer a couple of times, but Roxanne held out to do litigation. Ironically, she returned to her clerkship at Davis, Huebner, Johnson and Burt, where she had been fired a year earlier for being pregnant. The partners eventually offered her a full-time position, and with no other opportunities in sight Roxanne stayed on at the firm.[32]

Of course, this time around, Roxanne had an infant, but she was no longer pregnant, and the firm's partners were happy to welcome back the "energetic" young associate because she was "smart as a whip" and brought a "can-do attitude" to work every day. Her ability to put in the hours at work was due largely to Jim, who was supportive and whose jobs, especially once he got into real estate, gave him the flexibility to be a much more involved father than many at the time. "From the beginning," Roxanne told a reporter, "he's always been an equal parent. And a good one." At the same time, Roxanne had other assistance around the house. Her youngest sister Gina was thrilled to get out of her family's dysfunctional home in Excelsior, Minnesota, a suburb twenty miles west of Minneapolis—where she and Roxanne's parents and siblings then lived and where their father continued to be abusive—and help care for her new niece in that summer of 1966 and for several summers thereafter. It would have been a tight squeeze having Gina at their house on Carrie Avenue, but the couple bought a larger place right after Roxanne finished law school. Their new four-bedroom split-level home at 1623 Evans Street was about half a mile due south of their previous address.[33]

At Davis, Huebner, Johnson and Burt, Roxanne did a variety of legal work. She spent much of her time focusing on workers compensation cases under the direction of Fred Huebner but also worked with the firm's largest client, the Chicago and North Western Railway Company. Two incidents early on reflected the difficulties Roxanne and other women faced in their profession—it was an uphill battle to be taken seriously. In her first case, she represented the railroad in small claims court, but the judge, who was not used to seeing female attorneys, especially such young ones, did not believe twenty-two-year-old Roxanne was the lawyer. He called the firm to verify that she was an attorney, and from that point on Roxanne began carrying her certificate of admission to the Iowa Bar. At the same time, the partners at the firm decided that clients might respond better to correspondence from their new young associate if she signed her letters with the gender-neutral R. B. Conlin rather than Roxanne Barton Conlin. She refused, and the partners backed down.[34]

After roughly a year with Davis, Huebner, Roxanne was ready to move on. Harry Dahl, the Iowa industrial commissioner who administered Iowa's workers compensation service, hired her because of her experience with these cases. As one of several deputy commissioners, she worked alongside attorneys Barry Moranville, E. J. Giovannetti, and Frank Harrison investigating and settling work-related injury claims. Roxanne liked the job, and according to her colleague Giovannetti, "She took it very seriously, was meticulous about evidence, and was always fair."[35]

But Roxanne was one of the first women to hold a deputy commissioner position here, and in an awful twist, while trying to protect Iowa workers, she was sexually harassed on the job. Although widespread, sexual harassment was not publicly discussed or recognized as a problem. In fact, the term would not be coined until 1974, when it developed out of a consciousness-raising discussion led by feminist Lin Farley as part of a new field study course on women and work at Cornell University. From there, public awareness of the issue began to grow. Like so many others who dealt with similar incidents at the time, Roxanne was shocked and upset by the unwanted advance, but she also blamed herself, thinking she must have done something to cause it. With nowhere to turn, she kept quiet about the episode, but stress on the job increased.[36]

Meanwhile, she became pregnant again that spring, but she experienced more difficulties carrying the baby than she had the first time. This, coupled with an increasingly uncomfortable work environment, led her to quit abruptly in June 1968.[37]

For the next year and a half, Roxanne was a full-time wife and mother. That December, she gave birth to the couple's second child, a boy they named James Barton, J.B. Such a domestic existence, which Roxanne characterized as "at home with JB and Jackie, sleeping, eating, [and having] coffee with Jan"—Jan Macri, a neighbor and good friend—was a respite and a period of renewal for her. But being a stay-at-home mom was not part of her life plan, and as 1969 wound down, she followed up a lead and jumped back into the workforce on her own terms.[38]

Late that year, the Conlins were having dinner with friends Ben and Pam Cullison, when Ben suggested Roxanne join him at the Iowa Office of the Attorney General. Roxanne said she could not work for Attorney General Richard Turner, a Republican, but Cullison reminded her that he was a Democrat as well and that his political affiliation was not a major issue in the office. Turner, he said, just wanted good attorneys working for him. Roxanne was intrigued but noted that she was not ready to work full time, and again Cullison thought that Turner might be amenable.[39]

Roxanne met with Turner and pitched the idea of working for him part time. To her pleasant surprise, Cullison had been correct: Turner was interested. He hired her on a half-time basis with full benefits in December 1969, saying that they would reevaluate the situation two months down the road. The trial period came and went, nothing else was ever discussed, and Roxanne would stay there nearly seven years.[40]

From this new position, Roxanne was again on the move. She had overcome adversity and put together an impressive résumé in the legal field as well as in Democratic politics and the women's movement. She had married and had children, but while she cherished her family life, nothing could dampen her increasing activism on behalf of progressive causes and social justice. As she explained her simple but expansive goals to a *Des Moines Tribune* reporter in 1974, "The only thing I want to do is change the world."[41]

THREE

———

Change Agent

Roxanne had long been interested in effecting change, but during her first year of law school she thought the key to making a big impact was a degree from an elite institution. She applied to Harvard and Columbia and was admitted to both. Harvard, however, did not offer her any financial aid, which made it impossible for her to attend. Columbia provided her with scholarships, but the school would not allow her to live in its graduate student housing. Ironically, the ban she faced was not because she was female; rather, Roxanne was not permitted in the residential units because the nineteen-year-old did not meet the minimum age requirement of twenty-one.[1]

Columbia had been her first choice, and she was disheartened when it did not work out, but Roxanne had been wrong about needing a prestigious law degree to be a transformational leader. Indeed, staying at Drake and in Iowa could have been the best thing that happened to her. Here Roxanne had already begun building a network among attorneys and Democratic Party operatives, and here she was already being noticed for her intelligence, drive, and passion. At the same time, she had opportunities to get involved on the ground floor in areas that interested her, and like other successful people she jumped at the prospect. In her case, it was the women's rights movement that was taking off, and both personally and professionally Roxanne was smack in the middle of it, pushing for equality through existing groups, founding new organizations, fighting for changes in legislation, and rewriting sex discrimination law as the state's assistant attorney general heading up Iowa's civil rights division. Such activity led the *Des Moines Tribune* to call her "the most visible Iowa advocate of women's rights."[2]

Like many of her colleagues in the struggle for women's rights, Roxanne juggled many roles as assistant attorney general, political activist, wife, and mother as she tried to fit all the pieces of her life together. One key advantage she had in keeping her many plates spinning was the exceptional opportunity Richard Turner gave her to work as an assistant attorney general on a half-time basis. As she readily explained, "I was the world's only part-time assistant attorney general. I worked mornings, spent afternoons being a mom, and went back to work after [my children] went to bed."[3]

Her position at the attorney general's office began in late December 1969, when she joined fellow assistant attorney general and friend Ben Cullison on the state's lawsuit against a group of oil companies accused of "rigging prices on asphalt used on road and street improvement in this state." For Roxanne, this was trial by fire: she knew nothing about antitrust law. The case had started three years earlier, and Roxanne helped finish it by the end of January, with the oil companies agreeing to pay the state of Iowa $250,000 to settle the suit.[4]

Meanwhile, Turner looked to Roxanne to prosecute cases on behalf of the Iowa Civil Rights Commission, an agency established in 1965 to enforce the new Iowa Civil Rights Act. Roxanne was more than happy to do so. Defending the rights of others, especially the disadvantaged and those unable to fend for themselves, satisfied the core compulsion to protect people she had developed trying to shield her mother and siblings from her father's violence. As longtime friend Trudy Hurd put it, "Roxanne truly exists to help people who are less fortunate."[5]

Once she had read Iowa civil rights law, Roxanne realized that "every complaint" that came before the Iowa Civil Rights Commission "was resulting in a constitutional challenge," and it was therefore important to get a case before the Iowa Supreme Court. She got the chance with *Iron Workers Local 67 v. Hart* in 1971.[6]

The case involved Weitz Construction Company, which was building a new post office in Des Moines, and a local chapter of a trade union. The federal contract required Weitz to hire minority workers, but the company also had a contract with Iron Workers Local 67 to supply all iron personnel. The company tried to comply with federal regulations by working with the union to hire African American ironworkers, but Local 67 dragged its feet and obstructed the effort whenever possible. Weitz eventually faced a union-orchestrated sick-out that brought the job to a halt. A company official filed a complaint with the Iowa Civil Rights Commission, claiming the union had employed unfair labor practices. The commission investigated and, among other things, ordered the union to employ affirmative action efforts to recruit and hire minority workers. When the union refused, the case went to court, testing the constitutionality of the Iowa Civil Rights Act of 1965, which banned discrimination in employment or public accommodations based on race, religion, or national origin.[7]

When Roxanne took on the case, her life was threatened, and a cross was burned on her front lawn. But she persevered, and even though she remembered being "a really bad lawyer," she won, largely because "it was a very difficult case to lose." The court even suggested that Roxanne needed to hone her skills, writing in its opinion that her "evidence of pattern discrimination was not of that quality which makes an appellate court's work simple." It then listed several cases where attorneys had laid out detailed evidence of discrimination, something Roxanne should have done. Nonetheless, the Iowa Supreme Court upheld the constitutionality of the Iowa Civil Rights Act. Equally important for Roxanne and other feminist activists, it interpreted the act broadly, focusing on the law's intent to eliminate discrimination rather than its specific wording. This provided an opening for other types of discrimination cases. The court also upheld the power of the Iowa Civil Rights Commission to take action to meet the goals of the act. Specifically, according to historian

Sharon Lake, the "ruling allowed the ICRC to order institutional changes that would eliminate certain forms of sex discrimination more rapidly."[8]

Roxanne soon understood the importance of her position as the assistant attorney general overseeing the civil rights division. After the court's broad interpretation of the Iowa Civil Rights Act in *Iron Workers v. Hart*, she pushed to develop the state's law on sex discrimination, which had been added to the act in 1970. "We were at the very beginning," she realized. "The question of what the law meant was completely open." She began by drafting rules for her division that classified pregnancy discrimination as a type of sex discrimination. The Iowa Civil Rights Commission approved the new guidelines in 1972. She then actively pursued sex discrimination complaints in the commission and in court.[9]

Roxanne had begun laying the foundation for this work earlier, although she had not appreciated it at the time. From the late 1960s on, she had been building a network of female attorneys around the country who were promoting women's causes. This started shortly after she finished law school, while she was following *Weeks v. Southern Bell*. The 1966 sex discrimination case involved Leona Weeks, who claimed that her rights under the federal Civil Rights Act of 1964 had been violated when she was denied a promotion because she was a woman. National Organization for Women lawyer Sylvia Roberts took over the case and eventually won after several appeals in 1969. As the case moved through the system, Roxanne contacted Roberts, introduced herself, and offered her moral support. The two stayed in touch.[10]

Roxanne soon contacted others, and this informal network grew to include Ruth Bader Ginsburg, then a law professor at Rutgers and cofounder of the *Women's Rights Law Reporter*, the first law journal concentrating solely on women's rights, and Jane Picker, one of the first female law professors at Cleveland State University's Marshall College of Law and cofounder of the Women's Law Fund, an early nonprofit organization dedicated to fighting sex discrimination through education and litigation.[11]

The network was important for Roxanne, who understood that she and others in the group "were trying to work together to move the law forward." Once she became involved in her first sex discrimination case, she relied on the network to test ideas, discuss strategy, and exchange information on cases.[12]

Roxanne's first sex discrimination case came in the spring of 1971. Diane Kepner, a secretary at Homesteaders Life Insurance Company, believed she was fired because she "agitated for adding maternity benefits for employees to the group hospitalization insurance policy covering the firm's workers." As was common at the time, Homesteaders provided maternity benefits to wives of its male employees but not to its female workers. The firm was charged with "sex discrimination in awarding fringe benefits to male and female employees," and Roxanne argued that Kepner had been fired in retaliation for her activism.[13]

The following July, the Iowa Civil Rights Commission ruled in Kepner's favor, ordering Homesteaders to reinstate her and provide her with back salary for the seventeen months since she had been fired. More broadly, it demanded that the company cease its "discriminatory practices in the recruitment, hiring, classification, promotion and remuneration of employees in all of the conditions and privileges of employment." Specifically, the commission required the company to change its insurance coverage so that female employees received the same maternity benefits as wives of male employees.[14]

The victory was short lived, however. Homesteaders challenged the decision and, two years later, won when Judge John Hughes of the Fifth Judicial District Court of Iowa explained that firing Kepner had not been retaliatory and that the Iowa Civil Rights Commission did not have jurisdiction over the company's insurance programs under the Iowa Civil Rights Act. But while the case was being considered, Homesteaders had changed its insurance coverage to include maternity benefits for all employees. Because the policy had been changed, Roxanne chose not to appeal the case.[15]

In the meantime, she was involved in a number of other cases likely to move sex discrimination law forward. Early in the fall of 1971, the Iowa attorney general's office filed a complaint with the ICRC on behalf of Sally Huebner against American Republic Insurance Company. Huebner claimed that American Republic had a two-track system for its college-educated applicants, one for men and one for women. Males with bachelor's degrees were hired into a management training program, while female graduates were sent to the secretarial pool. Roxanne was eager to try the case because the firm's policy was "blatantly discriminatory." But Lex Hawkins, the attorney representing American Republic, and company officials realized that their hiring system was problematic and chose to settle. Huebner was put into the management training program and received back pay, while the firm's two-track hiring system was eliminated.[16]

During the Huebner case, Roxanne came into contact with Phylliss Henry, a woman interested in becoming a police officer. In 1970, Henry had returned to her native Des Moines from Isla Vista, California, after riots in that town led her to believe that her home state was a better place to raise her children. While she managed an apartment complex, Henry decided to take a course in police and community relations at Des Moines Area Community College. One day, the instructor told her there was federal money available through the Law Enforcement Assistance Administration that would cover the costs of tuition and books for the school's law enforcement program. Henry had long had an interest in police work, and she enrolled. She then began applying for jobs in Kansas City, Denver, and Dubuque, where she received the highest score on the written test, but no one hired her.[17]

A frustrated Henry got a boost in 1972 when the Equal Opportunity Employment Act extended the federal Civil Rights Act of 1964, prohibiting, among other things, gender discrimination in public employment. It was then that she applied to the Des Moines Police Department. To stop her application immediately, under orders from Chief Wendell Nichols, the department refused to weigh or measure her. The civil service office ordered it to do so, and Henry met the requirements of being at least 5 feet 9 inches tall and weighing at least 145 pounds. She also received the highest scores on the four civil service exams she took on the same day.[18]

But Henry continued to get the runaround, and a friend from church suggested she call Roxanne. Henry did, opening her conversation by saying, "I'm not a woman's libber . . . but I want to be a cop. I have children to support. I need a man's job, and I can do it." As she recalled, Roxanne was kind and even indulgent. She spent thirty minutes on the phone with Henry, carefully explaining the law and what police departments could and could not do in the hiring process. Henry would later learn that most of Roxanne's business calls lasted less than five minutes.[19]

From this point on, Roxanne became Henry's guardian angel, providing her with legal advice and moral support and acting as a sounding board as she encountered more roadblocks set up by the Des Moines Police Department. Henry was not notified of the place or time of the required physical agility test (then designed only for men) but fortunately learned of the test from a friendly civil service employee. She took it and passed it. When the department still dragged its feet, Roxanne called city attorney Phil Riley, who she said "understood the law." After talking with Roxanne, Riley informed Chief Nichols that Henry had to be hired, and in November 1972 she became the department's first female patrolman—the job title at the time. But that did not mean Henry was accepted. As Roxanne recalled, "She was criticized and ostracized and even choked into unconsciousness during physical training by other trainees. She was issued a male uniform and required to cut her hair 'like a man.'"[20]

The following March, after Henry completed her seventeen-week training at the police academy, she was recognized for "outstanding scholastic achievement." Chief Nichols, however, continued to make his opposition to Henry—and the idea of female police officers—clear, telling the *Des Moines Register* that if federal guidelines required women on police forces, "midgets may be next."[21]

Henry stayed at the police force for nine years, battling discrimination for much of her time with the department. Roxanne, however, remained in her corner, stayed in close touch with the city attorney, and kept pressure on the department, even threatening several lawsuits, although none was pursued. Henry was eventually promoted to master patrolman—the job title was changed to senior police officer after she and Roxanne filed a complaint with the Law Enforcement Assistance Administration. She advanced to sergeant in 1978. The two women remained in close touch, and down the road Henry would even work for Roxanne.[22]

Even as she helped ease the way for Henry's pioneering work as a Des Moines police officer, Roxanne continued to expand women's rights by taking on pregnancy discrimination. Her first case began in May 1972, when Linda Heinen, an elementary art teacher in the Johnston Community School District, a suburban district just north of Des Moines, contacted the Iowa attorney general's office. Heinen was pregnant and expecting her baby in October. She had challenged the district's policy requiring teachers to resign at the end of their fifth month of pregnancy with no guarantee of reemployment after the baby was born. Superintendent Louis Friestad proposed a compromise, which the school board approved. Heinen would step down at the end of the spring semester and would not teach in the fall. She would be reinstated in January 1973 at the beginning of the spring semester.[23]

Heinen did not think that was fair. She believed her rights were being violated and contacted the Iowa attorney general's office, where she was directed to Roxanne as head of its civil rights division. Roxanne agreed that the district's policy violated the Iowa Civil Rights Act. They filed a sexual discrimination complaint with the Iowa Civil Rights Commission and at the same time appealed the school board's decision. The board refused to change its position, so Roxanne represented Heinen at the commission's hearing in September. During the hearing, district officials struggled for reasons why Heinen should not be in the classroom that fall. Her principal testified that Heinen looked "less enthusiastic" after she became pregnant and said Heinen could not teach because she could no longer bend down to retrieve objects from the floor. Roxanne immediately jumped on the last comment and had Heinen stand up and touch her toes. Her client, Roxanne noted, could clearly meet the principal's stated physical requirement for teaching.[24]

In December 1972, Heinen and Roxanne won a big victory: the ICRC ruled that the Johnston Community School District was guilty of sexual discrimination when it blocked Heinen from teaching in the fall. It ordered the district to pay back wages for that semester and sick leave for the time she would have been unable to teach because of her baby's birth in October. Not surprisingly, the district appealed the decision, and the case was heard in Polk County District Court. The following December, Judge John Hughes, the same judge who had overturned the Homesteaders ruling, also overturned the ICRC decision, saying that Heinen had not faced discrimination. The district, Hughes concluded, was within its rights "to prohibit anything which would substantially interfere" with its students' education. If Heinen had taught that fall, he believed, her eight-week absence for maternity leave out of the eighteen-week semester would have harmed her students' education. Roxanne was frustrated but promised to appeal.[25]

Meanwhile, the same year Heinen filed her complaint with the ICRC, two teachers—Joan Parr and Judy McCarthy—in Cedar Rapids, 130 miles east of Des Moines, were required to take mandatory leaves when they became pregnant. Parr was not tenured, and she was fired; McCarthy was tenured and was therefore ordered to take compulsory leave with the understanding that she would be reinstated after her baby was born. Both filed discrimination complaints with the city's human rights commission, but when the commission was unable to get the women reinstated its director, Reverend Bill Cotton, contacted Roxanne and asked her to step in.[26]

Roxanne shepherded the Parr and McCarthy cases through the Iowa courts until the two were combined and heard before the Iowa Supreme Court. While the case was being considered, the United States Supreme Court weighed in on the issue with *Geduldig v. Aiello* in 1974, "remarkably," Roxanne recalled, holding that pregnancy discrimination was not sex discrimination—and thus did not fall under the equal protection clause of the Fourteenth Amendment—because "nonpregnant persons could include men and women and, therefore pregnancy discrimination was not sex discrimination." Put another way, scholar Sharon Lake explained the decision: "If all pregnant employees are treated alike, there is not sex discrimination."[27]

Roxanne, however, pushed progress for women forward once again by persuading the Iowa Supreme Court to see the situation differently.

In its 1975 decision in *Cedar Rapids Community School District v. Parr*, the Iowa Supreme Court became the first in the nation to hold that the school district's policy on pregnancy was, in fact, sex discrimination and violated the Iowa Civil Rights Act. This landmark decision put the court at odds with the U.S. Supreme Court, but it essentially ended pregnancy discrimination in Iowa and helped pave the way for the Pregnancy Discrimination Act of 1978, which amended the federal Civil Rights Act of 1964 to prohibit sex discrimination on the basis of pregnancy. In recalling the event years later, Roxanne commended the court: "The Iowa Supreme Court has always been for extending rights and protecting people. This is something we as Iowans should have great pride in."[28]

In light of this precedent-setting ruling, Roxanne and the Johnston Community School District negotiated a settlement in Linda Heinen's pregnancy discrimination complaint. The district paid Heinen $1,700 to cover a portion of the "back pay, sick pay, and hospital benefits" she would have received had she been allowed to teach until shortly before her baby was born. At the same time, Superintendent Friestad announced the district's new teacher pregnancy policy, which provided maternity leave and sick leave benefits to teachers on maternity leave and guaranteed those teachers a return to the classroom after their babies were born. Heinen was happy to end the standoff and pleased with the settlement. "I felt I had [the money] coming. I felt I was right, and I guess I was."[29]

Although Roxanne's penchant for battling discrimination against women was clear, her boss, Attorney General Richard Turner, thought that she was a solid attorney who was "equally aggressive" regardless of the case or its focus. He understood that Roxanne's zeal for fighting discrimination broadly ruffled feathers but was needed, even though the Republican Turner thought some of her ideas were a "little far-out liberal." And he frequently defended Roxanne, telling her, only a little tongue in cheek, that "if I didn't have a legislator in my office asking me to fire you, I knew you were out of town."[30]

Suggestive of her wide-ranging and vigorous defense of justice, Roxanne took several additional cases to the Iowa Supreme Court. Three were noteworthy, although she did not win them all. The first involved

Heriberto Zamora, an employee of Massey Ferguson who claimed he was fired in March 1970 because he was Mexican American. He immediately contacted the Iowa Civil Rights Commission, which began a number of discussions with the farm equipment company. With no resolution, Zamora filed a formal written complaint with the commission that August. It investigated, found in his favor, and ordered the manufacturer to reinstate Zamora with back pay and change its employment practices. Massey Ferguson appealed the order in district court, arguing that Zamora's written complaint had not been filed within the required ninety-day period. The court agreed with Massey Ferguson and dismissed the complaint.[31]

Roxanne appealed the decision to the Iowa Supreme Court, but the case remained focused on the technicality that the complaint had been lodged after the mandatory filing period was over, not on the discrimination issue. In 1973, the court found that the 90-day period was "an absolute requirement of the law" and upheld the decision of the lower court. Interestingly, because the case raised the question of a 90-day reporting period, the following year the Iowa legislature extended the period for filing a complaint for an alleged act of discrimination to 120 days.[32]

The second case, also settled in 1973, involved a discrimination charge as well. Leo Griggs was an African American who worked at Wilson-Sinclair Company, a Cedar Rapids meat-packing operation. He applied to the firm's all-white mechanical department, the only African American ever to do so. Entry into the department required applicants to pass three tests. Griggs passed the first two but did not meet the required score on the Bennett Mechanical Comprehension Test and was rejected. Actually, he had been applying to the department since 1962, when no tests were required, and he was rejected then as well.[33]

Griggs saw the testing procedure as discriminatory and filed a complaint with the ICRC in 1970. After investigating, it concluded that the tests were discriminatory and ordered Wilson-Sinclair to end its use of the Bennett test, move Griggs to the mechanical department, provide him with back pay, and begin an affirmative action hiring program. The company challenged the ruling in district court, which reversed the commission's ruling and threw out the complaint, arguing that Griggs and the commission had not shown that the Bennett test was used to prevent African Americans from moving into the mechanical department. Try as she might, Roxanne was unable to convince the Iowa Supreme Court otherwise, and in *Wilson-Sinclair Company v. Griggs* it upheld the lower court's decision.[34]

She had much better luck in a case against officials in Worth County, 130 miles north of Des Moines on the Minnesota border. Questions were initially raised in 1969 by local politician and Iowa representative Kenneth Logemann, who noticed extremely high mileage claims made by the county supervisors. This led the state auditor's office, the attorney general's office, and the Iowa Bureau of Criminal Investigation to look into the matter. It blossomed into a full investigation into the entire Worth County Board of Supervisors—Harvey Bartz, Arnold Buechele, and Boyd Harmon—which uncovered exaggerated mileage claims submitted for reimbursement, inappropriate use of county property and monies, and the acceptance of gratuities.[35]

A Worth County grand jury looked into the matter, but in January 1972 it concluded that there was not enough evidence to charge the supervisors with wrongdoing. At that point, the attorney general's office called for reopening the investigation and petitioned the Worth County District Court to hear the case and remove the supervisors.[36]

Roxanne pursued the case for the state, which took place that summer in Northwood, the Worth County seat. "It was a highly contentious atmosphere," she remembered. "The courtroom had a circus feel. Bill Pappas, the attorney for the supervisors, had a cheering section; I had a cheering section; and the *Globe Gazette* covered every detail, including what I wore each day."[37]

In laying out the state's argument for dismissing all the supervisors, Roxanne presented a large amount of evidence that they had misused county funds, accepted all-expenses-paid trips from businesses that had contracts with Worth County, and claimed illegitimate mileage and per diem expenses. For example, she told the court, "If they had driven the mileage they claimed for county business, they could have driven to the moon and back." Likewise, she found that the supervisors had collected per diem business expenses for time they were in the hospital, at ballgames, or at farm sales.[38]

After nearly a month, District Court Judge Blair Wood handed down a surprise ruling: he removed Boyd Harmon from office but dismissed the cases against Arnold Buechele and Harvey Bartz. The judge explained that there was "convincing evidence" that Harmon had "presented false claims for mileage," meriting his removal from office. But Wood felt the evidence against Buechele and Bartz was not as clear, although he said that the actions of all three supervisors "were close to the danger line," and he "did not condone" their "use of petty cash funds, the acceptance of expense-paid trips, or filing claims for each other when hospitalized."[39]

The attorney general appealed the decision, arguing that Buechele and Bartz should also have been removed from office, and Roxanne went before the Iowa Supreme Court to finish the job. She won. In December 1974, the court concluded that "the mileage claims submitted by both defendants were excessive" and necessitated their removal from office. It added that the gratuities they accepted and the slush funds they maintained were also illegal and warranted their ouster.[40]

Roxanne was well suited for her work at the attorney general's office. She was dedicated to protecting others and ensuring their civil rights, and she had the drive and energy to do so. At the same time, the job was good for her. It gave her the opportunity to sharpen her litigation skills, often before the state's highest court, and because the position remained part time, she had the time and flexibility to raise her children and advocate for women's rights.

Just as she had connected with other feminist attorneys around the country, Roxanne had also been building relationships with like-minded women in Iowa. One of these women was Virginia Watkins. By the late 1960s, Watkins's progressive bent had led her to advocate for civil rights and join the peace movement opposing the war in Vietnam. She also became part of a consciousness-raising group that, combined with her reading of Betty Friedan's *The Feminist Mystique*, developed and refined her emerging feminist thinking. In the midst of this awakening, Watkins joined the National Organization for Women in 1967.[41]

Two years later, in February, Watkins heard Betty Friedan speak at Drake University. She laid out her argument that culture and the media conspired to convince women that fulfillment came from caring for their husbands and children rather than pursuing their own interests. "You're expected to find a potentially successful junior executive to help find your identity, and then share the material goods furnished by a successful middle-class husband," not really "expected to be a person" with your own goals and desires. Friedan then talked about NOW and her interest in seeing local chapters established in Des Moines and across the country.[42]

It took Watkins "a year or two to work up the courage to try to organize a NOW chapter because this was something so new and controversial." She put together a list of other NOW members who lived in Des Moines (which included Roxanne) and added a few others, and late in 1970 she invited them to a meeting at her house in Clive, a western suburb of Des Moines, to discuss the creation of a NOW chapter. Those attending were Roxanne; community activist and philanthropist Louise Noun; her sister-in-law Dannie Rosenfield; Drake sociologist Sally Hacker; Pauline Johnson, another national NOW member; Kay Plymat, a nurse; Pamela Wilson, a writer and editor; and Louise Swartzwalder, a *Des Moines Register* reporter.[43]

The group met several times before announcing public meetings. That April, they held an organizational meeting at the city's Westside Branch Library that featured speakers Wilma Scott Heide and Mary Jean Collins-Robson, two national NOW directors. After that, the group began the chartering process, and in June the Des Moines NOW chapter was established, with Watkins named as president, Pam Cullison as vice-president, and Roxanne as vice-president for legal affairs.[44]

In the midst of her early activity with the local NOW chapter, Roxanne began thinking about the upcoming Iowa precinct caucuses and the presidential election in 1972. She had happily followed the career of Shirley Chisholm of New York, who in 1968 became the first African American woman elected to Congress. Chisholm was considering a run for the presidency, and Roxanne called her office to encourage her to do so. Chisholm formally announced her bid for the presidency in late January 1972. Shortly before that, Chisholm supporters in Des Moines established a campaign headquarters for her there and named Louise Noun and Edna Griffin, a well-known local civil rights activist, as cochairs of the state effort.[45]

Roxanne worked behind the scenes. Although Chisholm received less than 1.5 percent of the vote at the Iowa caucuses, Roxanne kept working for her at the Polk County Democratic convention and then at the party's state convention. Iowa ultimately sent four committed Chisholm delegates to the Democratic National Convention in Miami. There Chisholm, the first African American and the first woman to seek the presidential nomination from a major political party, garnered just over 5 percent of the delegate vote. George McGovern won the Democratic nomination but lost the general election to incumbent Richard Nixon.[46]

Meanwhile, the local chapter of NOW was not the only new women's advocacy group being established in Des Moines, and not surprisingly Roxanne was involved in both. As her commitments to these organizations—the Iowa Commission on the Status of Women and the Iowa Women's Political Caucus—grew, she became less active in NOW, even dropping her membership for a few years in the mid-1970s.

The Iowa Commission on the Status of Women's origins dated back to the early 1960s, when President John Kennedy created the President's Commission on the Status of Women. That body recommended governors create similar groups in their states, and Iowa governors Harold Hughes and Bob Ray both did so. Then in 1971, history teacher and feminist Cristine Whitgraf (Wilson after she remarried in 1972) and others worked to make the Governor's Commission on the Status of Women a permanent body, which would entitle it to state funding. Their efforts paid off the following year, when the Iowa General Assembly established the Iowa Commission on the Status of Women. That fall, Governor Ray named Wilson chair of the commission and appointed twenty-one other Iowans to the group, including her good friend Roxanne.[47]

Commission members jumped in, immediately working to better the lives of Iowa women. They initially chose to focus on education, child care, legal discrimination, and welfare, and they established task forces for each area designed to develop legislative priorities, which were forwarded to the governor and legislature. Roxanne worked with the legal discrimination group, and one of the first items it tackled was a review of the Iowa Code for gender-specific language that discriminated on the basis of sex. The task force used a computer to search the code for the words "woman, women, girl, girls, lady, ladies, man, men, boy, boys, wife, mother, mothers, husband, father, fathers, female, females, feminine, married, marries, marry, marrying, marriage, survivor, survivors." "The computer printout was thousands of pages and when piled up, it was over two feet tall," Roxanne remembered.[48]

Once sections of the code that included biased or discriminatory language were identified, Roxanne was charged with rewriting them in gender-neutral language. Then, in what appears comical today, as the bill was being considered there arose a controversy over a section covering beauticians, who at the time were not licensed to cut men's hair. The bill proposed revising this to allow them to cut men's hair. But many legislators opposed that change, and women's groups were tying up their representatives' phone lines demanding that they pass the entire bill. Brice Oakley, a Republican state representative at the time, phoned Roxanne to ask her to "call her people off."[49]

Roxanne refused, telling Oakley to "vote and then we'll be done." She and the commission were more committed to the other changes they were seeking in the code, and the haircutting topic was eventually set aside, but the rest of the bill—employing neutral references in place of gender-specific references—passed. In fact, many other legislative changes that the commission pushed (and that Roxanne had a hand in) passed in 1974 as well. The requirement of corroborating evidence of a rape victim's testimony was eliminated. Sex discrimination in housing sales or rentals became illegal, licensing procedures for child care facilities were developed, and inheritance laws were changed so that a widow no longer had to prove her economic contribution to take possession of an estate—it was now assumed that half of any property held in joint tenancy belonged to the surviving spouse.[50]

One of the major reasons for the commission's successes in 1974 and thereafter was the active support of the Iowa Women's Political

Caucus, the statewide chapter of the National Women's Political Caucus. Roxanne was the driving force behind its creation. Two years earlier, in July 1971, leading feminists of the time—including attorney and U.S. Representative Bella Abzug; Betty Friedan; Shirley Chisholm; Gloria Steinem, journalist, lecturer, and cofounder of *Ms.* magazine later in 1971; and Jill Ruckelshaus, a future commissioner for the U.S. Commission on Civil Rights—joined more than three hundred other women at a conference in Washington, D.C., to found the National Women's Political Caucus. The bipartisan organization was established to expand women's involvement in politics by identifying, promoting, training, and supporting female candidates for political office.[51]

Although Roxanne was aware of the NWPC's creation, she had not paid too much attention to it until she received a phone call from friend and feminist Ione Shadduck, an associate professor in physical education at Drake University, asking if she planned to go to the group's initial biennial convention in Houston in February 1973. That was the first Roxanne heard of the meeting, but she decided to go and was only one of two Iowans who attended. Here she met the "luminaries of the movement," including Abzug, Chisholm, and Steinem, and here, because she was well versed in parliamentary procedure, she became involved in drafting the organization's bylaws. Before leaving, women at the convention elected Texas attorney, Democrat, and politician Frances "Sissy" Farenthold as its first chair.[52]

Roxanne returned home to Iowa energized and interested in starting a state chapter of the organization, but she became busy with work at the attorney general's office. A few months passed before she sent handwritten letters—because, as mentioned previously, she never learned to type—to women from all over the state who she thought might be interested in forming such a group. The correspondence included an invitation and map to her Evans Street home on Des Moines's south side, where she planned an afternoon meeting on June 3, 1973. Thirty-four women—including Cristine Wilson; Louise Noun; Mary Louise Smith, a prominent Iowa Republican; Minnette Doderer, a Democratic state senator from Johnson

County; Lynn Cutler, a Waterloo Democrat who would become the first woman on the Black Hawk County Board of Supervisors and would later serve as vice-chair of the Democratic National Committee; and Dagmar Vidal, a member of the executive committee of the Democratic National Committee—joined Roxanne that afternoon.[53]

After some discussion, they formed the Iowa Women's Political Caucus, committed "to awaken, organize and assert the vast political power represented by women, who constitute a majority of voters," and "to reach out to every woman across the State, to assure her of first class citizenship and full and equal participation in the political process." They then drafted preliminary bylaws, named Roxanne as the organization's temporary chair, and began planning an initial state convention to be held that fall in Ames, forty miles north of Des Moines. In the meantime, Roxanne prepared a manual for organizing local caucuses throughout Iowa, and an additional statewide organizational meeting was held that July at Drake University.[54]

The three-day statewide conference was scheduled for September 28 to 30. The conveners enlisted two high-profile leaders from NWPC— Sissy Farenthold and Jill Ruckelshaus—as featured speakers and recruited Governor Robert Ray to offer opening remarks. Planned workshops throughout the weekend examined women's rights, child care, lobbying, and getting involved in the political process. Organizers expected 200 at the conference but were overwhelmed when nearly 700 women representing all the state's ninety-nine counties attended. "It was incredible," Roxanne recalled, "we really hit a nerve and met a need." Indeed, the Iowa Women's Political Caucus had. During its first year, the organization had a membership of roughly 1,000 and maintained a mailing list of 2,000, and by 1975 the *Ames Tribune* reported that it had "5,000 dues-paying members."[55]

This rapid growth made IWPC the largest women's organization in Iowa and the largest state chapter of NWPC until it was surpassed in 1980 by chapters in California and Texas. Roxanne attributed the group's early success to hard work, its low membership dues (three dollars a year at the time), and "our rigorous devotion to bipartisanship." Republican Mary Louise Smith agreed but added that "the impetus behind our success is . . . that women are finally becoming political." But she emphasized that it was "not non-partisan," believing that "everyone in the caucus should be involved in one of the political parties."[56]

Members of IPWC left their first state convention with a path forward. They formally adopted their bylaws and laid out their legislative priorities, which included banning sex discrimination in a variety of areas, removing gender-specific language from the Iowa Code, revising the state's rape and inheritance laws, and improving welfare benefits. Predictably, these goals aligned with those of the Iowa Commission on the Status of Women. And members elected Roxanne as IWPC's first chair. Shortly after the meeting, the group took its first public stand, endorsing seventeen women running in municipal elections across the state. Sixteen won, and although Roxanne doubted IWPC's endorsement made much difference, the organization took credit for these wins, and its significance grew in the public eye.[57]

Roxanne would head the group for two years, spending almost all her free time ensconced in its office near the capitol building at Executive Hills East, 1223 East Court Avenue. From there, she drafted and redrafted bills for the 1974 legislative session, often running across the street to the capitol to work with female legislators and lobby and cajole for passage of IPWC's agenda. And it was from this office that Roxanne and paid staffer Joan Von Stein organized the telephone trees that tied up phone lines and convinced legislators to back the prowomen legislation in 1974. With the exception of increasing welfare benefits to meet the minimum standard of need, the group achieved all its legislative priorities that year.[58]

That September, the group held its second annual conference in the Memorial Union at Iowa State University in Ames. Governor Ray again indicated his support for IWPC, this time by attending the fund-raiser on Friday evening, and Bella Abzug rallied the thousand attendees the following day. Roxanne was reelected as chair.[59]

Over the next few years, IWPC continued to push a progressive agenda, but it never did convince the legislature to increase welfare benefits. It did, however, win a big victory in 1976 by getting the state's sexual assault laws revised to make marital rape a crime when force or threat of force was involved. Meanwhile, in an effort to reach women where they lived, the group held twenty-four Women 2000: A New Voice for the Future conferences in communities all across the state over the course of 1975 and 1976. These seminars examined "public policies affecting women, the expanding role of women, and the future of society." A year later, IWPC took its message to teenagers when it began the annual Girls Leadership Camp, a workshop for high school girls.[60]

Roxanne was right in the middle of all this activity, traveling frequently to meetings throughout the state and making presentations for IWPC. To shorten travel time and make even more appearances at local caucus meetings possible and to fulfill a childhood dream of being a pilot, she began taking flying lessons. Roxanne loved flying and enjoyed the training, but she struggled with the scary intentional stall maneuver—a required part of the instruction to teach pilots how to recognize and recover from an engine stall—before she finally got her pilot's license.[61]

The license made Roxanne's life more convenient, especially with her work for IWPC as she continued to crisscross the state, often making twenty speeches a month on behalf of the organization. Linda Hanson, an early member of IWPC and the founder of the North Iowa Women's Political Caucus, believed Roxanne was essential to IWPC's creation, rise, and many accomplishments. "The time was ripe for such an organization in Iowa, and Roxanne was the right person to lead us. There was nobody else like her. Her passion and energy were infectious, she had strong leadership skills but was approachable, and she understood that we represented all women in the state, rich and poor, Republican and Democrat, those in the workforce and homemakers, and focused on inclusion. She was brilliant, well informed, and resolute, but she was also funny and had a great sense of humor. Maybe most important, she was a role model for all of us."[62]

With the Iowa Women's Political Caucus enjoying success, Roxanne began to think about bigger stages and greater challenges. An opportunity came in 1975 when Sissy Farenthold prepared to step down as chair of the National Women's Political Caucus. Roxanne chose to vie for the position.

Her boss, Attorney General Richard Turner, in fact, encouraged her to run, but she pledged to resign as an assistant attorney general if elected.[63]

Two others ran for the office: Democrat Dolores Delahanty, then vice-chair of NWPC, and Audrey Rowe, an African American Republican who was chair of the organization's chapter in Washington, D.C. Roxanne appeared to be the leading candidate as the group's conference opened on Friday, June 27. But according to Louise Swartzwalder, "party loyalties began to surface in the national race," and Republicans in attendance met to consider backing Rowe. Key Iowan Mary Louise Smith, at the time chair of the National Republican Committee, chose party loyalty over state affiliation and friendship with Roxanne, and when the election took place on Sunday Roxanne lost to Rowe by three votes.[64]

Linda Hanson was at the convention and recalled that most of the Iowa delegates "were dumbfounded and devastated" by Smith's support of Rowe, and Roxanne was "very disappointed" by the loss. Nonetheless, Roxanne remained committed to the Iowa Women's Political Caucus, serving as the keynote speaker, for example, at most of the Women 2000 conferences. She also stayed on at the attorney general's office, but her days there were numbered. Because of her very public activism on behalf of women, Roxanne was frequently in the news, and regardless of any particular article's focus, she was always identified as an assistant attorney general. This constant association of the attorney general's office with the women's cause, which was a contentious issue for many, drove conservatives crazy, and a growing number demanded that Turner dismiss her. The attorney general thought highly of Roxanne and had always supported her, but the pressure became too much, and in the fall of 1976 he told her she had to go. Roxanne understood. It was an amicable parting of the ways, so much so that Turner threw a big party for her when she left.[65]

She was now at a crossroads. Roxanne's success and high profile at the attorney general's office and the Iowa Women's Political Caucus had led many to see a political future for her. She did have such aspirations. While in high school, she told Frank Comito, whom she was dating at the time and who would become a prominent Des Moines attorney, that she intended to be governor of Iowa one day. As early as 1974, she thought of running for attorney general had Turner not sought the office again. She also considered seeking the Democratic nomination for the U.S. Senate that year, but she chose not to run when liberal Democratic congressman John Culver decided to run for the seat. Roxanne noted, "I didn't think I could beat Culver and nobody runs to lose." Thoughts of running came up again in the fall of 1976, but the timing did not seem right to her.[66]

Not ready to make any long-term commitments, Roxanne took a one-year consultant's position at the National Commission on the Observance of International Women's Year with the U.S. Department of State. Here under Catherine East, deputy coordinator of the Secretariat for International Women's Year at the State Department, she could continue her efforts on behalf of women, and although she had to travel to Washington, D.C., occasionally, she was able to do most of the job from Des Moines.[67]

Her intensity and exceptional intelligence coupled with, in her husband's words, her "phenomenal energies" were certainly important factors in Roxanne's very public successes. But so too was her marriage to Jim, whom daughter Jackie described as "completely committed to Mother." Jim explained that early on in their marriage "we made a commitment . . . that she already had an interest in politics and I had an interest in business. And we made a commitment to each other that we would leave the house each morning and that I would pursue as substantial an economic base as I could, and she would pursue a political base and when we came home, we would attempt to predicate our relationship, our family relationship on love and truth."[68]

Jim fulfilled this pledge, rising rapidly in the local world of real estate. After a couple of years with Cooper Homes, he moved over to Stanbrough Realty, an up-and-coming firm in the Des Moines market, in 1969. Three years later, he was noticed by Bill Knapp, owner of Iowa Realty, the largest real estate firm in the state, who recruited Jim as a sales manager focusing on the south side of Des Moines. Jim opened several sales offices for the expanding company over the decade, and Knapp remembered him as a "good manager." In 1968, Jim also began investing in real estate on his own; he and Roxanne bought five properties on Southwest Frazier Avenue, several blocks south of their home on Evans Street. With this stake in the market, he started buying additional properties by borrowing against these holdings. Jim continued the practice, commonly called pyramiding, and built a substantial real estate portfolio over the next few years.[69]

The Conlins were a two-career middle-class family at a time when less than half the nation's mothers worked outside the home, and Jim's financial success made it possible for Roxanne to work part time at the attorney general's office and pursue her political and social interests. He also remained involved at home, sharing parental responsibilities at a time when many fathers did not. It was Jim, for example, who woke the children up in the morning, gave them breakfast, and got them out the door to school. And unlike most other middle-class families of the period, the Conlins had a series of full-time housekeeper-nannies, beginning in the early 1970s, who kept the home in order and helped care for the children.[70]

Balancing family life and two careers was difficult, and as Roxanne remembered, "I don't think we so much as went to a movie for several years." Children Jackie and J.B., along with several stray cats that Roxanne adopted and a pair of miniature poodles named Jack and Jill, kept life in the Conlins' split-level home on Evans Street hopping. Once J.B. became interested in reptiles, an iguana and a boa constrictor named Harriet were added to the mix. At one point, Harriet became sick, and Roxanne had to come home daily from the attorney general's office to give it penicillin shots. "Snakes are not stupid," she recollected, "and the task became nearly impossible, but the snake recovered."[71]

Jackie was an active child, participating in Brownies with her mother and the YMCA's Indian Princesses program with her father. She also started dancing, taking lessons at the city's popular Betty Hill Dance Studios. J.B., meanwhile, had some difficulty. He was born with congenital esotropia—misaligned or crossed eyes—and required surgery and eye patches as a toddler to correct the problem. He would later struggle with dyslexia, much like his father had, but Roxanne hired a tutor to help him deal with this.[72]

J.B. was a handful. The rambunctious boy was expelled from preschool at Wakonda Christian Church for frequent fighting, and he recalled that he and Jackie "could be hard on our nannies." For example, in what conjures up a cartoonish image, after one nanny tried unsuccessfully to get J.B. to eat tomatoes, he poked her with a tack, and she chased him out into the yard with a frying pan in hand. Jim and Roxanne worked to channel J.B.'s boisterous behavior with activities such as Indian Guides, where Jim gave his energetic son the name Babbling Brook, and youth flag football.[73]

Extended family was important to the Conlins. They saw a lot of Jim's sister, Judy, who lived in Ames with her husband and two children, and Roxanne's youngest sister, Gina, who still lived with her parents in Excelsior and then Deephaven, western suburbs of Minneapolis. Gina spent several weeks each summer with Roxanne and Jim in order to help with the children and escape the incessant turmoil at home until she graduated from high school in 1973. Roxanne's mother and father had remained together, but because Bill's violence and verbal abuse of Alice persisted, the marriage was clearly on its last legs.[74]

Alice had been diagnosed with depression, a condition she had probably endured for some time. She tried various psychiatric treatments, including electroconvulsive shock therapy, but none completely removed the dark clouds, and she attempted suicide in 1970. Her children had her committed to the locked psychiatric ward at St. Mary's Hospital in Minneapolis. Shortly after she returned home, Bill walked out. From that point on, Roxanne had only sporadic contact with her father.[75]

Roxanne, Jim, and the children usually spent Thanksgiving and Christmas with family, sometimes Jim's sister and her family, but most often they celebrated holidays at Alice's home in Deephaven. Jackie and J.B. loved spending time there with their grandmother as well as their aunts, uncles, and cousins, and by the time they were in elementary school they spent a week or two each summer at their grandmother's home.[76]

A troubling incident shook the Conlin marriage in 1972 when Jim, who was an alcoholic, got into an argument with Roxanne when he was drinking. The fight escalated and became loud and animated to the point that Roxanne's violent childhood flashed before her. She saw signs pointing to a future she did not want, and she immediately moved out. She rented an apartment in West Des Moines, and the couple lived separately for six months, but ultimately Roxanne returned home, recalling that "I really loved him." Jim was lost without her, and before she came back she demanded that he quit drinking. He did, giving it up cold turkey, and the couple put the episode behind them.[77]

The Conlins moved on, with Jim renewing his commitment to ensuring that Roxanne's life was as comfortable and challenging as she wished. J.B. grew up seeing this dedication in everyday life, recalling, "I have never seen a man more devoted to a woman than my father is to my mother."[78]

The couple gradually returned to their normal rhythms and routines, but Roxanne opened the family's door to change a few years later when Debbie Conlin, Jim's sixteen-year-old daughter from his first marriage, moved into their home. Debbie had been a presence at Conlin family gatherings for the last ten years but had largely lived in and around Fort Dodge, a city one hundred miles northwest of Des Moines. Her mother, Janette Klein, was not prepared to raise children, so Debbie and Doug Klein, her half brother, were generally brought up by Debbie's maternal grandparents, Jim and Maude Jones, and her paternal grandparents, Cy and Evelyn Conlin.[79]

Janette briefly took the children and moved to New Orleans in 1965 before bringing them back to Fort Dodge the following year. She remarried in 1969, and the couple took the children to Iowa City, where Janette planned to get a college degree at the University of Iowa. But there she began experimenting with drugs and became an addict. In 1973, the family pulled up stakes again and moved to Humboldt, a small town eighteen miles north of Fort Dodge.[80]

Roxanne grew more and more concerned about Debbie's deteriorating situation and told her she could always move in with them in Des Moines. Debbie did so in 1975. Her arrival prompted the family to look for a larger house, which they soon found and purchased. They moved into the two-story contemporary frame home at 6116 Southwest Forty-Eighth Avenue (now McKinley Avenue) on the city's southwest side just east of Sixty-Third Street in 1976. Much to J.B.'s delight, it had a big yard and a swimming pool. As it turned out, the extra space would soon be needed even more than they had first realized.[81]

If Debbie's home life had been troubled, Doug's grew even worse after she left. Janette and her husband split up, and she and Doug moved back to Iowa City, where she fell deeper into the drug scene. Doug had already started smoking pot and hash, and in the increasingly unsavory environment he soon moved on to windowpanes and microdots, forms of LSD. Meanwhile, because he and his mother faced physical abuse from her new boyfriend, Doug spent much of his time on the streets, avoiding the violence at home by sleeping in cars or abandoned buildings. Debbie had kept in touch with Doug and knew of his worsening predicament. She went to Roxanne and asked if Doug could come for a visit. Roxanne compassionately agreed, and Doug packed all his belongings in a paper bag and took a bus to Des Moines.[82]

With his hair down the middle of his back and his Dashiki shirt, the fifteen-year-old stood out in the Conlins' upper-middle-class neighborhood, but Roxanne went out of her way to make Doug feel at home during his two-week respite from the streets. She and Jim even took him and the family on a trip to the Worlds of Fun amusement park in Kansas City. Of his stay, Doug remembered thinking, "So this is what a normal suburban family should be." As his visit wound down, Doug asked if he could stay permanently, and Roxanne said yes—even though she had two impressionable children in the house and knew that the move could create difficult and complicated situations. Eleven-year-old daughter Jackie was initially scared of the streetwise teenager, but she recalled his moving in as "that was what Mother did; she saved people." Doug eventually saw that Roxanne's act of kindness gave him a second chance.[83]

As the Conlin household was navigating the new territory of a blended family, Roxanne was recognized by two prominent women's magazines as a serious up-and-comer in the world of politics and policy. In 1975, *Redbook* named her one of "forty-four women who could save America," suggesting her for U.S. attorney general on its list of twenty-four "women we'll be hearing more about." The following year, *McCall's* asked a "panel of distinguished Democratic and Republican women to suggest women with outstanding qualifications for a position in the presidential cabinet and the Supreme Court." Roxanne was again selected as an optimal nominee for attorney general.[84]

Her rise had been rapid. In just six years, she had gone from a twenty-five-year-old assistant state attorney general to having her name kicked around as one who had the "talent and skill" to be U.S. attorney general. Roxanne did indeed have political ambitions, but at the time she was happy to be in positions that allowed her to generate change and better the lives of others. She had played an important role by heading up the newly formed civil rights division of the attorney general's office, where she took up discrimination claims, and with the Iowa Women's Political Caucus she had founded an organization designed to expand legal protections for women and get them involved in the political process.

Now in a short-term job as a consultant to the National Commission on the Observance of International Women's Year, Roxanne continued to push women's causes forward as she sought new challenges and opportunities. She would soon find them, breaking new ground for women over the next six years.

FOUR

———

Trailblazer

Roxanne once joked about her limited interest in homemaking. "Sometimes," she said, "I just want to stay home and have the whitest wash on the block—but it passes." Of course, doing laundry was not really an issue; she had a housekeeper to do that and other household chores. Doug Klein, whom Roxanne and Jim eventually adopted, added, "It would have been a waste of her time to be a domestic goddess. Her focus was where it needed to be—on helping people, those in unfortunate situations, those who had been abused, or those who couldn't speak for themselves."[1]

Just ten years out of law school, Roxanne had already enjoyed tremendous success fighting for equality and justice for Iowa's women and minorities, and as she later explained, she "had grown accustomed to having an impact." She also very much liked the limelight that accompanied her high-profile endeavors, which clearly scratched her childhood itch to be a performer. Now out of the attorney general's office, she looked for bigger challenges, where she could effect even greater change and remain in the public eye. She weighed her options during a short-term stint with the U.S. State Department's efforts on behalf of International Women's Year.[2]

By the late 1970s, there were numerous prospects for the former assistant state attorney general. But it was clear to those who knew Roxanne that decisions about her career path would be informed by, as sister-in-law Judy Conlin put it, "her irrepressible urge to change the world." Initially, she accepted an appointment in 1977 as one of the first women to serve as a United States district attorney. Here she developed a reputation as an aggressive prosecutor with a high success rate of putting away criminals. After Ronald Reagan won the presidency in 1980, Roxanne knew her days as a U.S. attorney were numbered, as she would be replaced by a Republican, and in a much more audacious step she considered throwing her hat into the political ring and running for governor of Iowa in 1982.[3]

Her year consulting for the National Commission on the Observance of International Women's Year began in fall 1976 and gave her a platform to continue advocating for women while she considered longer-term opportunities. One of the organization's initiatives was to develop booklets on homemakers rights in each of the fifty states. Although Roxanne had little time for or interest in homemaking herself, she knew that millions of American women were stay-at-home wives and mothers and thought it important that they be aware of their legal status. She therefore jumped at the chance to write about the topic, acting as lead author of Iowa's booklet and that of several other states while editing all the volumes.[4]

Although Roxanne knew Iowa law fairly well, her work preparing the homemakers rights pamphlets left her "with a sense of outrage." She summed up the current situation in Iowa: "The married woman whose husband refuses to support her or her children or who beats her or rapes her has little recourse but to divorce him. If she does, she stands only one chance in ten of receiving alimony, her child support is likely to be less than is necessary to provide even half the actual cost of rearing a child—and she may find that she cannot collect even that amount. Often she must seek public assistance." Roxanne softened the report's final paragraph, but the grim reality shone through: "No one is suggesting that the love and care of a wife or mother can or should be totally measured in dollars and cents. But we cannot continue to allow romantic notions of the occupation [of] homemaker to obscure the unique economic dependency of women who choose that career. . . . Women who choose to remain in their homes full-time are not protected—they are neglected. The time for a realistic reappraisal of the laws and practices affecting them is long overdue."[5]

Roxanne added this topic to her lecture repertoire as she was traveled throughout Iowa speaking on a variety of women's issues. Another key issue she addressed was the Equal Rights Amendment. The U.S. Congress had originally considered such a move fifty years earlier but did not act until 1972—following the Civil Rights Act of 1964 and the development of the women's movement—when it passed the ERA and sent it out to the state legislatures for ratification. Iowa was the fourth state to approve the proposed constitutional amendment, and by early 1973 thirty of the necessary thirty-eight states had passed the measure. With bipartisan support in Congress and President Gerald Ford's backing, it looked like the ERA was on its way to becoming law until opposition arose, led by conservative activist Phyllis Schlafly.[6]

Schlafly attracted adherents by arguing that the ERA would mean the end of the traditional family. She contended that its passage would take away a woman's right to stay home and care for her children, and it would also mean that women would face conscription and join men on the front lines of war. By 1974, just a little over a year after Schlafly entered the debate, the ERA's march toward ratification slowed, and over the next three years only five additional states had ratified the amendment, leaving it three states short of becoming law.[7]

In this increasingly contested atmosphere, Roxanne and Schlafly sparred in a long debate over the ERA on Des Moines radio station WHO in May 1977. At one point, according to *Des Moines Register* reporter Louise Swartzwalder, Roxanne "challenged Schlafly's interpretation of the ERA and told Schlafly her arguments amounted to 'baloney.'" Two rallies followed the broadcast. Two hundred opponents of the ERA gathered at the west steps of the Iowa capitol to hear Schlafly tell the crowd that their effort to stop the amendment reflected "the good principles we all believe," and she scolded supporters for "trying to cram ERA down our throats." On the south side of the statehouse, more than seven hundred supporters heard Roxanne say, "I just spent two-and-a-half hours with Phyllis Schlafly and I'm glad to be here with real women and real men."[8]

Despite the large number of states that had already ratified the ERA, Roxanne was clearly worried that the momentum behind the effort appeared to have slowed. In September 1977, at the National Women's Political Caucus's biennial convention in San Jose, California, she spoke at a workshop designed to assist ERA supporters in debating the issue with opponents. Perhaps more importantly, she put forward a resolution calling on the NWPC to focus its financial resources on the effort to ratify the ERA. The resolution passed, but it was for naught. Even though Congress extended the deadline for the ERA's ratification from 1979 to 1982, the amendment died, remaining three states short of the necessary thirty-eight to become law.[9]

Several months earlier, just after Roxanne had begun consulting for the State Department, Jimmy Carter won the presidency. Roxanne had volunteered for his campaign, and he had made it clear that he was interested in hiring women for important federal posts. This opened up several possibilities for Roxanne's future. The Women's Coalition, a national association of forty women's groups, sent the president-elect a list of women qualified for government positions. Roxanne's name was included. That plus the recent articles in *Redbook* and *McCall's* identifying her as one of a number of women qualified for cabinet-level positions stuck a chord, and Roxanne was considered for a couple of federal positions.[10]

First was as director of the Office of Civil Rights, then part of the U.S. Department of Health, Education, and Welfare. The agency was designed to enforce civil rights laws and antidiscrimination statutes, something that had been at the center of Roxanne's core values and work to date. She very much wished to continue such efforts and recalled, "I really wanted the job."[11]

She interviewed for the position with Larry Levinson, an adviser to HEW Secretary Joseph Califano, and others in February 1977.

Levinson came away impressed, seeing her as a top candidate: "Roxanne was exceptionally bright and very well organized and had a great deal of spirit." At one point, it was suggested that she consider the deputy director position, but Roxanne said she was not interested in the number 2 slot, fearing she "would not want to take every decision to somebody else." Ultimately, she was one of two finalists, but the job went to attorney David Tatel, now a judge on the U.S. Court of Appeals for the District of Columbia Circuit.[12]

There was an unsettling and ironic backstory to the process for Roxanne. During the interviews, she was asked questions that she saw as discriminatory, questions that would not have been asked of a male candidate, including, "What will you do with your children if you move to Washington, and what does your husband think of what you're planning to do?" Taken aback, Roxanne "was appalled" to be asked about this but tried to maintain her cool, although she snapped at the second question, "If you want to know what my husband thinks, here's his number, call him." While she felt the questions "were not intended to be offensive," she added facetiously, "I guess it was their concern for the children and husbands of the world."[13]

Much to her satisfaction, the *Des Moines Register* editorialized on the issue under the headline "For the Children's Sake?": "So the interviewers, perhaps subconsciously, viewed Conlin as a wife whose first concern should be to make her husband happy and care for her children, than as the excellent lawyer she is." It then wondered, "How many other talented women have been excluded from business and public life 'to save the children'?"[14]

Although disappointed, Roxanne did not have time to stew because she was also under consideration for U.S. attorney for the Southern District of Iowa. In January 1977, the Carter transition team had identified several possible candidates for the job. Top on the list was Roger Owens, a Polk County public defender who had been a Carter supporter and was a son of Edris "Soapy" Owens, an Iowa leader of the United Auto Workers. The senior Owens had "helped engineer Carter's surprise victory in the Iowa caucuses." Other contenders for the position included

Roxanne; John Fitzgibbons, currently an assistant U.S. attorney for the Southern District; and Dan Powers, a Drake University law professor. By April, a nominating commission set up by Iowa's U.S. senators Dick Clark and John Culver had interviewed all potential candidates and picked three, recommending Carter officials select Roxanne, Powers, or Frank Comito, a Des Moines attorney specializing in criminal law. *Des Moines Register* reporter David Yepsen thought the job would most likely go to Roxanne "because of her qualifications and because Carter has said he wants more women appointed to government jobs" or Powers "because of his former association with the Justice Department, where he was a trial tax specialist."[15]

In early June, the Department of Justice informed Roxanne that she was the designee for the job, although she did not receive official word from the administration until September. She was confirmed by the U.S. Senate on September 21 and formally sworn in the following month. The ceremony marked a historic event: Roxanne was the second woman to be confirmed by the U.S. Senate as a U.S. attorney—Virginia McCarty from Indiana was the first, sworn in two days before. And it was here that her two youngest children realized just how special their mother was. Eleven-year-old Jackie took notice when her teacher posted a newspaper article about Roxanne's new job on the classroom bulletin board, which held only important items, while eight-year-old J.B. was awed by the pomp of the event and all the people who turned out to see his mother take the oath of office.[16]

Roxanne resigned from the Iowa Commission on the Status of Women the following month to avoid any potential conflicts of interest. But she explained that her new federal attorney position would not stop her from pursuing her personal work as an activist fighting for women's rights and African American rights. This determination concerned some Iowa Democrats who had supported more mainstream male candidates for the job and believed Carter had made a mistake in the appointment. Clearly, Roxanne knew many would be watching her work as she made history as a U.S. attorney, and she understood that "when a woman in a public position does poorly, it reflects poorly on all women."[17]

Once ensconced in the U.S. Attorney's Office in Des Moines's classic revival-style U.S. Courthouse at First and Walnut Streets, Roxanne was careful to keep her politics out of her day-to-day operations, but she strove to increase diversity among her staff. Although she did not want to clean house when she began—choosing to keep current assistant U.S. attorneys John Fitzgibbons, Bill Scherle, and Kermit Anderson in place— there was immediately a position to fill because the office was authorized to have four assistant attorneys. Fitzgibbons left shortly thereafter, soon followed by Scherle, and Roxanne hired Christopher Hagen, Richard Blane, and Don Nickerson, the first African American to hold such a position in the Southern District; he would later become the first African American U.S. attorney in Iowa. When a fifth position was authorized, Roxanne recruited Amanda Dorr, the first woman to serve as an assistant U.S. attorney in the Southern District. Likewise, one of Roxanne's first legal interns at the office was a young woman named Eliza Ovrom, now a Polk County district judge.[18]

At the beginning of her tenure, Roxanne "set out to make a priority of prosecuting white-collar crime, particularly fraud, and being tough on other federal criminals, particularly drug traffickers." And she hit the ground running. That fall, as part of a nationwide effort, Roxanne and other federal attorneys began cracking down on students who were not repaying their federally guaranteed student loans. Defaults had gone up substantially over the past few years, leaving the federal government on the hook for millions of dollars. At the same time, she oversaw the successful prosecution of Walter Paustian, the former president of Donahue Savings Bank in Donahue, a small town just north of Davenport, 170 miles east of Des Moines. Paustian pleaded no contest to embezzling more than $80,000 from the bank, although its records suggested that it suffered losses of nearly $920,000 to embezzlement while he was its president, ultimately leading the small bank to collapse. Paustian was sentenced to eighteen months in prison, a harsh sentence for such a crime according to the *Des Moines Register*. William Stuart, the federal district judge who heard the case, explained that he intended the sentence to serve as a "deterrent to others."[19]

Bigger cases were in the offing. Roxanne handled a pollution lawsuit brought against Consolidated Packaging Corporation that had been filed in U.S. District Court by the Environmental Protection Agency in 1977. Charges focused on the firm's Crandon Mill, a wood pulp facility in Fort Madison accused of dumping pollutants into the Mississippi River. Interestingly, Michael Galligan, who would later become Roxanne's partner in a private law practice, represented the mill. The pulp turned that portion of the river pink, which Roxanne quipped "was just not a good color for the mighty Mississippi." The following May, she arranged an out-of-court settlement. Consolidated Packaging agreed to build a $2 million addition to its Crandon Mill, eliminating future pollution, and pay a $100,000 fine to federal and state governments. It also funded a scholarship program in environmental studies at Iowa State University. Of the deal, Roxanne proudly said, "This is the largest single penalty paid by anyone in the state of Iowa for pollution of the waterways."[20]

In 1979, she went after Mid-America Pipeline Company for its mishandling of the aftermath of a 1978 accident, when one of its liquid petroleum gas pipelines ruptured and exploded, killing three people near the small southeastern Iowa town of Donnellson. The firm was found guilty of not meeting federal requirements to keep a list of emergency personnel to be contacted in case of an accident, failing to train employees to handle emergency situations, and failing to coordinate training sessions with local firefighters and police forces. It was fined $4,000. But more importantly, this was the first time such a company had been successfully criminally prosecuted for violating federal pipeline safety regulations.[21]

Roxanne and her staff prosecuted a wide variety of cases. As former assistant U.S. attorney Kermit Anderson recalled, she was especially good at "cultivating the press and keeping the media's attention on her office's work." This included putting away bank robbers, jewelry thieves, a kidnapper, and other criminals, but her highest-profile efforts were in drug enforcement and a fraud charge against the head of the Iowa National Guard.[22]

Working closely with the U.S. Drug Enforcement Administration, the FBI, and state and local law officials, Roxanne and the assistant

U.S. attorneys aggressively went after drug dealers across the state. In September 1978, after a yearlong federal grand jury investigation, authorities in Des Moines and Cedar Rapids arrested thirty-four people for distributing an estimated "60 to 80 percent of Iowa's heroin traffic." Because the case was so big, Roxanne had to bring in extra help, first enlisting Bill Scherle, who had recently left her office to go into private practice, and later John Martin, an assistant U.S. attorney on loan from Kansas, as special prosecutors.[23]

The following January, twenty-six of those indicted were sentenced to prison terms that ranged in length from two to ten years, while five others received suspended sentences for their involvement in what officials called "the largest heroin distribution ring ever prosecuted in Iowa." As Roxanne would later explain, "We took every known heroin dealer in Des Moines and Cedar Rapids off the streets." She and her office later turned their attention to cocaine, and in the summer of 1980 Des Moines police and federal officials confiscated nearly four pounds of cocaine, the largest seizure of the drug in Iowa to date, and Roxanne put a man named Patrick Hartman in prison for drug trafficking. In 1982, while Hartman was serving his sentence at the federal penitentiary in Leavenworth, he was among fifty-three people indicted as part of an interstate ring that had been distributing cocaine since 1973.[24]

In another big case, Roxanne took on Major General Joseph May. In December 1977, she announced that May was the subject of a federal criminal investigation because of his alleged personal use of National Guard airplanes. May had resigned as the adjutant general of the Iowa National Guard several months earlier when the controversy arose, and although he reimbursed the guard $2,300 for his use of the equipment, a U.S. Army report recommended that he pay an additional $23,000.[25]

After more than a year of investigating the case, a federal grand jury issued an eighteen-count indictment against May, accusing him of "illegal personal use of military aircraft, then trying to cover up his action by lying to investigators and seeking to have records destroyed." The charges focused on twelve flights May made on National Guard aircraft, mostly to Florida but also to Chicago, Las Vegas, and New Orleans to meet his fiancée.[26]

Roxanne handled the nine-day trial herself, which took place in the summer of 1979; she characterized the case as one "of lying, cheating, and stealing, where May knew he was breaking the law and tried to cover up his actions." Raymond Rosenberg, May's lead defense attorney, countered that his client's actions were improper and violated military regulations, but such behavior was common and bore no criminal intent. After sixteen hours of deliberation, the jury found May guilty of eleven counts of "converting government property for his own use" and four counts "that charged him with lying about the trips and attempting to have certain flight records destroyed." He was sentenced to a year in prison and fined $5,000. Roxanne was pleased with the outcome: "I think it is not so much the length of the incarceration as it is the fact of incarceration—the loss of freedom." She would later add, "The importance of this case will be the concept of equal justice. No matter how high you are in the hierarchy, it doesn't insulate you from the law."[27]

The case was significant: it marked the first time that a high-ranking military officer had been tried or incarcerated for violating federal law. Perhaps more important for Roxanne, added to her successes in several prominent drug cases, it won over locally based FBI agents, who were initially skeptical of collaborating with a female U.S. attorney. Ed Mall, the special agent in charge of the agency's Des Moines office, later recalled, "We worked very well together. She knew her job." Al Overbaugh, an agent with the U.S. Drug Enforcement Administration, shared Mall's feelings: "She was hard on crime; definitely 'pro' law enforcement and willing to prosecute."[28]

While putting away criminals, Roxanne also made good on her pledge to continue working on behalf of the women's movement. A gifted public speaker who combined the serious topic of women's rights with humor, she often lectured at forums, rallies, and conventions throughout the state while remaining active in both the Iowa Women's Political Caucus and the National Women's Political Caucus. But that was not all. Described by her husband as leading "life full steam ahead," Roxanne used her boundless energy to teach a couple of courses at the University of Iowa College of Law.[29]

Her interest in teaching began when she was working on the homemakers rights pamphlets during her time with the National Commission on the Observance of International Women's Year. While researching the topic, she noticed that Iowa's law school did not have a course on sex discrimination law. This led her to contact the dean of the college, and after some discussion she developed such a course, one of the few offered by law schools at the time. It was set up as a once-a-week seminar. Roxanne taught the class twice, first in the fall of 1977 and again in the spring of 1979, using a book coauthored by Ruth Bader Ginsburg, *Sex-Based Discrimination: Texts, Cases, and Materials*. Meanwhile, she became a part-time student, taking courses at Drake University on her way to earning a master's degree in public administration, which she completed in 1979.[30]

All this activity limited Roxanne's time at home. When there and not working, she was usually in her family room with one or more of her children and perhaps Jim. There she unwound and relaxed by "watching mindless TV or reading trashy novels." She also kept busy tending her three hundred or so African violets, and because she was "very crafty," according to daughter Jackie, she sewed, hooked rugs, and knitted, often making baby sweaters and other items for friends and relatives. The house remained filled with pets, which by now included an all-white, 150-pound Great Pyrenees dog named Bear. Yet the number of pets always seemed to grow because Roxanne had a soft spot for strays, especially cats. Jim used to explain that there was a sign in their yard visible only to animals that read "free food and medical care, come right in."[31]

One pastime that took Roxanne outside the home and one she had adored since her teenage years was dancing. She was an outstanding dancer and especially loved the dramatic tango, but because Jim had no interest in the activity she struggled to find dance partners until David Butts returned to Des Moines. The two met in 1961, when he trained Roxanne to be an Arthur Murray dance instructor, and they became a popular couple for exhibition dances across Iowa. They began dancing regularly twenty years later once Butts was back in central Iowa. Generally, they danced together twice a month, usually at the Val Air Ballroom in West Des Moines or at the Lake Robbins Ballroom near Woodward, thirty miles northwest of Des Moines. Later they also danced at the Prairie Meadows Racetrack and Casino in the city's northeast suburb of Altoona and at the Croatian Slavic Center on Des Moines's south side.[32]

Roxanne also loved to jitterbug. While at a conference with other U.S. attorneys in Washington, D.C., she and a group of colleagues went out to a night spot called the Déjà Vu, and one of her friends entered her in the club's jitterbug contest. She won it and was named the 1981 jitterbug champion of the district. A few years later, Roxanne and her partner Butts offered jitterbug lessons as one of the prized items in several Des Moines charity auctions.[33]

Interestingly, Roxanne and Jim shared no hobbies. He once explained more generally, "We have our individual courses. We've always existed this way and it's very comfortable for us." While she pursued her interests, Jim enjoyed riding horses and motorcycles and briefly kept a boat at Lake Okoboji, but the real estate business was what consumed him. Jim remained at Iowa Realty, a vice-president in the commercial real estate division, but he was becoming more and more involved in his own real estate operations.[34]

In 1977, Jim formed Mid-Iowa Management Company to oversee his growing list of properties. He left Iowa Realty in 1981 and went out on his own, starting a second firm named the Conlin Company, a real estate brokerage business. Through these two enterprises, Jim bought, sold, and managed his own and others' properties. By 1982, Mid-Iowa managed 1,450 apartments and employed sixty people, while his brokerage operation had six on its sales force. According to *Des Moines Tribune* reporter David Elbert, Jim was viewed by those in the local real estate business as "someone who has 'come on very, very strong in the last two or three years.'" He had quietly grown wealthy. Mid-Iowa's rapid expansion made it the second-largest manager of apartments in greater Des Moines (Iowa Realty was first). At the same time, Jim had become the second-largest syndicator of real estate investor consortiums. These groups pooled their funds to purchase rental properties and received the tax benefits connected to property ownership of apartment buildings. Jim headed eight syndicates worth a total of $15 million.[35]

Meanwhile, Roxanne and Jim's children were growing up. Doug graduated from Lincoln High School in the spring of 1980 and went on to Drake University the following fall, where his sister Debbie was a senior. Fourteen-year-old Jackie started ninth grade at Dowling Catholic High School in West Des Moines in the fall of 1980, opting for the smaller school instead of Lincoln, while eleven-year-old J.B. began sixth grade at Brody Middle School on Des Moines's south side.[36]

Then that year's presidential election nudged Roxanne in a direction she had long wanted to pursue. With Ronald Reagan winning the White House in November, Roxanne knew her position as a U.S. attorney would soon go to a Republican appointee, and she would be out of a job. She would later joke: "U.S. attorneys serve at the pleasure of the president, and I did not please Ronald Reagan, but he didn't please me either."[37]

Finding a job would not be a problem. There were plenty of opportunities for Roxanne in either private practice or teaching, but she wanted something more. Roxanne loved leading, she loved bringing about change and bettering people's lives, she loved being in the public eye, and she yearned for a bigger stage. Thus, even as she worked in her lame-duck year as a U.S. attorney, she thought about testing the waters for her boldest pathbreaking move yet as she considered a gubernatorial run in 1982.

Her years of activity in the Democratic Party meant that Roxanne had many contacts within its circles, and she began discussing her possible campaign with numerous party figures. Early on, she consulted Jerry Crawford, a Des Moines attorney and state Democratic operative, who enthusiastically encouraged her to get in the race. She then began conferring with other prominent Polk County Democrats. The group included attorney Art Hedberg; close friend Cookie Brown; Marilyn Spina, a key figure in politics on Des Moines's south side; and, ironically, Ed Campbell, a longtime aid for governor and then senator Harold Hughes and the current head of the Democratic Party in Iowa, who would later become one of her adversaries in the party's primary. They all urged her to run, although Roxanne recalled that even these supporters were skeptical about her chances of winning. She then sought the advice of Don Rowan, the executive vice-president of the Iowa Federation of Labor and a big supporter of hers, and he suggested that before deciding she needed to talk to Tom Whitney.[38]

Whitney had been on Roxanne's list of people whose counsel she wanted, but she had not visited with him yet. She had known him since her days in the Iowa Young Democrats. Whitney was currently on the Polk County Board of Supervisors, was the past chair of the Iowa Democratic Party, and had run for governor in 1978, losing in the primary to Jerry Fitzgerald of Fort Dodge, then the majority leader of the Iowa House of Representatives. Roxanne called Whitney, and the two went to lunch. She told him she wanted to run for governor and wanted his help. Whitney was thrilled and felt she could win, but he would help only if she agreed to three conditions. First, he wanted ready access to Roxanne and her pledge to listen to him; second, if she won, he wanted carte blanche to seek out or create political opportunities for her nationally; and third, he would do her personal legal work. Roxanne concurred.[39]

In the midst of all these discussions, she also talked with Jim about throwing her hat into the ring, and as he usually did whenever Roxanne was passionate about a particular endeavor, he gave her his full support.[40]

Roxanne knew the odds were against her. There had never been a female governor in Iowa, nor had a woman ever run for the office from a major political party. Nationally, in fact, there had been only three female governors up to the mid-1970s, but all had been either wives or widows of former governors. The times, however, were changing. In 1974, Ella Grasso of Connecticut became the first woman elected as governor without any spousal ties to the office, and two years later the state of Washington elected Dixy Lee Ray as its governor. Fearless, according to numerous friends and associates, Roxanne had been breaking down barriers for years, and now as her term as U.S. attorney was waning, she thought the timing was right. Roxanne began laying the groundwork for a bid to be Iowa's next governor.

FIVE

———

Exploratory Effort

While Roxanne was testing the waters for a gubernatorial run, Dave Nagle, an attorney, influential Democrat, and soon state party chair, told her to "forget about running" because, he explained, the Equal Rights Amendment had never been ratified and the "liberal-women's agenda had been defeated." But such naysayers only motivated Roxanne. She had repeatedly been told that she could not do something because she was a woman. "That's what I was told when I was going into law," she recalled, "that's what I was told when I wanted to be an assistant attorney general, and when I was going to be U.S. attorney. I found such comments inspirational." Roxanne had flourished in these male-dominated areas, and her successes eased the way for other women to follow her.[1]

Now she had the governor's office in mind, but many were telling her she did not stand a chance. If history were a guide, Roxanne believed the odds were in her favor, because she had spent much of her life doing what others said she could not do. Thus in March 1981, six hundred days before the general election, she began exploring a campaign. However, she remained the U.S. attorney for the Southern District of Iowa—although she expected to be replaced in a few months—and this severely limited her behavior as a candidate. In her position, she could not announce her run for office, she could not raise money, she could not ask people for commitments, and she could not hire a staff.[2]

Fortunately, her job and her efforts on behalf of women's rights often required her to travel throughout the state, and because she was already a highly popular public speaker, Roxanne easily piggybacked her unofficial campaigning atop her work and advocacy. She did so by taking on additional speaking engagements and public appearances to increase her visibility and name recognition. And because of her careful cultivation of the press over the years, she continued to garner a great deal of coverage whatever she did, remaining a darling of the media.

Her unofficial campaign started March 1, 1981, when Associated Press reporter Roger Munns's story about Roxanne ran in several papers across the state. The article reviewed her work as U.S. attorney, and when Munns asked Roxanne about her future, she let it slip that she might just run for governor. Two days later she was in Red Oak, a county seat 120 miles southwest of Des Moines, where she visited with the Villisca Commercial Club. Here she floated a trial balloon about seeking the governorship.[3]

Such speaking engagements and public appearances became more frequent. Roxanne had it in mind to travel to all of the state's ninety-nine counties, making herself known to as many Iowans as she could. *Des Moines Tribune* reporter David Elbert described her early campaign efforts: "When she was done talking to police or lawyers about crime or to women about sexism, she hung around talking to Democrats about running for governor."[4]

That May, Roxanne served as the guest lecturer and grand marshal for VEISHEA, the annual student-run spring festival at Iowa State University. Serendipitously, the event's theme that year, "Pathways to Progress," fit perfectly with her efforts to become Iowa's first female governor.[5]

Work as a U.S. attorney kept her before the public as well, often on the front pages of newspapers. Perhaps the most memorable was a photograph of Roxanne at a press conference in June 1981, sitting behind more than $560,000 recovered from a $3.3 million Arizona bank heist. Several Des Moines men were suspected of the crime. One, Bruce Fennimore, arrested when the money was discovered, cut a plea deal. He ended up serving eight years of a twenty-year sentence before being paroled. The other two, David Grandstaff and Doug Brown, were arrested after Roxanne stepped down as U.S. attorney. Both were eventually acquitted of the crime.[6]

Meanwhile, Roxanne stepped up her campaign events, and soon Monica McFadden, a good friend, rising political operative, and active feminist, began accompanying her—as often as she could get away from work—as a volunteer campaign coordinator. Twenty-nine-year-old McFadden was smart, aggressive, and totally committed to Roxanne. The two had met when McFadden began serving as the Iowa Equal Rights Amendment campaign coordinator in early 1980. In addition to her work for the ERA, her political experience included local elections in Davenport, where her work with the Democratic Party there led to a sweep of the city council in 1979 and service as an Iowa regional campaign coordinator for Jimmy Carter's reelection bid in 1980. After Carter's defeat in November, McFadden settled down in Des Moines and took a job as the director of Community Telephone Counseling. She became head of the Polk County Women's Political Caucus in 1981.[7]

McFadden was initially Roxanne's entire campaign staff, doing everything from driving and scheduling events to handling the press. Later that spring of 1981 a second volunteer, Laura Ward, joined the campaign. She knew of Roxanne but had not met her until 1977. That May, Ward had called Roxanne to tell her that Cristine Wilson, a leading feminist and former teacher and mentor to Ward and a good friend of Roxanne's during her days on the Governor's Commission on the Status of Women, had been in a terrible auto accident and was in a coma. After that initial call, Ward and Roxanne visited often about Wilson—who remained in a coma until her death in 1991—and the two soon became friends, working together in the Iowa Women's Political Caucus.[8]

Ward, who worked as a legislative clerk at the Iowa General Assembly, began volunteering one or two evenings a week for Roxanne. Setting up shop in the Conlins' basement, she started putting together lists of potential supporters and calling people. Later that summer, two additional volunteers enlisted in the cause: Phylliss Henry, the woman who, with Roxanne's help, broke down the gender barrier at the Des Moines Police Department, and Roxanne's youngest sister, Gina, who had lived in Roxanne's basement on and off over the past few years. Gina had moved back and forth between Des Moines and Minneapolis since graduating from high school in 1973, partly to help Roxanne around the house but also because of continuing family troubles in Minnesota. Even though their father had left their mother in 1971, Alice still dealt with bouts of deep depression, and it was difficult for Gina to live with her.[9]

With a gradually growing all-volunteer operation, Roxanne pressed forward, moving from county to county introducing herself, shaking hands, and speaking. By mid-spring, names of five other Democrats— Don Avenson, minority leader in the Iowa House; Jerry Fitzgerald, former majority leader in the Iowa House and unsuccessful Democratic candidate for governor in 1978; U.S. Representative Tom Harkin; Harold Hughes, past Iowa governor and U.S. senator; and Tom Miller, Iowa attorney general—were being bantered about as possible gubernatorial candidates as well. On May 8, all except Hughes joined many other eastern Iowa Democrats gathered at the Townhouse Convention Center in Cedar Rapids. The event was intended to raise money for Ted Sovern, who had a large campaign debt from his unsuccessful 1980 bid to unseat Tom Tauke, Iowa's Second District congressional representative. The program featured a straw poll asking attendees to pick their nominee for governor. Miller, who was from the eastern Iowa city of Dubuque, won the poll with 92 votes, followed by Harkin with 52, Roxanne with 43, Fitzgerald with 33, Hughes with 19, and Avenson with 18.[10]

Roxanne "was delighted and surprised" at how well she had done, explaining, "Friday night was the first time I was in Cedar Rapids at a political function," and she was not disappointed by the winner, noting that "this is Miller's district." She remained in Cedar Rapids and spoke to the city's Downtown Rotary Club that Monday. Before her presentation, when a reporter asked if she were running for governor, she responded simply, "I haven't made up my mind. I'm still in my job so I can't make such a decision." She was aware, however, that she was not as well known as some of the other potential Democratic candidates, and she mentioned that she might resign earlier than October 7, when her term as U.S. attorney expired. Although unsaid, leaving her post early meant that she could devote more time and energy to her campaign.[11]

She continued with a heavy schedule of speaking engagements. In a sweep through southeastern Iowa, for example, Roxanne addressed the issue of white-collar crime with the Burlington Bar Association and a Keokuk Rotary group before talking with people at both programs about running for governor. She followed these up with a visit to the North Lee County District Courthouse in Fort Madison, where she again talked with local Democrats about seeking the nomination. Roxanne loved speaking to and meeting people and found her reception encouraging. "So far," she told a reporter in Fort Madison, "reaction across the state has been positive—surprisingly so."[12]

All seemed to be going well. Roxanne was somehow able to carry out her duties while unofficially campaigning for governor. But the Department of Justice soon saw her activities as a problem. In July Roxanne and her boss, Larry McWhorter, director of the Executive Office for United States Attorneys, were in Denver, where Roxanne was leading a seminar for incoming U.S. attorneys on working with grand juries. While there, McWhorter received a call from a superior in the attorney general's office, telling him that Roxanne needed to go because she was in effect campaigning for office, which was against the rules for U.S. attorneys. Politics probably played a part as well. In early 1981, Ronald Reagan appointee William Smith had taken over as attorney general, and the Republican did not want to look the other way while Democrat Roxanne campaigned for governor. Regardless, McWhorter passed along the news to Roxanne, who understood.[13]

After flying home, Roxanne held a press conference on July 24, announcing that she would be resigning as U.S. attorney effective August 31. Interestingly, Republican Richard Turner, Roxanne's friend and her former boss as Iowa's attorney general, would succeed her in the job after Kermit Anderson served as interim U.S. attorney. Roxanne added that she still had not decided to run for governor, but if she did, she did not believe that being a woman would hurt her. "I think the people of Iowa are fair," she noted. "I think I ought to be judged on the merits of my record."[14]

Nevertheless, being the first woman to seek the office from a major party "colored everything," remembered David Yepsen, who covered the campaign for the *Des Moines Register*. "Everything was new, and it took the press and the public time to get used to the idea of a woman candidate." Sexist comments and references crept into stories about Roxanne from the beginning. In May 1981, for example, a *Cedar Rapids Gazette* reporter played with the stereotype of a woman's interest in redecorating when he wrote of Roxanne: "She won't tell you that she is an unannounced candidate for governor . . . if you ask her about plans for redoing Terrace Hill," the Iowa governor's mansion. Then there was Robert Reiste, the editor of the *Ocheyedan Press*, a weekly in the small Iowa town 225 miles northwest of Des Moines, writing about whether Roxanne might choose "to toss a pretty bonnet into the political ring." He continued along these lines, describing her as "a smart lady who could also qualify as anyone's Mrs. America."[15]

Comments like these would have drawn Roxanne's ire in years past, but she now let them go, even identifying Reiste's editorial as her favorite among such pieces. She understood that she was unique as a gubernatorial candidate and that "if I want to seek this office, I'm going to have to deal with people's curiosity and fears about my being a woman."[16]

Most people encountering Roxanne on the campaign trail realized that she was no ordinary woman. In August, the Iowa Commission on the Status of Women had recognized Roxanne's many accomplishments by inducting her into the Iowa Women's Hall of Fame. Other honorees that year were agribusiness pioneer Mary Garst, feminist and philanthropist Louise Noun, and the late Mary Newbury Adams, one of the founders of the Iowa Federation of Women's Clubs and the Northern Iowa Suffrage Association in nineteenth-century Iowa.[17]

Roxanne's achievements made her a role model for many progressive women and those involved in the advocacy groups she had founded, such as the Iowa Women's Political Caucus, or other groups with which she had worked closely. She would look to these women for support once her campaign for governor became official.[18]

She was undoubtedly counting on this backing and was appreciative, but in September she told a gathering in Carroll, a northwestern Iowa city a hundred miles from Des Moines, that she would not run as a women's candidate because she could not get elected by such a narrow base. "It's clear to me," she said with a clever turn of phrase, "I have to do it as a woman candidate, but I can't do it as a women's candidate." And everywhere she went, she was asked how it felt to be a female candidate. She always replied, "Is there any other way for me to do it?"[19]

However, no matter how Roxanne tried to portray herself, being a woman running for governor guaranteed her large crowds and press coverage wherever she stopped to speak. By the fall, energy and enthusiasm were building around her campaign when results from the Iowa Poll, conducted by the *Des Moines Register*, ran in late September. It revealed that Harold Hughes—who was not yet in the race but was moving in that direction—was the most popular of the potential Democratic candidates—identified as Hughes, Tom Harkin, Roxanne, Tom Miller, and Jerry Fitzgerald. According to the poll, Hughes would give Governor Bob Ray the toughest race of all the Democrats—although he lagged behind the governor 52 percent to 37 percent, with 11 percent undecided—and he would defeat Terry Branstad, then the lieutenant governor, who had pledged to run if Ray chose to step down. Roxanne polled third among Democrats, behind Hughes and Harkin, and when compared to Branstad she trailed by 13 percent, 41 percent to 28 percent, with 31 percent undecided.[20]

A number of influential Democrats supported the idea of Hughes getting into the race. Key among them were Des Moines real estate mogul Bill Knapp, who had given the retired Hughes a job at Iowa Realty and brought him back to Iowa from the east coast in 1981, and Ed Campbell, former top aide to Hughes, key staffer to U.S. Senator John Culver, and at the time chair of the Iowa Democratic Party.[21]

The possibility of a Hughes candidacy clearly complicated the situation for other Democrats seeking the nomination. A week before the Iowa Poll was published, Tom Miller withdrew his name from consideration as long as Hughes was considering a run. Harkin soon followed, deciding to focus on his upcoming congressional race. Although Roxanne initially gave mixed signals about remaining in the race if Hughes chose to run, she stayed the course and continued to seek the nomination, while other potential candidates such as Jerry Fitzgerald, Don Avenson, and Lowell Junkins, a Fort Madison Democratic leader in the Iowa Senate, waited on the sidelines for a Hughes decision.[22]

Earlier in September, a Roxanne Conlin for Governor Committee had been established to raise funds for her campaign. But talk of Hughes getting into the race had hurt her ability to raise money, and in fact a Hughes for Governor Committee was soon created to fund his possible run. Still, by October 20, Roxanne's committee had received $20,550. The lion's share of the donations included a $14,000 loan from her husband.[23]

Roxanne used the loan from Jim to pay Cooper and Associates, a Virginia-based polling service, for a detailed analysis of her chances in the upcoming election. The firm's conclusions heartened her. It found that her statewide name recognition stood at 60 percent, up roughly 10 percent from estimates that spring. Even better, Roxanne told the *Des Moines Tribune*, Cooper and Associates were much more positive about her odds in the gubernatorial race than the earlier Iowa Poll. The pollsters believed their survey showed that Roxanne "could win a race against any Republican, including Bob Ray."[24]

Encouraged by this new poll, Roxanne used her close ties to the Iowa Women's Political Caucus to send a solicitation to its members in November. She opened the letter by recalling the beginning of the caucus in her living room eight years earlier. After recounting the progress they had made together fighting discrimination, Roxanne said that much still needed to be done, and she felt that she could better the lives of all Iowans by serving as their next governor.[25]

She noted that she had already logged more than 25,000 miles crisscrossing the state to visit every county. But she cautioned that more was required. "I must continue to travel, make calls, and do mailings," and such efforts required additional funds. In a postscript, Roxanne put it in dollars and cents: "A contribution of $500 will pay this month's phone bill. Fifty dollars will pay postage for 463 letters. A gift of $25 will cover my expenses for a day of travel." Then she closed, bringing the letter full circle with a flourish: "When the Iowa Women's Political Caucus celebrates its tenth anniversary, we can, if you help, all come back to my living room this time in Terrace Hill."[26]

As the letter went out, Roxanne went out as well, conducting a series of thirteen citizen forums throughout November, where she discussed key issues with groups around the state. She was in the midst of this tour when Hughes announced he would run. But there might be a problem, he told the press, with his eligibility. State law required a gubernatorial candidate to have been an Iowa resident for two years prior to the election. After Hughes left the U.S. Senate in 1975, he lived in Virginia and Maryland before returning to Iowa in April 1981, when he bought a home on five acres outside Norwalk, a small town just south of Des Moines.[27]

For Roxanne, Hughes's announcement "was most unsettling." But with the former governor and senator's candidacy in limbo, she ultimately chose to "lower her sights," telling the *Des Moines Tribune* in early December that she would seek the lieutenant governor's position if Hughes proved eligible to run for governor.[28]

The Hughes team sought a ruling from Iowa Secretary of State Mary Jane Odell, the state's top election official, on whether Hughes met the residency requirement to run for governor. Odell, a Republican, sought the advice of Attorney General Tom Miller, but he would not weigh in on the matter; he cited conflict of interest because he had supported Hughes's candidacy. Instead, the state hired Iowa attorney David Belin to counsel Odell. By the end of December, Odell ruled against Hughes, saying he did not meet the required residency terms to run for governor. Hughes chose not to contest the decision, and in early January 1982 he announced that he was withdrawing from the race.[29]

Roxanne breathed a sigh of relief, but there was instantly a new wrinkle. Even as Hughes was doing another interview immediately following the press conference where he pulled out of the campaign, Ed Campbell was just down the hall, telling other reporters he planned to announce his candidacy for governor in a couple of weeks. A longtime party insider, Campbell was associated with the conservative and more moderate wings of the Democratic Party. He formally threw his hat into the ring at the end of January, explaining, "Harold Hughes was the best candidate we could put forth. I happen to think I am next."[30]

A week later, Roxanne ended her yearlong exploratory effort by formally announcing her candidacy for the Democratic nomination for governor. Here she addressed the concerns of the many party regulars who still believed that being a woman from the liberal wing of the party was a serious handicap: "Iowans are ready for change. To suggest that they are not ready for a woman governor is to seriously underestimate the voters of this state . . . I trust them to judge me on the basis of my merits."[31]

If Roxanne's announcement was fully expected, Bob Ray's was not. On February 18, the fifty-three-year-old governor told a news conference he would not seek a sixth term because he was interested "in new challenges and adventures" and "might like to try new things." The move surprised almost everyone, even Terry Branstad, who was waiting in the wings to run if Ray did not. He announced his candidacy nine days later. Democrats, meanwhile, were emboldened by the turn of events. Jeffrey Cox, Johnson County Democratic chair, reflected the widespread belief: "There's been a great sense of hopelessness about beating Ray." His withdrawal, Cox believed, would make the election a real "horse race."[32]

Branstad would run unopposed in his party's primary, but just two days after he announced, Jerry Fitzgerald became the third and final Democratic candidate for governor. The stage was now set, the players were now all identified, and the curtain was about to go up on what could prove to be a historic race.[33]

Roxanne had waited a long time for this moment. She had talked about being Iowa's governor since she was a teenager, and she was now on the path to fulfilling her dream. But big questions remained. Were Iowa Democrats ready to nominate a woman as their gubernatorial candidate, and were Iowans in general ready for their first female governor?

Six

———

A Run for Governor

Roxanne knew the odds were against her, but she was optimistic as the official phase of her campaign got underway early in 1982. She had a head start on her opponents—she had spent much of 1981 introducing herself to voters in every corner of Iowa. She had generated a lot of interest and excitement because she was a woman seeking the office, and although she knew this had a downside, she hoped to use it to her advantage as well. With the primary three months away, however, it was clear that her opponents held some advantages.

First was Ed Campbell. A longtime Democratic political operative, Campbell knew the party and the key people within it. When former governor and U.S. senator Harold Hughes chose not to run, Campbell stepped right into the campaign apparatus that had been established for his former boss, and the well-connected businessman Bill Knapp served as his primary fund-raiser, aggressively going after money. Later in March, Hughes endorsed Campbell and even signed on as his campaign manager. But these apparent pluses also created some problems.[1]

Tom Whitney, then a Polk County supervisor and close adviser to Roxanne, remembered that Hughes's involvement often created strange optics at campaign stops: "The renowned, popular Harold Hughes with his great presence and booming voice often introduced Campbell at events. Ed had always been a behind-the-scenes guy. It just didn't appear quite right." Indeed, Campbell struggled to avoid being seen as a "substitute for Hughes." And while Knapp's support was valuable, Campbell—who had worked at Knapp's Iowa Realty for several years— faced being considered "Bill Knapp's candidate for governor."[2]

These issues aside, Campbell's campaign had greater fund-raising success than his rivals did, in large part because of Knapp's role. By the end of May, Campbell had amassed more than $234,000 compared to Roxanne's $169,300 and Jerry Fitzgerald's $85,500. Terry Branstad, meanwhile, had banked more than $200,000 in contributions. Although he could be happy about his war chest, Campbell faced an uphill battle from the start and never gained traction as a candidate.[3]

Fitzgerald got into the race late, and by the middle of March he still did not have any campaign staff. *Des Moines Register* reporter David Yepsen suggested that his loss to Ray in the 1978 gubernatorial race might have branded him a loser, but his home in Fort Dodge might make him appealing to rural voters opposed to his rivals from Des Moines.[4]

Most old guard party politicos went to work in either Campbell's or Fitzgerald's campaign, but Roxanne's was different. From the beginning of her exploratory effort, she had been using her connections and networking with various women's groups across the state, weaving together the beginnings of a movement. For nearly a year, Roxanne or Roxanne and Monica McFadden trekked across the state generating great enthusiasm among the women who became her core supporters. Once she formally announced her run for governor, many of these women rushed to volunteer, a number of them working at her campaign headquarters in the basement of the Flynn Building at Seventh and Locust Streets in downtown Des Moines. Interestingly, the building was owned by Jim Conlin. In 1998, Roxanne would rename it the Edna Griffin Building in honor of the African American civil rights activist who staged boycotts and sit-ins in 1948 after being refused service at the lunch counter of the Katz Drug Store there. A decade after the boycott, Roxanne's first job was as a fourteen-year-old waiter at this very lunch counter.[5]

Roxanne had been wooing Phylliss Henry, then volunteering for the campaign, to manage the growing ranks of volunteers. Henry had planned to leave the Police Department and return to school, but she finally agreed to Roxanne's offer. She delayed school and joined the campaign as a paid staffer that spring, serving as both volunteer coordinator and office manager. She was also put in charge of Roxanne's safety, handling threats against the candidate's life. Managing the office soon fell to someone else.[6]

Female volunteers were the lifeblood of Roxanne's campaign, rallying to the cause characterized by their candidate as "It's Our Turn." Here gender worked in Roxanne's favor. Traditionally, women carried out much of the mundane but critical work of politics at the grassroots level, and such was the case for Roxanne. They made phone calls, handled correspondence, mailed flyers, canvassed neighborhoods, and organized coffee klatches. Although Phylliss Henry had no political experience, she was an adept manager and was especially good at putting volunteers where their skills could best be employed.[7]

Women from all walks of life joined the effort. Two examples included LuAnn Olson and Charlotte Hubbell. Twenty-nine-year-old Olson, a laid-off Firestone worker and union activist, became Roxanne's driver. It was important that Roxanne have a female driver to avoid any appearance of impropriety and to confirm women's ability to do anything. Olson had replaced Drake basketball star Connie Newlin, who had driven Roxanne before basketball season started. Olson got along well with Roxanne, and she took care of the candidate on the road until the campaign sent her to Ottumwa to strengthen its position in the blue-collar city eighty-five miles southeast of Des Moines.[8]

Thirty-one-year-old attorney Charlotte Hubbell, meanwhile, was introduced to the campaign in 1981 by Julie Gammack, a local WHO radio talk show host and later a *Des Moines Register* columnist. She and her husband, Fred Hubbell, who had been living and working in New York, returned to his hometown when he took a position in his family's insurance business, Equitable of Iowa. Hubbell initially volunteered for Roxanne's campaign before joining the paid staff as her scheduler; she later headed the research operation. She left the campaign to have a baby that fall.[9]

Roxanne's headquarters buzzed with activity day and night. "I couldn't believe all the work these women were doing for Roxanne," recalled Tom Whitney. "I went to the office at 10:30 at night, and they would be working; I'd stop in at 2 in the morning, and they would be there. It was incredible; I'd never seen that sort of dedication and loyalty in a state campaign before." To make such long hours at the campaign office a bit easier, a volunteer installed a donated washer and dryer so the workers could wash clothes when they could not get home.[10]

The campaign was humming along, largely because of Roxanne herself and her success on the road. She had been vigorously engaged in retail politics for over a year, which she recalled was "the greatest fun ever." The performer in her loved giving speeches and holding forth at citizen forums, but she especially loved the nitty-gritty of local politics—shaking hands, kissing babies, visiting in town squares, and riding in parades. With these activities, she was winning Iowans over one by one.[11]

The long days on the hustings were physically grueling. Roxanne would make as many as twelve stops a day, often beginning at seven in the morning and not ending until midnight. Getting little sleep and not eating regularly, she subsisted by nibbling on peanuts, sesame sticks, and Hershey bars; she drank cups of Earl Grey tea, cans of Diet Coke, and an occasional glass of white wine; and she chain-smoked Triumph 100 cigarettes. Unlike many candidates who fought weight gain during campaigns, the 5-foot-4-inch 110-pound Roxanne lost close to 15 pounds by the time of the general election.[12]

It was clear that her hard work was paying off. Roxanne addressed the issues and began laying out her positions: she was a feminist who supported legalized abortion; she was tough on crime; she called for job training, more money for education, and support for the elderly; and she talked of increasing taxes on the wealthy. From her core support group of women and party liberals, she expanded her base to include young people and two key unions, the Iowa Federation of Labor and the state teachers union, the Iowa State Education Association. Yet the election remained about Roxanne, the woman running for governor. Her campaign wisely took advantage of this: in early spring green yard signs, bumper stickers, and election posters appeared with only her first name: RoXanne.[13]

In the meantime, Roxanne, Tom Whitney, and Jerry Crawford, another of her close friends and a political adviser, began talking about recruiting a campaign manager; they believed and Monica McFadden— who had essentially served in that capacity—agreed that for appearances they needed a male manager. They knew that a female candidate was a hard sell as it was; adding a female campaign manager to the mix would make it even more of a struggle. Yet many of the qualified political staffers in the state were already involved with other candidates, so the three agreed on Tom Chapman for the job. Chapman, from St. Louis, had experience running statewide campaigns in Missouri.[14]

When Chapman arrived in early March, Whitney pulled him aside and bluntly told him, "Roxanne is a force, and we're doing really well right now. You have one job here; just don't screw anything up." An Iowa Poll released in the middle of that month supported Whitney's rosy assessment. Twenty-nine percent of Iowa Democrats favored Roxanne for governor compared to 17 percent for Fitzgerald and 9 percent for Campbell. Even better, among all Iowans, Roxanne was ahead of Branstad 39 percent to 32 percent, a huge turnaround since the September Iowa Poll, which had her trailing the Republican. Also of interest, the data showed that being a woman "is neither helping nor hindering Conlin" as "her strength is equal among men and women in the test race against Branstad."[15]

Fund-raising, however, remained a problem, and that spring Roxanne borrowed an additional $50,000 from her husband. The loans were largely the extent of Jim's involvement in the campaign. He was not interested in politics, and because he had an unconventional sense of humor that could be off-putting to many, Roxanne had decided that he would not take an active public role in her campaign. Likewise, sixteen-year-old Jackie and thirteen-year-old J.B. sat out most political events, as did twenty-year-old Doug. Twenty-three-year-old Debbie, meanwhile, participated—interestingly, she had red hair like Roxanne, although she was Jim's daughter, not Roxanne's. Debbie was good with people, and she sometimes stepped in when Roxanne could not attend an event.[16]

Another Iowa Poll three weeks before the primary indicated that Roxanne's lead over her Democratic rivals was widening: 44 percent favored her, 25 percent Fitzgerald, and 15 percent Campbell. It also showed her remaining ahead in a projected matchup with Branstad, 45 percent to 38 percent, with the spread the same as the last poll but now with fewer undecided voters.[17]

Still, Roxanne was unhappy with campaign manager Chapman, often telling Whitney that he was not doing anything and that deputy manager McFadden, who had started at the campaign full time in January, was picking up the slack. Others in the campaign had similar feelings about Chapman, but Whitney was not concerned because everything pointed to a primary win. *Des Moines Register* political columnist Jim Flansburg thought Roxanne was on track as well: the headline for one of his May columns read "Conlin Looks Like Winner (unless She Trips Herself)." Roxanne was feeling good about her chances as well, but similar to Flansburg's comment she noted, "I'm striving not to shoot myself in the foot."[18]

She did not make any mistakes over the next few weeks, and the Iowa Poll proved correct. Roxanne won big. The turnout was particularly heavy, nearly 50 percent higher than expected. Roxanne carried eighty-six of the state's ninety-nine counties and won 48 percent of the vote to Fitzgerald's 31 percent and Campbell's 21 percent. She and her supporters were elated: she had become the first Iowa woman to be nominated for governor by a major political party. Roxanne addressed a thousand supporters gathered at the Hotel Savery just after midnight. Once the cheering died down, she explained that victory was sweet but the goal was to win the governor's seat in November: "This is only the first battle in a long war. The other side has the money, but we have the people. What we have to do is clear. We must commit the uncommitted, convince the unconvinced, and educate the ignorant. We must defeat those who would stand in the way of justice and progress."[19]

If the polls indicated that Roxanne's gender was no longer an important issue in the race, a feature in the *Des Moines Register* the day after the primary suggested otherwise. Under the headline "Candidate Conlin Learns to Cope with Image Game," reporter David Yepsen wrote an article about "behavior, grooming, and dressing rules . . . that apply to all politicians, but sexist or not, especially to women." Over the course of the campaign, Roxanne received frequent advice from well-wishers and opponents alike about how she should dress and wear her hair. Ultimately, according to Yepsen, she chose "colorless, shapeless clothes," a curly permed hairdo, and "subdued facial makeup." Roxanne took this approach to avoid distracting both female and male supporters. Then in a sexist twist, the *Register* did something it never would have done with a male candidate: it accompanied the story with six file photos showing Roxanne's changing hairstyles and makeup over the past ten years.[20]

Immediately following the victory, Roxanne announced that Tom Chapman was "burned out," and he left the campaign to return to Missouri. Both she and Chapman realized they had difficulty working together, and the parting was mutual. Still operating on the idea that she needed to have a male campaign manager, she went with Whitney's recommendation and looked to her recent rival, Jerry Fitzgerald. She offered him the job, but he declined. Then Whitney suggested John Fitzpatrick, the top aide to U.S. Representative Tom Harkin. Fitzpatrick was a former professor of political science at Iowa State University. Harkin recalled him as a "political genius." Roxanne asked Harkin if she could "borrow" Fitzpatrick to run her campaign. Harkin said yes, and Fitzpatrick agreed, planning to start in the beginning of July.[21]

Roxanne was riding high after the primary. A week and a half later, she gave a fiery speech at the Democratic state convention at Des Moines's Veterans Memorial Auditorium. There she rallied the crowd of three thousand by attacking Branstad and his "party of privilege," explaining that they were not the sole owners of the American dream. "Your bankroll can't buy it. Your tax shelters can't shelter it," she declared. "You've tried to monopolize the dream. You've tried to grab it all. But the dream only works when it is shared."[22]

A few days later, she and Tom Whitney went to the Democratic midterm national convention in Philadelphia. There Whitney ran into Senator Ted Kennedy, for whom he had worked during Kennedy's 1980 bid for the Democratic nomination for president. Kennedy asked him how Roxanne's campaign was going. When Whitney replied that things were great, Kennedy responded by saying, "If she wins, she is someone who will need to be reckoned with."[23]

Tom Whitney could not have agreed more. He had always thought Roxanne's political future was bright if she could just take the next step and win in November. But then things started to unravel: Roxanne indeed shot herself in the foot.

During the primary campaign, Roxanne had pledged to release a voluntary financial disclosure statement, but she had not done so because her complicated tax returns had not been completed. They had applied for and received an extension for filing from the Internal Revenue Service. The Conlins' returns were finished at the end of June, and the accountant gave Roxanne an overview, including the fact that the couple's net worth stood at $2.2 million, but because much of their wealth was invested in apartment buildings and real estate tax shelters, they owed no state taxes and paid only $2,995 in federal taxes. The accountant gave Roxanne the completed disclosure statement the following day, July 1.[24]

Roxanne's intuition, which she recalled "almost always served me well," told her the information was a political liability, but she should get it out to the public immediately, take her lumps, and hope the issue would pass. Without consulting key advisers such as Whitney and Fitzpatrick—the new campaign manager had just started that day—she gave the information to Jill Wiley, her publicity coordinator, to release that afternoon.[25]

The timing could not have been worse. The story broke in newspapers across the state on Friday morning, July 2, the opening of the Fourth of July weekend. Many Iowans woke to the *Des Moines Register*'s front-page headline: "Worth $2.2 Million, Conlin, Husband Paid No State Income Tax." The story became fodder for endless conversations around backyard barbeques, picnics, parades, and fireworks displays over the Independence Day holiday.[26]

Branstad pounced, saying he was "shocked" at Roxanne's disclosure, especially after she had recently railed against him and the Republican Party for using its "bankroll" and "tax shelters" to "monopolize the

[American] dream." His previously released financial statement put his and wife Christine Branstad's net worth at $105,000, showing that they paid $7,179 in federal taxes and $1,479 in state taxes in 1981. Governor Ray joined the attack, calling Roxanne's remarks "hypocritical." Ray's comment was a "real haymaker," recalled Jerry Crawford. "The governor was still immensely popular, and the words carried a lot of weight."[27]

The blows landed, and Roxanne's campaign was sent reeling. She explained that she and Jim were much like Iowa farmers, whose "paper wealth" was tied to their land or, in the Conlins' case, their real estate investments. Roxanne continued, saying it was a bad year for real estate, they had lost money on their investments, and therefore they did not owe state taxes. However, a growing number of Iowans were struggling in the recession, and Roxanne was a millionaire who had not paid taxes. Her explanations fell short.[28]

Two days later, the *Des Moines Register* ran a tough editorial on Roxanne's "tax dilemma." "Clearly," the paper's editorial board noted, "Conlin has a credibility gap and the campaign has a new issue, an issue not likely to go away." The words proved prophetic. Try as she might, Roxanne could not keep the issue at bay, and it kept cropping up throughout the rest of the campaign.[29]

Roxanne first had to deal with it on the road during the many Fourth of July events that had already been scheduled for her. Holiday picnics and parades, which should have been fun and easy campaigning, were anything but. Questions and comments about her taxes continued to hound her. She returned to her Des Moines headquarters early the following week demoralized, depressed, and exhausted. When she saw Whitney, she said she was ready to hang it up and withdraw from the race. Rather than talking her out of it, he talked her through the issue, and she ultimately decided to stay in and keep fighting.[30]

She came out the next weekend to give a speech at an American Federation of State, County and Municipal Employees picnic, where she said the tax issue had hurt, but she then gave a more detailed explanation that she hoped members would take back to their rank and file. Plans called for her to give similar speeches the following day in

Cedar Rapids and Fort Dodge in an effort to repair the damage and return the discussion to the real issues of the campaign. However, two days later, on Monday, July 12, the *Des Moines Register*'s front-page Frank Miller cartoon featured wealthy men on tire swings hanging from a tree labeled "Tax Shelter." On the swing labeled "Loophole" were the words "I'm voting for Roxanne! She is one of us!" Below the cartoon ran a story reporting that Democratic Party leaders believed that the tax controversy had "hurt her credibility as a candidate," and Fitzpatrick noted that fund-raising had taken a hit. Branstad maintained the pressure when he promised to release his tax returns, which showed he "paid his fair share."[31]

Soon green yard signs and bumper stickers began appearing. A spoof on the RoXanne signs, they said simply: TaXanne. Clever, direct, and to the point, the signs helped keep the tax issue alive. Inadvertently, Jim Conlin fanned the flames as well.[32]

In the middle of July, Jim agreed to meet with the *Des Moines Register* to discuss the couple's taxes and real estate tax shelters. But after conferring with Roxanne and Fitzpatrick, he abruptly canceled the interview. Then *Register* reporters noticed that Jim had planned to offer a seminar on real estate investments, which included a segment on property tax shelters. Ads for the course ran in the *Register*'s classified section earlier in the month, but the morning before the story appeared in the paper, Jim canceled the class scheduled for that evening.[33]

Unfortunately, the damage had been done. The incident kept public attention on the tax issue, and it became a topic of derision for the *Register*'s new opinion-page columnist, Patrick Lackey. The following week, he wrote, "Roxanne talked . . . about the unfairness of tax shelters, but when life presented her with a golden opportunity to act on principle, she wrestled with her principles and won. . . . Certainly the shelters she and her husband made the most of were just ones." Lackey continued, "Besides if James had paid taxes, he might have appeared professionally incompetent and even silly. Wouldn't you question the competence of someone who conducted seminars on avoiding taxes but paid taxes himself? Clearly, James was competent."[34]

As *Des Moines Tribune* reporter David Elbert so aptly put it, Roxanne and Jim had traveled on "parallel paths to success—she in politics and law, he in real estate and finance." They stayed out of each other's careers, and the arrangement worked well until that July, when "his success dealt a gutshot to the Democratic candidate for governor." Roxanne was exasperated. After roughly two weeks of talking about the tax issue failed to put the campaign back on track, she and her advisers decided she would stop discussing it.[35]

On July 29, Roxanne and Branstad held their first of four televised debates. This one focused on agricultural issues, and the *Sioux City Journal* characterized it as "pretty much ho-hum." Nothing in the debate seemed to change voters' minds. At about the same time, the Iowa Poll's end-of-July findings showed the dramatic impact that the "tax flap," as the *Des Moines Register* referred to it, was having on the race. Branstad now led Roxanne 49 percent to 37 percent, more than a complete reversal of the May poll that gave Roxanne a lead of 45 percent to his 38 percent.[36]

Six weeks later, on Saturday, September 11, Roxanne and Branstad butted heads in their second debate. The following morning, a *Des Moines Register* front-page story noted that both candidates were moving toward the middle as they sought to expand their base of support. The *Des Moines Tribune* later observed that Republicans and Democrats believed Roxanne performed better here than in the earlier debate but, not surprisingly, they split along party lines over who was the clear winner.[37]

Above the debate article in the Sunday *Register* ran the results of another Iowa Poll. As the story continued onto a second page, the headline proclaimed, "Tax Issue Still Hounding Conlin." The poll indicated that Branstad held an 11 percent advantage over Roxanne. Most noteworthy, 25 percent of Branstad supporters were characterized as anti-Roxanne voters, and the reason most often cited for their stance was the revelation that she had paid no state income taxes.[38]

Desperate to reverse her campaign slide, Roxanne reached out to good friend and political consultant Cathryn Simmons with a late night phone call in mid-September. The two met and grew close in the early 1970s through Democratic politics and the Iowa Women's Political

Caucus. Simmons, in fact, likely would have succeeded Roxanne as head of the IWPC had she remained in Des Moines, but her husband's job took him to Kansas City, and they moved to Missouri in the middle of the decade. There she became even more active in local campaign operations and began managing them, soon developing a reputation as a smart and effective political strategist.[39]

Roxanne opened the conversation with a question, "Do you want me to win this race?" When Simmons said yes, Roxanne replied, "Then you better get up here and fix this campaign because I'm losing." After thinking about it for a couple of days and talking with her husband, Simmons headed to Iowa. Since it was late in the game, Roxanne, Whitney, and Simmons agreed that Fitzpatrick would remain in place as the campaign manager, but Simmons would largely direct the campaign. She knew Roxanne well and understood that her campaign was different from traditional male political campaigns. In retrospect, Roxanne and some staffers thought they would have been better off under Simmons's guidance from the beginning.[40]

Simmons understood that she was not an Iowan and did not have the native perspective on the race. She also understood that she was stepping into a difficult situation very late in the game. Nevertheless, her outsider's point of view and her focus on the present and immediate future helped turn the campaign around.[41]

When Simmons arrived, she went out into the field to sample sentiment. She soon realized that they could turn people around and came to agree with Whitney's position that "people liked Roxanne; they were disappointed but ultimately wanted her to do well." Unfortunately, she recalled, "The campaign office was frozen," and the dedication that staffers had shown earlier had faded away. On one of her first mornings at Roxanne's headquarters, she was surprised that no one else was there, so she immediately posted a note requiring staffers to be in the office at 8:00 a.m. or face termination. Along with this discipline, she stressed that time was short and that everyone needed to stop dwelling on the tax debacle and any other past issues and move forward, concentrating on winning votes over the few weeks remaining.[42]

Next, Simmons asked Laura Ward to be Roxanne's permanent driver for the remainder of the campaign. Roxanne would be on the road a lot over the next month and a half, and Simmons felt she needed the stability and continuity of one driver, which she had not had for a couple of months since LuAnn Olson had been sent to win voters in Ottumwa. Campaign drivers were "much more than just drivers," Simmons noted. They were companions, confidants, and the go-to staffer as well, and Ward was completely dedicated to getting Roxanne elected.[43]

With Simmons's help, a reenergized Roxanne began to turn her campaign around. In early October, she proposed a $300 million Invest in Iowa bond issue to create jobs, rebuild crumbling roads and bridges, and fund energy and soil conservation measures. Given the poor economy and rising unemployment, the idea captured the imagination of both Democrats and Republicans. Roxanne immediately took to the road to tout the program, which resonated with voters and stopped or at least slowed questions about the tax flap. The move also pushed key union groups to throw their support behind Roxanne. Most notably, this included the United Auto Workers, which Roxanne and Simmons had been aggressively pursuing. In late September, they had even brought Ted Anderson, a UAW official and state senator from Waterloo, into the campaign.[44]

Meanwhile, a Branstad gaffe also helped Roxanne. At the end of September, he floated the idea of using his inaugural celebration to raise money for anti-abortion groups. He would later back away from the idea, but the suggestion raised questions about his judgment and ethics. This combined with Roxanne's new proposal and the apparent fading interest in her tax issue tightened the race. An Iowa Poll conducted in early October showed Roxanne pulling within 4 points of Branstad.[45]

Money began coming into Roxanne's coffers again, although the campaign was still running a deficit. With these limited funds, Simmons made a tactical decision: to counter Branstad's flood of television advertising, she put all her resources into television spots, forgoing any additional brochures, posters, or mailings. Meanwhile, the candidates faced off in two more debates in October. Neither made any major mistakes. Tom Whitney believed that Roxanne did well in the debates, coming off as "warm and knowledgeable," and he recalled that most observers gave her the edge in the contests.[46]

Between these two debates, the Iowa Democratic Party held its annual fund-raiser and rally, the Jefferson-Jackson Day dinner. Headlined by Senator Edward Kennedy, the gala should have given Roxanne and her supporters a big boost going into the two-week sprint before the election. Unfortunately, it did not. More than two thousand people gathered for the party, held at Iowa State University's Hilton Coliseum in Ames. After dinner and some preliminary speakers, Roxanne addressed the crowd.

Tom Whitney was with the press, where he hoped to get a sense of how reporters responded to the speech. He was especially interested in the reaction of *Des Moines Register* columnist and opinion maker Jim Flansburg and sat next to him. Roxanne began by comparing her campaign thus far to a baseball game. It was the ninth inning; the score was 11–10, and she was behind. "You may recall," she said, "that in about the sixth inning, I hit a line drive to center field, but as I was rounding second, I tripped over my tongue and fell flat on my face. In baseball, they call that an error. That is what we call it in politics, too." Laura Ward was with Roxanne when the candidate penned the speech earlier that day in the back seat of a small airplane as they headed to Ames from southern Iowa. She remembered that Roxanne was especially proud of this portion of her speech. "She was so happy with her baseball analogy even though she never cared for baseball."[47]

However, after reading the draft of the speech, Ward was worried about the next couple of sentences, but she did not feel it appropriate for her, a lowly driver, to comment. Following her baseball story, Roxanne told the audience, "You have forgiven me. The people of Iowa have forgiven me. And on November 2, we will win."[48]

Roxanne did not immediately realize it, but she had just shot herself in the foot again. Flansburg realized it. After the speech, he leaned over to Whitney and asked, "Tom, what the hell?" Shaking his head, Flansburg added, "She's dead; she's just dead." The columnist packed up to leave before Kennedy's address and told Whitney, "We're going to lead with the forgiven stuff . . . and it ain't going to be pretty."[49]

On his way out of the press area, Whitney received more bad news. Reporter Mike Owen stopped him and gave him a copy of that morning's *Quad-City Times*. Owen pointed out his story under the headline "Branstad: Conlin's Husband Shady," where Branstad raised the tax shelter issue again and questioned Jim's business ethics. Whitney took the paper and found Simmons, and the two of them went to tell Roxanne and Jim about the latest troubles. They found them with Laura Ward, pulled them into a vacant locker room, and told them to sit down.[50]

There Whitney and Simmons told the couple about Flansburg's belief that the speech would kill her campaign. The news hit Roxanne hard; she bent over with her head in her hands. Then came the second punch: the two advisers showed Roxanne and Jim the *Quad-City Times* story and said they expected to take some hits.[51]

The tax issue, which had been fading into the background, was back, and it was back at just the wrong time. A couple of days later, Governor Ray responded to Roxanne's Jefferson-Jackson Day speech, "I don't think she speaks for all of us. I don't think everybody has forgotten, nor do I think everybody has forgiven." Branstad, meanwhile, slipped in a comment on the tax issue whenever he had the opportunity.[52]

Amid the new discussion of the tax matter, state newspapers began publishing their gubernatorial endorsements. Branstad won the support of several significant dailies, including the *Cedar Rapids Gazette*, the *Muscatine Journal*, the *Sioux City Journal*, and the *Quad-City Times*, but Roxanne received the endorsement of the *Des Moines Register*, the state's largest and most influential paper. The backing was tepid, however. It was "a troubling choice," the *Register* wrote. "Neither Democrat Roxanne Conlin nor Republican Terry Branstad is a candidate we can enthusiastically endorse. Each has qualities that appeal to us, but others that concern us. Neither seems to possess that remarkable Ray talent for consensus for government that has served Iowa so well for 14 years. . . . On balance, Conlin comes closer to what we would hope to find in a new state leader than does Branstad. On that ground, but with less confidence than we would wish, we prefer Conlin for governor."[53]

Branstad, however, made some additional mistakes. In late October, he proposed converting Interstate 80 into a toll road. The statement caused quite a stir, and Branstad had to back away from it after Roxanne correctly explained that to do so, the state would have to repay the federal government 90 percent of its construction costs. She added that such a suggestion showed her opponent's "lack of judgment and foresight." A few days later, Branstad stuck his foot in his mouth again. In the midst of the farm crisis, he said, "A lot of the farmers I know that are in trouble today are the ones that were so greedy they wanted to buy every farm they could get their hands on back in the mid-1970s when farmland was going up in value. They've now got themselves into an over-extended situation." Again Roxanne took advantage, calling the remark "insensitive."[54]

The stage was now set. At the end of October, the *Des Moines Register*'s Iowa Poll showed Branstad holding a "razor thin" lead over Roxanne, 45 to 43 percent. The numbers gave Roxanne hope, and she was sanguine going into the election. So too was Whitney. Simmons liked the way things were trending but wished they had a few more days to campaign, although she thought they "might have it by a squeak."[55]

Roxanne and her family, staffers, friends, and other supporters gathered at the Hotel Savery on a mild election night to watch the returns. Campaign adviser Jerry Crawford was paying particular attention to numbers coming in from certain counties. Optimism soon turned to concern when he reported that early returns from Dubuque and Carroll Counties, then historically Democratic strongholds that Roxanne should carry by wide margins, were not good. They only grew worse because Branstad was running up big numbers across the state. With one-third of the vote counted, it became clear that the race was over, and at 10:30 p.m. Roxanne called Branstad to concede the election and wish him well.[56]

As it turned out, the election was not close. Branstad proved especially strong in the state's rural counties but also did well in traditionally Democratic urban ones. He took 53 percent of the vote to Roxanne's 47 percent. The loss was especially disheartening because Democrats took several top posts—lieutenant governor, attorney general, and state treasurer—and won control of both houses of the state legislature. Roxanne's loss was personal.[57]

What accounted for the election results? Undoubtedly, Roxanne's gender and the sexism of the time played a role, as did the tax flap. A year earlier, a polling firm's research had suggested that being a woman would cost Roxanne roughly 9 points in potential political races. Indeed, many of Roxanne's female supporters felt that she lost because she was a woman. Ultimately, it appeared, Iowans were not ready for a female governor in 1982 (or female representatives in the U.S. Senate and House, for that matter). Thirty-five years would pass before Lieutenant Governor Kim Reynolds became Iowa's first female governor, although she was appointed, not elected, when Terry Branstad, then the nation's longest-serving governor in history, stepped down to become the U.S. ambassador to China. Reynolds was then elected in her own right in 2018. Four years earlier, conservative Republican Joni Ernst broke Iowa's male monopoly on representation in Washington by becoming the state's first woman to be elected to the U.S. Senate. Democrats Cindy Axne and Abby Finkenauer followed as Iowa's first two women elected to Congress in 2018.[58]

Male supporters, Roxanne recalled, thought the tax matter cost her the election. It clearly was a major misstep. Branstad and his staff kept the issue in the news whenever possible, and Roxanne was never able to put the matter entirely to rest. She even unwittingly shone the spotlight on it two weeks before the election with her Jefferson-Jackson Day speech. The issue affected fund-raising, which nearly ground to a halt, and this limited the campaign's ability to advertise and sell Roxanne and her ideas. Worse, it gave many voters who may have been on the fence about voting for a woman a socially acceptable way to oppose Roxanne. These voters now had an out and could say, "I don't care that she's a woman, but this tax thing really bothers me. I just can't vote for her."[59]

But there were other factors as well. Inexperience hurt Roxanne. Although she had been active in many campaigns, she had never run for public office before, and Cathryn Simmons explained that being the candidate was an entirely new ball game. Roxanne admitted as much when she appeared on Iowa Public Television's *Iowa Press* program in late October 1982, observing that "perhaps" being a first-time candidate led to mistakes in her handling of the tax matter.[60]

At the same time, experience helped Terry Branstad, who proved to be a formidable foe. Also an attorney, Branstad won a seat in the Iowa House of Representatives in 1972, where he would serve three terms before running successfully for lieutenant governor in 1978. This background in both local and statewide campaigns gave him a familiarity with the election process and made him a hardworking, well-organized campaigner who maintained vote goals for every township and precinct. Over the course of several campaigns, Branstad had also put together a large professional staff. Moreover, his campaign was well funded, which allowed him to saturate the state with advertising, and he was able to tie himself to Bob Ray, the highly popular outgoing governor. For many, a vote for Branstad represented a continuation of Ray's moderate approach.[61]

Finally, according to David Yepsen, as an urban liberal from Des Moines Roxanne did not fit the profile of those Iowans most often elected to high office. With the exception of Bob Ray, who was also from Des Moines, Iowa voters preferred their statewide candidates to be from small towns or rural backgrounds and either conservative or at least moderate in their positions. Branstad, a conservative Republican from Leland and then Lake Mills, two small towns in Winnebago County, 130 miles north of Des Moines, fit the bill. So too did the first two women who broke Iowa's political glass ceiling: Senator Joni Ernst is a conservative Republican from Red Oak, a small town in southwestern Iowa about 120 miles from Des Moines, and Republican Governor Kim Reynolds is from St. Charles, a small town in Madison County 30 miles south of Des Moines.[62]

On election night, however, such explanations would have provided little solace. When it became clear that Branstad had won, Roxanne gave a gracious concession speech and remained poised as she circulated among her supporters in the Hotel Savery ballroom. But the loss proved extremely difficult. Her career had been an upward arc, filled with purpose, service, and success as she blazed new trails for women, battled discrimination, and helped people without a voice. She had long considered moving into politics, and becoming governor was something she had thought about since high school. That hope was dashed, and for one of the few times in her life she had to grapple with defeat and then reset as she searched for a new vocation.

Roxanne and her mother, Alice Barton, 1944. Courtesy of Roxanne Conlin.

Roxanne, 1945.
Courtesy of Roxanne Conlin.

Roxanne and her father, Bill Barton, 1945.
Courtesy of Roxanne Conlin.

Roxanne and kittens at a University of South Dakota trailer
park, ca. 1946. The Barton family lived here while Bill finished
his undergraduate degree. Courtesy of Roxanne Conlin.

Roxanne, 1950. Courtesy of Roxanne Conlin.

Roxanne on her first bicycle, 1953. She tried
to ride it home when the Floyd River flooded
her Sioux City neighborhood later that year.
Courtesy of Roxanne Conlin.

Roxanne, on the far left next to the Trails End sign, at a Girl Scout summer camp, 1955.
Courtesy of Roxanne Conlin.

The Barton family, 1958. Standing, left to right: Becky,
Rhonda, Roxanne, Rhoda, and Ray. Seated, left to right: Alice,
Gina, and Bill. Courtesy of Roxanne Conlin.

Roxanne on a modeling job, ca. 1960. Courtesy of Roxanne Conlin.

Roxanne, ca. 1962. Courtesy of Roxanne Conlin.

Roxanne at her Drake Law School graduation, 1966. Courtesy of Roxanne Conlin.

The Conlin family, 1969. Roxanne is holding infant son J.B., while husband Jim holds the couple's toddler, Jackie. Courtesy of Roxanne Conlin.

Roxanne in her office as an assistant state attorney general, 1974. Courtesy of Roxanne Conlin.

Roxanne and Bella Abzug, ca. 1975. Courtesy of the Iowa Women's Archives, University of Iowa Libraries.

Roxanne, her mother, and some of her siblings at her swearing in as a U.S. attorney, 1977. Left to right: Becky, Rhonda, Alice, Roxanne, and Ray. Courtesy of Roxanne Conlin.

The Conlin family and pets, 1980. Left to right: Jim, Roxanne, Doug, Jackie, Debbie, and J.B.
Courtesy of Roxanne Conlin.

Roxanne on the campaign trail, 1982.
Courtesy of Roxanne Conlin.

Roxanne with good friend Paulee Lipsman
during the 1982 gubernatorial campaign.
Courtesy of Roxanne Conlin.

Roxanne buttons from the 1982 campaign. Courtesy of Roxanne Conlin.

Des Moines Register cartoonist Frank Miller gave Roxanne this signed copy of his cartoon, which ran in the paper after Roxanne's primary victory in 1982. Courtesy of Roxanne Conlin.

Roxanne with former Iowa governor and then U.S. senator Harold Hughes, ca. 1982. Courtesy of the Iowa Women's Archives, University of Iowa Libraries.

Seven

Bouncing Back

Losing the gubernatorial race devastated Roxanne. "Inconsolable" was how sister-in-law Judy Conlin remembered her, as Roxanne spent most of the next eight months at home brooding, trying to get over the defeat. But family and friends supported her through this dark period. A particular group of women who called themselves the Survivors proved especially helpful to Roxanne, as did a return to political activity when she went to work for Senator John Glenn's short-lived bid for the presidency.[1]

Equally important was finding a new calling. Roxanne had always pursued work where she could help others, whether as a deputy commissioner handling workers compensation cases, an assistant Iowa attorney general fighting for civil rights, or a U.S. attorney going after white-collar criminals and drug traffickers. Service was one of the major reasons she had been so interested in becoming Iowa's governor. After turning down a number of job offers, Roxanne found her passion in plaintiff law when she joined the Des Moines firm of James and Galligan in October 1983. Here she took great pleasure in assisting those who had been wronged, and she grew very successful at it. She also became active in the national plaintiff attorneys' organization, the Association of Trial Lawyers of America, where she soon was a rising star.

As Roxanne was going through a transition, so too was her family. For a short time, Jim merged his business with Gene Stanbrough, a major real estate player in the Des Moines market, before going back out on his own. Their children, meanwhile, were finishing school, moving out, and starting lives of their own. Meanwhile Roxanne battled personal demons. She struggled to give up cigarettes and then received a very public wake-up call when she was arrested for drunk driving. Ultimately, though, a decade after losing the election, Roxanne was again on top, this time as the first female president of the Association of Trial Lawyers of America.

After her concession speech, Roxanne maintained an upbeat façade as she thanked supporters, hugged friends, and reassured those in tears. But after she left the hotel and was in the car with Jim and family, she broke down sobbing. The campaign had been draining, both physically and emotionally. Roxanne had set out to blaze another new trail and throw open the sexist doors of Terrace Hill. She had captured the imagination of women across the state, carrying their hopes and dreams of a more equitable Iowa. She was disappointed for herself, but her sadness went well beyond that. She felt she had let her supporters down; so many had done so much, and she had come up short. The burden of that responsibility weighed heavily on her.[2]

Cathryn Simmons, the de facto campaign manager, had returned to Missouri and her family immediately after the election, but she was worried about how Roxanne would deal with the loss and asked Laura Ward, Roxanne's driver, to stay on as her assistant for a few weeks. Ward closed down the campaign office and looked in on Roxanne, who recalled, "I was probably clinically depressed."[3]

Jim tried to help his disheartened wife by taking her away to Canyon Ranch, an exclusive resort and spa in Tucson. Unfortunately, governor-elect Terry Branstad was on the same plane. The retreat's various amenities probably helped distract Roxanne, but what she remembered was eating lots of food because she needed to gain back the weight she had lost during the campaign. This made her unpopular with a number of the other guests, many of whom were trying to lose weight.[4]

Getting away was good for Roxanne, but the dark clouds of defeat still hung over her when she returned to Iowa. Once back at home, she did not venture out much. "She hibernated for several months," said good friend Cookie Brown. Hidden away in her house, Roxanne spent her time trying to learn to cook and type. She did not master either. She also found some relief "in crafting and knitting." And because she was usually in a bathrobe and slippers, she wore out several pairs of floppy slippers.[5]

Sometimes, though, she was in her Reebok sneakers. Like thousands of other women across the nation, Roxanne had purchased *Jane Fonda's Workout Book*, the 1981 best seller, and the exercise video that accompanied it. With Fonda spouting instructions and encouragement from the video playing on her television, Roxanne exercised religiously over the next few months, toning her body into the best shape she had been in her life. The vigorous exercise helped keep her mind off the election loss.[6]

She also began talking about the defeat and other key events in her life to a group of women that good friend and jury consultant Hale Starr pulled together. Starr, who had lost her son in a car accident in 1980, had been toying with the idea of gathering several other female friends from different backgrounds and different careers who had survived difficult events in their lives. In Starr's mind, the women would form a support group. They would talk through their tragedies, but they would also discuss key issues of the day with the idea of publishing a book that would resonate with women across the nation.[7]

Starr initiated such a group in 1983 and dubbed it the Survivors. Six women took part. Besides Starr, the participants included Roxanne, who had lost the election; Joanne Fine, who had recently worked for Starr and was having memories of being sexually abused as a child; and Carol Baumgarten, Drake University's women's basketball coach, who was gay but had not yet come out. The other members were Elaine Symoniak, then on the Des Moines City Council, who had recently lost her bid for mayor, and Susan Terry, a West Des Moines businesswoman who had lost her husband in a construction accident in 1982.[8]

The group began meeting in early 1983, gathering once a month in their homes over the next year. Over food and wine, they talked about surviving loss but also about agreed-on topics such as love, marriage, sex, power, money, and politics. Starr recorded the meetings and then had the tapes transcribed. The transcripts were to be the primary source material for their proposed book, but after rereading what had been said, several members worried that their discussions were too revealing, and they all agreed to shelve the planned book.[9]

Nonetheless, the women grew closer because of their frank exchanges, and the get-togethers proved therapeutic for Roxanne, who began to rebound. Joanne Fine recalled that the "Survivors gave Roxanne a group who understood her feelings and were committed to staying with her and supporting her." In an unintended consequence, the friendships developed or deepened here led to several business relationships. In 1985, for example, Susan Terry (who owned a construction company) and Starr erected an office building to house their businesses and others at 1201 Grand Avenue in West Des Moines. That same year Fine, with Starr's backing, founded Keynote, Inc., a firm that marketed and arranged for speakers. Starr, Elaine Symoniak, and Roxanne were among the figures Keynote often booked. In 1987, Terry and her husband, Norton Gegner, collaborated with Roxanne and Jim and daughter Debbie and her husband, Kerry Anderson, in a Grease Monkey express lube shop franchise. Together they opened several more Grease Monkeys in the area over the next few years.[10]

As the Survivors began lifting her spirits, Roxanne's slow return to public life was initially marked by her performance at the Gridiron Show, Des Moines's advertising professionals' benefit to raise money for journalism and marketing scholarships. Typically, local celebrities provided the entertainment. The spring 1983 event featured, among others, newly elected governor Terry Branstad and first lady Chris Branstad, Des Moines Mayor Pete Crivaro, local restaurateur Babe Bisignano, WHO radio talk show host Julie Gammack, and *Des Moines Register* columnist Chuck Offenburger. But it was Roxanne who brought down the house. Channeling the singer and dancer she had long aspired to be, she strutted onstage in a flapper-style fringed black dress, fishnet stockings, and a feather boa and sang a reworded version of "Second Hand Rose" lampooning Branstad.[11]

Roxanne followed this with a dive back into politics. This time, however, she was not a candidate but part of Ohio senator John Glenn's campaign for president. She had gotten to know Glenn the previous year during her gubernatorial run, when he made a number of exploratory visits to the state in preparation for the Iowa caucuses in early 1984. She found him "funny, charming, and genuinely nice," and she was pleased with his pro-choice stand on abortion and his support for the Equal Rights Amendment. Roxanne was happy when Glenn announced his candidacy in April 1983, and over the next couple of months the Glenn campaign reached out to her for help. By June, she had decided to get back in the game and signed on to chair Glenn's national policy committee. At the end of that month, she publicly endorsed Glenn and announced her role in his campaign in a number of press conferences across Iowa. Interestingly, Monica McFadden, Roxanne's deputy campaign manager the previous year, was also involved in this presidential race, serving as the midwestern campaign coordinator for California senator Alan Cranston.[12]

In her unpaid position, Roxanne traveled on behalf of Glenn, discussed policy positions and strategy with him, and convened with other key supporters. But Glenn's candidacy never really caught on. Although a true American hero, he lacked charisma, and his message was unclear. He ran an abysmal fifth in the February Iowa caucuses, which former vice-president Walter Mondale won by a wide margin. Perhaps more important, Colorado senator Gary Hart came in second, establishing him as the alternative to Mondale. A week later, Hart surprised pundits by winning the New Hampshire primary, followed by Mondale and Glenn. The next month, Glenn dropped out of the race after a poor showing in the multistate Super Tuesday primaries, and Mondale would go on to secure the nomination.[13]

The primaries had not gone as Roxanne had hoped, but there were two positive aspects. First, the job proved especially good for her. It got her moving forward again and reignited her interest and engagement in Democratic politics, one of her lifelong passions. Second, another sexist barrier fell when Mondale selected Geraldine Ferraro as his running mate, making her the first female vice-presidential candidate of a major party. Women had organized an effort to elect her if Mondale did not nominate her, and Roxanne was among those in charge of carrying out the careful but ultimately unnecessary plan.[14]

Meanwhile, Roxanne had become active in the National Organization for Women's Legal Defense and Education Fund, a nonprofit independent organization founded in 1970 to "provide legal advocacy for women's rights." She joined its board in 1983 and served as a director over the next six years. Roxanne acted as its general counsel from 1985 to 1986 and its president from 1986 to 1988. Under her leadership, the group published its *State by State Guide to Women's Rights*. It also took up *Robinson v. Jacksonville Shipyards*, one of the first sexual harassment cases in federal court, which established the fact that "pornography in the workplace can create an unlawful hostile environment."[15]

But Roxanne needed more in her life. She needed a new career, one where she could make a difference. Hale Starr knew of Roxanne's search for fulfilling work, and she felt her friend was tailor-made to be a plaintiff trial lawyer. Starr mentioned this to Roxanne and told her about the Association of Trial Lawyers of America. An advocacy and lobbying group for plaintiff attorneys as well as one of "the Democratic Party's most influential political allies," ATLA in Starr's mind was perfect for Roxanne. Starr had planted the seed, and Roxanne considered these suggestions.[16]

Of course, attorneys across central Iowa were courting Roxanne, and she received several lucrative offers from some of Des Moines's most prominent law firms through mid-1983. None interested her. Then late that spring, attorney Dwight James invited her to lunch to discuss a job. He and Michael Galligan had been with the city's Dickinson Law Firm but left in 1980 to establish James and Galligan, a boutique practice specializing in plaintiff litigation. Both held Roxanne in high regard, and although she lacked civil law experience, James and Galligan agreed that she was an exceptional attorney whom they wanted to be part of their firm.[17]

Roxanne knew James through Democratic Party circles, and she was acquainted with Galligan because the two of them had opposed each other five years earlier when she as U.S. attorney had gone after Consolidated Packaging, which had retained Galligan, for polluting the

Mississippi River. Unlike her other job offers, this one intrigued her, and she met James and Galligan for lunch.[18]

James pitched joining the firm to Roxanne, telling her about the field of plaintiff law and the great satisfaction to be derived from standing up for clients who had been injured or wronged. The meeting went well, and as it turned out Roxanne did not require much persuasion. "It was as if a light bulb came on," she recalled, "and I realized doing this type of law was why I became an attorney. This was my path forward; this was what I was supposed to be doing." After Roxanne, James, and Galligan met several more times over the next few months to work out the details, she joined the firm in October on a part-time basis, agreeing to start full time whenever her work on John Glenn's campaign ended.[19]

Roxanne knew she had a lot to learn about plaintiff litigation and immediately dug into the field. James suggested she flip through the large number of ATLA journals, bound newsletters, and other publications in the firm's library. Besides being an important advocacy group, ATLA emphasized continuing education for its members. Its annual conventions always featured prominent trial attorneys offering seminars and workshops on various topics such as "trial tactics and techniques, psychology and persuasion in the courtroom, proof of damages, medical negligence, defending the criminal case, and professional liability." Many of these presentations were transcribed and included in the association's various publications, which Roxanne took home at night, digested, and repeated until she got through the entire collection. James marveled at her ability to absorb vast amounts of information rapidly: "Everyone said she was a genius, and she probably was. She was just like a sponge, soaking up and retaining everything she read."[20]

Roxanne had been thinking about ATLA since Starr described it. James was active in the group; he was a member of its board of governors and would head its Iowa state affiliate. Galligan was active in the state organization as well and would follow James as its president. Both understood the value of making contacts at ATLA, and James had had great success landing cases because of relationships he built in the organization. Both thought Roxanne would thrive in the group, and given her networking skills they believed the connections she would make could bring more business into the firm.[21]

James introduced Roxanne to ATLA, and she immediately made herself widely known as a passionate and hardworking member by volunteering for a number of committees. She moved up through the ranks quickly, soon chairing ATLA's consumer and victims' rights committee and its education department. This activity and her continuing networking paid off in the summer of 1988 when her ATLA peers elected her parliamentarian of their 60,000-strong organization, making her the first woman to hold an elective office in the association. This was a stepping-stone to the group's presidency. Robert Habush, a Milwaukee attorney, and Gene Pavalon of Chicago had both served as presidents of ATLA, and both agreed that Roxanne should be its first female president. They invited her to dinner and persuaded her to begin the process. Habush noted, "After you've been president and invested two years of your life, blood, and sweat, you get very fussy about who is going to be president in coming years. I have no qualms at all about Roxanne being president. She's a leader, which is not a characteristic many people have. She is politically astute, and she's an excellent lawyer."[22]

Back in Des Moines, Roxanne had been honing her skills in plaintiff law on several small cases when she got a big opportunity. Before she joined the firm, James and Galligan had taken a case referred to them by Oklahoma City attorney and ATLA member John Norman. It involved Ricky Gail, a young Cedar Rapids police officer who was badly injured in a car crash during a high-speed chase. Dwight James, Dennis Ogden, one of the firm's associates, and legal assistant Linda Hedlund had started working on the case before Roxanne came aboard. Once there, she became interested in the case, and because James was certain she could handle it, he handed it off to her.[23]

Early in the morning of September 13, 1981, police tried to pull over a suspect who had been drag racing another vehicle, but he eluded them and a chase ensued. Officer Ricky Gail was on duty, heard of the chase on his radio, and requested information on it. Unfortunately, the radio dispatcher provided him with incorrect details, and as Gail turned his squad car lights on and eased his vehicle into the intersection to intercept the fleeing suspect, he was looking the wrong way. The suspect's car—traveling 80 to 100 miles an hour without its headlights on—came from the other direction and broadsided Gail's car, totaling it. Gail was so badly injured that he was initially declared dead at the scene.[24]

Somehow, Gail survived and recovered. He spent five weeks in the hospital for a concussion and a number of broken ribs, which had punctured his lungs. He had also faced an infection and pulmonary emboli, which damaged his lungs. Nonetheless, nine months later, he was cleared to return to police work.

The driver of the vehicle that hit Gail, nineteen-year-old Ronald Clark, had been drinking all night and was clearly drunk at the time of the collision. Gail and his wife, Janet, ultimately turned to James and Galligan for legal counsel. Roxanne sued Clark, but she also sued 7-Eleven Food Stores and Western Convenience Stores, which had sold Clark beer that night. The case was long and complicated. First, Roxanne believed the actions of the two convenience stores fell under Iowa's dram shop law, which provided that those who sold alcohol to intoxicated people who went on to injure someone else were liable, but up to that point the law had been applied exclusively to bars. Roxanne argued, finally successfully, that convenience stores were liable for such actions as well.[25]

Second was the so-called fireman's rule—now referred to as the firefighter's rule—which held that public safety officials could not sue for injuries suffered in the line of duty. Roxanne would have to argue in a summary judgment motion and then in post-trial motions that the lawsuits were based on a violation of the dram shop law and not tied to the automobile chase.

Then there was the issue of Gail's medical condition. As Roxanne was interviewing fellow Cedar Rapids police officers about the case, she heard several say that they were concerned about Gail's health, which they believed had clearly deteriorated since he rejoined the force. He even passed out on occasion, and officers said "they feared for their own safety when working with him." In March 1985, Roxanne sent Gail back to Dr. James Boddicker, the pulmonary specialist who had cleared him for work in 1982. Boddicker ran new tests and concluded that Gail's lung capacity had declined more than 20 percent over the past two years. He now had difficulty breathing, could no longer lift more than ten pounds, and could only walk at a pace of 1.5 miles per hour—half a normal speed. Gail was judged to be permanently disabled because of his injuries, and he was forced to resign from the police force because he was not capable of doing the job.[26]

Meanwhile, two of the three defendants settled out of court prior to the trial. Clark's insurance company agreed to pay $60,000 (Clark's policy limit), while 7-Eleven Food Stores settled for $312,000. Western Convenience Stores offered only $25,000, and Roxanne's case against them proceeded to court. But she faced one more issue. A year before Gail was removed from the police force, he had been involved in a shooting where the suspect had been killed. Even though he was exonerated and found not liable in a civil trial, the judge in the case against Western Convenience Stores chose not to exclude this information from the jury, so Roxanne had to address the issue with all potential jurors during jury selection.[27]

After the jury was seated, the trial began in September 1985. A key element for Roxanne was establishing the fact that Clark was intoxicated at the time he bought beer from the Western Convenience store. Employees had denied selling alcohol to anyone who was intoxicated that night, and in his deposition Clark had testified that he was not drunk that night. There were no other credible witnesses, so prior to the trial Roxanne contacted Clark's attorney and asked to meet with his client. She told Clark, "You've done a great deal of damage. There isn't any way you can fix it. But you can tell the truth, and I don't think you've been doing that."[28]

Roxanne convinced Clark to take the stand, where he was her star witness. He admitted that he was drunk that night and that he had already consumed twelve beers when he stopped at the convenience store to buy a cold twelve-pack. He also explained that he had lied in his deposition because he was scared and was coming forward now to tell the truth, because "it's been four years, and I want to get this straight."[29]

If Clark's testimony was critical in establishing Western Convenience Stores' violation of the dram shop law, two others were important in explaining the lasting impact of Gail's injuries, which had forced him out of his chosen career. His psychiatrist described Gail's deep depression and listlessness after his mandatory removal from the police force. He testified that the intensely religious Gail believed he had done something to make God angry with him. Gail's father, a minister in the Open Bible Church, then testified that his son's new plan of following him into the ministry would require four years of study, and then he could expect to make only $10,000 to $15,000 per year, roughly one-half to three-quarters of his salary as a police officer.[30]

The ten-day trial ended with the Linn County District Court jury awarding Gail $1.16 million in damages. Roxanne was pleased. She observed that Gail had once been a robust 6-foot-5-inch police officer who loved his job and received awards and commendations for his work, but the crash had permanently transformed his life. "That was one of the reasons the award was so large," she said. "Here was a guy that was a great cop, and he can't be that anymore, not ever."[31]

Western Convenience Stores appealed, but in July 1987 the Iowa Supreme Court upheld the verdict. The big victory highlighted Roxanne's hard work, courtroom skills, compassion for her client, and understanding of plaintiff law. Just as James and Galligan had hoped, Roxanne began getting referrals and bringing in cases; she was named a partner in the firm in mid-1986. The following year, leaving their sixth-floor office in the Equitable Building at Sixth Avenue and Locust Street in downtown Des Moines, James, Galligan and Conlin moved into the first floor of the Plaza, a condominium and office tower several blocks east and south at Walnut and Third Streets. There Roxanne had custom glass shelves and grow lights installed in her office for a hundred or so of her prizewinning African violets.[32]

But even as she was engrossed in her work at the firm, Roxanne had not given up on the idea of public office. In June 1985, an Iowa Poll showed her with a large lead over other potential Democratic gubernatorial candidates: Attorney General Tom Miller, Lieutenant Governor Robert Anderson, Iowa Senate Majority Leader Lowell Junkins, and House Majority Leader Don Avenson. None of the five had announced his candidacy, but Roxanne believed Miller would run, and she had said she was leaning toward running for attorney general. She had not given up on being governor, but she thought that experience in a lesser office would help rehabilitate her image with Iowa voters.[33]

By October, Miller, Anderson, and Junkins were actively campaigning for the nomination, and Roxanne still planned to run for attorney general. Then Miller decided to seek reelection for his current job instead. Eyes again turned to Roxanne, who flirted with the idea of running for lieutenant governor rather than opposing Miller, but she eventually chose to stay on the sidelines in 1986. She noted that fall, "I have made my peace with the possibility that the time [for me to run] will not come again. I am now a partner in this law firm. I took that step with the recognition that this may be my home forever." Still, she closed no doors on elective office sometime in the future.[34]

Even as Roxanne was thinking about running for office, another case caught her attention. It involved Deborah Lynch, who had been inspired by trailblazer Phylliss Henry to become a Des Moines police officer, joining the force in 1981. Unfortunately, like Henry, Lynch was sexually harassed on the job. She routinely faced derogatory sexual comments about her body and requests to perform sex acts, and she frequently encountered pornographic images posted at police headquarters. Two particular officers in her squad, Timothy Lynch (unrelated to Deborah Lynch) and Merlin Nielsen, were especially flagrant in their sexual remarks to Lynch. Lynch reported these comments to her superior, Sergeant Dale Anderson, but nothing changed, and at one point Anderson flippantly suggested she talk to the wives of Lynch and Nielsen about their behavior.[35]

The comments and innuendos continued until one night when Lynch reached a breaking point. When Anderson and Timothy Lynch asked her why she had not been on duty the previous night, she said that her daughter had a sore throat, so she stayed home. Timothy Lynch responded by asking if she had been teaching her daughter how to perform oral sex. That was it: Lynch filed a formal sexual harassment complaint with the Police Department's internal affairs division in March 1985. In May William Moulder, chief of the Des Moines police force, found merit in her contentions that Timothy Lynch and Merlin Nielsen had violated the department's policy prohibiting sexual harassment. They were each suspended for thirty days and reassigned to a different squad. Sergeant Dale Anderson was suspended for fifteen days for his failure to provide adequate supervision.[36]

Still, problems persisted. After the officers were disciplined, Lieutenant Jack Rose told police officers at roll call that Lynch "had the department by the balls" and placed it in a difficult legal situation. He asked officers to look for any negative information on Lynch they could find. At the same time, he began singling Lynch out, ordering her to pick up human feces from a street "under the pretext of collecting evidence" and criticizing her hairstyle and fingernail length.[37]

Lynch had remembered how highly Phylliss Henry had spoken of Roxanne, and when things did not improve she made an appointment with the attorney. Roxanne initially thought a few phone calls to the city could rectify the situation, but when they did not she filed a complaint with the Iowa Civil Rights Commission in May, alleging that Lynch had faced sexual discrimination at the Police Department. The lewd remarks and retaliation against Lynch continued. In August, for example, when she requested backup on a call involving an armed suspect, coworkers delayed sending her assistance. The following month, Lynch sued the city and the three officers, Lynch, Nielsen, and Anderson, in Polk County District Court. She accused the officers of sexual harassment while charging the city with "failing to protect her right to work in an environment free of sexual harassment."[38]

After her preliminary investigation and with her fees at $1,500, Roxanne tried to get the city to settle the case, asking for only $10,000, but officials refused. She pushed repeatedly for an out-of-court settlement, but the city remained adamant and continued rejecting the idea, although Roxanne did negotiate an out-of-court settlement with the three officers involved. Meanwhile, the Iowa Civil Rights Commission "issued a right to sue letter" regarding her complaint, asserting that the city had sexually discriminated against Lynch in violation of the 1965 Iowa Civil Rights Act. Shortly thereafter, Roxanne filed the case, and all the judges in Polk

County District Court recused themselves because of the criminal cases they had to try with police officers as principal witnesses. Roxanne plunged ahead, deposing a large number of police officers and establishing the facts as she prepared to go to court. Because of the around-the-clock schedule of police officers, she took depositions whenever they were available, sometimes as early as 7:00 a.m. and sometimes as late as 11:00 p.m. Her extraordinary efforts amazed partner James, who noted, "I knew Roxanne was brighter than any other attorney, but she also outworked everyone."[39]

When the case finally went to trial in July 1988, it received front-page coverage in the *Des Moines Register*. Six months later, in December, District Judge Michael Streit ruled in Lynch's favor, finding that the city had both sexually discriminated against her and retaliated against her after she filed a complaint. "Lynch was required to work in an atmosphere pervaded by sexual harassment," he explained, which was "not only improper, but also intensely degrading." He then awarded Lynch $10,000 for her "mental anguish" and ordered the Police Department to put a department-wide training program in place to avoid sexual harassment in the future. He also ordered the city to pay Roxanne's legal fee.[40]

Roxanne was happy with the decision: "I'm hoping the city will accept the court's opinion and do what it should have done long ago. A massive educational effort is necessary to prevent this kind of conduct from reoccurring."[41]

A few months later, she submitted her bill to the city, noting that she and a colleague had worked more than eight hundred hours on the case and spent $23,000 of the firm's money on expenses. The total came to a whopping $158,000. Des Moines Mayor John "Pat" Dorrian said the taxpayers should not be expected to pay the outrageous fee, and the city council agreed, voting to appeal Streit's decision to the Iowa Supreme Court. But Roxanne defended her bill, telling the *Des Moines Register*, "I was appalled by the fees, too. But by God, I earned it." She also emphasized that the city had rebuffed her many efforts to settle the case early, which would have greatly reduced her fee.[42]

Streit would reduce Roxanne's bill to $90,139 (later increased by $5,000), putting the award in line with similar cases. However, he believed she was entitled to the still substantial fee because she had "ably and zealously represented her client . . . and expended substantial quantities of time in this representation." Not surprisingly, the city awaited the Iowa Supreme Court's decision before paying Roxanne.[43]

In 1990, the Iowa Supreme Court weighed in on Lynch's case. That April, a unanimous court upheld Streit's award to Lynch and his order that the Police Department institute a training program to eliminate sexual harassment. This marked the first time that the court saw a hostile work environment created through sexual harassment as sexual discrimination in violation of the Iowa Civil Rights Act. Then in December, the court approved Roxanne's $95,139 legal fee, observing that the city's "obstinate stance" had dragged the lawsuit out and resulted in the high fee. A *Register* editorial admonished the city "for ignoring numerous reasonable offers to settle [the Lynch case] out of court. . . . The city's handling of the suit was hard to figure out from the beginning. It seemed a clear case of sexual harassment, with ample evidence that male officers made Lynch's life miserable, and that her superiors ignored repeated pleas for help."[44]

Lynch cried when the Iowa Supreme Court upheld the lower court's decisions. "It wasn't about the money," she remembered, "it was about making things better for future female police officers." About Roxanne, Lynch said, "She was like a god. She took my case when few would have and gave a worker bee like me a voice. She didn't do it for the money or notoriety; she did it because it was the right thing to do."[45]

In April, before the Lynch case began in Polk County District Court, Roxanne faced sexual discrimination herself. Her good friend and attorney Jerry Crawford had invited her to a Monday dinner meeting at the Wakonda Club, a private country club on the south side of Des Moines. Unfortunately, he had forgotten that the main dining room was closed that night, and food was served only at the club's Men's Grill. When Roxanne arrived on the chilly spring evening, she was surprised to see Crawford and another guest waiting for her outside on the patio— Roxanne would not be allowed in the Men's Grill because of her sex. She asked the club staff for an inside table but was refused. Roxanne promised she would not make a scene and finally asked why she was being forced to sit outside. The bartender told her, "You can't come in because you are a woman."[46]

There were more important issues on the sexual discrimination front for Roxanne, but being barred from a portion of the club because of her sex annoyed her. She wrote a letter to the club president, Chester Woodburn, explaining that she had found her treatment insulting and telling him that she had talked to a number of club members who suggested they would resign if the policy continued. Then she jokingly told *Des Moines Register* columnist and friend Julie Gammack, "I might march on them."[47]

That autumn, the club bent its policy. In a club newsletter, Woodburn wrote that because "a small, but very vocal, coterie of women" had complained about being barred from the Men's Grill, it would now be open to them, although he noted that "ladies and their guests surely will feel more comfortable" in "the more cheerful ambiance" of other parts of the club.[48]

The following year, Roxanne landed a more pressing sexual discrimination case. Bonnie Campbell referred it to her in 1989 because Campbell was running for attorney general. It involved Linda Monohon, who began working as a secretary at George F. Rutledge and Company, a local reinsurance firm, in 1970 before rising to become one of the few female treaty brokers in the industry. When three of her associates—Roger Espe, John Burridge, and Frank Brunk—started a new company, Capitol Intermediaries, in 1979, they asked Monohon to join them. She did and became an assistant vice-president. She was shortly promoted to vice-president, even though she would later discover she was paid one-third to nearly three-quarters less than men in similar positions at the firm.[49]

Monohon had had a relationship with Burridge while both were at Rutledge and Company, but she ended it in the early 1980s. He did not handle the breakup well, sometimes completely ignoring her at work, sometimes leaving love letters on her desk. Meanwhile, Monohon wanted to be a single parent and have a child. When she became pregnant Burridge, who was not the father, proposed marriage, but she declined. When she returned to work from maternity leave in 1984, Monohon reported to Burridge, who began excluding her from meetings, meddled in her relationships with clients, and often talked about firing her.[50]

Such treatment left her feeling humiliated and ostracized. When her attempts to resolve the situation failed, she quit in 1985. Monohon was out of work for nearly two years and lost her home. She was eventually diagnosed with clinical depression and post-traumatic stress disorder and put on medication. She finally landed a position at Shelter Insurance, and it was at that point that she went to Campbell and decided to file a lawsuit. "There was no other recourse," Monohon believed, "I saw this was bigger than me. I felt I had to do it. It would have been, in some respects, far easier for me not to do it. But I don't know how I would have ever gotten out of that feeling of misery if I hadn't proceeded through the system."[51]

Roxanne claimed that her client had faced "outrageous conduct" while on the job. Specifically, she faced sexual discrimination and harassment at the hands of Roger Espe and John Burridge. Monohon sought $1.55 million in lost wages and medical expenses. She also sought $5 million in punitive damages for what Roxanne said was "reckless indifference to causing emotional distress."[52]

Because of Iowa law, a judge would decide on the issues of sexual harassment and discrimination, while a jury would decide on the matters of outrageous conduct and contractual issues. Roxanne believed it was one of the first times that a civil rights issue and a tort claim would be tried at the same time. In the spring of 1991, the jury found in favor of Monohon and ordered Espe and Burridge to pay her $1.3 million in lost wages and medical expenses. The jury also awarded her the entire $5 million that Roxanne had sought for damages. Of the jury's decision, Roxanne said, "This is every woman's story in one way or another. For the first time ever . . . a jury had the opportunity to say that sex discrimination is outrageous conduct and it better not happen anymore, not to our wives, not to our mothers, not to our daughters, not to my maybe soon-to-be-born granddaughter."[53]

Three months later, in September, Polk County District Judge Joel Novak rejected Monohon's claim that she had been sexually harassed. He acknowledged, however, that she had faced sexual discrimination by not being paid the same as her male counterparts and had been forced out of her job. Espe and Burridge appealed, and Roxanne ultimately agreed to a confidential out-of-court settlement. Yet with the Monohon and Lynch cases, Roxanne was putting Iowa businesses on notice: sexual harassment and sexual discrimination were unacceptable, and if she had anything to say about it, those who engaged in such behavior would face long and costly legal proceedings.[54]

As Roxanne was transitioning into plaintiff law, Jim and her children were experiencing changes as well. Jim's real estate business had been successful, but the recession that began in the late 1970s coupled with rising interest rates and unemployment made the market much more difficult. Some real estate firms closed, others downsized, and still others merged. In greater Des Moines, the number of real estate companies decreased by one-third from 1983 to 1985.[55]

This increased the competition between the state's leading real estate firm, Iowa Realty, and its major rival, Gene Stanbrough's First Realty. Stanbrough was a longtime figure in Des Moines's real estate business and had actually employed Jim early in his career. Stanbrough dealt with the changing market by expanding through acquisition, and in 1984 he approached Jim and made an offer for his three firms—Conlin Company Brokers, Mid-Iowa Management Company, and Conlin Securities Company. Late that year, Jim agreed to the deal, and his firms were added to Stanbrough's holding company, First Group.[56]

Jim became the head of Stanbrough's commercial real estate division as well as its property management firm and its real estate syndication business. Jim had a lot of autonomy in running these divisions, but he had gotten used to being his own boss, and a year and a half later he left Stanbrough and went back out on his own. In the spring of 1986, he established two companies, Equity Brokers Corporation, a real estate agency, and Regency Management and Investment, a property management company, to oversee those of his properties not included in the Stanbrough deal as well as those of others. The brokerage business struggled a bit, and Jim went back to Iowa Realty for a while in its commercial real estate division, but the property management business took off. It initially operated out of the breezeway in the Conlin home before relocating to an office complex. Jim hired his daughter Debbie, who had expressed an interest in the real estate business, to operate the property management company.[57]

After graduating from Drake in 1981, Debbie worked on Roxanne's campaign and then took a job at Polk County Social Services. She soon met Kerry Anderson through the First Church of the Open Bible in Beaverdale, a neighborhood northwest of Drake University. In June 1984, the two were married at the church in a large wedding officiated by Kerry's pastor father. A posh reception at the Hotel Savery in downtown Des Moines followed. The couple took up residence in northwest Des Moines near Anderson's All-Iowa Office Equipment store, which he owned and managed. Debbie continued with Polk County Social Services before joining her father's real estate business in 1986.[58]

Two years later, Debbie gave birth to a baby boy named Devin, Roxanne's first grandchild. Three years after that, in 1991, brother Colin was born, followed by sister Alexandria in 1993. The grandchildren changed Roxanne's life in many ways; perhaps most importantly, they provided the inducement she needed to quit her two-pack-a-day cigarette habit. Roxanne first tried to quit smoking in 1980, when she noticed how winded she was after dancing the jitterbug at a campaign fund-raiser. It was a false start, and she was soon back to smoking. She tried to quit repeatedly throughout the decade but always returned to smoking.[59]

In July 1991, Roxanne was taking care of Devin while Debbie was giving birth to Colin. She suddenly realized she "could not put that beautiful child's lungs in danger with secondhand smoke," and she quit that day. Roxanne chewed Nicorette gum and used Nicoderm patches to alleviate her craving for nicotine, but as legal assistant Linda Wickett remembered, "She often overdid it, using too many patches and gum at the same time; I was afraid she might have a stroke." Despite a long struggle, Roxanne kicked the habit, although she recalled that giving up cigarettes "was harder than anything else I ever did."[60]

The rest of the Conlin children were moving on and out as well. After a year at Drake University, Doug transferred to Iowa State University, where he majored in speech, focusing on film and video production. While in college, he had worked for Jim's Mid-Iowa Management Company mowing apartment complex lawns and acting as a leasing agent. Once he graduated, he held a wide variety of jobs—he waited tables, tended bar, sold stereo equipment, and worked for a filmmaking company called American Media in West Des Moines. In 1988, he headed to southern California for greater opportunities in the film and video business. There he worked for Propaganda Films, O Pictures, and Desert Music and did freelance work before starting Klein Films, which produced commercials and music videos.[61]

Daughter Jackie was soon out of the house as well, but she had a much bumpier ride. Jackie had always been rebellious, and as she described it, she "fell in with the wrong crowd in junior high." She began experimenting with alcohol when she was twelve and started taking amphetamines at Dowling Catholic High School. After graduating in 1984, she headed to the University of Iowa in Iowa City, 120 miles east of Des Moines, where her drinking and drug use only increased. By the fall of her sophomore year, she was also dealing with depression and an eating disorder and had stopped going to class. When she finally realized she needed help, she went to the registrar's office and dropped out. She then called her parents to pick her up and bring her home.[62]

Back in Des Moines, Jackie and her parents discussed treatment facilities. The counseling center at the University of Iowa had recommended a residential program at Timberlawn Psychiatric Hospital in Dallas. After doing more checking, all agreed the facility was the best option for Jackie. Once at the hospital, though, Roxanne had second thoughts about "leaving her vulnerable child with strangers," but she did it, believing it was for the best. Jackie spent a little over a year at the hospital, followed by another year at a halfway house across the street. By the time she was released, she had developed friendships in Dallas and decided to stay in the city. Unfortunately, she still had a drinking problem, although she was a functioning alcoholic, and she got a job in retail. Jackie stayed in the business until 1992 when, guided by her love of animals (clearly picked up from her mother), she established Park Cities Pet Sitter.[63]

J.B., meanwhile, struggled through school because of his learning disability but success in an economics course while at Dowling made him rethink his academic abilities. After graduating from Dowling in the spring of 1988, he began at the University of Iowa that fall. Here his academic success continued, and he majored in finance and marketing. However, J.B. often indulged in the school's active party scene until he was arrested in the spring of 1989 for drunk driving. Upset and embarrassed by the event, he pleaded guilty and received probation. The following semester, he decided to study abroad and went to the University of London. While there, he was able to do some sightseeing in Europe, which made him eager to see the world.[64]

Once back in Iowa, J.B. graduated in 1992 and then headed west. He initially stayed with Doug in Los Angeles before traveling east to Crested Butte, where he skied, removed snow from people's roofs, and worked in property management. He stayed through the winter. Then he headed to the Pacific, where he spent time in Hawaii, French Polynesia, New Zealand, and Australia before deciding to head home in the fall of 1993 and get into the real estate business. Jim got him a job at the Iowa Realty office at Sixty-Third Street and Grand Avenue in West Des Moines to learn the ropes, and J.B. soon obtained his real estate license.[65]

Although no children were at home now, Roxanne and Jim were not really empty nesters. By the end of the 1980s, four cats and another Great Pyrenees dog named Susan B. Anthony Conlin filled the home, where Roxanne often spent evenings—when she was not preparing for a case—knitting baby clothes for her first grandchild. She also enjoyed popular television shows of the time, including, not surprisingly, *L.A. Law* and *Designing Women*. When possible, Roxanne and Jim enjoyed Friday night dates, often taking in "mindless movies," Jim noted, "never one with a plot or one that requires any concentration." Sometimes the couple jetted off to New York City for long weekends.[66]

Big changes were about to take place at James, Galligan and Conlin as well. In July 1986, just after she became a partner, Roxanne went to the Association of Trial Lawyers of America annual convention in New York City. While there, she attended a presentation that soon changed the course of the firm. Dick Gerry, a prominent plaintiff attorney from San Diego, did a session on asbestos litigation, explaining that for decades asbestos firms knew of the potential dangers of asbestos exposure for workers handling it, but they hid the evidence. Specifically, he referred to a collection of documents known as the Sumner Simpson Papers, discovered during an asbestos-related lawsuit in the 1970s. The collection—made up of correspondence, internal memorandums, reports, and studies amassed by Sumner Simpson, the president of brake manufacturer Raybestos-Manhattan from 1929 to 1948—made it clear that the asbestos industry was aware of the health hazards of asbestos but had actively worked to cover up the evidence.[67]

The part of Gerry's presentation that really captured Roxanne's attention was a letter he displayed from one asbestos company manager to another, indicating that the industry knew of the dangers of asbestos but callously disregarded them. In September 1966, E. A. Martin of Bendix, a manufacturing firm that used asbestos in its products, such as automobile brakes, wrote to a manager at Johns Manville Canada, a supplier of asbestos. Martin was responding to a recent article in *Chemical Week* that listed automobile brake linings as a source of airborne asbestos. But he explained that another article from a different industry publication indicated that trees were also responsible for airborne contamination. The incongruity of the comparison struck a chord with many in the audience, Roxanne included.[68]

It got worse. Martin continued, showing a coldhearted indifference to those who worked with asbestos: "If you have enjoyed a good life while working with asbestos products, why not die from it. There's got to be some cause" of death. Roxanne recalled that the letter "made the hair on the back of my neck stand up." Taking on asbestos-related cases appealed to her longtime interest in providing justice for those who had been harmed, and once back in Des Moines she discussed the issue with her partners.[69]

Dwight James wondered about the potential financial risk of such lawsuits and gave the idea only lukewarm support. Michael Galligan, however, was fully supportive, and the firm began investigating taking on asbestos cases. Roxanne was soon in touch with South Carolina trial attorney Ron Motley, a friend she had met through ATLA and a leading figure in lawsuits against the asbestos industry, and he referred a number of cases to them, mostly concerning union workers.[70]

Ultimately, the cases involved 250 Iowa plumbers, pipe fitters, and sheet metal workers, making the undertaking massive and complicated. Preparation was lengthy and expensive. It required extensive investigation to identify which asbestos firms were responsible in each particular case, and the firm had to depose large numbers of plaintiffs and representatives from asbestos companies and hire expert witnesses.[71]

By 1988, work on the asbestos cases was in full swing, and they were consuming more and more of the firm's time. The costs of mounting such cases piled up, and the firm took on a growing debt to cover the expenses. This led to significant changes at the firm. Bill Wickett, who had been on a partner track, missed the variety of law the firm had been practicing before it became involved in asbestos work. Furthermore, Galligan told him, although they hoped to make Wickett a partner, they could not do so until the firm's high debt was brought down when some of the asbestos cases were settled. Wickett decided to leave in December 1988, initially joining Mark Goodrich in his practice before going to work for Patterson Law Firm. Dennis Ogden, the other associate attorney, left as well, deciding plaintiff law was not for him. He took a job at Belin Law Firm.[72]

Dwight James also left in 1988. He had not been completely sold on doing asbestos work, but more importantly he wanted to practice with his son, Fred James, who had finished law school the previous year and worked at the Polk County Attorney's Office. The two set up a practice together in the Equitable Building. Meanwhile, the firm had been adding other young attorneys to assist with the asbestos work, and by 1989 Galligan and Conlin included three associates, Michael Maxwell, Jay Irwin, and Carmen Eichmann.[73]

Roxanne had three big asbestos cases go to court the following year, but even after lengthy and costly preparation they did not all go her way. In February, she represented Thelma Knight, an East Moline, Illinois, woman whose husband had died of lung cancer in 1988 after working forty years as a pipe fitter. The lawsuit maintained that Barron Knight's years of working with products containing asbestos caused his cancer and death. His widow was seeking damages for "loss to his estate and loss of consortium for herself and her children." Thirty-three companies were originally named as defendants, but only four—Owens Corning, Celotex, Carey Canada, and Lincoln Electric—remained when the trial began. After four weeks of testimony, the Clinton County jury found that Knight was largely at fault because it believed his heavy smoking caused the cancer. While the jury did find that all the defendants except Lincoln Electric were at fault as well, it awarded Thelma Knight no damages.[74]

In July, it looked like Roxanne had a huge victory. A Des Moines jury awarded her clients, Joe and Beverly Beeman, $6.5 million in an asbestos injury case estimated by assistant court administrator Ron Branam to be one of the largest civil awards at that time in the Polk County Courthouse. Joe Beeman claimed that he had lung damage from using products containing asbestos manufactured by the Keene Corporation and Johns Manville while working as a pipe fitter and plumber. Roxanne saw the verdict as significant and said bluntly, "A jury . . . has told a corporation that you can't kill people without paying the piper."[75]

However, two months later, in September, Judge James Brown reduced the award by more than $5.6 million because, he said, the jury should not have assessed Keene $5 million in punitive damages since the corporation did not show intent or disregard for others. He further reduced the $600,000 that the jury had assessed Johns Manville for "loss of life expectancy" and cut the amount of future medical expenses by $70,000. Roxanne appealed, but in 1993 the Iowa Supreme Court upheld the judge's decision. Ultimately, the Beemans' $830,000 award was sizable—$1.62 million today—but it was nowhere near the original amount, which would be $11 million today.[76]

That same September, just a week before the judge reduced the Beemans' award, Roxanne lost a similar asbestos case. This client, Carl Christiansen, Jr., also a plumber and pipe fitter, claimed that his exposure to asbestos had left him with lung damage diagnosed as asbestosis. But like Barron Knight, he had been a longtime smoker, and the defense successfully argued that the asbestos companies should not be held responsible for his disease. The jury therefore ruled that Keene and the Manville Asbestos Disease Compensation Fund did not have to pay Christiansen anything for damages.[77]

The expense of taking these cases to court coupled with decisions that went against them or were appealed meant that Galligan and Conlin's significant debt kept growing. So much so, in fact, that in December 1990 the firm unsuccessfully tried to withdraw from nineteen asbestos cases to be heard in Black Hawk County District Court because its finances were stretched too thin. It was at that point, Roxanne believed, that the partnership was saved from bankruptcy by a court-sponsored statewide asbestos litigation settlement conference.[78]

The conference was the brainchild of John Nahra, a Scott County District Court judge. He came up with the idea when thirty-four asbestos cases were lined up to be heard in his court. After discussing the matter with colleagues, Nahra became convinced that such a conference might avoid "judicial gridlock" not only in his district but across the state as well.[79]

Nahra took his plan to Des Moines–based U.S. District Magistrate Judge Celeste Bremer, who liked the idea but suggested adding federal asbestos cases as well. Nahra agreed. He then convinced attorneys for the plaintiffs (Roxanne and Galligan were principal among them) and the defendants to sign on and persuaded a number of state and federal judges to participate. Bremer arranged for the conference to be held in February 1991 in downtown Des Moines at the Hotel Fort Des Moines. After details were worked out with fellow justices, the conference began on Thursday, February 7. It drew several thousand participants, including plaintiffs, representatives from all the asbestos firms being sued, and attorneys for both sides.[80]

By all accounts, the two-day conference was hugely successful. Nahra believed that roughly 90 percent of the cases brought to the Des Moines meeting were resolved, while Bremer recalled that it settled the claims of about nine hundred people. Roxanne and Galligan were thrilled; they disposed of most of their remaining asbestos cases, getting good settlements for their clients, and were able to pay down a sizable portion of the firm's mounting debt.[81]

But by that time another issue besides the debt was straining the relationship between Roxanne and Galligan. He worried that his partner's growing time commitment to the Association of Trial Lawyers of America would distract her from her casework. Ever since Roxanne had been elected parliamentarian in 1988, she had been on track to be the organization's president. She was elected vice-president in 1990 and ran unopposed for president-elect the following year. Galligan asked her to postpone seeking the office for a year, until they had dispatched their remaining asbestos cases, but Roxanne refused. She had great confidence in her ability to handle her work at the firm and her ATLA obligations. Further, she felt it was too late for her, as the first woman to make a bid for the office, to step away.[82]

Roxanne served as president-elect of ATLA in 1991 and would begin her presidency the following August. It was a huge honor—not only would she be the first woman to hold the office, she would be the first Iowan to do so as well. But Galligan saw it as detrimental to the firm, and the partnership broke up early in the summer of 1991. Roxanne Conlin and Associates was born, although Roxanne and Galligan remained good friends and continued to share the same office space at the Plaza.[83]

In the midst of her very public professional life, Roxanne had some personal and private struggles. In 1989, she was diagnosed with dysplasia, which predisposed her to cervical cancer. Her gynecologist, Dr. Norman Rinderknecht, tried several surgical procedures to remove the abnormal cells from her cervix, but when those failed he told Roxanne that she would need a hysterectomy. Before she could schedule it, however, Jim faced serious health problems.[84]

He developed a large gastrointestinal stromal tumor in his abdomen. As J.B. recalled, "Dad was putting weight on in his stomach, and we thought it looked like a beer belly, but he didn't drink. We teased him about it but then felt terrible when we discovered it was a tumor." When the tumor began bleeding in April 1990, Jim was rushed to Mercy Hospital in downtown Des Moines, where he underwent emergency surgery to stop the bleeding and remove the tumor. His heart stopped twice during the procedure, but he was successfully revived and made it through the surgery. He was in critical condition, so Roxanne arranged to have a room at the hospital and stayed there for the remainder of Jim's two months in the hospital. He required another major surgery to repair the damage to his intestines and spent most of this time in the intensive care unit.[85]

After Jim recovered, Roxanne had her hysterectomy, which led to menopause. The two experiences were physically and emotionally draining for Roxanne, but unfortunately they were followed the next year by the death of her close friend and longtime legal secretary, Phillis Porter. Roxanne grieved over the loss, which hit her both personally and professionally. Later she darkly joked that after Porter died, "For weeks, we didn't even know how to sue somebody."[86]

Friends surmised that these troubles might have led to the increase in Roxanne's drinking. Given her family history with an alcoholic father and having dealt with Jim's alcoholism, Roxanne was well aware of the problems associated with drinking, but she drank socially. However, after J.B.'s drunk driving arrest, he noticed that his mother was drinking more often and more heavily. J.B. eventually talked with Jackie about it, and when she was back in Des Moines, the two siblings confronted their mother, telling her she was drinking too much and needed to quit. Roxanne listened but did not hear them. She was not an alcoholic, she told herself; she did not drink every day, she only drank wine, she rarely had hangovers, and she never missed work because of drinking.[87]

Roxanne "drank blithely on." One of her favorite watering holes was the Kaplan Hat Company, a restaurant in the burgeoning Court Avenue entertainment district on the south side of downtown Des Moines. There on a Tuesday evening in June 1992, she joined two attorneys from her office and her law clerk after work to review cases and coordinate their calendars. After several hours and "a few glasses of wine," Roxanne left the restaurant about 9:00 p.m. and started driving home. Off-duty Johnston police officer Dale Waller was on his way home when he saw Roxanne's Lincoln Continental heading south from the I-235 freeway onto Sixty-

Third Street. He was behind her when he noticed her driving erratically, so he followed her and called the West Des Moines police for backup.[88]

When Roxanne realized she was being followed by an unidentified car, she initially thought to drive to the West Des Moines Police Department, but it had recently moved, and she was not sure of its new location. She decided to go home, pull into her garage, close the door, and call 911. However, when she arrived, Jim was watering flowers in the front yard, so she stopped in the driveway and confronted the driver, who had pulled in behind her. As she did so, a uniformed West Des Moines police officer, Jody Hayes, arrived.[89]

Hayes asked Roxanne if she had been drinking, and Roxanne said yes, but she refused to take the field sobriety test and called attorney Jerry Crawford. He soon arrived and talked with Roxanne and the police. She was then arrested, and the officer began putting handcuffs on her. Jim started toward the officer but Crawford quickly stopped him, and Roxanne was taken to the West Des Moines police station. She was charged with first offense drunk driving and processed, her mug shot was taken, and she was released a couple of hours later. The following day she, Crawford, and Maggi Moss, another Des Moines attorney and a good friend of Roxanne's, drafted a statement explaining that Roxanne was deeply embarrassed by her actions, accepted full responsibility, planned on pleading guilty, and was ready to accept the consequences.[90]

What Roxanne was not ready for was the *Des Moines Register*'s front-page coverage of her arrest the next morning. Worse, editor Geneva Overholser decided to include Roxanne's mug shot as the story continued inside the front section of the newspaper. The move angered Roxanne, but she was buoyed by the reaction of *Register* readers. Letters to the editor poured in, expressing outrage at the article's front-page placement and the decision to run Roxanne's mug shot. One wrote, "The *Register*'s story and picture of Roxanne Conlin set Iowa journalism back at least a century"; another called it "the worst of tabloid journalism"; and one sardonically said, "Thank you so much for the mugshot of Roxanne Conlin. I haven't seen one of those since the one of Charles Manson."[91]

Maggi Moss initially handled the case. Roxanne pleaded guilty to drunk driving and received a year of probation. The judge also ordered her to undergo a substance abuse evaluation and perform forty hours of community service. Roxanne fulfilled the latter by writing a pamphlet for people who had to represent themselves in domestic violence cases. She also underwent her evaluation, thus completing all the requirements to have her probation lifted. But more important for the long term, she admitted she was an alcoholic and promised her family she would quit drinking. She had her last drink the night of the arrest.[92]

But the case did not go away. The following September she was back in court, when the judge who had sentenced her, Patricia Houlihan, contended that Roxanne had not attended the driver's training program ordered as part of her probation. Roxanne and her lawyer, now prominent criminal attorney Al Parrish, argued that she had never been informed of this requirement and had never received such an order in writing. Judge Thomas Mott was brought in when Houlihan recused herself. Mott was known to be tough on drunk drivers, often sentencing these offenders to jail. Throughout the proceedings, two uniformed deputy sheriffs sat in the courtroom, apparently expecting, Roxanne thought, to take her into custody. But that did not happen. Mott extended Roxanne's probation another year and required her to take the driving course. By March 1994, she had completed the necessary training, and Mott discharged her from probation.[93]

By the early 1990s, Roxanne's rebound was complete. She had come a long way since her painful loss to Terry Branstad in 1982. Recovery from the defeat had taken nearly a year, but Roxanne ultimately came storming back, affecting the lives of others in new ways. She found her true vocation in plaintiff law, where she could speak for the voiceless and protect those who could not protect themselves. Here she continued her crusade for women, fighting against sexual harassment and discrimination, and here she took on companies, corporations, and government institutions that harmed individuals or treated them unjustly.

Peers took notice of Roxanne's fine work in the courtroom. The *National Law Journal* recognized her as one of the top ten trial lawyers in the nation in 1989, and two years later the same publication named her one of the hundred most influential attorneys in the country. Likewise, her election as the first female president of the Association of Trial Lawyers of America was a huge victory that represented the respect Roxanne had garnered from her colleagues in trial law. Although these accolades were certainly tempered by the embarrassment of her drunk driving arrest and all that it entailed, Roxanne handled that situation with grace, and she never drank again.[94]

Recognition went well beyond legal circles. The Iowa Women's Archives opened at the University of Iowa in the fall of 1992. Leading Iowa feminist Louise Noun explained its importance: "If we do not consciously collect these bits and pieces of Iowa history through women's eyes, a very valuable part of our state's heritage will be lost." Curator Kären Mason noted that this was a first: no other state at the time had archives devoted to women, and no one was surprised when it was announced that one of the significant collections at the new archives was the Roxanne Barton Conlin Papers.[95]

Roxanne was only forty-eight years old, and she was just hitting her stride. She had much to do and remained as committed as ever to "changing the world." Such a focus was reflected in her wry comment after she narrowly avoided a terrible car accident: "I'm too busy to die. I had so much to do that day that dying would really mess it up." Perhaps it was Paulee Lipsman, a close friend and onetime client, who best captured Roxanne's drive and motivation: "As long as there are people who need her help, as long as bigotry and discrimination exist, Roxanne will continue to fight."[96]

EIGHT

———

Hear Me Roar

One of Roxanne's greatest strengths was her passion for justice. "It was unmistakable; you can't buy that kind of zeal," noted former partner Dwight James. Good friend and lawyer Maggi Moss highlighted this characteristic as well: "Roxanne's passion for helping people and victims is clear. She believes in her clients 100 percent and tells their stories from her heart and soul. She wins trials by keeping juries riveted without spin or exaggeration." She only took cases in which she strongly believed, and then according to Paige Fiedler, one of Roxanne's former clerks and now a successful attorney, "she worked harder than anyone I know" on behalf of her clients.[1]

This passion was clear in one of Roxanne's essays as president of the Association of Trial Lawyers of America. Here she opened her playbook, advising her colleagues, "Do everything possible to win every single case. Hire the best experts. Take the best depositions. Spend every minute and every dollar needed to win. Don't skimp. Don't hesitate. Turn over every rock. Tie up every loose end. Do your utmost."[2]

Such fervor spilled over into other areas of Roxanne's life as well. She did nothing half-heartedly. Whether working with organizations in which she was involved, helping people or animals in need, marking special occasions, or building her dream house, Roxanne had, in the words of sister-in-law Judy Conlin, "the tendency to go big."[3]

This was certainly evident in her participation in ATLA. Regardless of the setting, Roxanne had always aggressively promoted the interests of women and minorities, and her activity in this prominent, largely white male organization was no different. As she rose through its ranks, she gradually changed the face of the association. She was initially successful in 1989, winning increased minority representation on ATLA's education advisory group as well as requiring that all the organization's education programs had to include female and minority speakers. But her first attempt to increase diversity at the association's top fell short. Roxanne had proposed that ATLA's Minority Caucus, which she had created, and its Women Trial Lawyers Caucus each be empowered to elect two representatives to the group's board of governors. She was upset when the measure failed: "The racial and sexual hostility I saw outraged me. I told everyone there I didn't want to be president of an organization that was governed by an all-white, almost all male board."[4]

Roxanne redoubled her efforts, working behind the scenes over the next couple of years to "get people on the same page" and garner support for her plan. Finally, as president-elect, she shepherded an amendment to the organization's bylaws increasing the representation of women and minorities on the board. It was adopted at the fall board meeting in 1991, nine months before Roxanne became ATLA's president at its Washington, D.C., convention the following July. Her family came to the event to see Roxanne make history when she was installed as the first female head of the association. Close friends such as Susan Terry, Hale Starr, and Joanne Fine also attended, and they joked about the august occasion, referring to it as "Roxanne's coronation."[5]

Like a coronation marking the crowning of a sovereign, Roxanne's installation was a formal affair. But rather than presiding in a monarchical, conservative manner, Roxanne continued to shake things up, to push the doors of access open. She immediately addressed the issue of inclusiveness in her first presidential column in ATLA's August 1992 newsletter: "The watchword of the '90s is diversity, and so it is for ATLA. We want not only justice for all but equality for all. . . . Our membership and leadership increasingly reflect the changing face of the nation and particularly, of the legal profession. Women, African Americans, Hispanic Americans, Asian Americans, Native Americans and others long excluded from power are joining those who have guided the profession for so long." Then, explaining its importance and value, she wrote, "Diversity strengthens us by increasing our numbers. Diversity strengthens us by broadening our ideas. Diversity strengthens us by opening our eyes and hearts to all that needs to be done."[6]

Roxanne poured herself into the job, frequently giving speeches, participating in forums, attending regional meetings, raising money, and lobbying on ATLA's behalf. In particular, she successfully fought against a federal product liability bill that would have limited liability for defective products that injured or killed their users. She recalled that her battle against the bill led conservative commentator Rush Limbaugh to attack her by name, and she still grins when she thinks of it. Roxanne traveled so often that flight attendants on two major airlines knew her by name, and she collected enough miniature hotel soaps, shampoos, and the like to supply all Iowa shelters for battered women and the homeless for a year.[7]

Her promotion of women in ATLA included developing a directory for female trial lawyers to encourage networking. According to attorney Howard Nations, then treasurer in charge of membership drives, her presidency led to a surge in women inquiring about joining the organization. He added that Roxanne won over a lot of male support because inclusion to her did not mean the exclusion of white males. Pam Liapakis, a prominent New York trial attorney and then secretary of ATLA, said of Roxanne, "She's really started a revolution in ATLA."[8]

Just as Roxanne had made noise when she entered ATLA, she left its presidency in the same manner. For her swan song at the organization's 1993 annual convention, which denoted the end of her term, she recruited major figures to speak. She envisioned a program with only women, scheduling a long list of headliners. This included Janet Reno, the recently appointed U.S. attorney general; Ann Richards, the colorful Democratic governor of Texas; and Anita Hill, a law professor at the University of

Oklahoma who became famous for testifying that she had been sexually harassed by Clarence Thomas, then being considered for the U.S. Supreme Court (he would go on to be confirmed). But she eventually decided to add her close friend and role model Morris Dees, cofounder of the Southern Poverty Law Center. When she introduced him, Roxanne joked that he was her token male speaker. To enjoy the festivities and help her celebrate, she flew her entire law firm staff out to San Francisco.[9]

In an even bigger and perhaps more fitting addition to the program, Roxanne hired pop singer Helen Reddy to perform at the convention. Reddy was famous for her 1972 hit "I Am Woman," widely viewed as the unofficial anthem of second wave feminism—essentially the women's movement from the 1960s up to the 1980s. Women in the audience went wild and Roxanne beamed when Reddy took the stage and belted out the iconic lyrics: "I am woman, hear me roar, in numbers too big to ignore . . ."[10]

During her ATLA presidency, Roxanne was away from her office often and relied heavily on her law clerks and her legal assistants to research and work up the firm's cases, readying them for trial or settlement. As her presidential term was winding down, she was preparing for the *Falczynski v. Amoco Oil Co.* trial—an employment discrimination and disability claim—scheduled for that July. However, the floods of 1993 brought Des Moines to a standstill for roughly two weeks in the middle of the month, when many areas of the city were cut off, the city's water works flooded, and Des Moines was without running water. With the Des Moines Courthouse unusable, Judge Larry Eisenhauer initially tried to postpone the trial. When Amoco's attorneys said that they could not reschedule the hearing for another two years, Eisenhauer searched for another courtroom in the district, but none was available.[11]

Then Roxanne came up with a novel idea. She suggested holding a bench trial at the Marriott Hotel in West Des Moines, where she had reserved one of the last available rooms. The judge did not want to delay the trial two years and thought this a good idea. The defense counsel, Condon McGlothlen and Michael Warner from the Chicago firm of Seyfarth, Shaw, Fairweather and Geraldson, agreed not only to the idea but to split the cost of the room as well. Hotel staff removed the beds and brought in additional tables and chairs, arranging the space to approximate a mini courtroom. Besides allowing the trial to proceed as scheduled, the location was important from a practical standpoint. Although West Des Moines was hard hit by the flooding, its own water works remained up and running. Hence each afternoon, after the judge called a recess for the day, all the trial participants who lived in Des Moines took turns showering in the hotel room before heading home for the evening. Dawn Stockton, Roxanne's clerk who participated in the trial, remembered that while she was grateful for access to a shower, she was always the last to do so, and there were never any towels left.[12]

Unfortunately, the trial did not go as Roxanne had hoped. An immigrant from Poland, Danuta Falczynski had taken a job in Amoco's accounting department in 1988. She received satisfactory evaluations, but her supervisors thought she was slow at her work and moved her to a data entry position. There Falczynski felt she faced different treatment than native-born employees, and she lodged a complaint with the firm's human resources department. Falczynski also started experiencing health problems. A doctor initially diagnosed her problem as bronchitis and allergies, but treatment did not alleviate the symptoms. Falczynski continued to miss work because of medical appointments or because she did not feel well. After missing more work than Amoco's policy allowed, she received a warning, but after more absences she was terminated in the fall of 1990. Shortly after being fired, Falczynski was diagnosed with a rare form of asthma.[13]

Falczynski hired Roxanne and sued Amoco, claiming that she had encountered discrimination and then was terminated because of her national origin and her disability. After several days in the motel room hearing, however, Judge Eisenhauer dismissed her claims, concluding that her termination was based on "excessive absenteeism in violation of [Amoco's] policy rather than because of her national origin or any disability."[14]

Roxanne appealed the ruling, contending that people could not be fired for things related to their disability and that, in Falczynski's case, her absences from work were largely medical appointments related to her health problems. The case went up to the Iowa Supreme Court, becoming the first disability discrimination claim it heard. In 1995, the court agreed that Falczynski's dismissal was based on company policy, not on discrimination due to national origin, and upheld that part of the decision. But once the lower court had decided that Falczynski's termination was proper, it did not address the disability claim. The Supreme Court therefore remanded that part of the decision back to a lower court. Two years later, the appeals court ruled that Falczynski's asthma did not affect her job performance and was not a disability under the Iowa Code.[15]

Roxanne suffered another loss in 1995 as well when an Iowa Supreme Court decision went against her in a medical malpractice case. Her competitive nature and belief in her clients made such defeats difficult. Roxanne once noted, "I can recite from memory every case I have lost and the date when it happened. . . . We try other cases. We win some, and we lose some. When we lose, we survive. But we never forget."[16]

These setbacks only made Roxanne work even harder on future cases. Beginning in 1995, she had a new tool to assist her: she bought a Toshiba laptop computer. It was a big step for Roxanne, particularly because it required her to type, something she had adamantly refused to learn years earlier because she feared the skill would doom her to a career as a legal secretary. She never became a good typist, however, and continued to rely largely on Peggy Dupre, the legal secretary who had replaced Phillis Porter and who would remain with Roxanne until 2008.[17]

Besides Dupre, Roxanne's support staff included legal assistants Pat Ewing, Donna Emmerson, and Shelley Johnson, who specialized in organizing documents in big cases. When Emmerson retired in 1997, she was replaced by Linda Wickett, who had previously worked for James, Galligan and Conlin and was happy to join Roxanne again. At the time there were four law clerks, largely from Drake University, because Roxanne hoped they could work over their summers. Roxanne depended on her clerks and delegated a great deal of work to them, including such important tasks as contacting clients, writing legal briefs, taking depositions, and assisting with trial preparation.[18]

Most were initially intimidated by her. Former clerk and then associate Melinda Ellwanger recalled, "I was completely in awe of her and terrified of her at the same time." Dawn Stockton agreed, remembering that Roxanne talked very fast and expected everything to be done perfectly. But when Stockton eventually became more comfortable in the office, she and the scores of clerks who followed saw Roxanne as a true mentor: "She built up our confidence and helped us make our own way. We had a lot of access to the real work of being a lawyer and a lot of opportunities to observe Roxanne." Former clerk and then associate Tom Duff added, "She not only trained and taught us to be good attorneys, she stressed the importance of caring for clients and making a difference."[19]

When Roxanne began adding associates, she looked to Tom Duff in 1993. He had clerked at James, Galligan and Conlin in the late 1980s and moved to Virginia before returning to Des Moines. Next was Melinda Ellwanger, who had clerked for Roxanne in the early 1990s and stayed on as a part-time associate. Finally, Roxanne hired Tiffany Klosener, an attorney from Kansas City who had followed her husband to Des Moines. With this team, Roxanne won a number of significant cases over the next few years, largely in the areas of employment discrimination and sexual harassment and discrimination.[20]

Work in these areas was briefly interrupted when Roxanne's love of animals and long association with the Animal Rescue League led her to join attorney Maggi Moss in a puppy mill case. In September 1995, eighty-one dogs were seized from Jean Davenport, a dog breeder from rural Union County, sixty-five miles southwest of Des Moines, because of the kennels' filthy conditions. Davenport's troubles had started that spring after a Des Moines television station aired an undercover video of her stitching up a screaming dog without anesthesia. Following the video, Davenport surrendered her license to sell dogs, but she maintained her kennels.[21]

After the Union County sheriff's department removed the dogs from the property, it turned them over to the Animal Rescue League of Iowa to care for them. Davenport was charged with selling dogs without a license and animal neglect. The seizure of the dogs, however, created another issue. The ARL, at the time headed by Roxanne's sister-in-law Judy Conlin, needed legal custody of the dogs before it could put them up for adoption. League attorney Maggi Moss therefore sued Davenport for custody of the dogs and the cost of their care and brought in Roxanne to assist. During the trial, Roxanne had to leave the courtroom every time the horrific video of the helpless animal was shown. Polk County District Judge Ray Fenton ultimately ordered Davenport to relinquish ownership of the dogs but then instructed the ARL to auction them off. Moss and Roxanne were thrilled that the dogs would be going to good homes, although the ARL would have preferred individual adoptions. Still, Judy Conlin noted, "If we can be sure these animals get good homes, then that makes me feel great."[22]

The puppy mill hearing received widespread local media attention, but the *Des Moines Register* questioned the extensive coverage, pointing out that a concurrent Polk County trial of a father accused of child endangerment—his daughter had died from shaken baby syndrome—received no coverage. The story frustrated Roxanne and Moss, who replied with a letter to the editor. They observed, "No one can or will equate child abuse or death with animal abuse and death. Human life will always have the highest priority." Nevertheless, they explained, "Iowa ranks high in the United States for 'puppy mills.' These facilities breed thousands of dogs, all living in disgusting, graphic, primitive, and deplorable conditions. They have no human interaction, and are caged in their own feces and often diseased. If they live, they face an existence of torture, pain, and suffering." Puppy mills, they concluded, "are inexcusable, sickening, and a major blemish in any civilized state. One of the ways to educate the public and to fight the mills is the media."[23]

The following year, Roxanne won two age discrimination suits. She had always been drawn to cases where she perceived an injustice, but now her own age—she had turned fifty in 1994—clearly gave her even greater empathy for those who unfairly lost their jobs because of their advancing age. That was what happened to Edward Bleimehl, who had worked for IBM for twenty-eight years as a sales representative, an account manager, and eventually a regional manager. After Eastman Kodak bought IBM's copier business in 1988, Bleimehl was asked to stay on as a senior marketing representative. But three years later, in 1991, younger managers fired the fifty-four-year-old, claiming that he did not meet sales goals. In court, Roxanne told a much different story. Bleimehl's supervisors worked to get rid of him by increasing his sales goals to unreachable heights—much higher than those of younger sales managers—taking away part of his territory and his best customers, and denying him the chance to operate in a newly opened sales territory adjacent to his. He was fired, and the only other sales manager over fifty years of age was forced into retirement. Bleimehl was replaced by a much younger manager, whose territory was expanded and sales targets reduced.[24]

Then in his mid-fifties, unable to find a steady job, Bleimehl retained Roxanne as his attorney. The three-week trial took place in the spring of 1996. After deliberating for two days, the jury found that Bleimehl had been wrongly fired and awarded him $1,029,000, one of the largest amounts in an age discrimination lawsuit in federal court from Iowa's Southern District. The following year, a judge set aside the jury's finding of willfulness, which allowed him to decrease the amount of damages, and reduced the award to $855,000, but he added 10 percent interest annually from 1993 and awarded Roxanne attorney fees of $329,000.[25]

Roxanne's other age discrimination case involved Arlene Gallion, a thirty-year employee of Cerro Gordo County, 120 miles north of Des Moines, who was fired in January 1992. Then the county's deputy auditor, Gallion was told that her termination was the result of needed budget cuts because the county had lost money in the Iowa Trust Fund scandal that had been uncovered a month earlier.[26]

The forty-nine-year-old Gallion retained Roxanne and initially sued the county for breach of contract. When the judge dismissed the case because he ruled no contract had existed, she filed an age discrimination suit with the Mason City Human Rights Commission. After reviewing the case, the commission turned the matter over to administrative law judge Kristin Johnson in the fall of 1996. While it was true that the county faced serious budget problems because of the trust scandal— although all of its $3 million investment was later recovered—Roxanne showed that the decision to fire Gallion was made before news of the scandal broke, and her client was terminated because of her "high age-related salary." The judge agreed that Gallion had been unjustly fired due to her age. Roxanne was happy with the decision, "not just because it compensates Arlene economically, but also because it vindicates her."[27]

Gallion was awarded $162,000 in back pay and future earnings as well as $15,000 for emotional distress. Attorney's fees and costs were to be determined in a separate proceeding, but before that took place the county settled with Gallion, paying her a total of $200,000, which included attorney's fees and costs. Roxanne had initially offered to settle the case for $10,000 but had been rebuffed.[28]

Meanwhile, the Iowa Civil Rights Commission saw the number of sexual harassment cases in the state more than double over the first half of the decade, rising from 97 in 1991 to 262 in 1997. A commission spokesperson believed the spike occurred for three reasons: the federal Civil Rights Act of 1991 allowed plaintiffs claiming sexual harassment or discrimination the right to have jury trials and to collect monetary damages; greater education made people aware they had legal recourse for such treatment; and large settlement cases attracted public attention. Roxanne had long crusaded for protecting women from sexual harassment and discrimination, and it surprised no one that two of her biggest cases of the decade involved these issues.[29]

The first case involved Linda Channon, who started at United Parcel Service right out of high school, moving up over twenty-two years from a part-time loader on the midnight shift to a center manager making $80,000 a year. Along the way, she endured and ignored inequities in pay and other forms of discrimination and harassment until an incident in fall 1993, when she broke up a shouting match between driver Richard Olson and one of her managers. The driver pushed Channon up against a large and dangerous piece of moving equipment while screaming at her and twice poking his finger into her breast.[30]

She immediately demanded that Olson be fired. He was, but he appealed his termination, and UPS management reinstated him. Olson then began stalking Channon. The attack had traumatized her. Channon suffered from anxiety after the incident, recalling, "I couldn't get myself back together after the attack." She sought counseling through a UPS employee assistance program, but the situation at work only got worse. Channon faced retaliation from male UPS managers; a promotion she was slated to get was taken away, and then she was transferred from job to job. As Roxanne put it, "The people above her refused to provide her any protection, then started being critical of her and her efforts in a way that was simply unfair." A doctor diagnosed Channon with post-traumatic stress disorder in 1996 and recommended she leave her job. She did and went on medical disability.[31]

Channon had been slow to take action against UPS. Following the attack, she held out hope that the company would protect her and improve her job situation. When it was clear that this was not going to happen, her therapist suggested she contact an attorney and recommended Roxanne. Channon called her office, talked to associate Tom Duff, then hand-delivered a written account of all incidents of sexual harassment she had endured at UPS. She feared Roxanne would not believe her and would not take the case. Two days later on a Sunday, however, Roxanne called her and explained the 180-day statute of limitations period for filing federal Equal Employment Opportunity Commission and Iowa Civil Rights Commission complaints. The time to sue was about to run out. When it did, Roxanne said, UPS would fire Channon, and she would have no recourse. Channon "reluctantly" agreed to have Roxanne draft a complaint and planned to decide whether to sign it the next day. At work on Monday, she discovered that Roxanne had been right: the company planned to terminate her. She signed the complaint, which they filed just one day under the wire.[32]

The sexual harassment and discrimination trial against UPS began in early January 1998 before Judge Arthur Gamble in Polk County District Court. In moving testimony, Channon described the long-standing discrimination she had endured at the company, and Roxanne presented evidence showing that her client was paid $4,000 less per year than her male counterparts. Channon also provided details of Olson's harassment. Backing up Channon's assertions, other female UPS managers and employees testified to confronting similar discrimination and unfair pay practices at the company. The UPS managers who testified for the defense claimed that Channon was moved from job to job because she was incompetent. Roxanne impeached them all, using Channon's superior job evaluations and the statistics UPS kept on all its functions. Included in these statistics was proof that Channon had outperformed male employees in similar positions. The jury deliberated for four days after the nearly five-week trial before returning a huge verdict for Channon, which became the lead story in next morning's *Des Moines Register*. The headline read, "Polk [County] Jury Socks UPS: $80 Million Awarded in Bias Case."[33]

The jury agreed with Roxanne that UPS had maintained a hostile work environment, disregarding Channon's charges of harassment and then punishing her for making them. It also found that her wages had been less than those of men in similar positions. It awarded Channon $528,000 in compensatory damages, which included past and future medical costs, back and future pay, and emotional distress, plus $14,600 in an equal pay claim. Then, as the *Register* reported, "in a stinging blow to UPS," the jury ordered the company to pay $80.2 million in punitive damages, an extraordinary amount.[34]

Channon was elated by the result: "It will heal a lot of old hurt from a lot of people. It gives me and the other women a sense of worth that we hadn't felt when we tried to resolve this through the company." Roxanne was happy as well but knew that the federal cap on punitive awards was $300,000. Although she would challenge it, the judgment would likely be drastically reduced. However, she saw the $80 million verdict as a strong message to corporations that they would be forced to pay for discrimination.[35]

That spring, as they expected, legal experts saw the award decreased: Judge Gamble cut the total judgment to $500,000. Roxanne and UPS both appealed the case, which was heard by the Iowa Supreme Court in 2001. It revised the district court's judgment, restoring the original $528,000 amount in compensatory damages and the $300,000 ceiling for punitive damages; with interest, the total amounted to nearly $1.2 million. The company was also ordered to pay Roxanne's fees for seven years of work, totaling $694,000.[36]

However, Roxanne did much more than win the case for Channon. As the two were preparing for trial, the attorney told Channon that she was smart and that she "needed to do more than move boxes for UPS." After planting the seed, Roxanne made Channon promise to go back to school and then consider law school. Channon had a few college credits but thought that at forty-six, she was too old to finish school. Roxanne said she had gone through college in three years and thought Channon could do it in two. She finally took the advice, and in the spring of 1998 she enrolled at Upper Iowa University while taking a full load of classes at Des Moines Area Community College as well. She was given some life experience course credit at Upper Iowa and earned additional college credit by taking a number of College-Level Examination Program standardized tests. With Roxanne's constant encouragement, Channon finished her undergraduate degree in public administration in one year.[37]

As Roxanne cheered her on, Channon completed law school at the University of Iowa in May 2002 and began practicing law in Des Moines. She was effusive about her attorney, friend, and mentor: "Roxanne had much more confidence in me than I had in myself. . . . She was the wind beneath my wings. I literally owe my life to Roxanne."[38]

The year after Channon's initial hearing, Roxanne won another big verdict in federal court in a sexual harassment and racial discrimination case against Iowa Beef Processors. Her client, Sheri Sawyer Madison, worked at an IBP plant in Perry, a small city forty miles northwest of Des Moines, for ten years. During that time, she had been passed over for more than twenty promotions, which all went to less qualified white men. Madison also encountered sexual harassment by her coworkers, who disapproved of her marriage to an African American man who also worked at the plant. They referred to her mixed-race children as monkeys and zebras, yelled obscenities and racial epithets at her, groped her breasts and buttocks, and rubbed up against her. Thomas Hanson, IBP's attorney, denied that Madison lost any promotions because she was a woman and claimed that she readily participated in what he termed horseplay at the facility by swearing and hitting coworkers in the groin.[39]

During the nearly four-week trial, Madison refused to consider the possibility of losing and rejected any efforts at settlement. The jury sided with Roxanne, awarding Madison $2.4 million, although this was soon reduced to roughly $1.64 million (plus attorneys' fees and costs) because of the $300,000 cap on sex discrimination damages. Iowa Beef Processors appealed all the way to the U.S. Supreme Court, which affirmed the decision in 2002. Roxanne then settled for a confidential amount. Through all the appeals, Madison insisted on continuing to work at IBP. Roxanne recalled worrying about her client's safety: "I felt a little nauseated every day at 2:30 p.m., which was when Sheri went to work, because I knew she would be with people who hated her, and they had ready access to knives."[40]

Meanwhile, in another lawsuit against UPS, Roxanne helped shape Iowa law by clarifying the issue of individuals' liability for their own discriminatory acts. The case involved Wendy Vivian, who had started working at UPS in 1994 as a part-time driver with the promise of soon moving to permanent full-time employment. But her supervisor refused to give the African American woman a route of her own, while white males hired after her were given full-time work. Vivian also contended with racist slurs on the job. Supervisor Gerry Madison fired her, but she appealed her termination. She was reinstated, only to be fired again a month later. Vivian contended she had faced discrimination at the company and was terminated because of her race and sex. She hired Roxanne, who saw yet another opportunity to take on not only UPS but also the company manager who had discriminated against Vivian.[41]

They filed suit in federal court against UPS and Gerry Madison, claiming that Vivian had faced "repeated acts of racial and sexual discrimination" in violation of Title VII of the federal Civil Rights Act of 1964 and the Iowa Civil Rights Act of 1965. Roxanne settled the case with UPS but continued with the suit against Madison. He filed a motion to dismiss the complaint against him, claiming that the Iowa Civil Rights Act did not hold supervisory employees liable. Because federal courts in Iowa had split on this issue and because there was no unqualified precedent on the subject from the Iowa Supreme Court, U.S. District Judge Ronald

Longstaff certified the question of whether a supervisory employee was "subject to individual liability for unfair employment practices . . . under the Iowa Civil Rights Act" to the Iowa Supreme Court.[42]

In the fall of 1999, the Iowa Supreme Court decided that yes, any person, not just an employer, who discriminated against another in a job setting was subject to discrimination claims under the Iowa Civil Rights Act. With that, all Iowa managers were put on notice that they could be held personally responsible for their actions in the workplace, and Roxanne had helped shape more progressive employment throughout the state. She then settled the case with Madison following the decision.[43]

Such effort garnered Roxanne more recognition, and in 1998 the *National Law Journal* named her one of the fifty most influential female lawyers in America, putting her alongside the likes of Gloria Allred, Janet Reno, and Elizabeth Warren. Indeed, Roxanne thrived on her work and the public spotlight it often attracted, but she found comfort and recharged in her private realm, which she saw as "an escape from my life and my job."[44]

At the center of this refuge was Jim, who was always there to support her although he did not share most of her passions, especially politics. This briefly changed in 1993, when Jim uncharacteristically dove into the Des Moines City Council race. Because his business interests—Regency Management and Investment Company, which owned and managed condominiums, apartments, and retail buildings, and his recently established construction firm, the Phoenix Group—focused on Des Moines, he closely followed the city council's actions and decisions. He had even considered running for a seat several years earlier but could not because he and Roxanne then lived outside the city limits.[45]

This changed in the early 1990s, when Des Moines annexed their neighborhood, and Jim again thought about running for city council. He was especially unimpressed with popular local politician George Flagg, who had been the at-large representative since 1980, and decided to run against him. Roxanne thought it was a terrible idea, explaining, "He was definitely not temperamentally suited to run for office." He too readily spoke his mind, and as son J.B. recalled, "He would say things in jest, with a straight face, that others did not find funny."[46]

On the plus side, Jim emphasized his business experience during the campaign, saying he knew how to balance budgets and bring efficiencies to organizations. He also offered some interesting proposals, including banning firearms in the city and merging government services with other municipalities to cut down on costs. He even outraised Flagg more than three to one, accumulating nearly $19,000 to finance his campaign compared to his opponent's $6,000.[47]

But much as Roxanne had feared, Jim became his own worst enemy, making headlines for the wrong reasons. Before a city council meeting that Jim planned to attend, for instance, he and Flagg engaged in a conversation that devolved into a loud argument. It ended with Jim yelling at his opponent, "You're out of your goddamn mind!" Then as Flagg, who was a large man, walked away, Jim said, "Go to Weight Watchers." In another exchange in a candidate forum, Flagg accused Jim of running a "phony poll," and Jim returned fire when introducing himself: "My name is Jim Conlin, and the previous speaker is a phony." The two then argued back and forth about who had been out of town during the city's historic floods the previous July.[48]

It was a rough-and-tumble, ugly race. Jim did not comport himself well or impress those who turned out at the polls, and Flagg easily defeated him, winning 62 percent of the vote. Although Jim felt he "had been enriched by the [campaign] process," he made it clear that he was finished with politics, and the bid for public office was his last. Roxanne was relieved and "said a silent prayer of thanks."[49]

If Jim's run was but an aberration, Roxanne's plans to celebrate a marriage milestone in a grandiose manner were not. Thirty years earlier, in 1964, she and Jim had rushed to the altar just two weeks after meeting. The wedding, officiated by a justice of the peace in a dingy room, was anything but romantic. "It was all we had time and money for," Roxanne remembered, but it was not what she had envisioned. "As a child of the fifties," she noted, "I was raised on the Cinderella myth . . . and expected and intended to have an enormous wedding wearing a white gown with a long train and attended by numerous bridesmaids."[50]

Now with the wherewithal to do so, Roxanne staged the extravagant wedding of her dreams, where she and Jim would renew their vows on their thirtieth wedding anniversary. She began thinking about the idea shortly after their twenty-fifth anniversary, initially hoping to have the service in the Catholic Church to please her mother. Since Jim had been married before, the church required him to get an annulment. Roxanne, Jim, and friend and attorney Jerry Crawford, therefore, went to see a Des Moines priest about the matter. The conversation did not go as planned. Jim could not remember where exactly his first marriage had taken place—such information was necessary for the annulment—and when the priest said he had additional questions, Roxanne said she had some questions for him. With that, she started peppering him with questions about the church's stand on women. The three left the meeting without any annulment in the works. Soon afterward, Roxanne discussed the "rewedding" with her mother, who told her she did not care about it being in the Catholic Church, and Roxanne began making other plans.[51]

The storybook ceremony took place in Des Moines's Plymouth Congregational Church on Saturday evening, March 19, two days shy of the couple's anniversary. With trumpets sounding, Roxanne walked herself down the aisle in an elegant, "one-of-a kind, European-designed wedding gown." At the front of the church, she joined Jim, who was in tails. Next to Roxanne were her bridesmaids: daughters Debbie and Jackie and Sara Quinn Ketcham, a friend from her teen years who had stood up for her at her original wedding. Jim was flanked by his groomsmen: sons Doug and J.B. and Tom Groff, his best man thirty years ago.[52]

The thousand guests included businesspeople, attorneys, politicians, women's rights activists, colleagues, former clients of Roxanne's, and family members. All of Roxanne's siblings and their families came as well as her parents, although her relationship with her father remained strained.[53]

A sumptuous reception, with large ice sculptures and a huge cake, followed in the downtown Hotel Savery ballroom. Roxanne topped off the fairy-tale occasion with a two-week honeymoon in Paris. She told Jim she had always wanted to go to Paris on her honeymoon and was going to do just that. She asked him if he wanted to come along. Jim went, even though he hated to fly, and joked that he would try to convince the pilot to taxi all the way to France. While some die-hard feminists might have looked askance at the big rewedding, Roxanne considered it completely within her feminist framework: "Equality means you get to do what you want. It never has meant that you don't like men in general or one in particular or that you don't adore children or that you don't want to wear a long white dress at your wedding. I have always rejected such doctrinaire feminism, which suggests you have to be a certain way. It's all about choosing. And I'm choosing to have a big wedding."[54]

The year after Roxanne and Jim celebrated their marriage, there were two significant changes in the Conlin family. First, son Doug got married. He had grown tired of Los Angeles and returned to Des Moines in 1993, where he began working in computer software for Century Systems. That year, he met Julie Harned, a receptionist at a local architectural firm, and the two started dating. The couple bought a house together on Terrace Drive in Des Moines in April 1995, and the following month they got married in the downtown Younkers Tea Room, where Julie wore Roxanne's wedding dress. Much to Roxanne's delight, they soon had two children: a son, Gavin, in 1996 and a daughter, Geneva, in 2000.[55]

The same month of Doug's wedding, his sister Debbie divorced after nearly eleven years of marriage. She and her husband, Kerry, had gradually grown apart, especially since she had begun to question their once-shared conservative religious views. Meanwhile, Debbie's knack for the real estate business and management had led her to enjoy success at her father's Regency Management, where she soon became its president. She had pushed the company's expansion and hired good people. However, after being largely uninvolved in the company since its inception, Jim stepped back into its operations in 1988, and he and his daughter began to butt heads. Disagreements over the direction of the real estate company as well as their struggling Grease Monkey franchises soured their relationship.[56]

Debbie soon left Regency and established Anderson Properties, and she and Kerry purchased homes, refurbished them, and then either rented or sold them. Debbie continued this after the divorce but tired of it by 1999, when she began looking for a new direction and a fresh start. That year, she packed up her three children and headed to Ithaca, New York, and Cornell University, where she enrolled in a real estate master's program.[57]

While Doug and Debbie were going through several transitions, J.B. and Jackie were largely experiencing more of the same. J.B. continued at Iowa Realty, learning various aspects of the business of selling real estate, but he also worked on projects under Jim's umbrella of companies. Jackie, meanwhile, remained in Dallas, where she had been building her pet-sitting business, but a phone call she made to her parents led to another big change for Roxanne and Jim.

Years earlier, when Jackie was beginning high school, she briefly dated eighteen-year-old Johnny Kime. The two remained good friends after they stopped dating, and they stayed in touch over the years. Johnny had had a difficult childhood. When Jackie met him, his notorious father, John "Jack" Kime, was serving time at the state prison in Fort Madison for a string of robberies. Kime would be released in 1982 but returned to prison in 1995 when U.S. District Judge Ronald Longstaff, who believed Kime was one of the most dangerous criminals he had ever known, sentenced him to seventy-five years in prison for drug trafficking and firearms charges. His mother, meanwhile, had been a nurse, but she was also a drug addict. At some point, Johnny Monroe Kime decided to dissociate from his father as much as possible, and he legally changed his name to Johnny Monroe.[58]

Jackie and Johnny had remained good friends and talked on the phone with some regularity, but one particular call in the mid-1990s worried her. Johnny was battling depression, she recalled, and he sounded desperate. He had no money and no food. Jackie immediately called her parents and asked them to check on Johnny, who happened to be living in one of Jim's apartment buildings. They did, and at Roxanne's insistence they brought Johnny home to live with them. He lived with the Conlins for a few years, doing odd jobs around the house and working for Roxanne as her driver. Johnny essentially became another member of the family, and Roxanne wanted to give him opportunities he had not had. She eventually convinced him to go to law school at the University of Iowa. She footed the bill and bought him a car.[59]

Sadly, Roxanne's efforts to help Johnny fell short. His depression deepened after he finished law school in 1998, and he sought help from a therapist in Des Moines. But he remained despondent and committed suicide the following spring. The tragedy hit Roxanne especially hard, and she still has trouble talking about Johnny Monroe today. Worse, she had to deal with the deaths of both her parents at roughly the same time.[60]

In December 1998, her father died of cancer in Phoenix, where he had been living for several years. Roxanne's youngest sister, Gina Finkelstein, was the only one of his six children with him when he died, and although Roxanne had booked a flight to Phoenix when she heard he was near death, she never made it. She had had a complicated relationship with her father. She had never forgiven him for the physical and verbal abuse he had perpetrated on the family. Likewise, he had never forgiven her for calling the police and having him arrested almost forty years earlier when he was in a rage. After she went to college, she did not see her father often, and in fact she remained afraid of him. Years later, however, when her father needed financial assistance, she and her brother Ray, who was then CEO of Great Clips, helped him with his living expenses and even bought him a house.[61]

Still, the pent-up anger toward her father gnawed at her, and the thought of seeing him again actually made her physically sick. With a fever of 102 degrees, Roxanne could not make the trip to see her dying father. However, she along with the rest of her siblings did attend his memorial service at Huber Funeral Home in Eden Prairie, Minnesota. Well-wishers packed the room, and a number of people spoke at the funeral, eulogizing Bill Barton as a brilliant man with a great sense of humor. Amid all the positive comments, Ray leaned over to Roxanne and whispered, "Gosh, I wish I'd known that guy!" "Me, too," was Roxanne's reply. Barton's body was cremated, and his ashes were interred in his hometown of Huron, South Dakota.[62]

Roxanne had mixed emotions about her father's death. Her sister Becky Hudlow may have expressed these difficult feelings best, saying, "I think all of us [children] were actually relieved when he died." But Roxanne and all her siblings deeply mourned the loss of their mother, who passed away the following December. Alice had been struggling with emphysema and generally poor health for a number of years, and by that

October her doctor wanted to send her to hospice. Yet Alice said she was not quite ready to die and remained in her home in Deephaven. Roxanne and Jim went up a couple of months later to enjoy Christmas with her.[63]

The next day, Alice called daughters Becky and Gina, saying she was especially short of breath and needed help. An experienced nurse, Becky had connections with hospice and was able to get stronger medication for her mother. Ray, who was in Colorado at the time, returned to Minnesota. Meanwhile, a hospice nurse visited Alice on December 27, and later that day Alice announced she was going into a coma and did so. Roxanne headed back to Minnesota as well. When she arrived, her mother came out of the coma and said, "Good. You are here. I love you." Then she slipped back into the coma. Roxanne and her five siblings sat around the kitchen table sharing stories about their mom as they laughed and cried. They were all with her when she passed away peacefully at home on December 29.[64]

The funeral took place two days later at St. Therese Catholic Church in Deephaven. In lieu of flowers, Alice had requested that people bring food for the poor to her funeral. She said she loved flowers, but she would be dead and the food would make a difference. Boxes and bags of groceries surrounded her casket: more than 1,500 pounds of food, which fed approximately 1,700 people. Following the service, Alice was cremated with one of her beloved dogs, which had recently died, and interred at Resurrection Cemetery in nearby Shorewood.[65]

Roxanne had been close to her mother and was not ready to let her go. To ease the pain of loss and hold on to her memory, she brought home a portion of her mother's ashes along with a small fiberboard chest that her mother had painted and repainted over the years. The ashes now sit atop the modest piece of furniture in a grand closet in Roxanne's bedroom, a daily comfort and a constant reminder of her mother.[66]

Shortly before her father died and before she faced the loss of Johnny Monroe and her mother, Roxanne took a step back into the political arena when Democratic governor-elect Tom Vilsack asked her to chair the state's Democratic Party. Although she had insisted that she had made peace with her career outside of politics, she still harbored a deep desire to lead and to effect change through politics. When she accepted Vilsack's offer, some wondered if this was Roxanne's first step toward another run.[67]

Then, just four short months later, in March, Roxanne abruptly resigned as chair. In announcing her departure, she said she simply did not have time to head the party, run her law practice, and spend time with her family. But there were murmurs about the real reason Roxanne had resigned: she was furious that two days earlier, the Iowa Finance Authority had turned down her husband's application for $500,000 in tax credits to build a ninety-two-unit, low-income apartment complex. Jim had applied with seventy-two other developers for $3.5 million in tax credits. According to Darlene Jeris, the Vilsack-appointed director of the IFA, the top twenty were funded, and Jim's proposal fell into the second tier. The *Waterloo Courier* immediately added another wrinkle to the story. It noted that the Conlins had donated $33,500 to the Vilsack campaign, 1.2 percent of the total he raised, and turning down Jim's housing proposal sent "a signal that the Vilsack administration will not mix business and politics."[68]

Roxanne was livid. When she resigned as chair of the party, she told the governor she was "completely flummoxed" by the IFA's rankings; Jim had always presented strong proposals and had received tax credits six times since 1991 under the Branstad administration. The event led to a break between Roxanne and the governor, and she did not speak to him again for several years. "I was mad as a hornet," she recalled. "James was treated unfairly, and you don't mess with my husband."[69]

She immediately began investigating the IFA's procedures for distributing tax credits and found problems with its rules for evaluating and ranking proposals. Specifically, she thought Jim's project had been unfairly graded. For example, she noted, the previous year under the Branstad administration an application from Jim was accepted. In a key section, it had received five points—the highest score for local support— with a letter of recommendation from Des Moines's mayor. This time, armed with the same letter of support from the mayor, Jim's project scored zero in this section, while a project on which Jeris had consulted received five points in the local support section with an identical letter of recommendation from the mayor. Five points were also available if the project had a local developer, but inexplicably Jim did not receive any points in this category either.[70]

Roxanne filed a formal complaint with the Iowa Finance Authority, arguing against its decision because it had never legally adopted rules to govern its selection process, and it had scored Jim's project unfairly. Two other developers denied tax credits followed suit. Mark McCormick, lawyer for Larry Tuel, former director of the IFA and then director of the Iowa Housing Corporation, filed a formal complaint along the same lines as Roxanne's about the IFA's denial of tax credits to four IHC projects. Developer Lew Weinburg filed a complaint because his plan to convert the historic Warrior Hotel in Sioux City into low-income housing failed to receive tax credits, even though the IFA ranked the application fourth out of seventy-three submissions.[71]

Faced with the three complaints, the IFA debated what to do. Finally in June, its board members agreed with Roxanne and McCormick that their rules were indeed flawed and that it was therefore not possible to review individual cases fairly. They decided to throw out their evaluation process, revoke all the tax credits issued in March, rewrite their rules, and rescore the original submissions.[72]

As discussions went forward within the IFA, a public feud broke out between Roxanne and Jeris when Roxanne that claimed the IFA director harbored hostility toward her and her husband. Besides the unfair handling of Jim's recent application, she noted that Jeris was then auditing three of Jim's last five tax credit projects, while only 20 percent of such projects were to be audited in any one year. Moreover, the IFA could not "replicate the scoring or explain it" for the funded projects. Finally, Roxanne had a sworn statement from local attorney Patricia Wengert saying that she had overheard Jeris at the Latin King, a popular restaurant on Des Moines's east side, brag about being the one "who took Roxanne Conlin out."[73]

Jeris strongly denied the charges. At a public meeting in late September, she eyed Roxanne and said, "I'd like to announce a cease-fire at this meeting. This [IFA issue] should not be reduced to a ridiculous personality conflict between you and me. Obviously you don't think I'm qualified, nor competent, nor fair enough to run this agency." Roxanne did not back down, replying only, "I did not declare this war. I say to you, put away your guns."[74]

The quarrel had calmed down and then faded away in November by the time the IFA had rewritten its rules and rescored its tax credit applications. Fourteen developers who had originally received tax credits had them reinstated, while five did not. The latter were replaced by five proposals initially turned down, including Jim's ninety-two-unit Deer Ridge development in Des Moines. Roxanne happily recalled, "When the projects were rescored, James's came out first." The following spring, Roxanne was happy to learn that after only fifteen months on the job, Jeris left the IFA and Iowa to move to New York with her husband.[75]

This was not the only building project that captured Roxanne's attention. There was another even closer to her heart, and as was her inclination, here she would go lavishly big. By the mid-1990s, Roxanne began searching for a grand home, symbolic of how far she had come in the world. The hunt was prompted in 1995, when the Iowa Department of Transportation relocated Sixty-Third Street between Grand Avenue and Army Post Road and then widened it to a four-lane highway. The repositioned highway required the removal of several homes to the west of the Conlins' property on what is now McKinley Avenue, east of the new Highway 28. Roxanne always liked the rural feel of the area, but when the highway construction changed this, she was ready to move.[76]

She looked at dozens of homes but soon zeroed in on the city's old money enclave south of Grand Avenue and just west of downtown. Here Des Moines's movers and shakers of the early twentieth century had congregated in opulent mansions, and here many of the city's elites remained. Roxanne found several homes that interested her, but Jim did not want to move and dragged his feet at every opportunity. That became especially difficult in 1997, when Roxanne came across a three-story redbrick, Georgian Colonial mansion. Situated on one and a half acres south of Grand Avenue on Thirty-Seventh Street, the home had been built in 1912 by Henry C. Wallace, the journalist and later U.S. secretary of agriculture under presidents Warren Harding and Calvin Coolidge. Curiously, two other U.S. secretaries of agriculture would live in the house: Henry C.'s son, Henry A. Wallace, who would serve as secretary of agriculture, vice-president, and U.S. secretary of commerce from 1933 to 1946, and then E. T. Meredith, founder of the Meredith publishing firm and briefly secretary of agriculture under President Woodrow Wilson in 1920 and 1921.[77]

Roxanne was especially attracted to the structure's timeless elegance. Jim viewed it in a different light. Although neither blanched at its price— over $500,000, a hefty amount at the time in the Des Moines housing market—Jim saw it as an old house, requiring several hundred thousand dollars of renovations followed by constant repairs and updates. He finally told Roxanne that if she passed on it, he would build her the home of her dreams. She agreed, and later that year they found and bought the perfect lot and a half on a new cul-de-sac in Southern Hills, an upscale subdivision on the city's southwest side just north of Park Avenue. The acre and a half's northern edge abutted Des Moines's Water Works Park, one of the largest urban parks in the nation, and offered a spectacular view of the expansive woodland.[78]

Here Roxanne's dream home would eventually go up, but the project took a number of years. Roxanne had a number of requirements for the structure. Because she planned to entertain on a lavish scale—something she had always desired but never had the space to do—she wanted a huge formal living room, a grand double staircase, and the ability to shut off a large portion of the home for pets, rescued animals, and foster cats. As for personal touches, Roxanne only wanted one bedroom in the home, a giant closet the size of three standard bedrooms, and a large round table in the dining room, "so no one sat at the head of the table." She, Jim, and J.B., who would act as the general contractor on the project, worked with several designers and architects before choosing Environmental Design Group and architect Dennis Hansen.[79]

Construction finally began in 2001 with Conlin Construction Services (originally called the Phoenix Group) building the luxurious $1.25 million brick home, which boasted more than 10,000 square feet of living space. Fortunately, from J.B.'s perspective, the two-story stone-trimmed residence included three bedrooms, two more than Roxanne felt necessary, because he had convinced her that having only one bedroom would make the eventual sale of the house extremely difficult. It was completed in 2004, and soon, as Roxanne had wanted, she began entertaining on a grand scale, often holding large charitable and political fund-raisers at her home.[80]

Roxanne had indeed roared through the 1990s. She was at the top of her game and she loved what she did. She was widely respected, very well compensated, and beginning to enjoy the hard-won fruits of her labors. Yet it was never about the dollar for Roxanne. As longtime associate Tom Duff recalled, she was driven "to right wrongs or correct bad things that happened to people, even if she did not make money."[81]

Over the decade, Roxanne marched forward. She pushed open the doors for other women to take up leadership roles in the Association of Trial Lawyers of America. She took on complicated employment and sexual discrimination and harassment cases, winning far more than she lost and expanding protections for workers. Likewise, she finally felt comfortable being excessive, enjoying over-the-top celebrations and building a splendid new home. At the same time, she faced losses in court and had to cope with the deaths of her parents and Johnny Monroe. She also abruptly stepped away from chairing the state's Democratic Party and possibly rehabilitating her political career to battle unfair treatment of her husband.

Roxanne seemed to be right where she wanted to be. However, she remained haunted by her failed gubernatorial bid of 1982, and the itch to win public office grew. These two threads—standing up for the underdog and fulfilling her unquenched political ambition—would dominate the next years of her life.

NINE

—

Taking on Icons

Like Don Quixote, Cervantes's seventeenth-century character who strove to fight injustice, Roxanne had long championed equal rights and fair treatment for all. But unlike the delusional Quixote, who imagined himself a knight and believed he was battling giants rather than the windmills he was actually attacking, Roxanne fought the real giants she saw running roughshod over everyday Iowans. In 2000, therefore, she went after Microsoft, the technology colossus, filing a class action lawsuit on behalf of thousands of Iowans. She thought the company abused its monopoly power by forcing customers to pay higher prices for their software than they would have in a competitive market. In the midst of this case, she assisted her friend, former law clerk, and fellow attorney Paige Fiedler who was battling her own giant, Iowa State University, in a sexual harassment lawsuit. Both these efforts paid off with Roxanne helping negotiate a large settlement with Iowa State and, after seven years of trial, arranging a huge settlement with Microsoft.

Shortly after this, Roxanne returned to the political stage, where unfinished business remained, and another giant loomed on the horizon. Iowa's senior U.S. senator, Republican Charles "Chuck" Grassley, was up for reelection in 2010. The popular politician had been in the Senate since 1981. Roxanne relished the idea of being the one to defeat him, and now in her mid-sixties, she believed this was her last opportunity to run.

Before Roxanne focused on either the tech company or the senator, she decided to relocate her office. Jim had been pushing her to move from the downtown office in the Plaza that she still shared with former law partner and close friend Michael Galligan to her own office in his six-story Griffin Building several blocks west at Seventh and Locust Streets. Roxanne did need more space, and the Plaza office was a bit awkward because it had not been reconfigured after Roxanne and Galligan split their practice into two separate firms. But Roxanne was not comfortable with change, Fiedler recalled. For instance, she had never learned to pump her own gasoline; as late as the 1990s, she always searched out stations that still had attendants to provide the service before Fiedler taught her boss the skill. Moving was another adjustment that seemed too big.[1]

Jim, however, continued to press the idea, explaining that the entire sixth floor was available. Here Roxanne could have an expansive office of 7,000 square feet, more than double the size of her office at the Plaza, and she could design it just as she wanted. She also understood Jim to say that it would be cheaper than her office at the Plaza, but he meant that her cost per square foot would decrease although the total cost would go up because the office was so much larger than the one she was leaving. Despite the misunderstanding and her sense of being overcharged, which stuck in her craw for months, Roxanne went ahead and signed the lease.[2]

To ease the transition and because she had always liked the feel of her office in the Plaza, Roxanne used many of the same design cues and color combinations, including similar dark blue carpet and the same wooden millwork and pillars, throughout her new sixth-floor office in the Griffin Building. She also hired a feng shui designer to ensure the creation of a harmonious environment. There were some key additions, most noticeably, the animals.[3]

First was the aviary. Roxanne had gotten the idea years earlier when she took a deposition at the hospital in Knoxville and fell in love with its aviary. She also noticed the calming effect the chirping birds had on patients and visitors and hoped to provide a similar atmosphere for clients in her office. Legal assistant Linda Wickett contacted Living Design, a South Dakota company responsible for the hospital's installation, and had the firm build a small aviary outside Roxanne's office. Roxanne enjoyed it so much that she soon had Living Design build a large aviary outside the conference room. Twenty exotic songbirds—all with individual names—filled the space, which over the years included diamond doves, canaries, blue capped waxbills, orange weavers, white-hooded nuns, and zebra and society finches. A 150-gallon saltwater aquarium with colorful tropical fish added to the office's peaceful ambience.[4]

Roxanne and her staff moved into their new space in June 2000. Cats soon resided at the office as well. Roxanne's long love of animals had resulted in her actively fostering kittens for the Animal Rescue League of Iowa. When they turned two months old, the kittens were returned to the league to be adopted. Roxanne kept most of the foster kittens at home, but when there were too many for the house, the overflow stayed at the office. Two cats became permanent residents: Emma Grace, who had cerebral palsy and whom Roxanne fostered and kept, and Ginger, an injured cat whom Peggy Dupre, Roxanne's legal secretary, had nursed back to health.[5]

There were other residents in the office as well. Ever since Roxanne started her own firm in 1991, she had welcomed staffers' children into the office. Most were babies, who usually went to day care by the time they were toddlers. Over the years, her office hosted more than fifteen babies. The move made Roxanne's firm one of the few law practices around the country to open its doors to children, and it was a small part of her effort to help young women in her office have it all.[6]

Because she now had plenty of space, Roxanne maintained two personal offices at the Griffin Building, a formal one for visiting with clients, which had "a gilded chair, a Louis XV desk, and a Victorian fainting couch, upholstered in silver-and-gold brocade," and a more practical work office, usually in some disarray with files all about and a cat scratching post. However, unless it was necessary for Roxanne to be in the downtown office, she often worked from home. To facilitate this, one of her clerks or associates delivered a brown cardboard banker box filled with the files and memos she needed to review to her home and left it on the front porch. Roxanne, who preferred to work late into the night, would go through the material, do what was required, and then repackage the box with files, notes, memos, and directives to staff. Jim would return the box to the downtown office the following morning, then go to his Conlin Properties office one floor below. The system would then repeat itself.[7]

Four months before moving into the new office space, Roxanne took a step down another new path when she filed a lawsuit against Microsoft. Although she did not realize it at the time, the case would end up dominating her life for years. The federal government's case against the technology behemoth that began in the late 1990s had motivated Roxanne to take action. The U.S. Department of Justice had argued that Microsoft had abused its market dominance in software operating systems for personal computers to hurt competitors and had therefore violated the Sherman Antitrust Act. In the fall of 1999, U.S. District Judge Thomas Penfield Jackson agreed, issuing a two hundred–page "findings of fact" that concluded: "Microsoft has demonstrated that it will use its prodigious market power and immense profits to harm any firm that insists on pursing initiatives that could intensify competition against one of Microsoft's core products."[8]

The case dragged on for another two years, but Judge Jackson's findings opened the door for plaintiff attorneys across the country to go after Microsoft. The following year, more than two hundred class action lawsuits were filed against the company, all essentially claiming that its anticompetitive practices hurt consumers. One was Roxanne's.

Although she was not an antitrust attorney, standing up to Microsoft, which she had come to believe had taken advantage of Iowans for years, appealed to her desire to use the justice system to protect people. As Roxanne was considering the situation with the software firm, Joe Comes, a good friend of J.B.'s, talked with her about some legal issues with his Des Moines–based vending machine company. By happenstance, the conversation turned to Microsoft. Roxanne told him of the antitrust cases against the business and the potential for one in Iowa. She explained her belief that Microsoft had restrained trade with its Windows 98 operating system. Without competition, it had overcharged Iowans for software. Comes said he used a computer running Windows 98, and if she wanted to pursue a class action case against the software giant, he was willing to be the named plaintiff.[9]

Thus, with Comes as the class representative in the case, Roxanne went forward. She filed a state class action lawsuit in February 2000 and asked that the case be tried in Polk County District Court.[10]

Not surprisingly, a Microsoft spokesperson responded by first saying that such lawsuits ultimately hurt consumers. The company, he said, "brought computers to the masses. When you attack, you are talking about raising prices." He added that the company would oppose trying the case in Iowa, preferring to group it together with the scores of other lawsuits into one case.[11]

In March, some Iowans made it clear that they opposed the lawsuit by writing letters to the editor of the *Des Moines Register*. John Metz from the western Des Moines suburb of Waukee, for example, called Roxanne's effort "high tech ambulance chasing," while Roger Underwood of Ames, forty miles north of Des Moines, said he thought Windows 98 "an excellent product" and did not feel that Microsoft "had swooped into the market and ravaged me as a consumer."[12]

Roxanne responded to the letters with one of her own, writing that a "well-regarded federal judge had determined that Microsoft had violated federal antitrust law" and had found that "everyone who had purchased Windows 98 . . . paid about $40 too much just because Microsoft restrained trade." After noting that successful capitalism required a level playing field, she concluded, "If a state judge agrees, Microsoft owes Iowans some money. The authors of the March 13 letters are certainly free to send their shares back to Bill Gates."[13]

Microsoft's initial move was to have the case dismissed because "indirect purchasers" of the software had filed it. In this case, indirect purchasers were those who bought Intel-based personal computers— produced by, for instance, hardware manufacturers like Hewlett-Packard or Dell—which came with Windows already installed. Under federal antitrust law, only direct purchasers, those who bought the product straight from the manufacturer—in this case, those who purchased the software from Microsoft and installed it on their computers—could sue in federal court or most state courts, including Iowa, which had followed federal law up to that point. Attorneys for Microsoft, therefore, filed a motion to dismiss the case.[14]

Roxanne knew the law, but she wanted to change it and see her case move ahead. She argued against the motion, explaining that anyone hurt by illegal monopolistic practices should be able to sue. The district court, however, sided with Microsoft, and that July it dismissed the case because indirect purchasers could not sue under Iowa law. Tenacious as ever, Roxanne appealed the decision despite long odds and Microsoft's tough team of experienced attorneys, including David Tulchin, Joseph Neuhaus, and Sharon Nelles, top commercial litigators from Sullivan and Cromwell, one of the nation's leading law firms.[15]

It was nearly two years before the Iowa Supreme Court weighed in, but for Roxanne the wait was worth it. In June 2002, in a 5–2 decision, the court reversed the lower court's ruling and reinstated the lawsuit, "making it," wrote the *Des Moines Register*, "the first antitrust ruling in any state favoring 'indirect purchasers.'" Microsoft was disappointed; a company spokesperson noted that the ruling broke with what had been taking place in other state courts, such as recent decisions in New Hampshire and Rhode Island, where lawsuits against Microsoft by indirect purchasers had been thrown out. Roxanne was "so surprised we won. It was just Joe [Comes] and me against Microsoft!" She could not have been happier, explaining, "What's most important here is that consumers have a direct remedy against violations of Iowa's antitrust laws, when in most states they do not."[16]

Bob Brammer of the Iowa attorney general's office called the ruling "a momentous decision," setting a precedent for future class action suits in Iowa. While Roxanne saw the ruling's significance for the future, she focused on the present and was pleased to have overcome a major hurdle in her fight against Microsoft. Others were interested as well. Attorneys from across the country started calling Roxanne, wanting to help her with the case. Most suggested they could assist her in concluding it with a quick settlement, but to Roxanne those offers did not seem to have her clients' best interests in mind. Then she got a call from Richard "Rick" Hagstrom, an attorney in Minneapolis who was pursuing a lawsuit against Microsoft in Minnesota. He took a different approach.[17]

An attorney with the firm of Zelle, Hofmann, Voelbel, Mason and Gette, Hagstrom specialized in antitrust litigation. He suggested that he and Roxanne visit in person to discuss their respective cases. She agreed, and in December 2002 the two met in Mason City, halfway between Des Moines and Minneapolis. They immediately liked each other and had a productive conversation.[18]

Hagstrom said that Microsoft had monopolies with several products besides Windows 98—past operating systems and application software such as Word and Excel—and should face liability in these areas as well. He then explained that while prosecuting a case for only Windows 98 might be more straightforward, Microsoft would fight all lawsuits aggressively. Therefore, to make her case worthwhile—a case Roxanne had naively estimated to be worth only $100,000—Hagstrom suggested that she bring additional Microsoft products into the lawsuit as well, which would push estimated damages into the range of several hundred million dollars. Finally, the antitrust attorney said that such a case would be much too big for a sole practitioner, and he proposed the two work together on the case—as he and his firm were already doing in the Minnesota Microsoft case and had done in a similar lawsuit in California.[19]

After several weeks and more discussion, Roxanne and Hagstrom agreed to partner as co–lead counsels on the Comes lawsuit. Then, as Hagstrom had proposed in their first conversation, Roxanne enlarged the case by amending her complaint to include two classes of plaintiffs: those who had purchased Microsoft operating systems and those who had purchased application software. The trial court certified the two classes, Microsoft objected and appealed again, but the Iowa Supreme Court upheld the decision in a May 2005 ruling.[20]

Even as the Microsoft litigation was picking up, Roxanne still made good on an earlier pledge to help Paige Fiedler, who was now a plaintiff attorney, with a sexual harassment case. It involved Julie McElroy, a graduate student at Iowa State University in the mid-1990s, who charged education professor Lynn Glass with sexual harassment. McElroy claimed that Glass, for whom she worked as a research assistant, made unwanted advances that included kissing her and placing his hands on her thighs. In the spring of 1995, the two traveled to Moscow with a group of ISU students. Once there, she discovered that Glass had booked a one-bedroom suite for the two of them. McElroy was unable to make other room arrangements, and against Glass' wishes she moved her bed into the suite's living room. During the month-long trip, Glass confiscated her passport and her money, insisted on discussing his sex life with her, and massaged her neck and feet without her consent.[21]

Anxious and depressed over the ordeal, McElroy filed a formal complaint with ISU's Affirmative Action Office when she returned. An investigation ensued, finding that Glass had "violated the university's policy against sexual harassment" as well as "created a hostile employment and academic environment, and interfered with McElroy's academic progress." It was recommended that he be suspended for six months without pay, take a course on sexual harassment, and have no contact with McElroy. The dean adopted the recommendations, although he increased the suspension to an entire year, and the president started the process to fire the tenured faculty member. At the same time, however, tests revealed that Glass had terminal colon cancer, and at his request the university dropped all actions against him.[22]

Initially, the university had ordered Glass to avoid contact with McElroy, but he ignored the directive and stalked her. He continued doing so after the penalties were lifted, and his department, which believed he had been falsely accused, retaliated against McElroy by cutting the number of classes she taught and demoting her from temporary instructor to graduate assistant, thus reducing her pay. McElroy became "absolutely petrified to go to work" and dropped out of the graduate program in 1997. Doctors diagnosed her with depression and post-traumatic stress disorder, and she never completed her doctorate.[23]

Dismayed at the state university's lack of action, McElroy sought legal counsel at Parrish Law Firm in Des Moines. There she met with

Fiedler, and in November 1997, six months after Glass died, she filed a lawsuit against the state and the university for sexual harassment in employment and education. "Instead of protecting her from Glass when she complained, McElroy alleged the defendants retaliated by changing the terms of her employment. McElroy claimed she suffered psychologically and physically as a result."[24]

The trial took place in June 1999. Fiedler sought $1 million in damages for McElroy and thought she had a strong case. Roxanne kept close track of the trial, and Fiedler called her regularly for advice, help, and moral support. Fiedler had been frustrated when the judge excluded a great deal of important evidence. She was even more upset when the judge gave incorrect instructions to the jury, requiring it be proved that sexual harassment had affected McElroy's employment. Much to Fiedler's dismay, the jury found that Iowa State University had acted properly and declined to award any damages.[25]

Fiedler was distraught, but Roxanne assured her that she had handled the case properly. She thought the judge's errors led to the outcome and agreed that if Fiedler won an appeal for another trial, Roxanne would serve as co-counsel. As Fiedler had hoped, the Iowa Supreme Court found in McElroy's favor in 2001 and sent the case back to the lower court. At that point, Fiedler sought a settlement, but Iowa State was not interested, and the second trial took place in June 2003. This time, Fiedler and Roxanne worked together and used Roxanne's office as their headquarters. During the three-week trial, Roxanne's great drive and stamina were on display. She and Fiedler worked late every night, but generally around 11:00 p.m. Fiedler would tell Roxanne she had to go home to get some sleep before being in court the next morning. Roxanne's retort was always the same, "What, you're leaving? It's not even midnight." "And she meant it," Fiedler noted, "she was horrified that I wasn't putting in the hours."[26]

This jury heard evidence not allowed in the first trial, including the testimony of numerous other women whom Glass had also sexually harassed. With Roxanne by her side, Fiedler was more confident in the courtroom, and because she was especially adept at addressing juries, Roxanne made the closing argument. A much different result ensued. The jury found for McElroy and awarded her more than $3 million in damages.[27]

It was the largest sexual harassment verdict against Iowa State to date. After the win, McElroy said, "I thought I'd have this huge sense of victory and relief, but I really haven't. Mostly, I feel sad that it takes a huge award like that to make change happen." But the case continued. The university appealed, and in June 2005 the Iowa Supreme Court overturned the verdict on a technicality. As the court explained, "McElroy failed to exhaust her administrative remedies with respect to her federal and state retaliation-in-employment claims. Therefore these claims were not properly before the district court. Because the jury returned a general verdict, a new trial is required on all surviving claims. On remand, the plaintiff shall have the right to have her entire case tried to a jury."[28]

There was the silver lining for Roxanne. She had cross-appealed, arguing that McElroy was entitled to a jury trial, which had not been allowed to that point, because of her claims under the Iowa Civil Rights Act. Here the court agreed with her, setting a new precedent, and once again Roxanne had helped shape Iowa law, giving plaintiffs options they had not previously enjoyed. The third McElroy trial, however, never took place. Fiedler and Roxanne settled the case in 2006 for $2 million plus attorneys' fees, and McElroy's long ordeal finally ended.[29]

Meanwhile, in 2004, Roxanne had the opportunity to assist in the Minnesota class action lawsuit against Microsoft. Early that year Rick Hagstrom, Roxanne's co–lead counsel in *Comes v. Microsoft*, called Roxanne and asked if she would be interested in helping try *Gordon v. Microsoft*, which Hagstrom had filed. It was the first consumer class action case against Microsoft to go to trial, and Roxanne readily agreed to help.[30]

Hagstrom and his co–lead counsel, Dan Hume of New York City–based Kirby, McInerney and Squire, sought $425 million in damages on behalf of Minnesota consumers, and the trial began in March 2004. However, since neither attorney had much trial experience, presenting the case in court fell largely to Roxanne, who had only a few weeks to prepare. Hagstrom and Hume had built a strong case, which included much more evidence and testimony than employed in the federal government's case against Microsoft in 2001. Key expert witnesses included Stanford University antitrust economist Roger Noll, who explained that Microsoft's illegal monopoly allowed it to overcharge Minnesota consumers for its products. Then a former manager from a small computer manufacturer told the jury that Microsoft billed his firm based on the number of computers it shipped, whether or not they included Microsoft software. Therefore, he explained, it did not make sense for the company to install any other software besides Microsoft products.[31]

Six weeks into the trial, Hagstrom's team and Microsoft's attorneys began settlement talks, which concluded with a preliminary agreement a week later on April 19. Hagstrom noted, "It has been a hard-fought battle, and both sides were putting forth their best efforts. We're very pleased with the resolution on behalf of Minnesota class members." Microsoft denied any wrongdoing but agreed to provide up to $174.5 million in vouchers for Minnesota consumers to purchase computer equipment or any software, including non-Microsoft products. Individuals could claim up to $100 in vouchers; those with receipts for their Microsoft products could claim more. The settlement also stipulated that half the funds not claimed—eventually amounting to more than $50 million— would go to Minnesota schools. In addition, Microsoft paid $2.5 million to the Minnesota Legal Aid Society and $5 million to the University of Minnesota's Institute of Technology, taking the total settlement up to $182 million. Finally, Microsoft was required to pay $48 million in plaintiff attorneys' fees and expenses.[32]

By that time, Microsoft had resolved a number of the legal problems that had dogged it since 1999. It had already settled antitrust cases with nine other states as well as the District of Columbia, costing the firm more than $1.5 billion. This figure included a $1.1 billion settlement in California, where Hagstrom had been involved. Moreover, Hagstrom remained a thorn in Microsoft's side as he still had two similar class action suits against the firm pending, one in Wisconsin and the one in Iowa. Ultimately, Hagstrom reached a favorable settlement in the Wisconsin case in September 2006 before it went to trial—with Microsoft paying out up to $224 million—but the Iowa case was moving toward trial.[33]

The Minnesota trial provided a wealth of information about Microsoft and laid a strong foundation for the Iowa case. It also served as somewhat of a dry run for Roxanne, giving her ideas of what did and did not work well against Microsoft's defense team. One of her key takeaways from the experience was that she needed hooks to help the jurors navigate through the highly technical testimony they would hear in the Iowa trial. These hooks ended up being stories Roxanne developed, designed to hold the jury's attention while describing complicated and esoteric matters about computer technologies and antitrust issues.[34]

Through hundreds of pretrial discovery requests and tens of motions, Roxanne and Hagstrom had compelled Microsoft to turn over a vast quantity of material related to its past antitrust cases. This resulted in the company sending more than 25 million pages of evidence to Roxanne's office. The documents came in several formats, including paper and electronic versions, but few had been converted into searchable electronic documents via optical character recognition, which was then in its infancy.[35]

Ironically, Roxanne, one of the least technologically adroit attorneys at the time, embraced technology to battle the software giant. Without a rapid and accurate way to search through the millions of Microsoft documents, the overwhelming mass of material would be of little use in the trial. This huge cache offered a great deal more information than had been available for the Minnesota case, and Roxanne wanted access to all the evidence possible. When outside vendors estimated it would cost roughly $2 million to convert the documents into a usable format, law clerk Andrew Smith told Roxanne he thought he could do it at a fraction of the cost. A self-described computer nerd, Smith had worked for a small internet provider in high school and college, where he learned the Linux operating system and eventually managed and administered the company's servers. This background proved to be a serendipitous bonus; no one at the law firm had been aware of it when Smith interviewed for a clerkship in 2004.[36]

Smith began by searching for a product he could run that used optical character recognition to scan all the material Microsoft had provided and convert it into searchable documents. Early on, he came across Vividata, a small Berkeley, California, company devoted to document imaging software. Smith called the firm, explained what he needed, and asked if it had software available to handle the large task. "Yes," responded the employee, who seemed puzzled by the question. He then explained that Vividata had only a few clients, even fewer that had done such big projects, but these included the Central Intelligence Agency, the National Security Agency, and Google. This convinced Smith that he had found the right vendor, and he easily persuaded Roxanne to buy Vividata's software and printer and scanner drivers as well as twenty computers, printers, scanners, and storage drives.[37]

Smith set up his operation four floors below Roxanne's office on the vacant second floor of the Griffin Building at the end of 2005. Here he wired the computers and other hardware into a cluster and wrote computer code to automate the scanning software. Smith's system grabbed an image, scanned it, and then ran it through the Vividata software, which created a searchable text alongside a copy of the original document. These were stored on large hard drives, and the process continued around the clock, seven days a week, making its way through the millions of Microsoft documents.[38]

Although automated, the system sometimes encountered difficulties or even crashed, so Smith had to keep close tabs on its operation. Once, for instance, the building's central air-conditioning stopped working. This was potentially a serious problem because the computers generated a great deal of heat, and they required cool temperatures to function properly. Smith ran out, bought two window air conditioners, and installed them on his second floor, maintaining the room's low temperatures and keeping the computers humming along. For Roxanne, Smith's computer efforts were "indispensable." "He built me a supercomputer like NASA had," she explained, "and babysat it around the clock for months. . . . Microsoft was floored when they realized what we had done. They had nothing like it."[39]

After putting together the computer cluster, Smith created a database for the mass of information. As always, Roxanne emphasized organization and insisted on having all the documents she might need for the trial readily retrievable. Thus, as the Microsoft pages were made searchable, they were reviewed for certain topics identified by Roxanne and Hagstrom and then filed in appropriate categories and cross-referenced in a variety of ways, including topic, date, authorship, and witness.[40]

Reviewing, tagging, and filing all these documents as well as preparing for the trial in general required Roxanne to beef up her staff. Starting in 2005, she increased the number of law clerks from four to six and added a number of part-timers solely responsible for data entry. She also hired local attorney Jean Mauss, who had clerked for her several years earlier. Meanwhile, current clerk Brad Beaman finished law school, passed the bar, and stayed on to see the Microsoft case through.[41]

In addition to Roxanne's team, there was co–lead counsel Rick Hagstrom plus his group of eight to ten Zelle attorneys. They began gearing up, initially working on the case from Minneapolis until October 2006, when they moved down to Des Moines and set up shop on the fourth floor of the Griffin Building. Roxanne was largely responsible for organizing the trial and presenting the case in court, while Hagstrom and the deep resources of the Zelle firm did much of the needed research, handled most of the motions, provided the expertise on antitrust issues, and recruited expert witnesses.[42]

In early November 2006, shortly before the trial began, Roxanne enjoyed two victories. Scott Rosenberg, the Polk County district judge who would hear the case, ruled in her favor on her motion to call Microsoft executives Bill Gates, the firm's founder and then chair of the board, and Steve Ballmer—who had succeeded Gates as the company's president in 1998 and as CEO in 2000—as witnesses in her case, even though they would also appear as Microsoft witnesses. Three weeks later, she had another motion granted: the judge would allow her to show Bill Gates's ten-hour videotaped deposition taken by attorney David Boies in 1998 for the *United States v. Microsoft* case.[43]

This videotape was important. Even though Microsoft had faced a number of antitrust lawsuits, as an individual Gates maintained a near-heroic status and a stellar reputation, especially after he and his wife founded the beneficent Bill and Melinda Gates Foundation in 2000. In December 2005, for instance, *Time* magazine named Bill and Melinda

Gates and rock musician Bono persons of the year for their global philanthropic efforts and activism. But the deposition depicted Gates as anything but heroic. "Here," wrote New York Times columnist Adam Liptak, "his demeanor . . . reflected, many thought, the callow, arrogant and recklessly aggressive corporate culture at Microsoft."[44]

Roxanne wanted the jury to see this Gates—an unlikable figure determined to crush the competition. Hagstrom recalled that showing the videotape was "a no-brainer." He had used parts of it in the Minnesota trial. Meanwhile Hale Starr, Roxanne's friend and her jury consultant on the case who had been showing parts of the deposition to focus groups, reported how effective it was in turning people's positive views of Gates into negative ones.[45]

However, there were two pretrial setbacks as well. First, Microsoft persuaded Judge Rosenberg to rule against Roxanne and Hagstrom's effort to increase the damage estimate from $329 million to $452 million. Second, the judge denied Roxanne's attempt to introduce a new type of damage claim—loss of innovation—in which she suggested that Microsoft's market dominance squelched others' ability to create superior software products.[46]

Jury selection began on Monday, November 13. Some 450 people were called as potential jurors. Ultimately, eighty were interviewed. Starr assisted Roxanne and Hagstrom in culling the group. But there was a surprising twist for Roxanne at the outset. Theresa Zagnoli—then a partner at the Chicago-based research firm of Zagnoli McEvoy Foley—who had been a good friend of Roxanne's and had learned the trial consulting business at Hale Starr's company, had joined the Microsoft team for the trial and was assisting with their jury picks. Roxanne was shocked and felt betrayed; she did not speak to Zagnoli again. Nevertheless, the jury selection process ground on for several days, and after a break for Thanksgiving, the jury of seven men and five women was seated late the following week.[47]

With thousands of exhibits prepared and a number of significant witnesses lined up—including Gates and Ballmer as well as Nobel Prize–winning economist Joseph Stiglitz, Stanford University antitrust expert Roger Noll, and John Constant, an English software engineer who had been part of the team that developed the Digital Research, Inc., operating system on which Windows was based—Roxanne was ready for what was expected to be a six-month trial. She had drafted a series of stories designed to explain to the jury in a straightforward and compelling manner Microsoft's predatory activity over the past twenty years, which by crushing the competition had allowed it to overcharge Iowa consumers. Each of the nine narratives focused on a particular software or hardware company, including well-known ones like IBM, Linux, and Netscape and lesser-known ones like GO Computers, Acer, and Digital Research, Inc./Novell.[48]

By the time the case went to trial, three additional named plaintiffs had been added to Comes: Pat Larsen, Riley Paint, Inc., and Skeffington's Formal Wear. Class members in the lawsuit included Iowans who had purchased Microsoft Windows, MS-DOS, Word, Excel, or Office software or a personal computer with any of this software preinstalled between May 18, 1994, and June 30, 2006.[49]

After Judge Rosenberg gave the jury a day and a half of detailed instructions, Roxanne and Hagstrom began their opening statement, estimated to take three to five days, on Friday, December 1. After Hagstrom's brief remarks, Roxanne told the jury, "Microsoft didn't come into Iowa and do things directly" to increase prices, "they acted to destroy competition" by using "illegal choke holds, one on input and one on output." With competition broken down, the company was free to charge higher prices for its products.[50]

Roxanne then explained that she would sum up Microsoft's illicit activities with nine stories that described how the tech giant weakened or destroyed its competitors through illegal techniques. She illustrated these activities with a "computer-generated" image of fifteen icons, each identifying an illegal strategy Microsoft had pursued, for example, "exclusionary contract," "technical sabotage," "buying out the competition," and "espionage."[51]

Key witnesses, Roxanne observed, would describe how these tactics resulted in such a loss of competition in the state that Iowans overpaid by as much as $330 million. She also promised to prove that Bill Gates was not the upstanding figure most of the jurors believed him to be. Roxanne closed her statement that day by beginning a detailed summary of her nine stories, starting with the tale of DRI/Novell.[52]

Judge Rosenberg stopped Roxanne after four hours and adjourned court for the weekend. She picked right up the following Monday, and she and Hagstrom—although Roxanne did most of it—completed laying out their case and closed their opening statement on Friday. It took roughly twenty hours and spanned six days; some wondered if it was the longest opening statement in Iowa's history. Trial consultant Hale Starr was "horrified at the idea" of the lengthy, detailed opening because "juries are generally not made up of people interested in details of antitrust issues and Microsoft," and she worried Roxanne would lose the jurors at the outset. "I had never seen an attorney attempt such a thing, but it was brilliant," and Roxanne pulled it off with aplomb.[53]

Attorney David Tulchin began his opening statement by explaining, "The real issues are not complicated. No one in Iowa has been harmed by anything the plaintiffs can show that Microsoft has done. It is the plaintiffs' burden to prove to you that they were overcharged. The evidence will show that the price is not too high. That there is no overcharge." Tulchin and the other Microsoft attorneys took three more days to complete their opening statement because, as he initially said, "there was a lot in [Roxanne and Hagstrom's] opening statement that was fictional or openly misleading," and they needed "a few days to set the facts straight."[54]

In the midst of these opening statements, Roxanne changed her trial strategy. She initially told the jury that she was putting Gates and Ballmer on the witness stand in early January. However, to avoid requiring the executives to make a second trip to Iowa as defense witnesses later in the trial, the judge agreed to let the Microsoft attorneys question them when Roxanne was finished. Roxanne did not like this idea; she felt it would interrupt the presentation of her case and allow Microsoft to begin its defense early. Rather, she decided, she would question the two when they came to Iowa later as defense witnesses. In Gates's place, she planned to show his 1998 videotaped deposition, which she felt offered a better portrait of his feelings about competition than she would get from questioning him in person.[55]

She elected to open her case by showing the entire ten-hour deposition. The strategy was "extremely important," thought Andrew Smith. It knocked Gates down a peg or two, "quickly dispelling the myth that he was a perfect person." The lingering effect was also critical, as Roxanne and her team thought the negative view of Gates would color the rest of the evidence and ultimately the trial. Actually, the timing could not have been better: two days after Roxanne finished with the videotape, the court recessed two weeks for the holidays. Thus, as jurors took a break from the trial and went about their holiday preparations, they could not help but ruminate over the unflattering self-portrait that Bill Gates had painted.[56]

The trial resumed on January 4, 2007, with Roxanne continuing the first story she had begun before the recess: one that focused on DRI/ Novell and Microsoft's effort to eliminate them as a competitive threat. A month later, she was still on this first of her nine planned narratives. Neither Roxanne and Hagstrom nor Microsoft—whose army of attorneys on the case included two in-house lawyers and twenty-six others from the white-shoe firms of Sullivan and Cromwell and Heller Ehrman—had shown any interest in settling. Trial watchers believed it would drag on into summer.[57]

But on February 11, a chilly, flurry-filled Sunday afternoon, Roxanne and Rich Wallis, Microsoft's associate general counsel, met covertly at Des Moines's south side Perkins Restaurant on Fleur Drive. Over omelets and chocolate malts, the two agreed to settle the case. They had met privately from time to time over the course of the trial, and according to Wallis they "had a good working relationship." The meetings had been kept secret from all but a very few—each side wished to avoid distracting its team if a settlement was not reached. They hammered it out on Tuesday, and the next day, February 14, the two presented the settlement as a Valentine's Day gift to Judge Scott Rosenberg.[58]

When the judge told the jury that a settlement had been reached and the trial was over, "they started to file out . . . and after about four of them were out of the courtroom," Wallis noted, "you could hear this 'Wooo!' But you could tell they were surprised. They expected this to go on for months. It's like they left in the middle of the movie." Attorney Jean Mauss, who was completely unaware of the settlement talks, had the same feeling: "We were geared up and did not see an end in sight. It was like being hit by a truck."[59]

Details of the agreement came out in April, and experts called it the largest legal settlement in Iowa to date. Microsoft agreed to pay up to $179.95 million to Iowans who had purchased its operating systems or software packages from May 1994 to June 2006, making it the largest Microsoft class action settlement on a per capita basis. Unlike all previous Microsoft settlements, individuals would be given cash, while volume purchasers would still receive vouchers good for any type of computer hardware or software. Then, much like the Minnesota settlement, half of the unclaimed proceeds—approximately $70 million—would go to Iowa public schools for technology upgrades. The Iowa Department of Education received $1 million to administer the technology program, and Microsoft paid $1 million in unclaimed proceeds to Iowa Legal Aid.[60]

The big win also meant large legal fees. Roxanne and Hagstrom calculated that they and their teams—lawyers, paralegals, and law clerks—had devoted more than 117,000 hours to the case over the past seven years. That plus their nearly $8 million in expenses came to over $75.5 million. In August, Judge Rosenberg approved their legal fees at an even $75 million, a record for a civil case in Iowa. That averaged out to approximately $575 per hour, compared to the $300 to $400 per hour that top attorneys at Des Moines's largest firms charged. As co–lead counsels, Roxanne and Hagstrom billed at $750 per hour plus a 43 percent risk premium—fairly standard fees for plaintiff attorneys working complicated cases, because if they lost the case they would not receive any compensation—taking their hourly rate to $1,072.50, while paralegal and law clerk rates ranged from $120 to $180 per hour.[61]

Some complained about the exorbitant amount, given that the average individual Iowa claimant received $90 from the settlement, but Des Moines attorneys largely defended the fees. Nick Critelli, a past president of the Iowa Bar Association, felt they were appropriate given the "extremely complex and extremely risky" case. Others explained that attorneys in larger cities such as New York were then billing over $1,000 per hour. In that context, Thomas Drew, a local lawyer and chair of the Iowa Bar Association's litigation section, felt Roxanne's hourly rate might even have been low. "Roxanne Conlin," he observed, "is not just one of the finest trial lawyers in Iowa, she's a world-class litigator."[62]

The Microsoft victory was a huge achievement among Roxanne's many and continuing accomplishments, but her lifelong goal of succeeding in the political arena still eluded her. Even though she had tamped down the urge to seek office, the compulsion remained, but she was approaching her mid-sixties and felt that the window of opportunity for such a run was almost closed. Then, a year and a half later, she was approached about running for the U.S. Senate.

In January 2009, Governor Chet Culver—son of John Culver, whose decision to run for the Senate in 1974 had caused Roxanne to change her mind about running—picked Michael Kiernan, longtime friend, adviser, and then a Des Moines city council member, to serve as the new chair of the Iowa Democratic Party. Three days later, shortly after the party's central committee made it official and elected Kiernan chair, the new Democratic leader was asked if the party would field a candidate who could offer a real challenge to entrenched Republican senator Chuck Grassley. His glib response was, "You know what, [I] just got on the job five minutes ago. Give me a day or two."[63]

Actually, it did not take Kiernan much longer than that. He already had Roxanne Conlin in mind. "She was the ideal candidate," he thought. "Roxanne was the smartest person I knew, she had the gravitas, she had the name recognition, she could raise money, and she had a genuineness and a compassion that would resonate with voters." He scheduled a meeting with her in early February, and there in her Griffin Building office he suggested she run for the U.S. Senate, even though she had recently told the *Des Moines Register* that "was not something I'm going to do." He recalled that the visit was brief, largely because he realized he had caught Roxanne off guard. Roxanne remembered thinking, "He had lost his mind." "You must be kidding me," she told him, "why would I do such a thing?" But the two continued meeting, talking, and e-mailing about it over the next few months, and as she gave the idea greater consideration, Roxanne recalled, "Grassley continued putting his foot in it."[64]

Meanwhile, two other Democrats had entered the race. Fifty-nine-year-old Bob Krause, a former state legislator and federal transportation official from Fairfield, a small city in southeastern Iowa, announced his candidacy in March. Five months later Tom Fiegen, a fifty-year-old attorney and former state senator from Clarence, a small town in Cedar County in eastern Iowa, entered the race as well. Neither one, however, had any chance of defeating the iconic Grassley.[65]

As journalist Michael Gartner explained, Grassley had been "in elective office continuously for 50 years—in the [state] legislature, the House of Representatives and since 1980 the United States Senate"— and he had always "been immensely popular, for reasons that confound Democratic pros who say he's far more conservative than Iowa voters realize." By the fall of 2009, Gartner and others noted, Grassley's approval rating had plunged rapidly—tumbling from 75 percent in January to 57 percent in November—largely because of his role in the debate over what became Obamacare. He was one of the so-called Gang of Six, a bipartisan group of the Senate Finance Committee working on a compromise health care bill. Here he angered constituents on the Tea Party right for working toward a bipartisan bill, and then when he voted against the Finance Committee's bill, he angered independents and Democrats.[66]

Grassley had also made a number of questionable remarks. One regarded a proposal in the health care bill that had Medicare paying for a doctor's visit for end-of-life planning, which would entail discussions about hospice care or living wills, for example. Here Grassley picked up on former Alaska governor Sarah Palin's line of thinking of "death panels" and said, "In the House bill there is counseling for the end of life. You have every right to fear. You shouldn't have counseling at the end of life, you should have done that 20 years before. [You] should not have a government run plan to decide when to pull the plug on grandma."[67]

With Grassley looking vulnerable for the first time in years, Roxanne was moving toward throwing her hat into the ring, but it was against the advice of her family, who unanimously opposed her running. "We reminded Mom of how painful her loss to Branstad was and the near impossibility of beating Grassley," remembered son J.B. Close friends like political confidant Jerry Crawford also disliked the idea.[68]

By late summer, rumors were swirling about big name Iowa Democrats getting into the race. These included U.S. Representative Bruce Braley; Barry Griswell, retired CEO of Principal Financial Group; and Fred Hubbell, former CEO of Equitable of Iowa and then an executive of the ING Group who was serving as the interim state economic development director. Christie Vilsack, Iowa's former first lady, and Roxanne were being discussed as possibilities as well. Kiernan added to the speculation. In September, he suggested there was a mystery candidate: "a first-round draft pick," as he put it, who would soon become a candidate for the Senate. "I'm going to tell you here today," Kiernan announced on Iowa Public Television's *Iowa Press* program, "Chuck Grassley will be in for the race of his life."[69]

Braley, Griswell, and Hubbell all soon said they were not running, while Roxanne and Vilsack both left the door open. By October 22, *Des Moines Register* political columnist Kathie Obradovich wrote that either woman "would be a strong competitor against Grassley." That same day, in an exclusive interview from her home, Roxanne told *Register* reporter Thomas Beaumont that she would most likely run for the Senate. She explained that she had never quite abandoned her political ambitions after her 1982 gubernatorial loss and felt that now was the right time to run again, especially because of Grassley's positions on health care. "I never thought I'd run again. But in my lifetime I don't ever want to say, 'If only I had followed my heart.' What has changed for me is Grassley."[70]

Four days later, Vilsack told reporters that she was not entering the race, and Kiernan explained that Roxanne had been the mystery candidate all along. She formally entered the race on November 9 when she filed the necessary paperwork with the Federal Election Commission. Roxanne did so with her eyes wide open. She knew she was taking on an Iowa icon and her chances of victory were slim.[71]

She announced her candidacy with an online video. The two-minute film began by depicting her humble beginnings and difficult childhood. Roxanne narrated the video, describing her long legal career battling "drug dealers, corrupt politicians, and corporations who violated the public trust" as a U.S. attorney and her work in private practice, where she had given a voice "to everyday people who had none." Such work, she noted, of "taking on the special interests has been the cause of my life. I'm running for U.S. Senate to take the fight to Washington." She concluded: "Join me in taking on this fight, because the special interests have had their turn, now it's our turn." Missing from the video was any mention of her 1982 gubernatorial run or her class action lawsuit against Microsoft, and there was no mention of Grassley, although Roxanne did suggest that "career politicians" in the nation's capital were a big part of the problem.[72]

There were two other Democrats vying for the party's nomination, but most considered Roxanne the de facto Democratic candidate. The day after she entered the race, for instance, the *Waterloo Courier*'s front-page story on her announcement ran under the headline "Conlin Takes on Grassley."[73]

Roxanne hit the ground running. Advisers suggested she look nationwide for experienced political strategists to run her campaign. She interviewed a number of people, but no one clicked with her until she talked to Mark Daley. By the time she announced her candidacy, she had selected Daley as her campaign manager. Then based in Iowa, Daley had most recently served as Hillary Clinton's communications director for much of her 2008 presidential run. He and Roxanne originally met several years earlier, becoming better acquainted when Daley founded One Iowa, the state's leading lesbian, gay, bisexual, and transgender organization, in 2005. After that, he had done some public relations work for Jim's real estate company and had helped Roxanne with the press after the Microsoft settlement.[74]

Paulee Lipsman was another key figure on Roxanne's team, serving as the full-time volunteer deputy campaign manager. Roxanne and Lipsman were close friends, first becoming acquainted years earlier when Roxanne was running for governor and Lipsman was head of the Scott County

Democrats. Lipsman had initially worked as a radio and television reporter in the Quad Cities before moving over to politics; she served as Tom Harkin's in-state finance director during his first bid for the U.S. Senate in 1984. Tragically, that summer Lipsman was raped in her Des Moines apartment by a man who came in through a sliding glass window that did not lock. Lipsman had contacted her landlord several times, including three times in writing, about her defective window. Repairs were never made, and the rapist was never caught. Roxanne soon filed a lawsuit against the landlord on Lipsman's behalf. The two held a news conference, and Lipsman called on landlords to take action to protect female tenants from rape. The case was ultimately settled out of court, and much as Roxanne had so often done before, it opened up a new branch of law: third party criminal negligence.[75]

From 1989 until 2010, Lipsman worked for the Democratic research staff of the Iowa House of Representatives. This work with the Democratic legislative caucus gave her a thorough understanding of Iowa politics. Lipsman proved to be an insightful adviser and strategist and a tireless campaign worker for Roxanne. "She provided a calming presence," Daley recalled. "During stressful moments, her peaceful nature would overpower the emotions in the [campaign headquarters] and keep us focused on the mission." Perhaps most important for Roxanne, "Lipsman was the only person who would tell me the truth, even when it was very hard to hear."[76]

Daley and Lipsman knew Grassley's approval ratings had plummeted, but they also knew he remained popular, and a Roxanne victory remained a long shot. A *Des Moines Register* Iowa Poll taken in November showed Grassley easily defeating her 57 percent to 30 percent, with 10 percent undecided. Roxanne confirmed this reality at a rally late that month: "I don't want you to be under any illusion of any kind. This is an uphill race. I am the underdog."[77]

Making matters worse, incumbent Grassley had a campaign war chest of $4.4 million from the outset. "We were running against money and tradition," Daley recalled, and Roxanne believed she needed to raise $10 million to be competitive. Nonetheless, she planned to refuse any money from political action committees. Often sponsored by corporations, trade associations, or labor unions, these organizations pool donations from individuals in the hope of influencing elections. Roxanne viewed these funds as tainted, and she did not want to appear beholden to such interests. Campaign manager Daley disagreed. He thought the campaign should take PAC money because "it was perfectly legal, Grassley would continue taking it, and we'd be leaving money on the table."[78]

But Roxanne stood firm and did not take any PAC money. Nevertheless, she and her campaign outraised Grassley in the first quarter of 2010. Roxanne spent a lot of time on the phone soliciting larger donations, many from plaintiff attorneys around the country. Volunteers were active on the phone bank, reaching out to everyday Iowans. Through March, the campaign raised $630,000 to Grassley's $614,000. Equally impressive, 78 percent of the donations were at the $100 or less level. In addition to the funds she raised, Roxanne contributed $250,000 of her own money to the campaign, which increased the amount amassed over this first quarter to $880,000 and the total raised since the campaign started to $1.48 million. Yet this amount paled in comparison to Grassley's then $5 million.[79]

Fortunately, Roxanne was largely able to keep at least one eye on Grassley from the start because her primary opponents were not expected to give her much of a race. There was little surprise in June, therefore, when she won the Democratic nomination by a wide margin, carrying 78 percent of the vote to Krause's 13 percent and Fiegen's 9 percent. In her victory speech, Roxanne promised to "fight for every single Iowan every single day" as opposed to Grassley, who she said had lost touch with Iowans. After five terms in the Senate, she continued, he "deserves a rest."[80]

Now focused on the general election, Roxanne called for cutting the $1.7 trillion deficit with a program that included ending tax breaks and subsidies to big businesses, which shipped jobs overseas, and going after companies that evaded federal taxes. She proposed creating jobs by enlarging groups like AmeriCorps, increasing middle-class purchasing power by allowing such families to defer $5,000 in taxes, and expanding Head Start, and of course she remained firmly pro-choice. At the same time, she opposed tax cuts to the wealthy and any plan to privatize Social Security.[81]

Just like her run against Branstad in 1982, Roxanne adored being out on the campaign trail shaking hands, kissing babies, and talking with Iowans. "That was my favorite thing to do," she recalled, "I drew such energy from the people." But in an era when, according to party chair Michael Kiernan, "money equaled message," Roxanne needed to spend an inordinate amount of time on the phone fund-raising, which she quickly grew to hate. This kept her from stumping and led her to quip, "I used to be a highly respected trial lawyer, now I'm a telemarketer."[82]

Too much time on the phone turned Roxanne morose, sometimes causing her to lash out. When that happened, Lipsman generally righted her. The close friend and confidant pulled Roxanne aside and told her, "Roxanne, you're being a bitch." She then gave her dear friend specific examples of her poor behavior. Roxanne listened and realized what Lipsman said was true, and she worked hard to get through her fund-raising calls on an even keel. She and her staff ultimately did enjoy success in raising money, but the total of $3.1 million—which included another $750,000 from Roxanne, taking her contribution to the effort to $1 million—fell well short of the $10 million she said she needed to keep the race competitive. Grassley, meanwhile, raised $7.7 million on top of the $4.4 he initially had in the bank.[83]

Money raised by Roxanne and her campaign funded some television advertising. One of Roxanne's favorite commercials featured two of her grandchildren, Gavin and Geneva Klein, telling viewers that Roxanne "was a fighter . . . who took on corporations . . . dishonest politicians . . . big oil and big business." They promised viewers she would "hold Washington accountable . . . and tell it to you straight" because "she's one tough grandma!" Unfortunately, this ad and Roxanne's others were drowned out by the deluge of Grassley's advertising, which inundated the airwaves.[84]

Grassley remained well ahead in the polls, although his 20-point February lead had dipped to 9 points in May, according to a poll by KCCI, Des Moines's CBS-affiliated television station. Then the Rasmussen Reports poll suggested it rebounded to 17 points by mid-June. From

July until the election, Grassley never made an appearance that was open to the public. In September, the Iowa Poll showed him ahead by a wide margin, 61 percent to Roxanne's 30 percent. With this overwhelming lead, Grassley had no reason to accept Roxanne's invitations for head-to-head televised debates, despite the *Des Moines Register*'s editorial encouragement and a full-page ad in the paper demanding one as well.[85]

Nevertheless, Grassley did agree to a joint one-hour forum on Des Moines radio station WHO in late October, which was rebroadcast statewide by Iowa Public Television on a delayed basis. Roxanne performed well, but Grassley did not make any serious mistakes, and as the *Register* wrote five days later, Roxanne had "not moved the needle at all since September."[86]

Sadly for Roxanne, the polls proved accurate. She and her campaign team had seen the tide turn away from them late that spring, and they were unable to slow it down. Grassley won big in November, taking 65 percent of the vote to Roxanne's 33 percent. She was obviously disappointed by the loss, but she was not devastated as she had been after her defeat in 1982. "I do not want to be sad about the outcome tonight," she told her supporters at the downtown Hotel Fort Des Moines, but "I must admit that being the first runner up again is not very satisfying." Roxanne blamed her loss on the "anti-Obama, anti-Democrat" attitude that had swept the nation. That mood certainly played a role, but taking on Chuck Grassley, a giant among Iowa politicians, might have been an insurmountable task. As Jerry Crawford remembered, Roxanne and her staff "made no fundamental mistakes in the campaign." However, like Crawford and Roxanne's family, some believed it had been a mistake to have entered the race in the first place.[87]

Yet this was something Roxanne had needed to do. She had never completely given up on elective office after her loss to Branstad—she had considered running for office several times since, but the timing was never right. As she explained on the eve of entering the race against Grassley: "I expected to be in public office. I expected to run the state of Iowa. That is always what I thought would happen." The defeat to Grassley hurt. It cost Roxanne the $1 million she contributed to her campaign and at least $500,000 in lost law firm income, but it did finally provide closure. Roxanne had sought public office to lead and to contribute, but it was now clear that was not in her future. She put the idea to bed and returned to her law practice. From here, she knew, she would continue to contribute, she would continue to take on giants, and she would continue working to better society one case at a time.[88]

Left to right: Hale Starr, Roxanne, Susan Terry, and Joanne Fine at the 1992 Association of Trial Lawyers of America convention, where Roxanne was inducted as the organization's first female president. Courtesy of Susan Terry Knapp.

Roxanne speaking at National Bar Association meeting, ca. 1993. Courtesy of Roxanne Conlin.

204

Roxanne, Helen Reddy, and Jim Conlin at the 1993 ATLA convention.
Courtesy of Roxanne Conlin.

Roxanne with one of her favorite cats, 1996. Courtesy of Roxanne Conlin.

Left to right: Maggi Moss, Paige Fiedler, and Roxanne after the puppy mill case, 1997.
Courtesy of Roxanne Conlin.

The funeral of Roxanne's mother, Alice Barton, 1999. She had requested food donations rather than flowers at her memorial, and bags and boxes of groceries surrounded her coffin at the service.
Courtesy of Roxanne Conlin.

Left to right: Trudy Hurd, Sara Quinn Ketcham, and Roxanne, ca. 2000. The three met in high school and remained good friends. Courtesy of Roxanne Conlin.

Left to right: Attorneys Bud Hockenberg, Michael Galligan,
David Brown, and Roxanne, 2000.
Courtesy of Roxanne Conlin.

Songbirds in Roxanne's office aviary, ca. 2005. Courtesy of Roxanne Conlin.

Roxanne and former Iowa governor Robert Ray, 2008. Courtesy of Roxanne Conlin.

208

Roxanne and all her sisters on a cruise, 2009. Left to right: Rhoda Olsen, Rhonda Richmond, Roxanne, Becky Hudlow, and Gina Finkelstein. Courtesy of Roxanne Conlin.

The Conlin family, 2009. Standing, left to right: Connie Newlin, Debbie Conlin (now Newlin), Doug Klein, Julie Klein, Judy Conlin, J.B. Conlin, Courtney Conlin, and Jackie Conlin. Seated, left to right: Debbie's daughter Alexandria Anderson, Roxanne, Gavin Klein, Geneva Klein, and Jim. Courtesy of Roxanne Conlin.

Roxanne and grandsons Colin (left) and Devin Anderson, 2009. Courtesy of Roxanne Conlin.

Roxanne during her U.S. Senate campaign,
2010. Courtesy of Roxanne Conlin.

Roxanne and Jim in Australia during a cruise, 2011. Courtesy of Roxanne Conlin.

Roxanne helping with an ESL class in a Conlin property, 2014. Courtesy of Roxanne Conlin.

Roxanne conferring with Paige Fiedler at Godfrey trial, 2019. Courtesy of Stephen Gruber-Miller/ The Register via Imagn Content Services, LLC.

Roxanne's client Chris Godfrey in front of a copy of the *Des Moines Register* with its headline announcing the victory in his discrimination lawsuit, 2019. Courtesy of Chris Godfrey.

Roxanne and her dance partner David Butts dancing at Roxanne's seventy-fifth birthday party, 2019. Courtesy of Whitney Warne.

TEN

——

Changing Pace

After the Microsoft settlement, Roxanne thought about slowing down. The seven-year case had exhausted her. "I will not take anything like that again. It was all-consuming, seven days a week, 16, 18, 20 hours a day for almost two full years up to and including the trial." Work had indeed dominated her life, but there was a discernible change following this big case. Roxanne reduced the size of her staff, pursued fewer cases, took more vacations, especially ocean cruises, and became more interested in philanthropic endeavors. Other activities outside of work picked up as Roxanne spent more time with her children and grandchildren, and she remained active in Democratic Party politics. But such pursuits were interrupted by a stroke in 2013.[1]

The decade or so prior to Roxanne's stroke, which had been an eventful period for her, had been both busy and transitional for her adult children as well. Debbie, the oldest, had taken her two sons and her daughter to Ithaca in 1999, where she pursued graduate work at Cornell University. After completing her master's in real estate, she stayed on another year and a half and added another master's degree, this one in hospitality management. The following January 2003, Debbie moved to San Francisco. She initially worked at Starbucks before finding a job at

Deutsche Bank in its commercial real estate division as a leasing and property director. It was during this time that Debbie realized she was gay and started dating women.[2]

Before Debbie headed to California, she and Roxanne met at Zanzibar's, a Des Moines coffee shop. There Roxanne tried in vain to convince her daughter to move back to Des Moines. While the two were talking, Connie Newlin, the owner of Pro Search, Inc., a local headhunting firm, walked by. Roxanne and Newlin had known each other for years; Newlin had briefly served as Roxanne's driver during the 1982 gubernatorial campaign while finishing her college career as a standout basketball player at Drake University. Roxanne introduced Newlin to Debbie, and then, not yet aware her daughter was a lesbian, said, "Connie, maybe you can find Debbie a man!" Debbie recalled being embarrassed but said nothing.[3]

After a few years in the Bay Area, Debbie was ready to come home. Roxanne suggested she contact Newlin about finding a job in Des Moines. She did, and the two visited at Zanzibar's while Debbie was in town in January 2008. Debbie told Newlin she had been mortified by her mother's comment several years earlier because she had been attracted to Newlin. Newlin suggested they go out on a date. They did and began a long-distance relationship for several months before Debbie moved back to Des Moines. Newlin helped her land a position at DuPont Pioneer in its corporate real estate division.[4]

In August 2012, three years after the landmark Iowa Supreme Court decision in *Varnum v. Brien*, which legalized same-sex marriage in the state, the couple married in an intimate ceremony. Although the two kept Newlin's house in Waukee, a western suburb of Des Moines, they moved to California in 2013. After a brief stint back in Iowa in 2015, they returned to California the following year.[5]

Unlike his sister, after returning from Los Angeles several years earlier, Doug had remained in Des Moines and continued in the computer and software development business. By the early 2000s, he was working as the director of business services at ABC Virtual Communications, a West Des Moines e-business consulting firm. But he had always had an independent streak and an entrepreneurial bent, which had earlier led him to establish his own video production business. By 2003, he was ready to try another venture and gambled that he could turn his love of classic American muscle cars—high-performance sports cars from the 1950s through the 1970s—into a successful business. He and partner Robert Munoz kept their day jobs, took out loans, and established American Dream Machines, a classic car dealership specializing in muscle cars. The business was located in the back half of the old Packard automobile dealership and more recently Dave Ostrem Imports at Fifteenth and Locust Streets in downtown Des Moines.[6]

Seven months later, the building went up for sale, and the partners bought it, putting their showroom on a distinctive black-and-white checkerboard tile floor behind the plate glass windows facing north onto Locust Street. With classic rock music playing in the background, the showroom displayed beautifully restored classics such as Cadillacs, Chevrolet Corvettes and Camaros, Pontiac GTOs, Ford Mustangs, and Plymouth Challengers. The business immediately attracted a lot of attention. In fact, Doug said, "We have fingerprints all over our windows every night. We have people walking around and just peering in at the cars." Fortunately, people were buying, too.[7]

The business soon took off. Doug quit his job at ABC Virtual Communications, bought out his partner, and brought wife Julie into the business. By 2013 he could boast, "We're actually one of the largest muscle car shops in the country, probably the world." At that time, his inventory ranged in price from $17,000 to $100,000, with out-of-state buyers, including celebrities such as Randy Travis and Kid Rock, accounting for most of his sales. Billy Joel patronized the business as well, buying a classic 1973—the year his megahit "Piano Man" came out—burgundy Volkswagen Beetle he had noticed in the showroom while in Des Moines for a concert in the spring of 2008.[8]

While Doug had been reestablishing himself in Des Moines, Jackie had remained in Dallas. An entrepreneur herself, she continued operating her successful pet-sitting business. Toward the end of the 1990s, she began a romantic relationship with Laurie Gibbons, a highly successful sales director for OnDisplay, an e-business software company, before it was sold to Vignette in 2000. Gibbons was promoted and transferred to San Francisco later that year. Jackie, meanwhile, was tiring of her business and ready for a change. in 2000, she sold Park Cities Pet Sitter to employee Joette White and followed Gibbons to San Francisco.[9]

Jackie loved the Bay Area, but the move did not solve her drinking problem, which only worsened when she and Gibbons broke up two years later. Single again, Jackie returned to the retail industry, taking a job at a Saks Fifth Avenue store in San Francisco. She tried to quit drinking several times but failed. Still, Jackie remained functional, and because she had always had an eye for fashion, she became one of Saks's leading in-house personal shoppers. Here she encountered a number of style consultants and realized that was something she would like to do.[10]

She launched Jackie Conlin, Personal Style Consultant, in 2003, but she was still battling her drinking demons. A therapist gave her anxiety medication, but Jackie was soon abusing this as well. She continued drinking until she hit bottom in 2007. Afraid she might die, Jackie knew she needed help and made arrangements to check herself into San Rafael's Bayside Marin Treatment Center, one of northern California's leading substance abuse treatment centers. She drank for the next seven days, showed up drunk to be admitted, and began her sobriety the following day, July 4, 2007. This time rehab worked, and Jackie has remained sober since that personal Independence Day. Once clean and sober, she paid much greater attention to her nascent small business, which began to thrive. Nine years later, with her parents providing part of the down payment, Jackie bought a condominium in San Francisco, where she currently resides with her two rescued Great Danes.[11]

Son J.B. continued selling real estate for Iowa Realty, but over the course of the 1990s he began doing more and more work for Conlin Properties, especially in the area of construction. Early the following decade, as Jim was approaching his mid-sixties, he began talking with J.B. about the future of the family firm. Jim was considering promoting J.B. to the company's vice-presidency. But Kris Saddoris had much more experience at the firm and in the real estate business in general, and she was better prepared for the job. J.B. and Saddoris discussed the situation, and they decided the company would be best served if they jointly held the position as co-vice-presidents.[12]

The two pitched the plan to Jim, who liked it, and in September 2006 J.B. became a full-time vice-president of Conlin Properties. Saddoris also advanced to a vice-presidency, with the idea that the two would gradually take over the day-to-day management of the company as Jim eased out of these operations and focused on the firm's development division. Saddoris initially shouldered more of the work as she also mentored the younger Conlin.[13]

The following month, J.B. married his longtime girlfriend, Courtney Briese. They met on a blind date two and a half years earlier, and much like Roxanne and Jim, the two immediately fell for each other. At the time, Courtney worked for Principal Financial Group, but she would go on to try retail merchandising, the bakery business, and real estate before following the advice of sister-in-law Jackie and starting a style consulting business in 2012.[14]

Roxanne was aware that the two could not afford the wedding they desired, and she intervened early in the process, telling J.B. that she and his father wanted to pay for a grand Salisbury House wedding and Des Moines Club reception. Shortly before the wedding, J.B. worried about the cost when he saw a number of large bills arriving. But Roxanne immediately consoled him, "We have plenty of money, J.B. You're only going to do this once, and we are happy to take care of all this. Enjoy the day, or it will make it less enjoyable for your dad and me." Reassured, J.B. and Courtney relished their wedding.[15]

Their only regret was the fact that the end-of-October ceremony fell just a few weeks before the Iowa Microsoft trial began. Roxanne was in full trial preparation mode and could not enjoy the day as they and she would have liked. Before any trial, Roxanne explained, she became laser-focused on the case: "All I can think about is the trial. I don't sleep, I don't eat, and I become incredibly antsy." Unfortunately, this was only compounded by the size and scope of the impending trial, and Roxanne left the reception after only a couple of hours.[16]

That fall, J.B. and his colleague Saddoris settled into their new positions at Conlin Properties, but after several years as co-vice-presidents, both became convinced that Jim was not ready to give up control of the company, and he had been making daily decisions without consulting them. After trying to work through the situation, they ultimately decided to leave the company. Saddoris took a job at Hubbell Realty in West Des Moines, and J.B. decided to pursue his master's degree in business administration at the University of Iowa. Before leaving, however, the two met with Jim and worked to hire their replacements. After months of interviewing, they hired two people to replace them, but neither lasted very long. Jim then promoted Beth Ehlers, already at Conlin Properties, to vice-president, and he hired Bret Mills from the Iowa Department of Economic Development as the other vice-president in 2011. Mills would be elevated to president the following year.[17]

After J.B. finished his MBA in 2012, he wanted to do something on his own, away from Conlin Properties. He tried consulting, without much success, and helped Courtney with real estate, which reminded him how much he liked the business. Jim, meanwhile, remained concerned about the company's succession and wanted to bring J.B. back into the fold. The two started talking about such a move in November 2013, and the following month J.B. accepted a newly created job at Conlin Properties as its chief operating officer with what he believed was commensurate authority to go with the title. Jim stayed on as CEO.[18]

With three of her four children and all of her grandchildren living in town for much of this period, Roxanne loved hosting family events and spoiling her grandchildren. By far everyone's favorite gathering was her extravagant Easter celebration. Her palatial home was decked out for the holiday with elaborate Easter baskets and scores of stuffed animals, many of which were animated and could sing and dance. After a brunch or lunch, either at the Conlin home or at the downtown Des Moines Club, the grandchildren eagerly awaited Roxanne's illustrious Easter egg hunt.[19]

Sometimes assisted by Jim and J.B., Roxanne scattered ninety-nine colorful plastic eggs about the Conlins' large home. She held the event indoors because of her severe hay fever and allergies. However, unlike most such hunts, where the eggs generally contained candy, these eggs were filled with money—a variety of bills ranging from $1 to $100 or, in a nod to feminism, Susan B. Anthony silver dollars. Sister-in-law Judy Conlin's grandchildren participated as well, and she recalled that the event was so popular that grandchildren refused to age out even when they became young adults. One was twenty-three before he finally decided he was too old for the hunt.[20]

Judy Conlin felt the Easter celebration captured the "fun-loving generosity" of Roxanne and Jim. For son Doug Klein, it was just another indication that they were "great" grandparents when they had the time.[21]

In fact, one of the reasons Jim had promoted J.B. and Saddoris in 2006 was his desire to step away from daily management duties, so he and Roxanne could "spend more personal time pursuing international travel and our political and philanthropic interests." Roxanne was fully on board after her Microsoft victory the following year. Luxurious travel soon ensued with an African trip in March 2009 followed by a Mediterranean cruise later that year. Her Senate bid kept the couple close to home, but after the loss Roxanne and Jim were back on a cruise ship, this time from Lisbon to the Canary Islands.[22]

Early on, they became devotees of Crystal Cruises and were soon taking two or three cruises a year to destinations such as Alaska, Mexico, Argentina, the Caribbean, Japan, Australia, New Zealand, the British Isles, and Africa. Besides lavishly appointed ships and first-class excursions, Crystal Cruises offered a service that set it apart from most of its competitors. Its Ambassador Dance Host program provided professional male dancers who danced with single women or women with partners who did not dance. This made the cruise line especially appealing to Roxanne, who took great pleasure in jitterbugging and fox-trotting her nights away as she sailed the high seas.[23]

Roxanne also occasionally traveled with her sisters. In 2009, she and Becky, Rhoda, Rhonda, and Gina took a Mexican Riviera cruise. Several other "sister cruises" followed with all but Rhonda, who did not enjoy the cruise ship experience, taking part.[24]

If longer vacations and cruises were new for Roxanne, involvement in local and statewide Democratic Party politics was not. She had remained a staunch supporter of female candidates, providing financial support for many and often holding fund-raising events for them in her office or home. She hosted the Polk County Democrats Women's Event—an annual gala begun in 2000 to highlight Democratic women holding or running for office in Polk County—at her office in 2002. Once her grand home was finished, she opened it up for the occasion in 2005, 2011, 2013, 2014, and 2017.[25]

Roxanne also played an important role in state and national politics, cochairing Senator John Edwards's Iowa campaigns for president in both 2004 and 2008. Everything about Edwards appealed to her. Like Roxanne, he was a self-made millionaire; he had taken up the law and become one of the country's leading plaintiff attorneys; and he represented the progressive wing of the Democratic Party. The two had met in the early 1980s through the Association of Trial Lawyers of America and grew to be good friends.[26]

Edwards had burst onto the political scene by winning a U.S. Senate seat in North Carolina in 1998. A couple of years into his term, it became clear that the young, handsome, and smooth-talking freshman senator had presidential ambitions when he set up a political action committee to raise money. Edwards also began visiting Iowa, testing the waters for a possible presidential run. If he did so, the race would begin in the state because of its first-in-the-nation caucuses, the initial test of contenders for each party's nomination.[27]

During this exploratory phase, he kept in contact with Roxanne—who enthusiastically supported an Edwards run—and courted other Democratic Party activists. On New Year's Day of 2003, he announced his bid for the presidency, and four weeks later Roxanne and attorney Rob Tully, both former chairs of the Iowa Democratic Party, were named cochairs of his Iowa campaign. The two focused on landing endorsements, bringing in big donors, and helping Edwards lay out the broad outlines of his statewide strategy. Day-to-day management of the operation fell to campaign manager Rob Berntsen and political director Aaron Pickrell.[28]

The campaign leased space for its headquarters in Jim Conlin's Griffin Building in downtown Des Moines. Although Edwards had gotten a relatively early start campaigning, he was clearly an underdog as he faced a field of more experienced and better-known Democratic politicians. These included former Vermont governor Howard Dean, Missouri congressman Richard Gephardt, Massachusetts senator John Kerry, Ohio congressman Dennis Kucinich, and Carol Moseley Braun, a former U.S. senator from Illinois, although she would drop out shortly before the caucuses.[29]

By late spring, Edwards was generally running fourth or fifth in the polls, but one Democratic activist noted that he had "some heavy hitters [referring to Roxanne and Tully] with him" and he should not be counted out. Roxanne spent a lot of time making appearances for Edwards, and she relished the experience. She recalled, "I liked it, I really did. I just loved those people out there. Iowans are really good, smart, caring people." Actually, Roxanne's time on the campaign trail made her briefly contemplate a run against Senator Chuck Grassley in 2004. But with the ongoing Microsoft case, she decided against challenging the senator at that time.[30]

Roxanne believed Edwards's blue-collar background and self-made success would resonate with Iowans, especially rural voters. As she had hoped, after the candidate made a number of sweeps through the state, his poll numbers began to surge as the caucus date neared. It still looked like he would come in fourth, but the race had tightened. Dean was leading, followed by Kerry, who was moving up in the polls. Gephardt was third, and Edwards followed, although he was advancing as well. Kucinich was running far behind.[31]

Edwards's momentum continued through caucus night. Kerry won with 38 percent of the vote, but Edwards came in second with 32 percent. Dean took 18 percent, Gephardt 11 percent, and Kucinich 2 percent. Gephardt dropped out of the race, and Dean would drop out the following month. Kerry went on to win the nomination, and in July he picked Edwards as his vice-presidential nominee. Roxanne was delighted with the news. Although she understood that running mates rarely determined an election outcome, she thought that Edwards might play an important role. "You saw what sort of connection he has with the people of Iowa," she said. "It's a tribute to him being a trial lawyer and someone with charisma." Roxanne felt that Edwards's magnetic personality would give him a "very real, human connection" with voters all across the nation.[32]

Nevertheless, the Kerry-Edwards ticket came up short, and incumbent president George Bush and his vice-president Dick Cheney won in a close race in November. The election had made Edwards a national figure, however, and he ran for the presidency again in 2008. Roxanne and Tully cochaired this Iowa effort as well. In early January of that year, Edwards again placed second in the Iowa Democratic caucus. This time he trailed Senator Barack Obama but ran ahead of Senator Hillary Clinton. But his bid for the presidency quickly went downhill from there when he placed third in the primaries in New Hampshire, South Carolina, and Florida. Edwards suspended his campaign at the end of January.[33]

Roxanne was sorry to see Edwards pull out of the race but remained impressed with him until that August, when he finally admitted that the year-old allegations that he had had an extramarital affair with filmmaker Rielle Hunter were true. But he vehemently denied that Hunter's baby, born in February 2008, was his. The story was made that much worse because his wife, Elizabeth, was dealing with a return of breast cancer, which had metastasized and was not curable. Two years later, in January 2010, Edwards publicly admitted that he had fathered Hunter's child. Elizabeth soon separated from her husband, and she died that December.[34]

Roxanne was distraught over the scandal, but because Edwards had been a close friend she thought she knew, the deception made her especially angry. After he admitted the affair, she did not speak to him for years. "Like so many people, he fooled me," she noted in 2010. "The sense of betrayal and disappointment is overwhelming."[35]

Besides her work on behalf of Democratic candidates, Roxanne gave generously to the party. From 1990 to 2010, she and Jim contributed $360,000 to federal candidates and political action committees, including those of the Association of Trial Lawyers of America and the American Association for Justice, EMILY's List, the Gay and Lesbian Victory Fund, and the National Organization for Women. Most of the donations were made by Roxanne.[36]

The Iowa Democratic Party was the largest recipient, getting $72,000 from the Conlins, while the Association of Trial Lawyers of America and the American Association for Justice got $48,000. Iowa Senator Tom Harkin and Representative Leonard Boswell were the top individual beneficiaries of the couple's donations. Over the same period, Jim gave $4,200 to Republican candidates and groups, including, interestingly, $1,500 to Senator Grassley in 2004.[37]

The couple had also become more interested in philanthropic giving, especially after Roxanne won the Microsoft case and Jim began contemplating moving away from day-to-day operations at Conlin Properties. Roxanne had always been generous. Her giving reflected the idea of tithing, one of the few remnants of her Catholic upbringing that stuck, she said, although her donations went to various nonprofits instead of the church.[38]

In her public life, Roxanne sought out and thrived in the spotlight, but she helped friends and various nonprofits without seeking public recognition. Friend, attorney, and former law clerk Paige Fiedler recalled her giving money to homeless people while the two were at a conference in San Francisco. Fiedler observed, "Roxanne was very generous with her money. If you had a good cause, she would contribute," but she did so quietly, and "you won't be able to find anyone who can tell you about all her donations."[39]

Des Moines attorney Alfredo Parrish recounted one such story of Roxanne's kindheartedness at the 2017 memorial service for Polk County District Judge Don Nickerson. Roxanne had hired Nickerson as an assistant U.S. attorney in 1978, the first African American to hold the position in Iowa, and the two became good friends. Nickerson went on to be the first African American to serve as the U.S. attorney for the Southern District of Iowa before being appointed a Polk County judge. In 1992, doctors discovered he had a brain tumor. Radiation treatment was not successful, and many, including Roxanne, feared he was giving up hope. She contacted mutual friend Mark Bennett, then a U.S. magistrate judge, and told him "in no uncertain terms" that his "mission was to get Don [to agree to go] to the Mayo Clinic" for a second opinion. Roxanne had already made an appointment for him.[40]

Bennett passed along the message and said that if Nickerson did not go, he would have to explain himself to Roxanne. Nickerson half-jokingly responded: "I would rather go to Mayo than face the wrath of Roxanne." She arranged for a private plane to fly him there, where a specialist determined that Nickerson required surgery. The operation saved his life.[41]

Besides helping people in need, Roxanne always had a soft spot when it came to animals, especially cats, and as noted previously she and Jim actively fostered Animal Rescue League of Iowa kittens until they were old enough to be adopted. Roxanne and Jim also gave generously to the league and other such organizations that assisted with unwanted pets or helped people who could not afford needed medical treatment for their animals.[42]

In 2007, Roxanne and Jim established two philanthropic funds at the Community Foundation of Greater Des Moines—the Conlin Family Iowa Charitable Giving Fund and the Roxanne and James Conlin Fund—and Roxanne put $500,000 in each after the Microsoft victory. The couple continues to contribute to these funds, which they decided would be devoted to efforts supporting basic human needs rather than brick-and-mortar projects. In the years to come, many of these programs would be associated with Jim's affordable housing communities.[43]

It was Judy Conlin, Roxanne's sister-in-law, who suggested the first opportunity. There were many non-English-speaking immigrants living in the Conlins' properties, and Judy, then the executive director of the Iowa International Center, proposed that Roxanne and Jim offer on-site English as a Second Language classes (and provide child care during class time). The couple liked the idea and began funding a pilot program at their Deer Ridge apartment complex on Des Moines's south side in 2012. The experiment was a success, and with Roxanne and Jim agreeing to cover a majority of its costs, the Iowa International Center continued ESL classes at Deer Ridge.[44]

Educational programs focusing on children living in the Conlins' properties followed. The couple soon began providing transportation for young children of their neediest residents to and from their apartments to preschool, and starting in 2014 they sponsored a summer reading program—conducted by IOWAREADS, a nonprofit literacy improvement organization—at their properties, which generally hosts forty to fifty children annually.[45]

As J.B. Conlin gradually took on more and more responsibility at the company, he also helped his parents work with nonprofits and direct their philanthropic efforts. For instance, he found a way to assist some who could not ordinarily afford an apartment. Several years earlier, he had become acquainted with Toby O'Berry of Iowa Homeless Youth Centers. After a number of discussions, J.B. and O'Berry brought Conlin Properties and Youth Shelter Services, IHYC's parent organization, into a partnership. Beginning in 2017, nine young adults who could not meet the regular credit requirements or the monthly fees to rent an apartment were moved into Conlin complexes. A portion of their rent was paid by Youth Shelter Services, and the tenants were given access to YSS counselors and special Conlin managers to help them navigate the experience and keep them in the housing. Six young families followed, joining the program in 2019 and moving into Conlin apartments.[46]

In 2018, a representative of the Community Foundation contacted J.B. about Eat Greater Des Moines, a central Iowa nonprofit. It was developing a pilot program to provide good-quality food to those in need through a food recovery program, and the Community Foundation thought the Conlins might be interested in supporting the effort. They were. Roxanne and Jim provided funding for the pilot plan in 2018. Kum and Go, a Des Moines–based chain of convenience stores, donated food nearing its expiration date to Eat Greater Des Moines. The nonprofit then transported this food several times a week to four Conlin apartment complexes offering affordable housing to those on fixed or lower incomes. There the food was stored in newly purchased community room refrigerators and made available to residents on a first come, first served basis.[47]

Roxanne made two other significant gifts independently and separate from those funded by the Conlins' Community Foundation accounts. Because of the domestic violence she and her mother, brother, and sisters had faced in her childhood home, Roxanne had been a longtime supporter of the Iowa Coalition Against Domestic Violence. She began thinking of creating a program with the organization to honor her mother and support survivors of domestic violence. Roxanne worked with the coalition to develop the Alice Barton Scholarship program in 2011 and initially funded it. She then asked brother Ray, then CEO of Great Clips, and sister Rhoda, then president of the company, if they would help with the scholarship. They agreed, and the three siblings have committed to funding the project with $63,000 annually, which provides up to sixty scholarships a year in honor of their mother. The awards pay for tuition, books, fees for classes, and other expenses in support of recipients' education and job-training efforts, including child care and transportation.[48]

At the announcement of the program, Roxanne observed, "I know at a deeply personal level the debilitating effect of family violence. When someone you love hurts you, it destroys trust and confidence. Education was the way out of poverty for all of us. Our family hopes that, through these scholarships, in the name of our beloved mother, we can reach out to others and give them the chance to secure a safe future for themselves and their families."[49]

Then Roxanne gave back to her alma mater, Drake University, in 2015 when she pledged $1 million to the law school. Since she remembered how tight money was when she was in law school, she directed her donation to a scholarship fund designed to meet emergency needs of students.[50]

Three years earlier Kim Baer, a friend, local attorney, and then the president of Variety—the Children's Charity of Iowa, asked Roxanne if she would serve as the club's honorary chair for the year. Although a supporter of Variety, Roxanne had a number of commitments and declined. Baer soon came back with another proposal: would Roxanne be the subject of a fund-raising celebrity roast? Roxanne agreed, and the "roast and toast" was scheduled for Thursday evening, February 28, 2013.[51]

But on Tuesday morning, two days before the roast, Roxanne fell when getting out of bed. The right side of her body was numb, and she had difficulty maintaining her balance. Unfortunately, she was alone in the house because Jim had just left to take some foster kittens ready for adoption back to the Animal Rescue League. She crawled into the bathroom and faced the mirror, looking for telltale signs of a stroke. Nothing was wrong with her face, and she could smile. By happenstance, however, a day earlier Roxanne had taken a deposition in a wrongful death lawsuit involving doctors who had failed to diagnose a stroke, and she was well aware of the variety of stroke symptoms.[52]

She called 911, told the operator she was having a stroke, and asked for an ambulance. She then called Jim and J.B. Unfortunately, a surprise storm had hit the city early that morning, dumping heavy snow and making travel on central Iowa's roads slow and difficult. It took the ambulance fifty minutes to make it to Roxanne's house. J.B. arrived at the same time—the usual ten-minute drive took forty-five minutes because of the storm. Jim met them at Iowa Methodist Medical Center in downtown Des Moines.[53]

At the hospital, doctors immediately did a CT scan to make sure Roxanne was not having a hemorrhagic stroke. She was not, but the doctor said there were signs of a previous stroke, although Roxanne had no idea she had ever had one. Meanwhile, with doctors discussing her situation and possible next steps, Roxanne believed she was having an ischemic stroke, where arteries in the brain are constricted or blocked, which drastically reduces blood flow to parts of the brain. She insisted they begin tissue plasminogen activator treatment, which dissolves blood clots and improves blood flow to the brain. Fortunately they did, and fortunately it worked.[54]

Roxanne felt better. Local news outlets reported that she had suffered a mild stroke but had spent Tuesday afternoon responding to e-mails. J.B. posted a message on her Facebook page that day, writing that she was fine and thanking all her well-wishers for their concern. Roxanne even believed she could make the roast on Thursday.[55]

But the reality of her condition soon became apparent. The next day, she was unable to get out of her hospital bed because the right side of her body was not functioning properly. The roast was postponed, and Roxanne spent another six days at Iowa Methodist before being sent to the adjacent Younker Rehabilitation Center. One of her greatest worries while at the hospital was that she might not be able to dance anymore. David Butts, her longtime dance partner, tried to put her fears to rest when he visited her. He took Roxanne down to the cafeteria and shifted some tables out of the way, and the two danced, although Butts largely held her up as they moved across the floor.[56]

After six additional days of rehabilitation, Roxanne was finally discharged. She went home to continue a grueling schedule of daily physical therapy on an outpatient basis. The sessions focused on her hand-eye coordination as well as her mobility and balance issues. They gradually decreased to an every-other-day basis, and by early May she had fully recuperated save for a noticeable limp, which slowly disappeared over the coming months. Soon, much to her delight, she was back on the ballroom floor dancing with David Butts.[57]

The roast was rescheduled for May 15. That evening, a few hundred of her friends and colleagues gathered at the downtown Des Moines Marriott Hotel to honor Roxanne, make jokes at her expense, and raise money for Variety in silent and live auctions. Emceed by longtime friend Jerry Crawford, the event featured a number of roasters offering comments about Roxanne. These included Senator Tom Harkin and Congressman Bruce Braley, who sent videotaped speeches, as well as good friends Cookie Brown, Jacquie Easley, and Susan Terry Knapp, state senator Mike Gronstal, former colleagues Melinda Ellwanger, Tom Duff, and Paige Fiedler, husband Jim, brother Ray, and sister-in-law Judy.[58]

The evening was a success, and Roxanne enjoyed it immensely. There were lots of laughter, applause, and money raised for Variety, but most of all the event signaled the sixty-eight-year-old's recovery, more so actually than the audience realized. Although her speech had never been affected by the stroke, Roxanne had worried that the episode might have diminished her ability to practice law. Therefore, a couple of weeks before the roast, she had a neuropsychologist run a battery of tests, and much to her relief the results showed that her mental abilities had not been impaired at all. Thrilled, she jumped right back into her current cases and actively pursued new ones that interested her. [59]

A comment she made about retirement in 2007 was now more germane than ever. "I will never retire," she explained. "Why would I? Unless health or something like that forces me to. I have absolutely no intention of ever leaving the practice of law. They can carry me out with my boots on." Her stroke had tested this remark, but it was clear that Roxanne had every intention of standing by it. [60]

Roxanne had altered her trajectory after the Microsoft case and had become more interested in philanthropy and travel. She shrank the size of her firm, yet she could not quite step away from the law. She took fewer cases, and she interrupted her practice when she ran for the Senate in 2010, but she was back at it after her defeat that fall. It was in her essence, and it was not something she could live without. Roxanne remained, as Iowa senator Mike Gronstal said at her roast, "a rock star when it comes to standing up for people's rights." [61]

Eleven

Ever the Advocate

Sixty-eight years old in 2012, Roxanne was growing increasingly aware of her own mortality, especially because both her parents died at seventy-five. Even though she maintained a much healthier lifestyle than either her mother or father—she had quit smoking and drinking and worked out regularly with a personal trainer—she felt a mounting urgency to continue making a difference. Her stroke the following year only heightened this resolve. "I consider many of the clients we serve heroes and they are the reason I get up each morning and my inspiration to continue fighting to make sure that their voices are heard," she explained in 2017.[1]

An increasing number of Roxanne's clients were involved in third party criminal negligence cases. Her interest in the area started in the mid-1980s when Paulee Lipsman, her good friend and a rape victim, filed a lawsuit against her landlord for failing to fix a defective window lock in her apartment, which had allowed her attacker to enter. Such cases involved not only apartment or hotel owners, who could be liable for third party criminal activity on their premises if their facilities lacked adequate security for tenants or guests, but business owners in general could also be liable if they did not provide satisfactory safety measures for their employees or customers. Likewise, schools that failed to protect their students from injury or sexual exploitation because of lack of security, poor staff training, or insufficient supervision could be liable as well.[2]

Roxanne became an evangelist for this developing branch of law. She soon drafted a speech on the topic, "Rape, Robbery, and Murder: What Civil Lawyers Can Do to Help the Victims of Crime," and began delivering the talk to bar associations around the country. She also pushed the American Association for Justice to create a litigation group focusing on inadequate safety, which offered training in the field.[3]

One recent such case involved "Jane Doe," a middle school student in Clinton, Iowa, and teacher Christopher Nielsen, who in 2014 began inappropriately contacting the juvenile on social media and giving her gifts. He eventually lured her into sexual intercourse on several occasions. Doe's parents sensed something was wrong and contacted police about what they thought was "an uncomfortable relationship" Nielsen had developed with their daughter. Police investigated and arrested Nielsen for sexual abuse and sexual exploitation. In June 2017, he pleaded guilty to third-degree sexual abuse and received a ten-year sentence; he also pleaded guilty to sexual exploitation by a school employee and received an additional five years in prison for that charge.[4]

Shortly thereafter, Doe's parents, Kaylyn and Jeffery Dickinson, contacted Roxanne, and that October they filed a lawsuit against the Clinton Community School District and Clinton Middle School, charging them with "negligent hiring, supervision and retention, and premises liability." Some months later, in May 2018, Roxanne and the school district agreed to a $2.25 million settlement. The district also overhauled its policies, procedures, and staff training to ensure the safety of its learning community.[5]

Other important cases fell within Roxanne's more traditional areas of practice. In 2012, she filed a disability lawsuit against the University of Iowa on behalf of her client, Janis Perkins, for discrimination, retaliation, and failure to follow procedures. Perkins began working at the university in 1994; three years later, she became the first director of its study abroad program. Under her leadership, the program took off, but Perkins was dealing with an autoimmune disorder and depression that required treatment and intermittent absences from work. Still, she received positive evaluations and was promoted to assistant dean of international programs in 2010.[6]

Nevertheless, the following year, Perkins was dumbfounded when she received a performance improvement plan highlighting her alleged shortcomings. This came two months after she had gone through a job review, which did not mention any of these allegations. Perkins also claimed that two of her superiors "spent the next four months bullying, harassing, and discriminating against her."[7]

Their actions pushed Perkins into a deep depression that required hospitalization. She retained Roxanne as her attorney and returned to work. University officials told Roxanne the school was interested in an agreement leading to Perkins's departure. The following month, the university announced a reorganization consolidating its international programs and eliminating the position Perkins had held.[8]

Perkins sued, claiming the reorganization failed to follow university procedures and "was a mere pretext for terminating [her] based on her disability." The lawsuit dragged on until 2015, when Roxanne and university lawyers worked out a settlement. The university denied any wrongdoing but agreed to pay Perkins $150,000 in compensation for lost wages, emotional distress, and legal fees.[9]

Roxanne also took another precedent-setting pregnancy discrimination case in 2012. She had already advanced the cause of pregnant women with her win in the landmark *Cedar Rapids Community School District v. Parr* in 1975. In that case, the Iowa Supreme Court had ruled that the district had sexually discriminated because it treated pregnant employees differently from other staff members. Since that time, the Iowa legislature had weighed in on the issue in 1987 when it amended the Iowa Civil Rights Act. A new provision in the employment section called the disabilities caused by a worker's pregnancy temporary. A later addition required employers to provide employees disabled by pregnancy with a leave of absence.[10]

This time, Roxanne's client was Karen McQuistion, the only female firefighter in Clinton, a city on the Mississippi River in eastern Iowa.

She became pregnant in 2011, and that May she asked Chief Mark Regenwether to put her on light duty, which did not involve fighting fires or responding to emergencies. McQuistion did not have a pregnancy-related condition that qualified as a disability, and because the city offered light duty only to those injured on the job, the chief refused.[11]

McQuistion remained on regular duty fighting fires until the end of September, when she was no longer able to fit into her protective gear, and her doctors recommended she cease working fires because of potential exposure to toxic conditions. She took a leave of absence, receiving her salary until her accrued sick time and vacation days were gone, then went without pay. McQuistion had her baby in January 2012 and returned to work on regular duty that March. In the meantime, she had hired Roxanne and filed a suit against the city, claiming pregnancy discrimination and violation of her equal protection and due process rights under the Iowa Constitution.[12]

The district court sided with the city, explaining that the city had not discriminated because it denied light work to both pregnant employees and nonpregnant disabled employees who had not been injured on the job. The court added that McQuistion's situation was not similar to Clinton police officers given light duty when they were pregnant, because the city's police force had a union contract calling for light duty in those situations, while the fire department did not. McQuistion appealed.[13]

Before the Iowa Supreme Court in March 2015, Roxanne argued that pregnancy was a temporary disability eligible for accommodation under Iowa law. She explained that under city rules, firefighters could receive light duty for injuries that happened on the job, and pregnant city police officers were entitled to light duty because of their union contract. "What that tells us," she concluded, "is that light duty is available, that light duty is possible, that there is no imposition on the city that is not reasonable. There is no undue hardship on the city to provide temporary light duty work for women, who are temporarily disabled as a result of pregnancy."[14]

As the Iowa justices were considering the case, the U.S. Supreme Court ruled on the issue in *Young v. United Parcel Service*, writing that if special consideration is given to any worker, those same accommodations must be provided to a pregnant worker unless the employer can prove that doing so would be extremely burdensome. On December 24, 2015, the Iowa Supreme Court overturned the lower court's decision on pregnancy discrimination, essentially aligning with the U.S. Supreme Court. It was a big victory for McQuistion. The Iowa Supreme Court sent the case back to the lower court, ordering it to reevaluate its findings by comparing McQuistion's treatment with "all those temporarily disabled, not just those injured on the job."[15]

Here again, Roxanne had improved the lives of pregnant working women. Shortly after the decision and before the Iowa district court returned to the case, Clinton officials and Roxanne agreed to a settlement that covered McQuistion's economic losses, emotional distress, and attorney's fees and costs. Then the city revised its policies, ensuring that any pregnant employee "be given light duty when she was unable to perform her regular duties according to her physician, without exhausting sick leave or any other leave."[16]

Meanwhile, a situation of alleged age and race discrimination had drawn Roxanne's attention to Mason City, 120 miles north of Des Moines. African American Lionel Foster, the only director of the city's Human Rights Commission since 1978 and the only full-time African American employee of the city up to that time, lost his job in July 2013 when the city council reduced the commission's annual budget from $143,000 to $15,000. The council explained that the cut put the budget in line with commissions in cities of comparable size. Foster was highly regarded across the state. Governors Terry Branstad and Tom Vilsack had both recognized his work, and he had recently been inducted into the Iowa African American Hall of Fame. The seventy-five-year-old believed the budget cut was a ruse to get rid of him, and he hired Roxanne, whom he had known for years because they both worked in the field of civil rights. In September, Foster filed a complaint with the Iowa Civil Rights Commission, charging age and race discrimination. He also claimed that the move was retaliation for the many civil rights investigations he had led against local business supporters of Mason City's mayor.[17]

The following April, the Iowa Civil Rights Commission granted Foster the right to sue the city. In June he did just that, charging the city, its Human Rights Commission, Mayor Eric Bookmeyer and City Administrator Brent Trout, all six city council members, and three human rights commissioners with the same violations described in his earlier complaint. He added other charges, including denial of due process and equal protection, as well. Two months later, a district judge dismissed all these new counts but upheld the allegations of age and race discrimination, allowing the lawsuit to move forward. Both sides were prepared to go to trial, but by December Roxanne and attorneys for Mason City's insurer settled the case for $240,000.[18]

Shortly before Foster filed his initial complaint, Roxanne had become involved in a headline-grabbing story of bullying in Des Moines. In April 2012, Grand View University student Cameron Fagen and several friends were horsing around in a common room in one of the school's dormitories. The roughhousing took a horrible turn when Fagen's six dorm mates, all Grand View basketball or football players, pushed him to the floor, wrapped him in a discarded piece of carpet, and secured it with duct tape. His arms and legs were completely restrained, and his feet did not reach the floor.[19]

With Fagen immobilized in the carpet, the athletes stood him up in a corner of the room and proceeded to punch and kick him. They beat him with a broom handle, then laid him down, rolled him across the room, and stood him up again. This time he fell forward. He landed on his chin, breaking it in two places. Fagen remained on the floor bleeding until a friend helped him get out of the carpet. He was taken to Des Moines's Mercy Hospital, but because of the severity of his injuries he was transferred to the University of Iowa's hospital in Iowa City.[20]

A security camera captured the entire thirty-eight-minute episode. Grand View disciplined the students involved, expelling most. By September, Fagen had recovered and transferred to another school. He had also retained Roxanne and filed a lawsuit against Grand View University and his six attackers. The school was charged with negligence as well as failing to monitor the common room and stop the attack and leaving the carpet remnant in the room. The students were charged with bullying and assault. Fagen sought monetary damages for his injuries, physical and mental pain, and physical and mental disability as well as medical expenses for care and treatment.[21]

In a deposition, Fagen mentioned he had been treated for anger management issues in elementary school, and because he claimed mental pain and suffering from the assault, attorneys for the defendants asked him to sign a waiver giving them unrestricted access to all his medical records, not only those pertaining to the incident. Fagen refused. The district court ordered him to do so, and Roxanne appealed the decision to the Iowa Supreme Court.[22]

The Iowa Supreme Court reversed the lower court's order in 2015. It argued that a trial court should not automatically require access to all of a plaintiff's mental health records because of the claim of emotional distress. Rather, the defendant must show that the requested records are likely to contain information relevant to the case. It was a significant win for Roxanne and her colleagues in plaintiff law, limiting a defense attorney's nearly automatic access to all of a litigant's mental health records. Roxanne quickly settled the suit after the Iowa Supreme Court decision, getting $125,000 from Grand View for her client. In addition, each of Fagen's assailants agreed to apologize and donate $1,000 to antibullying organizations.[23]

On the heels of settling the Fagen case, Roxanne joined what became a massive class action lawsuit. In September 2015, the Environmental Protection Agency accused Volkswagen of manipulating emissions tests on hundreds of thousands of its diesel automobiles, which according to the *Des Moines Register* exposed "people to harmful pollutants at 40 times the acceptable [federal] standard." The German automaker admitted to installing software on its "clean" diesel vehicles designed to trick regulators into believing that the cars met clean air standards, and it agreed to cooperate with investigators.[24]

The revelation led lawyers across the country to file lawsuits against Volkswagen. That was when Rick Hagstrom, a Minneapolis attorney and Roxanne's partner in the Iowa Microsoft case, called her to discuss the situation. Hagstrom had great respect for Roxanne and thought they had worked well together against the software giant. He now proposed they work together again, this time against Volkswagen. Hagstrom suggested that he and Roxanne each file a class action lawsuit against the automaker in their respective states.[25]

Although Roxanne much preferred working on behalf of individuals, VW angered her by misrepresenting its vehicles as environmentally green and taking advantage of its consumers. She had also liked working with Hagstrom, and she agreed to collaborate with him on the effort. As planned, he filed a suit in Minnesota, and Roxanne filed *Jamieson et al v. Volkswagen Group of America, Inc.*, in November 2015.[26]

As Hagstrom expected, their cases, along with the five hundred other lawsuits filed against VW, were consolidated through a federal case management procedure called multidistrict litigation. This process speeds up the litigation of complex civil suits sharing common questions in various district courts. U.S. District Court Judge Charles Breyer would oversee the case in San Francisco. After the consolidation, Roxanne and Hagstrom both applied to be on the plaintiff steering committee—the group of attorneys to be appointed by Breyer and charged with helping arrange a settlement between VW and the thousands of consumers in the class action lawsuit. Roxanne and Hagstrom had agreed to work together if either was named to the committee.[27]

One hundred fifty law firms applied for twenty-two committee slots. Roxanne was among those selected; Hagstrom was not. Interestingly, the committee also included David Boies, one of the most renowned litigators in the country. Roxanne best knew him for his work years earlier as the U.S. Justice Department attorney who had taken the famous ten-hour deposition of Bill Gates for the federal government's case against Microsoft. Roxanne had used the videotape of this deposition to great effect in her case against the software maker.[28]

Two other names popped up in conjunction with the litigation. John Edwards, the well-known attorney, former U.S. senator, vice-presidential nominee, and two-time presidential candidate whose Iowa campaigns Roxanne had chaired, had applied for a slot but was not named to the committee. Meanwhile Robert S. Mueller, former FBI director and the special counsel who investigated Russian interference in the 2016 election, was named special master—an attorney appointed by a judge to provide expert advice and assist in bringing the case to a conclusion. Breyer tasked Mueller with mediating the talks with Volkswagen.[29]

The committee worked with amazing alacrity and efficiency, meeting several times over the next few months in San Francisco and often discussing matters via conference calls. This, combined with Volkswagen's desire to restore customer confidence quickly and Judge Breyer's refusal "to allow the litigation to bog down," led to an agreement in principle between the steering committee and the automaker in April. Two months later, in June 2016, a preliminary settlement was in place.[30]

Under the terms of the agreement, Volkswagen would pay $14.7 billion to settle the case, making this one of the largest consumer class action settlements in U.S. history. Roughly $10 billion would go to buying back or repairing autos involved in the lawsuit as well as providing additional compensation to the owners of the vehicles; $2 billion was earmarked for government agencies for environmental mitigation; and another $2.7 billion would be directed to an Environmental Protection Agency fund to pay for the deleterious environmental impact of the vehicles involved in the lawsuit.[31]

Judge Breyer approved the settlement in October. It was by far the largest civil settlement by an automobile maker to date—seven times larger than the General Motors suit that paid out $2 billion to customers for defective ignition switches and ten times larger than Toyota's $1.4 billion settlement for faulty accelerators. It fell $4 billion shy, however, of the largest civil settlement in U.S. history—BP's $18.7 billion agreement settling claims for its 2010 oil spill in the Gulf of Mexico. The BP case, however, was not a consumer class action lawsuit. Roxanne was delighted but also shocked that she and the steering committee were able to reach a deal so quickly, calling the settlement "a land speed record for a class action lawsuit."[32]

This rapidity stood in stark contrast to what Roxanne would describe in 2017 as "the case of a lifetime," which dragged out over a number of years. The client was Chris Godfrey, who had clerked for her in the late 1990s before finishing law school and going into workers compensation and employment law, first as a corporate attorney for Iowa Beef Processors and then in private practice. In January 2006, Governor Tom Vilsack nominated him to serve the remaining three years of a six-year term as the Iowa workers compensation commissioner. He was forced to withdraw the nomination because of the strong opposition from Republicans because Godfrey was gay. Vilsack immediately reappointed him to serve as an interim commissioner, and when Chet Culver became governor a few months later, the Democratically controlled Senate confirmed Godfrey to the post. Two years later, Governor Culver reappointed him to a full six-year term that would expire in 2015. The Iowa Senate confirmed Godfrey in 2007 and in 2009 with nearly unanimous bipartisan votes.[33]

The following year, Republican Terry Branstad defeated Culver and returned to the governorship in January 2011 after a twelve-year hiatus. A month before being sworn into office, Branstad asked for resignations from a number of state directors and appointees, including Godfrey, a standard practice for incoming governors. Godfrey refused because his term was fixed by statute and he did not serve at the governor's pleasure.[34]

Branstad could not fire Godfrey, but he and his staff—chief of staff Jeffrey Boeyink, legal counsel Brenna Findley, communications director Timothy Albrecht, and Iowa Workforce Development director Teresa Wahlert—made several more efforts to push the commissioner out. None succeeded. Finally, in July 2011, Boeyink and Findley met with Godfrey at Branstad's direction one final time and asked again for his resignation. Boeyink threatened Godfrey with a reduction in his salary if he declined. He turned the governor down yet again, and Branstad cut Godfrey's pay from $112,000 to $73,500, the lowest level legally permissible, before he even got back to his office.[35]

The governor's office gave Godfrey no reason why he was being asked to resign. There was nothing said about his job performance, no discussion about the fact that he was a Democrat among Republicans, no hint that certain business leaders had pressured the governor to appoint a commissioner friendlier to business, and no reference to Godfrey being the only openly gay department head in the Branstad administration.[36]

The commissioner was determined to remain on the job to protect the integrity of his office, but he felt he was facing discrimination and unfair treatment. Godfrey had been in touch with his friend and mentor Roxanne, keeping her apprised of the ordeal, since it began. He asked her for legal help the day after his pay was cut in July. Roxanne immediately contacted Branstad's attorney, Brenna Findley. Roxanne explained that if the administration restored Godfrey's salary and left him alone to do his job, he would consider the matter resolved. Findley replied that the governor did not intend to return his pay to its original level.[37]

At that point, Roxanne declared "all-out war." She was convinced that her client had been wronged, and as always she was laser-focused on winning a legal solution. In January 2012, she filed a $1 million lawsuit on Godfrey's behalf against the state of Iowa, Branstad, Lieutenant Governor Kim Reynolds, Boeyink, Findley, Albrecht, and Wahlert for defamation, harassment, sexual discrimination, and extortion.[38]

Then, in an unusual twist, Branstad went with Des Moines private practice attorney George LaMarca rather than the Iowa attorney general's office to defend the administration. Attorney General Tom Miller concurred, understanding that some of his staff might be called as witnesses and knowing the governor's "strong preference to retain outside counsel."[39]

Branstad and his administration said that discrimination was not a factor and that they were not aware Godfrey was gay until after his salary had been reduced. They claimed the major reason for requesting his resignation was to appoint their own person to the post. That September, the Iowa attorney general issued a scope of employment motion saying that the governor and his staff had acted within their legal job duties when they reduced Godfrey's pay. This meant that Godfrey could sue only the state, not the individuals, but Iowa law forbade the state being sued for defamation, a key part of the lawsuit. His defamation charge was dismissed, and in November a district judge said the attorney general's scope of employment decision was not subject to judicial review.[40]

Roxanne was undeterred. She believed the attorney general's action blocked Godfrey's claims without allowing him due process, and she moved to have the issue addressed by the Iowa Supreme Court. She explained, "We want a decision from the court on this important issue, which basically deprives a person who is defamed by any employee of the state of a remedy."[41]

She got her day in court and won big in June 2014. In a landmark decision, the Iowa Supreme Court agreed with Roxanne, allowing the case against Branstad and his administration to move forward. The court wrote that the attorney general's scope of employment ruling should not be the final word in the Godfrey case and that state employees could be individually liable if they were not acting in the scope of their employment. It then said that the individuals named in the lawsuit—Branstad, Reynolds, and the staffers—could not be removed until a judge did so. Roxanne applauded the decision, which allowed Godfrey's case to go forward. "It's important because nobody's above the law," she observed. "That's a bedrock principle of Iowa jurisprudence. Everybody is accountable for their own action and that includes the governor, the lieutenant governor and members of the staff who defame other people.[42]

By this time, the case had cost the state $525,000 in attorney fees, and these would only go up as it headed toward trial. In his "Civic Skinny" column in *Cityview*, journalist Michael Gartner captured the feeling of a growing number of politicians and attorneys when he wrote, "The state is nuts if it doesn't try to settle the Chris Godfrey lawsuit right away." Unfortunately, it did not. Two months later, Godfrey resigned his state position and accepted a federal appointment in Washington, D.C., as chair and chief judge of the Employees' Compensation Appeals Board. In his letter of resignation, he wrote that he had withstood "unwarranted influence, intimidation and retaliation." But he continued to pursue the lawsuit.[43]

The following spring of 2015, Polk County District Judge Brad McCall dismissed the constitution-based claims of the lawsuit. The decision meant that Godfrey could not sue government officials for alleged violations of his civil liberties protected by the Iowa Constitution.

Specifically, Godfrey claimed his due process and equal protection rights were violated when his reputation was besmirched and his salary decreased for partisan political reasons or because he was gay.[44]

After discussions with Godfrey, Roxanne appealed the decision to the Iowa Supreme Court. George LaMarca found the move "puzzling" since the suit was still moving forward, because Godfrey had made other claims for damages under the Iowa Civil Rights Act. But Roxanne saw an opportunity to develop the law in an area where she had sought change for twenty years. She felt that Iowans should be able to "seek a remedy in damages under the Iowa Constitution when the government trampled on those rights" guaranteed by that document.[45]

The Iowa Supreme Court heard the appeal in September 2016. Nine months later, in June, a divided Supreme Court ruled for the first time that Iowa citizens could sue state officials and seek monetary damages for violations of their civil rights guaranteed by the Iowa Constitution. It was a huge victory for Roxanne, for Godfrey, and for future plaintiffs who believed that the government had violated their constitutional rights.[46]

The case went back to district court, where the trial was set for January 2019. Yet four months earlier, in the fall of 2018, seventy-three-year-old George LaMarca, the attorney for Branstad and the other state officials being sued, withdrew from the case because of poor health. Judge Brad McCall ultimately delayed the trial until June to give the new attorney, Frank Harty, a partner in Des Moines's Nyemaster Goode law firm, time to prepare his defense. LaMarca billed the state just over $1 million for his six and a half years of work.[47]

The Godfrey case remained uppermost in her mind, and Roxanne looked forward to the trial. Godfrey, however, felt they had already enjoyed success, given Roxanne's two big victories in the Iowa Supreme Court. Months before the rescheduled trial was to take place, he explained, "We have already won" because "all Iowans . . . now have a mechanism to hold government itself from being abusive toward its citizens."[48]

By the time jury selection started in the first week of June, Reynolds, Albrecht, and Wahlert had been dropped from the lawsuit, leaving the state, Branstad, Findley, and Boeyink as the remaining defendants. Following a two-day process, the jury was seated, and the long-awaited trial finally began on Wednesday, June 5, at the Polk County Courthouse.[49]

In his opening statement, Frank Harty explained that the governor asked Godfrey to resign as the Iowa workers compensation commissioner because he was considered hostile to business interests. "The most important fact," he said, "is that Terry Branstad didn't know that Chris Godfrey was gay when he made the decisions at issue in this case."[50]

Roxanne countered: "The state, through Terry Branstad, discriminated against Chris Godfrey because he is, and has been for a very long time, an openly gay man." The circumstantial evidence would prove, she continued, that Branstad knew Godfrey was gay. Roxanne noted that the highly charged political atmosphere of the time was important to understand, reminding the jury of the antigay Iowa Republican Party platform of 2010, which included strong stands against same-sex marriage and adoption by same-sex couples, when Branstad was head of the party. This followed the unanimous Iowa Supreme Court decision of the previous year legalizing same-sex marriage. She finally observed that no other executive officers during Branstad's six terms as governor had had their salaries cut. "Chris Godfrey had his salary reduced by 35 percent," she told jurors, and "the only person who had his salary reduced is an openly gay executive officer."[51]

But the trial then took an unexpected turn. After spending four days in the courthouse, Roxanne had trouble breathing. She had a history of chronic obstructive pulmonary disease and believed her current respiratory difficulties were caused by dust and other airborne particulates created by the ongoing renovation of the 112-year-old courthouse. A month earlier, in fact, she had asked that the trial be moved to another building to accommodate her health issue, but the motion had been denied. On Thursday evening Jean Mauss, one of her former law clerks and a local attorney she had hired in December to help with the case, had contacted Paige Fiedler, another former clerk of Roxanne's, and Kim Baer, a friend. Both were prominent plaintiff attorneys in town, and Mauss alerted them to Roxanne's worsening condition.[52]

By the next morning, it was clear that Roxanne could not continue with the trial, and Mauss urgently texted Fiedler to meet Roxanne and her at Nyemaster Goode. Fiedler did, and they called Jim to pick up Roxanne and take her to the hospital. Mauss, Fiedler, and Godfrey then met with the judge and opposing counsel to explain the situation. Fiedler took over as lead counsel until Roxanne could return, and the trial resumed that afternoon.[53]

Roxanne was released from the hospital the following day but was confined to her home through Sunday, June 16. That did not stop her from keeping close track of the trial, however. Mauss remembered that Roxanne remained in frequent contact that first weekend, "reminding us of tasks that needed to be completed or explaining issues regarding the order in which witnesses should be called." After the trial resumed on Monday, Roxanne read the transcript each night and talked to Fiedler, Mauss, and Godfrey by conference call each afternoon after the trial recessed for the day.[54]

Her illness resulted in three more twists in and around the trial. On Monday morning, June 10, son J.B. went into the courtroom before the trial was in session with a technician from a local environmental testing company. He wanted to test the courtroom's air quality, hoping to prove it was unhealthful. J.B. refused to leave when asked to do so by a Polk County deputy sheriff and was arrested for "interfering with official acts." Nonetheless, Polk County officials continued to say that their monitors did not indicate any problem with the building's air quality. Roxanne, meanwhile, filed another motion requesting reasonable accommodation and a change of location. At the same time, Fiedler said she intended to ask for a mistrial if the trial were not relocated to allow Roxanne to participate. "We believe," she said, "that the plaintiff is being prejudiced each day and each hour by Ms. Conlin not being in the courtroom with her knowledge and experience and understanding of the facts and the law of this case."[55]

Then came the dramatic showdown that was not to be. With Roxanne still sidelined, she could not question Terry Branstad, the former governor and current U.S. ambassador to China who would be in town only on

Friday, June 14, to testify. Roxanne and Branstad, of course, had faced off thirty-seven years earlier when he defeated her in the hotly contested 1982 gubernatorial election. The questioning of Branstad fell to Paige Fiedler.[56]

In his testimony, Branstad told the jury that he did not know Godfrey was gay until threatened with the lawsuit and explained that he had asked for his resignation because he had heard negative comments about the commissioner from business groups during the campaign. But Fiedler did get Branstad to admit that he was unaware of the exceptional number of cases Godfrey's office had handled and that the fees businesses paid for workers compensation claims had fallen during Godfrey's time in office. Fiedler also continued to talk of the political climate of the time and played a recording of Branstad from 2010 saying he had been "really shocked" by the Iowa Supreme Court's decision legalizing same-sex marriage and believed "it needed to be overturned with a constitutional amendment."[57]

Although she had had very little time to prepare, Fiedler rose to the occasion, wrote Michael Gartner, the "Civic Skinny" columnist for *Cityview*: "She couldn't have done any better. She was in total command. She flummoxed the governor. Several times he preferred to talk about his accomplishments as governor rather than answer her questions. Several times, Judge McCall had to remind Branstad that he needed to answer Fiedler. Several times, he simply couldn't."[58]

The following week, Roxanne and her team finally succeeded in getting the trial relocated. On Thursday afternoon, June 20, it was moved to the Jasper County Courthouse in Newton, thirty-five miles east of Des Moines. The new venue brought Roxanne back to the courtroom, and a week after Branstad testified, she called her client to the stand. Godfrey told a much different tale, saying the governor had tried to push him out of his job because he was gay. He explained he had "felt personally attacked" after "being asked to resign twice" and then having his "pay slashed." Godfrey said he brought the lawsuit because he "needed justice."[59]

Other witnesses followed, and Roxanne masterfully wove their stories and thousands of evidentiary documents together into a powerful narrative that laid out the case for discrimination. After six weeks spent in two courthouses, the jury agreed with Roxanne, finding that

Branstad, his attorney Brenna Findley, and the state had discriminated against Godfrey, and it awarded him $1.5 million in damages. The other remaining defendant, Jeffrey Boeyink, Branstad's chief of staff, was not held responsible.[60]

Godfrey felt vindicated: "The jury heard my sexual orientation was clearly a motivating factor. This is a win for me and it's a win for the entire gay community in Iowa. It shows that we have sexual orientation in the Civil Rights Act in Iowa for a reason and nobody, not even Terry Branstad, is above the law." Roxanne saw that a wrong had finally been righted. "It's important, indeed critical, that every employee of the state of Iowa be treated fairly, that they be treated like a full human being. That did not happen to Chris Godfrey." She explained, "This was about the way that the governor of the state of Iowa treated a very extraordinarily great workers compensation commissioner, and the jury held that the reason he was treated like that is because he's gay." She continued, "We all agree that's wrong."[61]

The $1.5 million jury award was believed to be the largest ever given to an Iowa plaintiff in a sexual orientation discrimination case. In fact, expert Greg Nevins, an attorney for Lambda Legal, a national group fighting for gay and transgender rights, said the award was the biggest he could remember in a civil rights case focused on sexual discrimination.[62]

In addition to the award, Iowa taxpayers would also be responsible for attorneys' fees and expenses. Roxanne's bill—for her team of attorneys and legal assistants for seven-plus years—came to just over $4 million, while the defense's fees were thought to exceed $2 million. However, the case did not appear to be over. Shortly after the award, defense attorney Frank Harty said he expected to appeal the decision, and two weeks later he filed a motion to overturn the jury's verdict. Harty and his associates referred to the case as a "show trial" and argued in part that Branstad had the authority to cut Godfrey's salary; the jury award was "excessive"; some evidence, such as the Republican Party platform of 2010, should not have been admitted; and there was not enough evidence provided in the trial to prove that Branstad knew Godfrey was gay when he pushed him to resign.[63]

Roxanne, meanwhile, remained certain of the justice of the jury's verdict and promised to respond to the motion. She noted, "The jury decided that Governor Terry Branstad discriminated against Chris Godfrey because he was gay and then retaliated against him after he refused to resign. That is the fact that was decided by the jury and that cannot be overturned."[64]

A few months later in November, Judge McCall rejected the state's motion to overturn the jury's verdict, but later that month, Governor Kim Reynolds decided to appeal the Godfrey case to the Iowa Supreme Court. Roxanne thought the state's move was "deeply dumb," and pledged to keep fighting on Godfrey's behalf. "There comes a time when they should pack it in," she explained. "I will retry this case until the end of my days if necessary. I believe strongly in the principle and I believe strongly in the man and we will fight to the bitter end."[65]

As the continuing Godfrey case makes clear, Roxanne remains committed to doing what she has done for years: standing up for the injured and mistreated regardless of the odds. Good friend and attorney Jerry Crawford explained her success: "When you combine Roxanne's brain with her work ethic, you have an unstoppable force. To top it off, she's one hell of a nice person—at least when she's on your side!" Maggi Moss, another close friend and attorney who had recently retired from the practice of law to focus on her horse-racing business, marveled at her longtime role model's ongoing work in the profession. "I just got burned out," she noted, "the trials, the research, dealing with real-life tragedies; it's physically and mentally exhausting, but Roxanne's stamina is incredible. She's still at it, and she's thriving." Decades earlier, Roxanne's compassion compelled her to fight for others. Doing so today remains her life's purpose.[66]

CONCLUSION: NINE LIVES

"I want to be relevant," Roxanne told daughter Jackie when she was considering a 2010 run for the U.S. Senate. The statement was telling. This burning desire had driven her since childhood. As a youngster, she had conflated relevancy with fame and aspired to be an actor. A high school English teacher altered her course by convincing the teenager to pursue the law, where she could combine her intellect with her flair for the dramatic. This was her ticket to relevancy, which soon intersected with her desire to effect social reform. Through the law and the opportunities it opened, Roxanne would push Iowa to be a more progressive and just place.[1]

Roxanne became relevant almost from the get-go, first bursting onto the public stage as president of the Polk County Young Democrats in her late teens. She has remained in the limelight to this day. But she has differed from many other agents of change by proving to be transformational across a variety of settings in a variety of roles. Like her beloved cats and their fabled nine lives, Roxanne has lived multiple lives, acting as a catalyst for significant change in each.

This interest in making an impact first manifested itself in the early 1960s when the teenager joined the Polk County Young Democrats. Tom Whitney, a longtime friend, an attorney, and then a rising local party leader, recalled meeting Roxanne at the time: "It was immediately clear she was something special." A few years later Patti Huston, a legal secretary at Roxanne's first job out of law school, remembered thinking similarly that the young lawyer's raw intelligence and can-do attitude "destined [her] for greatness."[2]

Indeed, Roxanne's razor-sharp mind and big heart set her apart. Added to these attributes is her supreme self-confidence. Melinda Ellwanger, a longtime associate attorney for Roxanne, noted, "Roxanne has no self-doubt, literally none. She knows where she wants to go and how to get there." Laura Ward, a campaign worker and Roxanne's driver during her 1982 gubernatorial bid, called this her "tenacious certainty." Once she became "filled with a conviction that she was absolutely right," Ward said, there was no stopping her.[3]

Backing up this drive and total self-assurance is Roxanne's indefatigable energy. Amanda Dorr, an assistant U.S. attorney who worked for Roxanne while she served as the U.S. attorney for the Southern District of Iowa, recollected her endless energy: "She wore me out. I don't know how she did all she did. She was a force of nature."[4]

With the Polk County Young Democrats, Roxanne immersed herself in statewide politics, connected with party activists, and rose to head the organization in 1964. She has remained active in the party, serving in various capacities including chairing a number of state political campaigns, chairing the state's Democratic Party, and hosting countless fund-raisers over the years.

She joined the Office of the Attorney General in 1969 and found meaning in protecting everyday Iowans and in heading the Iowa Department of Justice's new civil rights division. She was head of it because, as she often joked, she was the only one in it. She fought race and sex discrimination. Her successes included ousting the entire Board of Supervisors of Worth County for misuse of public funds and winning the landmark *Cedar Rapids Community School District v. Parr* case when the Iowa Supreme Court held that firing pregnant teachers violated the Iowa Civil Rights Act.

At the same time, the ardent feminist founded and then chaired the Iowa Women's Political Caucus, the state affiliate of the National Women's Political Caucus. Intended to raise women's political awareness and increase their participation in the process, the IWPC became the largest state chapter of the NWPC before chapters in California and Texas overtook it. As head of the organization, Roxanne revised the Iowa

Code, replacing all biased language with gender-neutral terminology, and she rewrote Iowa's inheritance and rape laws to make them more equitable for women.

A pioneering stretch as one of the nation's first female U.S. attorneys followed. Here she was especially tough on white-collar crime and drug trafficking. Some of her noteworthy efforts included taking down General Joseph May, head of the Iowa National Guard, for public corruption. She also went after and prosecuted the largest heroin distribution ring in Iowa to date. She unequivocally proved that a woman was up to the U.S. attorney's job, and she paved the way for others to follow.

The pathbreaking achievements continued when Roxanne threw her hat into the Iowa gubernatorial ring. She became the state's first female candidate for governor from a major political party. She won the Democratic primary but lost the general election to Terry Branstad. Iowa may not have been ready for a female governor, but a key mistake during the campaign seriously damaged her chances of winning. Regardless, Roxanne had not gotten the desire for political office out of her system, and in 2010 she aspired to be the first female U.S. senator from the state. She fell short here as well, but she opened the door for Iowa women seeking higher office. As of 2019, Iowa had its first female governor, its first female U.S. senator, and its first two female representatives in the U.S. House—half of its congressional delegation.

By the early 1980s, Roxanne had found her true calling in plaintiff law, which satisfied her natural penchant for helping and protecting others. She quickly became one of the nation's top trial lawyers. Yet even that was not enough. She was soon rattling cages and pushing for change in the Association of Trial Lawyers of America, now the American Association for Justice, the national organization of trial lawyers. After she joined the group, she began moving up through its ranks until she shattered another glass ceiling and became its first female president in 1992. Six women have succeeded her in heading the organization since Roxanne's trailblazing term.[5]

Roxanne's relevance has only grown over her thirty-five-plus years in plaintiff law. She remains on the lookout for cases that address important legal or constitutional issues where she hopes to advance the law for all by winning new legal precedents. Former clerk and current client Chris Godfrey noted, "She takes on big causes and fights for real people . . . making Iowa a safer place to live and work regardless of who you are."[6]

Roxanne continues to make a difference by standing up for those injured by others. Her compassion and commitment, coupled with her single-mindedness in winning clients' cases and her great success at it, keep her in great demand. She still receives 1,200 to 1,500 calls a year for legal assistance because, as local real estate magnate and philanthropist Bill Knapp put it, "If you need a trial attorney, you need Roxanne."[7]

Over the years, there has always been another demand on Roxanne's time: she has been preoccupied with the hundreds of kittens she has fostered for the Animal Rescue League of Iowa. During the lengthy Microsoft trial in 2006 and 2007, she stopped taking the kittens, which led ARL executive director Tom Colvin to grumble about the drawn-out ordeal. "We need her for more important things," he said.[8]

He need not have worried. The trial ultimately ended, normalcy resumed, and Roxanne, who had loved kittens since childhood, returned to her important work as the ARL's leading foster mom.

Although Colvin undoubtedly valued Roxanne's commitment to caring for the kittens, his comment was a bit tongue-in-cheek. Roxanne has played many more significant roles over the last fifty years, positively affecting the lives of countless Iowans in a wide variety of ways. Yet like Colvin, most view her through a narrower lens and see only particular aspects of her life. Today she is largely known as a fierce and highly successful plaintiff attorney and trial lawyer, frequently pursuing groundbreaking cases as she continues to represent victims and the voiceless.

Years ago, when Roxanne discovered she could register and purchase URLs, she bought eight or ten and kept two. Their names only underscore her avocation of bettering the lives of others by bringing and winning lawsuits on their behalf. The website addresses that now take people to the Roxanne Conlin and Associates home page are Suethebadguys.com and Somepeoplejustneedtobesued.com. Indeed, when Dick Calkins, former dean of Drake Law School, wrote that "that lawyer is worthy who lightens the burden of others," he could have been describing Roxanne.[9]

But the law is only the basis for a few of Roxanne's nine lives. Her advocacy on behalf of women informs others. Louise Noun, a leading Iowa feminist and champion of civil liberties, saw her from that perspective: "Roxanne Conlin is the name that immediately comes to the fore when you mention feminism." Roxanne's feminism and her quest for equal rights go to her very core and continue to push her to break down barriers and improve the lives of women across the state and the nation. Leading the way for others, she has become a role model for many young women. As a wife, mother, grandmother, attorney, feminist, political activist and political candidate, ballroom dancer, and foster mom for kittens, she has led a full and accomplished life, epitomizing the phrase "having it all."[10]

Of course, Roxanne is far from finished. At seventy-five, she is going strong, having survived, in her words, "poverty, violence, and multiple sexists along the way." Seeking justice and seeking equal rights remain her two guiding principles, and she still relishes the fight: "I love to win, and I particularly love to win in areas where no person has gone before."[11]

A NOTE ON SOURCES

Much of this book is based on publicly and privately held manuscript collections, the most important of which are listed below, as well as interviews, telephone conversations, and correspondence with people who have known Roxanne over the course of her life.

Papers

J.B. Conlin Papers. Private collection, Des Moines, Iowa.
Roxanne Conlin Papers. Private collection, Des Moines, Iowa.
Roxanne Barton Conlin Papers. Iowa Women's Archives, University of Iowa Libraries, Iowa City, Iowa.
Melinda Ellwanger Papers. Private collection, Las Vegas, Nevada.
Linda Hanson Papers. Private collection, Indianola, Iowa.

Interviews, Telephone Conversations, and Correspondence

Kermit Anderson. Telephone conversation with author, 4 December 2017. Correspondence with author, 19 December 2017.
Deborah Lynch Babb. Telephone conversations with author, 3 April, 17 December 2018.
Kim Baer. Correspondence with author, 28, 29 September 2018.
Raymond Barton. Telephone conversation with author, 9 May 2017. Correspondence with author, 7, 8 July 2017.
Brad Beaman. Telephone conversation with author, 21 August 2018.
Carmela Brown. Interview by author, Urbandale, Iowa, 17 July 2017.
David Butts. Correspondence with author, 11 December 2017.
Richard Calkins. Interview by author, Urbandale, Iowa, 19 September 2018.

Bonnie Campbell. Correspondence with author, 7 January, 12 April 2018; 22 March 2019.

Jackie Conlin. Telephone conversations with author, 20 September 2017; 3 April 2018. Correspondence with author, 27 June, 4 October 2018.

J.B. Conlin. Interviews by author, Des Moines, Iowa, 3 October 2017; 2 March 2018. Telephone conversations with author, 18 June, 28 September 2018. Correspondence with author, 24 October 2017; 2, 13, 29 March, 5, 21 May, 18 June, 22 July, 25, 30 September, 3, 20 November 2018; 28 January, 3, 25 February 2019.

Judy Conlin. Interview by author, Clive, Iowa, 30 October 2017. Correspondence with author, 17 December 2017; 6 July, 8 October 2018.

Roxanne Conlin. Interviews by author, Des Moines, Iowa, 2 May, 26 June, 5 September, 18 December 2017; 10 January, 11 April, 1 June, 14 September, 27 December 2018; 4 February 2019. Correspondence with author, 25 April, 20 May, 3 June, 21 July, 24 October, 5 December 2017; 25 March, 11 April, 4 May, 16, 23, 26 July, 14 November, 17, 19, 22 December 2018; 4 February, 2, 11 March, 10 December 2019.

Jerry Crawford. Telephone conversations with author, 18 April, 13 June 2018.

Mark Daley. Telephone conversation with author, 7 September 2018. Correspondence with author, 14 September 2018.

Judy Beller Dennett. Telephone conversation with author, 16 May 2017.

Tom Duff. Interview by author, West Des Moines, Iowa, 7 June 2018. Correspondence with author, 23, 26 July 2018.

Peggy Dupre. Correspondence with author, 26, 27, 28 July 2018.

Larry Eisenhauer. Telephone conversation with author, 13 June 2018.

Melinda Ellwanger. Telephone conversation with author, 12 July 2018. Correspondence with author, 23 May, 12 July 2018.

Paige Fiedler. Interview by author, Johnston, Iowa, 10 May 2018. Correspondence with author, 25 May, 28 September, 31 October 2018; 30 July 2019.

Joanne Fine. Telephone conversation with author, 27 February 2018.

Regina Barton Finkelstein. Telephone conversation with author, 17
    May 2017. Correspondence with author, 21 May 2017; 5 January,
    7 May 2018.
E. J. Giovannetti. Telephone conversation with author, 10 August 2017.
Chris Godfrey. Correspondence with author, 18 November 2018; 20
    February 2019.
Richard Hagstrom. Telephone conversation with author, 8 August
    2018.
Linda Hanson. Interview by author, Indianola, Iowa, 27 October 2017.
Tom Harkin. Correspondence with author, 5 January 2018.
Linda Heinen. Telephone conversation with author, 2 January 2019.
Phylliss Henry. Telephone conversations with author, 22 September
    2017; 10 January 2018. Correspondence with author, 4, 5 October
    2017; 12, 17 January, 20 July 2018.
Charlotte Hubbell. Interview by author, Des Moines, Iowa, 13
    December 2017.
Rebecca Barton Hudlow. Telephone conversation with author, 1 June
    2017. Correspondence with author, 27 June 2017; 21, 24 June
    2018.
Trudy Hurd. Interview by author, Des Moines, Iowa, 9 November
    2017.
Patty Huston. Telephone conversation with author, 20 July 2017.
Dwight James. Interview by author, Des Moines, Iowa, 12 February
    2018.
Noelle Johnson. Correspondence with author, 22 December 2017.
Sara Quinn Ketcham. Telephone conversation with author, 15 June
    2017.
Michael Kiernan. Telephone conversation with author, 10 September
    2018.
Doug Klein. Telephone conversation with author, 8 November 2017.
    Correspondence with author, 9 November 2017; 28 March, 16
    June 2018.
Michael Kline. Telephone conversation with author, 14 October 2019.
Bill Knapp. Interview by author, West Des Moines, Iowa, 28 April
    2017.
Susan Terry Knapp. Interview by author, West Des Moines, Iowa, 28
    February 2018.

Rox Laird. Correspondence with author, 3 January 2018.

Katherine Lincoln. Correspondence with author, 19 December 2017.

Jean Lloyd-Jones. Telephone conversation with author, 8 September 2017.

Kären Mason. Correspondence with author, 18 July 2018.

Jean Mauss. Telephone conversation with author, 13 August 2018. Correspondence with author, 31 July, 5 August 2019.

Amanda Dorr Meers. Telephone conversation with author, 5 December 2017.

Angie Meyer. Correspondence with author, 30 July, 19 September, 15, 16 November 2018; 7 August 2019.

Maggi Moss. Telephone conversation with author, 10 April 2018.

Linda Channon Murphy. Correspondence with author, 30 May 2018.

John Nahra. Telephone conversation with author, 20 April 2018.

Debbie Conlin Newlin. Telephone conversations with author, 21, 23 December 2018.

Dennis Ogden. Interview by author, West Des Moines, Iowa, 9 March 2018.

Rhoda Barton Olsen. Telephone conversation with author, 23 May 2017. Correspondence with author, 3 July 2017; 5 October 2018.

Gary Ordway. Telephone conversation with author, 24 July 2017.

Patty Barr Petty. Telephone conversation with author, 15 May 2017.

Janey Piersall. Correspondence with author, 2 July 2018.

Melanie Ritchey. Correspondence with author, 23 April 2018.

Cathryn Simmons. Telephone conversation with author, 8 January 2018.

Andrew Smith. Telephone conversation with author, 30 July 2018. Correspondence with author, 30 July 2018.

Hale Starr. Telephone conversation with author, 29 January 2018.

Larry Van Werden. Telephone conversation with author, 12 July 2017.

Laura Ward. Telephone conversation with author, 4 January 2018. Correspondence with author, 14 January, 18, 20 July 2018.

Jeffrey White. Correspondence with author, 18 April 2018.

Tom Whitney. Interview by author, Clive, Iowa, 19 January 2018.

Bill Wickett. Telephone conversation with author, 16 March 2018.

Linda Hedlund Wickett. Telephone conversation with author, 6 March 2018. Correspondence with author, 7 August 2018.

Dawn Stockton Yager. Telephone conversation with author, 22 May 2018. Correspondence with author, 22 May 2018.

David Yepsen. Interview by author, West Des Moines, Iowa, 11 December 2017.

NOTES

Introduction: On a Mission

1. David Yepsen, quoted in Peter Lattman, "Law Blog Lawyer of the Day: Roxanne Conlin," *Wall Street Journal*, 15 February 2007, https://blogs.wsj.com/law/2007/02/15/law-blog-lawyer-of-the-day-roxanne-conlin/.

2. Roxanne Conlin, interview by author, Des Moines, Iowa, 14 September 2018.

3. Ibid., 2 May 2017.

4. Ibid., 14 September 2018.

5. Gary Ordway, telephone conversation with author, 24 July 2017, and Larry Van Werden, telephone conversation with author, 12 July 2017. For the quotation, see Christine Riccelli, "And Justice for All," *dsm*, May–June 2016, 47.

6. *Des Moines Tribune*, 27 June 1974, and Brad Beaman, telephone conversation with author, 21 August 2018.

7. Linda Hanson, interview by author, Indianola, Iowa, 27 October 2017.

8. Andrew Smith, telephone conversation with author, 30 July 2018.

9. On boxing shorts, see Roxanne Conlin, correspondence with author, 19 December 2018. Quotation from Lattman, "Law Blog Lawyer of the Day."

1. A Rocky Beginning

1. Gross national product numbers and median income from William B. Friedricks, *The Real Deal: The Life of Bill Knapp* (Des Moines:

Business Publications Corporation Inc., 2013), 54. Quotation from John Diggins, *The Proud Decades: America in War and Peace, 1941–1960* (New York: W. W. Norton, 1988).

2. Baby boom numbers from Friedricks, *The Real Deal*, 54.
3. David Halberstam, *The Fifties* (New York: Fawcett Columbine, 1993), 508.
4. See Roxanne Conlin's reminiscences in "Biographical Material for Shotwell," 9, and Walt Shotwell, "The Fabulous Feats of a Fan Dancer: The Many Survivals of Roxanne Conlin," unpublished manuscript, n.d., 3. Both documents are in the Roxanne Conlin Papers, private collection held by Roxanne Conlin, Des Moines, Iowa; hereafter cited as Roxanne Conlin Papers.
5. For background on Roxanne's mother's side of the family, see Genevieve Osborn, "Family History of Edward Muraine and William Louis Madden," unpublished manuscript, n.d., Roxanne Conlin Papers. For information on the Barton side of the family, see the Barton Historical Society, Barton Database, https://www.bartonsite.org/. On Bill, Ray, and Grant Barton, see Roxanne Conlin, interview by author, Des Moines, Iowa, 2 May 2017. For more on the agricultural depression of the 1920s, see David Danbom, *Born in the Country: A History of Rural America* (Baltimore, Md.: Johns Hopkins University Press, 1995), 176–196.
6. On South Dakota and the drought, dust storms, and the Great Depression, see Herbert Schell, *A History of South Dakota* (Lincoln: University of Nebraska Press, 1968), 277–297, and Catherine McNicol Stock, *Main Street in Crisis: The Great Depression and the Old Middle Class on the Northern Plains* (Chapel Hill: University of North Carolina Press, 1992), 17–40. On Bill skipping a grade, see Roxanne Conlin, interview, 2 May 2017, and on his graduating with the class of 1940 a month shy of his seventeenth birthday and attending Huron College, see the *Evening Huronite*, 10 September 1943.
7. See Osborn, "Family History," 32.
8. Ibid., 35, and *Evening Huronite*, 23 February, 22 June 1943.
9. On hasty marriages during World War II, see Jane Mersky Leder, *Thanks for the Memories: Love, Sex, and World War* (Westport, Conn.: Praeger, 2006), 17–19. For details of the wedding, see the *Evening Huronite*, 10 September 1943.

10. *Evening Huronite,* 21 March, 10 May, 6 September 1944, and Roxanne Conlin, interview, 2 May 2017. For details on the 97th Infantry Division, see http://www.97thdivision.com/historyp1.html.
11. See http://www.97thdivision.com/historyp1.html.
12. Ibid., and *Daily Huronite,* 10 June 1945, 14 February 1946.
13. Quotation from Michael C. C. Adams, *The Best War Ever: America and World War II* (Baltimore, Md.: Johns Hopkins University Press, 1994), 150. See also Tim Madigan, "Their War Ended 70 Years Ago: Their Trauma Didn't," *Fort Worth Star-Telegram,* http://www.star-telegram.com/living/health-fitness/article44049570.html. On Bill's drinking and gambling during the war and the observation of Eleanor Madden Cleary, see Roxanne Conlin, interview, 2 May 2017.
14. On the divorce rate and the difficulties of veterans adjusting to civilian life, see Madigan, "Their War Ended 70 Years Ago," and Steven Mintz and Susan Kellogg, *Domestic Revolutions: A Social History of American Family Life* (New York: Free Press, 1987), 153–155.
15. Marion William "Bill" Barton, "Recollections of Roxanne's Early Childhood," unpublished typescript, n.d., 1, Roxanne Conlin Papers.
16. On the G.I. Bill—officially the Servicemen's Readjustment Act of 1944—see Lizabeth Cohen, *A Consumers' Republic: The Politics of Mass Consumption in the Postwar Age* (New York: Vintage Books, 2004), 137–146, and David Kennedy, *Freedom from Fear: The American People in Depression and War, 1929–1945* (New York: Oxford University Press, 1999), 787.
17. On the University of South Dakota's University Park, see Sarah Hanson, "University Park and Beyond," Archives and Special Collections Blog, University Library, University of South Dakota, https://archivesandspecialcollections.wordpress.com/category/vets-villa/. On the Barton family in the trailer park, see Barton, "Recollections," 2–4. Quotations from Conlin, "Biographical Material," 1–2.
18. Barton, "Recollections," 2.
19. Ibid. Quotation from Conlin, "Biographical Material," 1.
20. Barton, "Recollections," 4–5.
21. *Daily Huronite,* 7 December 1948, and Roxanne Conlin, interview, 2 May 2017.

22. On the job at W. A. Klinger, see *Polk's Sioux City Directory, 1950* (Omaha: R. L. Polk and Co., 1950), 42. On the births of the other Barton children, see Rhoda Barton Olsen, telephone conversation with author, 23 May 2017.

23. On Sioux City representing the good years and for the first quotation, see Rebecca Barton Hudlow, telephone conversation with author, 1 June 2017. Roxanne's quotation from Conlin, "Biographical Material," 11. See also Roxanne Conlin, correspondence with author, 3 June 2017.

24. Roxanne Conlin, interview, 2 May 2017, and *Sioux City Journal*, 2 February 1982.

25. Ibid. See also Raymond Barton, telephone conversation with author, 9 May 2017, and Rebecca Barton Hudlow, telephone conversation.

26. See Rebecca Barton Hudlow, telephone conversation, and Roxanne Conlin, interview, 2 May 2017.

27. Conlin, "Biographical Material," 6.

28. On the Bartons getting a television set, see ibid., 9. On the impact of television on the decade, see Doris Kearns Goodwin, *Wait Till Next Year: A Memoir* (New York: Touchstone, 1997), 120–122. Quotation from Rebecca Barton Hudlow, telephone conversation.

29. Conlin, "Biographical Material," 12–14.

30. Roxanne Conlin, interview, 2 May 2017, and Patty Barr Petty, telephone conversation with author, 15 May 2017.

31. Raymond Barton, telephone conversation, and Rhoda Barton Olsen, telephone conversation. On the flooding of the Floyd River and Leeds in 1953, see the *Chicago Tribune*, 9 June 1953, and http://www.siouxcityhistory.org/disasters/96-floyd-river-flood-1953.

32. Roxanne Conlin, "Biography—Tape 2," transcript of Roxanne's reminiscences, n.d., 2, Roxanne Conlin Papers.

33. *Ninth Report of the Iowa Library Commission for the Biennial Period July 1, 1916 to June 30, 1918* (Des Moines: State of Iowa, 1918), 6. Quotation from Patty Barr Petty, telephone conversation.

34. For the quotation and more about performing on *Canyon Kid's Kid Corner*, see Judy Beller Dennett, telephone conversation with author, 16 May 2017. For more on the television program, see the *Sioux City Journal*, 31 January 2014, 6 March 2016. For Roxanne's

changing ambitions, see Conlin, "Biographical Material," 1, 11, and Roxanne Conlin, interview, 2 May 2017.

35. Roxanne Conlin, interview by author, Des Moines, Iowa, 26 June 2017.

36. Roxanne Conlin, correspondence with author, 26 July 2018; *Sioux City Journal*, 18 August 2002, 12 June 2010; and https://www.graceland.com/blog/elvis-presleys-tour-dates-in-1956/.

37. Roxanne Conlin, interview, 26 June 2017. See also Raymond Barton, telephone conversation; Rebecca Barton Hudlow, telephone conversation; and Rhoda Barton Olsen, telephone conversation.

38. On changing jobs and moving, see Roxanne Conlin, interview, 2 May 2017, and Rebecca Barton Hudlow, telephone conversation. See also *Polk's Sioux City Directory, 1956* (Omaha: R. L. Polk and Co., 1957), 25, and *Polk's Clinton City Directory, 1957* (Kansas City: R. L. Polk and Co., 1957), 140.

39. Roxanne Conlin, interview, 26 June 2017; Conlin, "Biographical Material," 17; and *Clinton Herald*, 26 April 1958.

40. Conlin, "Biographical Material," 17.

41. Ibid., and Roxanne Conlin, interview, 2 May 2017.

42. Rebecca Barton Hudlow, telephone conversation; Rhoda Barton Olsen, telephone conversation; Raymond Barton, telephone conversation; and Roxanne Conlin, interview, 2 May 2017. See also *Polk's Des Moines City Directory, 1959* (Kansas City: R. L. Polk and Co., 1959), 66. On the products Hot Spot made, see http://www.unionhistories.com/books/ibew-347-history-book-web.pdf, 15. On St. Joseph Academy, see https://www.dowlingcatholic.org/history. St. Joseph's merged with Dowling Catholic High School in 1971, and its facility at 3200 Grand Avenue was purchased by the College of Osteopathic Medicine, now Des Moines University.

43. Walt Shotwell, "Roxanne 1," transcript of interview with Roxanne Conlin, n.d., 2–3, Roxanne Conlin Papers.

44. Ibid., 8; Sara Quinn Ketcham, telephone conversation with author, 15 June 2017; Roxanne Conlin, interview, 2 May 2017; Roxanne Conlin, correspondence with Walt Shotwell, 3 March 2007, Roxanne Conlin Papers; and Becky Kolosik, "Giving a Voice to the Voiceless: Meet Roxanne Conlin," *WOW: Women of Worth*, February–March 2017, 6.

45. Conlin, "Biographical Material," 21, and Sara Quinn Ketcham, telephone conversation.
46. On Roxanne working, see Roxanne Conlin, interview, 2 May 2017, and the *Des Moines Tribune*, 27 June 1974, 15 January 1982. First quotation from Regina Barton Finkelstein, telephone conversation with author, 17 May 2017; second quotation from Sara Quinn Ketcham, telephone conversation.
47. Conlin, "Biographical Material," 19–20, and Roxanne Conlin, interview, 2 May 2017.
48. Quotation from Shotwell, "Roxanne 1," 8.
49. Rhoda Barton Olsen, telephone conversation, and Roxanne Conlin, interviews, 2 May, 26 June 2017.
50. Ibid.
51. Rebecca Barton Hudlow, telephone conversation, and Roxanne Conlin, correspondence with author, 20 May 2017. On Luther Glanton, see Hal S. Chase, "Glanton, Luther T., Jr.," in *The Biographical Dictionary of Iowa*, ed. David Hudson, Marvin Bergman, and Loren Horton (Iowa City: University of Iowa Press, 2009), 189–191.
52. *Polk's Des Moines City Directory, 1962* (Kansas City: R. L. Polk and Co., 1962), 46; *Polk's Des Moines City Directory, 1963* (Kansas City: R. L. Polk and Co., 1963), 46; Roxanne Conlin, interview, 2 May 2017; Roxanne Conlin, correspondence with author, 25 April 2017; Raymond Barton, telephone conversation; Rebecca Barton Hudlow, telephone conversation; Rhoda Barton Olsen, telephone conversation; and Regina Barton Finkelstein, telephone conversation.
53. Roxanne Conlin, correspondence, 3 June 2017; Roxanne Conlin, interview, 2 May 2017; and Rebecca Barton Hudlow, telephone conversation.
54. Michael Kline, telephone conversation with author, 14 October 2019, and Roxanne Conlin, interview, 2 May 2017.
55. Shotwell, "Roxanne 1," 9–10; Roxanne Conlin, interview, 26 June 2017; and *Polk's Des Moines City Directory, 1963*, 46.
56. For the quotations, see the *Des Moines Tribune*, 27 June 1974, and "Roxanne Proves Career and Family Can Mesh," *Central Iowa Commuter*, 28 April 1982, 3. See also Roxanne Conlin, interview, 26 June 2017.

57. *Des Moines Register*, 24 March 1964; *Des Moines Tribune*, 3 February 1982; and *Fairfield Ledger*, 2 March 1982.
58. Roxanne Conlin, "Memorandum Regarding Wedding," 26 February 2014, Roxanne Conlin Papers.
59. Ibid. Second quotation from the *Des Moines Tribune*, 15 January 1982. See also Roxanne Conlin, interview, 2 May 2017.
60. Quotation from the *Des Moines Register*, 10 January 1994.
61. Conlin, "Memorandum Regarding Wedding."
62. Quotation from Walt Shotwell, transcript of interview with Roxanne Conlin and Jim Conlin, 12 April 2007, Roxanne Conlin Papers. See also Roxanne Conlin, correspondence with Walt Shotwell, 29 April 2007, Roxanne Conlin Papers; *Des Moines Register*, 26 March 2017; Roxanne Conlin, interview, 2 May 2017; and Sara Quinn Ketcham, telephone conversation.

2. Raising Her Consciousness

1. First quotation from the *Fairfield Ledger*, 2 March 1982; second and third quotations from the *Des Moines Register*, 9 June 1982.
2. See https://www.americanbar.org/content/dam/aba/administrative/legal_education_and_admissionsto_the_bar/statistics/jd_enrollment_1yr_total_gender.authcheckdam.pdf.
3. Quotation from the *Fairfield Ledger,* 2 March 1982.
4. Susan E. Martin and Nancy C. Jurik, *Doing Justice, Doing Gender: Women in Legal and Criminal Justice Occupations* (London: Sage Publications, 2006), 110.
5. Gary Ordway, telephone conversation with author, 24 July 2017.
6. *Times-Delphic* (Drake University student newspaper), 9 February 1982.
7. Larry Van Werden, telephone conversation with author, 12 July 2017, and Gary Ordway, telephone conversation.
8. Walt Shotwell, transcript of interview with Roxanne Conlin and Jim Conlin, 12 April 2007, Roxanne Conlin Papers, private collection held by Roxanne Conlin, Des Moines, Iowa; hereafter cited as Roxanne Conlin Papers.
9. Jim's quotation from the *Des Moines Register*, 10 January 1994.

10. *Des Moines Register*, 10 June 1982; Roxanne Conlin, correspondence with author, 21 July 2017; and *Polk's Des Moines City Directory, 1965* (Kansas City: R. L. Polk and Co., 1965), 170.

11. *Des Moines Register*, 10 January 1994; Carmela Brown, interview by author, Urbandale, Iowa, 17 July 2017; and Roxanne Conlin, interview by author, Des Moines, Iowa, 26 June 2017.

12. Carmela Brown, interview, and *Des Moines Tribune*, 27 June 1974.

13. Patty Huston, telephone conversation with author, 20 July 2017.

14. Roxanne Conlin, correspondence, 21 July 2017.

15. See Roxanne Conlin to Walt Shotwell, 30 August 2007, Roxanne Conlin Papers; Roxanne Conlin, interview, 26 June 2017; and Louise Noun, *More Strong-Minded Women: Iowa Feminists Tell Their Stories* (Ames: Iowa State University Press, 1992), 121.

16. Roxanne Conlin, interview by author, Des Moines, Iowa, 2 May 2017. Quotation from transcript of Roxanne and Jim Conlin, interview by Walt Shotwell, 12 April 2007, Roxanne Conlin Papers.

17. Roxanne Conlin to Walt Shotwell, 30 March 2007, Roxanne Conlin Papers.

18. Transcript of Roxanne and Jim Conlin, interview by Walt Shotwell, 12 April 2007, Roxanne Conlin Papers, and Carmela Brown, interview. First quotation from http://www.vfa.us/ROXANNE%20BARTON%20CONLIN.htm; final exam story and quotation from the *Fairfield Ledger*, 2 March 1982.

19. Quotation from https://www.veteranfeministsofamerica.org/legacy/ROXANNE%20BARTON%20CONLIN.htm.

20. See Noun, *More Strong-Minded Women*, 122, and Barbara J. Love, *Feminists Who Changed America*, 1963–1975 (Urbana: University of Illinois Press, 2006), 92.

21. Roxanne Conlin, "Biography—Tape 2," transcript of Roxanne's reminiscences, n.d., Roxanne Conlin Papers.

22. Roxanne Conlin, interview, 2 May 2017; *Daily Plainsman*, 19 June 1966; *Des Moines Register*, 13 April 1964, 9 May 1966; and *Dubuque Telegraph Herald*, 10 May 1965.

23. *Des Moines Register*, 13 April 1964, and *Dubuque Telegraph Herald*, 10 May 1965. See also Roxanne Conlin, interview by author, Des Moines, Iowa, 4 February 2019.

24. Roxanne Conlin, résumé, 7 May 2007, Roxanne Conlin Papers.
25. *Des Moines Register*, 31 May, 1, 2, 3 June 1964.
26. For more on Willie Glanton, see the *Des Moines Register*, 7, 12 July 2017, and https://www.americanbar.org/content/dam/aba/migrated/women/margaretbrent/10/glanton.authcheckdam.pdf.
27. Roxanne Conlin, interview, 2 May 2017, and Gary Ordway, telephone conversation.
28. *Des Moines Register*, 24 March 1964. For Glanton's hiring of Roxanne as her campaign manager and the quotation, see "Willie Glanton Talks about Roxanne Conlin," 23 October 2009, YouTube video, https://www.youtube.com/watch?v=UKVU3WcbcSc.
29. *Des Moines Register*, 2 June 1964, and *Cedar Rapids Gazette*, 4 November 1964. First quotation from the *Carroll Times Herald*, 11 July 1964; second quotation from Judy Conlin, correspondence with Walt Shotwell, 19 July 2006, Roxanne Conlin Papers.
30. *Des Moines Register*, 12 July 2017, and Roxanne Conlin, interview, 26 June 2017.
31. *Daily Plainsman*, 19 June 1966, and Larry Van Werden, telephone conversation. For the story about Roxanne intentionally not learning to type, see the *National Law Journal*, 18 December 2001, http://www.nationallawjournal.com/id=900005524901/Roxanne-Barton- Conlin?slreturn=20170609182756.
32. Roxanne Conlin, correspondence, 21 July 2017, and Noun, *More Strong-Minded Women*, 122. Dial Finance later merged with Norwest Bank and eventually became part of Wells Fargo.
33. Quoted phrases about Roxanne from Patty Huston, telephone conversation; Roxanne's statement about Jim from "Roxanne Proves Career and Family Can Mesh," *Central Iowa Commuter*, 28 April 1982, 3. And see Regina Barton Finkelstein, telephone conversation with author, 17 May 2017; Roxanne Conlin, correspondence, 21 July 2017; and *Polk's Des Moines City Directory, 1967* (Kansas City: R. L. Polk and Co., 1967), 193.
34. *Fairfield Ledger*, 2 March 1982.
35. E. J. Giovannetti, telephone conversation with author, 10 August 2017.
36. See Reva B. Siegel, "Introduction: A Short History of Sexual Harassment," in *Directions in Sexual Harassment Law*, ed. Catharine

A. MacKinnon and Reva B. Siegel (New Haven, Conn.: Yale University Press, 2003), 8.

37. Roxanne Conlin, interview by author, Des Moines, Iowa, 5 September 2017.
38. "Life Chronology," Roxanne Conlin Papers.
39. Roxanne Conlin, interview, 5 September 2017.
40. Ibid.
41. *Des Moines Tribune*, 27 June 1974.

3. Change Agent
1. Roxanne Conlin, interview by author, Des Moines, Iowa, 5 September 2017.
2. *Des Moines Tribune*, 15 January 1982.
3. "Roxanne Proves Career and Family Can Mesh," *Central Iowa Commuter*, 28 April 1982, 3.
4. Roxanne Conlin, interview, 5 September 2017, and *Des Moines Register*, 3, 7, 9, 10 January 1970.
5. Walt Shotwell, transcript of interview with Trudy Holman Hurd, n.d., Roxanne Conlin Papers, private collection held by Roxanne Conlin, Des Moines, Iowa.
6. Sharon M. Lake, "The Accidental Feminist: Iowa's Breastfeeding Firefighter and the National Struggle for Workplace Equity," Ph.D. dissertation, University of Iowa, 2010, 358.
7. Iowa Civil Rights Commission, *Annual Report, 1971*, http://publications.iowa.gov/1641/1/annual71casestudies.html, and *Iron Workers Local 67 v. Hart*, 191 N.W. 2d 758 (1971).
8. First quotation and information about the settlement from Roxanne Conlin, interview, 5 September 2017. Second quotation and details of opinion from *Iron Workers Local 67 v. Hart*, 191 N.W. 2d 758 (1971). Third quotation from Lake, "Accidental Feminist," 359.
9. Lake, "Accidental Feminist," 359–360.
10. Roxanne Conlin, interview, 5 September 2017. On Sylvia Roberts, see obituary, http://obits.theadvocate.com/obituaries/theadvocate/obituary.aspx?pid=173795348, and on Roberts and the Weeks case, see Flora Davis, *Moving the Mountain: The Women's Movement in America since 1960* (Urbana: University of Illinois Press, 1999), 61–64.

11. On Ruth Bader Ginsburg and the *Women's Law Review*, see https://web.archive.org/web/20080708192947/http://pegasus.rutgers.edu/~wrlr/index.html, and on Jane Picker, see https://www.law.csuohio.edu/sites/default/files/currentstudents/gavel/Vol60Issue2.pdf.
12. Quotation from Lake, "Accidental Feminist," 360.
13. First quotation from Roxanne Conlin, interview, 5 September 2017. For more on the case and the second quotation, see the *Des Moines Register*, 12 June 1971.
14. *Des Moines Register*, 15 July 1972.
15. Iowa Civil Rights Commission, *Annual Report, 1974*, http://publications.iowa.gov/1555/1/annual74hearings.html, and Roxanne Conlin, interview, 5 September 2017.
16. Lake, "Accidental Feminist," 360, and Roxanne Conlin, interview, 5 September 2017.
17. Phylliss Henry, telephone conversation with author, 22 September 2017, and *Des Moines Register*, 9 January 1972. See also Louise Noun, *More Strong-Minded Women: Iowa Feminists Tell Their Stories* (Ames: Iowa State University Press, 1992), 180–194.
18. Phylliss Henry, telephone conversation, 22 September 2017, and Roxanne Conlin, interview, 5 September 2017.
19. Phylliss Henry, telephone conversation, 22 September 2017. Quotation from Roxanne Conlin, http://www.roxanneconlinlaw.com/Articles/My-Clients-My-Heroe.shtml.
20. On talking to Riley and for the quotation about him, see Roxanne Conlin, interview, 5 September 2017. Roxanne's quotation from Roxanne Conlin, correspondence with author, 11 March 2019. For more on Henry's hiring, see the *Des Moines Tribune*, 31 October, 27 November, 26 December 1972, and the *Des Moines Register*, 7 November 1972.
21. *Des Moines Register*, 23 March 1973.
22. Phylliss Henry, telephone conversation, 22 September 2017, and Roxanne Conlin, interview, 5 September 2017.
23. Linda Heinen, telephone conversation with author, 2 January 2019, and *Des Moines Tribune*, 17 May 1972.
24. Linda Heinen, telephone conversation, and *Des Moines Tribune*, 6 June 1972. For the quotation and the comment about Heinen's inability to bend over, see the *Des Moines Tribune*, 3 October 1972.

See also Roxanne Conlin, correspondence with author, 22 December 2018.

25. Linda Heinen, telephone conversation. For more on the ICRC ruling, see the *Des Moines Register*, 9 December 1972. On Hughes's decision, see the *Des Moines Tribune*, 20 December 1973.

26. The United States Attorney's Office for the Northern District of Iowa press release, "Women's History Month Commemorated," 19 March 2015, https://www.justice.gov/usao-ndia/pr/women-s-history-month-commemorated; *Cedar Rapids Gazette*, 20 March 2015; and Iowa Civil Rights Commission, *Annual Report, 1974*.

27. *Geduldig v. Aiello*, 417 U.S. 484 (1974), and Lake, "Accidental Feminist," 362, n. 184. Roxanne's comment from Roxanne Conlin, correspondence, 22 December 2018.

28. *Cedar Rapids Community School District v. Parr*, 227 N.W. 2d 486 (1975). On the Pregnancy Discrimination Act, see https://www.eeoc.gov/eeoc/history/50th/thelaw/pregnancy_discrimination-1978.cfm. Roxanne's quotation from the *Cedar Rapids Gazette*, 20 March 2015.

29. *Des Moines Register*, 28 August 1975.

30. First quotation from the *Des Moines Tribune*, 15 January 1982; second quotation from the *Des Moines Tribune*, 27 June 1974; and third quotation from Roxanne Conlin, interview, 5 September 2017.

31. *Iowa Civil Rights Commission v. Massey-Ferguson, Inc.*, 207 N.W. 2d 5 (1973). On the extension of the time period for filing a complaint, see the Iowa Civil Rights Commission, *Annual Report, 1974*.

32. Iowa Civil Rights Commission, *Annual Report, 1974*.

33. *Wilson-Sinclair Company v. Griggs*, 211 N.W. 2d 133 (1973).

34. Ibid.

35. *Mason City Globe Gazette*, 6 April 1972.

36. Ibid., 10 April 1972.

37. Roxanne Conlin, interview, 5 September 2017.

38. Ibid., and *Mason City Globe Gazette*, 17, 19 August, 5 September 1972.

39. *Mason City Globe Gazette*, 18 October 1972.

40. *State v. Bartz*, 224 N.W. 2d 632 (1974), and *Mason City Globe Gazette*, 18 December 1974.

41. Noun, *More Strong-Minded Women*, 31–32.

42. *Des Moines Register*, 27 February 1969.

43. Noun, *More Strong-Minded Women*, 33–34.

44. *Des Moines Register*, 25 April 1971.

45. Roxanne Conlin, interview by author, Des Moines, Iowa, 4 February 2019; *Des Moines Register*, 19 January 1972; and Shirley Chisholm, *The Good Fight: A Moving and Hard-Hitting Statement by the Woman Who Ran for President in 1972* (New York: Harper and Row, 1973), 48.

46. See Roxanne Conlin, interview, 4 February 2019, and Shirley Chisholm to Roxanne Conlin, 28 January, 23 March 1972, Shirley Chisholm folder, box 45, Roxanne Barton Conlin Papers, Iowa Women's Archives, University of Iowa Libraries, Iowa City, Iowa.

47. *Des Moines Register*, 28 October 1972. For a list of all the commissioners, see *Iowa Commission on the Status of Women, First Annual Report*, 1 February 1972, 2.

48. *Iowa Commission on the Status of Women, Second Annual Report*, 14. Roxanne's quotation from Roxanne Conlin, correspondence, 22 December 2018.

49. Roxanne Conlin, interview, 5 September 2017; Noun, *More Strong-Minded Women*, 126.

50. *Iowa Commission on the Status of Women, Third Annual Report*, 1 February 1975, 7. See also the *Muscatine Journal*, 25 May 1974; *Des Moines Tribune*, 27 June 1974; and Noun, *More Strong-Minded Women*, 126.

51. Barbara Louise Burrell, "A New Dimension in Political Participation: The Women's Political Caucus," M.A. thesis, Iowa State University, 1975, 24, 30.

52. See *NWPC* 2, the newsletter of the National Women's Political Caucus, February–March 1973, Linda Hanson Papers, private collection held by Linda Hanson, Indianola, Iowa; hereafter cited as Linda Hanson Papers. The other Iowan attending was Mary Lou Houston, a representative of Dubuque's NOW chapter; see Noun, *More Strong-Minded Women*, 7, 124. Roxanne's quotation from Roxanne Conlin, interview, 5 September 2017.

53. Noun, *More Strong-Minded Women*, 124; Burrell, "A New Dimension in Political Participation," 30; and Roxanne Conlin, interview, 5 September 2017.

54. Ibid. Quotation from the Iowa Women's Political Caucus state convention program, 28–30 September 1973, Linda Hanson

Papers. See also press release, "Statewide Meeting Iowa Women's Political Caucus," 3 July 1973, and "Organizing Manual for Local Caucuses," 1973, Linda Hanson Papers.

55. See the Iowa Women's Political Caucus state convention program, Linda Hanson Papers, and the *Ames Tribune*, 23 May 1975.

56. Information about the IWPC's growth from the guide to the Iowa Women's Political Caucus records, http://collguides.lib.uiowa.edu/?IWA0019; Roxanne's quotation from Roxanne Conlin, interview, 5 September 2017; and Smith's quotation from the *Cedar Rapids Gazette*, 27 September 1975.

57. Noun, *More Strong-Minded Women*, 125, and *Mason City Globe Gazette*, 29 September 1975.

58. Roxanne Conlin, interview, 5 September 2017, and *Cedar Rapids Gazette*, 22, 23 September 1974.

59. Ibid., and *Ames Tribune*, 23 September 1974.

60. *Des Moines Register*, 29 September 1975; *Waterloo Courier*, 30 September 1975; *Cedar Rapids Gazette*, 28 December 1978; and https://www.legis.iowa.gov/docs/shelves/code/ocr/1977%20Iowa%20Code%20Supplement.pdf. Quotation about the Women 2000 conferences from the *Estherville Daily News*, 30 April 1976, and for more on these events see, for instance, the *Burlington Hawk Eye*, 18 April 1975; *Fort Madison Evening Democrat*, 17 April 1975; *Des Moines Register*, 9 May 1976; *Dubuque Telegraph Herald*, 17 April 1975; *Mason City Globe Gazette*, 7 April 1975; *Ottumwa Courier*, 31 May 1975; *Jefferson Bee*, 23 August 1976; and *Spirit Lake Beacon*, 6 May 1976. See also the Women 2000: A New Voice for the Future program, 12 April 1975, Linda Hanson Papers, and http://findingaids.lib.iastate.edu/spcl/manuscripts/MS652.html.

61. Iowa Women's Political Caucus newsletter, 1 April 1974, 1, Linda Hanson Papers. See also Carmela Brown, interview by author, Urbandale, Iowa, 17 July 2017, and Roxanne Conlin, interview by author, Des Moines, Iowa, 27 December 2018.

62. *Des Moines Tribune*, 27 June 1974. For the quotation see Linda Hanson, interview by author, Indianola, Iowa, 27 October 2017.

63. *Des Moines Register*, 13 March 1975.

64. Ibid., 27, 28 June 1975; *New York Times*, 30 June 1975; and Noun, *More Strong-Minded Women*, 127, 153–154.

65. For the first quotation see Linda Hanson, interview; for the second quotation see Roxanne Conlin, interview, 5 September 2017. See also the *Des Moines Register*, 20 October 1976.

66. Statement about Roxanne telling Comito she wanted to be governor from the *Des Moines Tribune*, 15 January 1982. For her interest in political positions, see the *Des Moines Tribune*, 27 June 1974, and the *Des Moines Register*, 20 October 1976.

67. Roxanne Conlin, interview, 5 September 2017, and *Des Moines Register*, 20 October 1976.

68. Jim Conlin's quotation from the *Des Moines Tribune*, 15 January 1982, and Jackie Conlin's quotation from Jackie Conlin, telephone conversation with author, 20 September 2017.

69. *Des Moines Tribune*, 16 September 1982.

70. On the American family and the issue of working mothers, see the Pew Research Center, "The American Family Today," 17 December 2015, http://www.pewsocialtrends.org/2015/12/17/1-the-american-family-today/. And see Roxanne Conlin, interview, 5 September 2017, and Jackie Conlin, telephone conversation, 20 September 2017.

71. Roxanne Conlin, correspondence, 24 October 2017; J.B. Conlin, correspondence with author, 24 October 2017; and Jackie Conlin, telephone conversation, 20 September 2017.

72. Ibid.

73. Roxanne Conlin, interview, 5 September 2017; Jackie Conlin, telephone conversation, 20 September 2017; and J.B. Conlin, interview by author, Des Moines, Iowa, 3 October 2017.

74. Judy Conlin, interview by author, Clive, Iowa, 30 October 2017, and Regina Barton Finkelstein, telephone conversation with author, 17 May 2017.

75. Regina Barton Finkelstein, telephone conversation; Rebecca Barton Hudlow, telephone conversation with author, 1 June 2017; and Rhoda Barton Olsen, telephone conversation with author, 23 May 2017.

76. Judy Conlin, interview; Jackie Conlin, telephone conversation, 20 September 2017; and J.B. Conlin, interview, 3 October 2017.

77. Roxanne Conlin, interview by author, Des Moines, Iowa, 26 June 2017.

78. Quotation from J.B. Conlin, interview, 3 October 2017.
79. Debbie Conlin Newlin, telephone conversation with author, 21 December 2018, and Doug Klein, telephone conversation with author, 8 November 2017.
80. Ibid.
81. Debbie Conlin Newlin, telephone conversation, 21 December 2018; Roxanne Conlin, interview, 26 June 2017; Jackie Conlin, telephone conversation, 20 September 2017; J.B. Conlin, interview, 3 October 2017; and Judy Conlin, interview.
82. Roxanne Conlin, interview, 26 June 2017; Debbie Conlin Newlin, telephone conversation, 21 December 2018; and Doug Klein, telephone conversation.
83. Ibid., and Jackie Conlin, telephone conversation, 20 September 2017.
84. Frances Farenthold, "44 Women Who Could Save America," *Redbook* 144 (April 1975), 82–83, 134, 36, 38, 40, and Janet Chan, "Right Now: 44 Qualified Women for the Cabinet and the Supreme Court," *McCall's* 104 (November 1976), 37–38.

4. Trailblazer

1. First quotation from the *Des Moines Tribune*, 27 June 1974; second quotation from Doug Klein, telephone conversation with author, 8 November 2017.
2. Quotation from the *Cedar Rapids Gazette*, 1 March 1981.
3. Quotation from Judy Conlin, interview by author, Clive, Iowa, 30 October 2017.
4. Roxanne Conlin, interview by author, Des Moines, Iowa, 5 September 2017. See also Roxanne Barton Conlin, "The Legal Status of Homemakers in Iowa" (Washington, D.C.: National Commission on the Observance of International Women's Year, 1976). For all the booklets, see boxes 89–94, Roxanne Barton Conlin Papers, Iowa Women's Archives, University of Iowa Libraries, Iowa City, Iowa.
5. Quotations from Conlin, "Legal Status of Homemakers in Iowa," 23–24. See, for example, the *Cedar Rapids Gazette*, 3 January, 8, 21 February, 11 March, 24 April 1977.
6. On the ERA, see Mary Frances Berry, *Why ERA Failed: Politics, Women's Rights, and the Amending Process of the Constitution*

(Bloomington: Indiana University Press, 1986), and Jane J.
Mansbridge, *Why We Lost the ERA* (Chicago: University of Chicago
Press, 1986).

7. On the slowing of the ERA's move toward ratification, see http://
www.equalrightsamendment.org/states.htm.

8. *Des Moines Register*, 17 May 1977.

9. Ibid., 10, 11 September 1977.

10. Ibid., 24 March 1977.

11. For the quotation and background, see Roxanne Conlin, interview,
5 September 2017. See also the *Des Moines Register*, 24 March 1977.

12. *Des Moines Register*, 24 March 1977.

13. Ibid., 25 April 1977.

14. Ibid., 1 May 1977.

15. On the first list of possible candidates, see the *Ames Tribune*,
18 January 1977. Quotation about Soapy Owens from the *Des
Moines Register*, 26 September 1998. Second quotation and the
commission's selections from the *Des Moines Register*, 8 April 1977.

16. *Des Moines Register*, 3 June, 17 September, 11, 29 October 1977;
Jackie Conlin, telephone conversation with author, 20 September
2017; and J.B. Conlin, interview by author, Des Moines, Iowa,
3 October 2017.

17. *Des Moines Register*, 4 November 1977, and *Burlington Hawk Eye*, 13
August 1979. Quotation from the *Des Moines Register*, 9 June 1982.

18. Kermit Anderson, telephone conversation with author, 4 December
2017; Amanda Dorr Meers, telephone conversation with author,
5 December 2017; *Des Moines Register*, 1 November 2017; and
Roxanne Conlin, correspondence with author, 5 December 2017.
See also the *Iowa Official Register* 58 (1979–1980), 110, and the
Iowa Official Register 59 (1981–1982), 119. When Richard Blane
and Don Nickerson left to pursue other opportunities, Roxanne
hired Ron Kayser and Terry Wright.

19. Quotation from the *Cedar Rapids Gazette*, 25 July 1981. On the
crackdown on student loan defaulters, see the *Des Moines Register*,
15 October 1977, and the *Cedar Rapids Gazette*, 27 October 1977.
On the embezzlement case, see the *Des Moines Register*, 12 October
1977, and for the sentence and the second quotation, see the *Des
Moines Register*, 22 November 1977.

20. *See the Burlington Hawk Eye*, 12 May 1978. For the first quotation, see Roxanne Conlin, correspondence with author, 11 March 2019. For the settlement and the second quotation, see the *Burlington Hawk Eye*, 16 May 1978.
21. *Des Moines Register*, 18 July 1979, and *Cedar Rapids Gazette*, 30 October 1979.
22. Kermit Anderson, telephone conversation, 4 December 2017.
23. Quotation from the *Fort Madison Daily Democrat*, 6 September 1978. For more on the arrests and case, see the *Cedar Rapids Gazette*, 6, 7, 8 September 1978; Amanda Dorr Meers, telephone conversation; Kermit Anderson, correspondence with author, 19 December 2017; and Roxanne Conlin, interview by author, Des Moines, Iowa, 18 December 2017.
24. On the heroin case, see the *Cedar Rapids Gazette*, 28 January 1979. On the cocaine case, see the *Cedar Rapids Gazette*, 26 July 1980, and the *Fairfield Ledger*, 7 July 1982. Roxanne's quotation from the *Cedar Rapids Gazette*, 1 March 1981.
25. *Des Moines Register*, 7 December 1977.
26. *Cedar Rapids Gazette*, 26 January 1979. For the quotation, see the *Burlington Hawk Eye*, 3 August 1979.
27. On the trial and verdict, see the *Burlington Hawk Eye*, 5 August 1979, and the *Des Moines Register*, 8 August 1979. For the sentencing and Roxanne's first quotation, see the *Cedar Rapids Gazette*, 7 September 1979; for the second quotation, see the *Cedar Rapids Gazette*, 1 March 1981.
28. *Des Moines Tribune*, 15 January 1982.
29. For a sample of Roxanne's activities on behalf of women during the period, see the *Ames Tribune*, 27 September, 21 November 1977; *Burlington Hawk Eye*, 18 March 1981; *Des Moines Register*, 10, 22 September 1977; and *Cedar Rapids Gazette*, 25 August 1978, 15 March, 18 June, 23 August, 25 October, 2 November 1980. See also Roxanne Conlin, interview, 5 September 2017. Jim's quotation from the *Des Moines Tribune*, 15 January 1982.
30. Roxanne Conlin, interview, 18 December 2017; Noelle Johnson, correspondence with author, 22 December 2017; University of Iowa College of Law course offerings, 1977–1979, University of Iowa College of Law; and Katherine Lincoln, correspondence with

author, 19 December 2017. For the textbook Roxanne used, see Kenneth M. Davidson, Ruth Bader Ginsburg, and Herma Hill Kay, *Sex-Based Discrimination: Texts, Cases, and Materials* (St. Paul, Minn.: West Publishing Co.), 1974.

31. For the first quotation, see Roxanne Conlin, interview by author, Des Moines, Iowa, 4 February 2019. For Roxanne's hobbies, crafts, and the second quotation, see Jackie Conlin, telephone conversation, 20 September 2017. See also Judy Conlin, interview, and Carmela Brown, interview by author, Urbandale, Iowa, 17 July 2017. For Roxanne's statement about Jim, see "Roxanne Proves Career and Family Can Mesh," *Central Iowa Commuter*, 28 April 1982, 3, and for Bear, see the *Des Moines Tribune*, 6 October 1981.

32. On dancing, see Judy Conlin, interview; Trudy Hurd, interview by author, Des Moines, Iowa, 9 November 2017; Roxanne Conlin, interview, 18 December 2017; and David Butts, correspondence with author, 11 December 2017.

33. On the jitterbug contest in Washington, D.C., and Roxanne's jitterbug lessons as auction prizes, see the *Des Moines Register*, 14, 26 April 1984, 29 April 1987.

34. On Jim's hobbies, see Judy Conlin, interview. Jim's quotation from the *Des Moines Register*, 10 June 1982.

35. *Des Moines Tribune*, 5 September 1982.

36. Roxanne Conlin, interview, 5 September 2017.

37. Roxanne Conlin, interview, 18 December 2017.

38. Ibid.; Jerry Crawford, telephone conversation with author, 18 April 2018; and Tom Whitney, interview by author, Clive, Iowa, 19 January 2018.

39. Tom Whitney, interview.

40. Roxanne Conlin, interview, 18 December 2017.

5. Exploratory Effort

1. First quotation from the *Washington Post*, 1 June 1982; second quotation from the *Des Moines Tribune*, 15 January 1982.

2. *Cedar Rapids Gazette*, 12 May 1981.

3. See the Associated Press story in the *Cedar Rapids Gazette*, 1 March 1981, and the *Sioux City Journal*, 1 March 1981. On visiting

with the Villisca Commercial Club, see the *Des Moines Register*, 29 October 1982, and Roxanne Conlin, interview by author, Des Moines, Iowa, 18 December 2017.

4. *Des Moines Tribune*, 5 May 1982.

5. *Des Moines Register*, 6 May 1981.

6. *Des Moines Register*, 12 June 1981. A book on the robbery appeared in 1993, although Roxanne was not interviewed for it; see Debra Weyermann, *The Gang They Couldn't Catch: The Story of America's Greatest Modern-Day Bank Robberies—and How They Got Away with It* (New York: Simon and Schuster, 1993).

7. On Monica McFadden and her background, see the *Washington Post*, 7 March 1983; *Chicago Tribune*, 13 July 1993; *Des Moines Register*, 6 November 1980, 25 January 1981, 9 July 1982; *Des Moines Tribune*, 20 January 1981; Roxanne Conlin, interview, 18 December 2017; and Laura Ward, telephone conversation with author, 4 January 2018.

8. Roxanne Conlin, interview, 18 December 2017; see also Laura Ward, telephone conversation.

9. Ibid.; Phylliss Henry, telephone conversation with author, 10 January 2018; and Regina Barton Finkelstein, correspondence with author, 5 January, 7 May 2018.

10. *Cedar Rapids Gazette*, 10, 24 May 1981.

11. Ibid., 12 May 1981.

12. *Fort Madison Daily Democrat*, 22 May 1981.

13. Roxanne Conlin, interview, 18 December 2017.

14. Quotation from the *Des Moines Register*, 25 July 1981; see also the *Cedar Rapids Gazette*, 25 July 1981. On Turner, see Kermit Anderson, telephone conversation with author, 4 December 2017; *Iowa City Press-Citizen*, 17 December 1981; and *Waterloo Courier*, 2 December 1981.

15. David Yepsen, interview by author, West Des Moines, Iowa, 11 December 2017. First quotation from the *Cedar Rapids Gazette*, 12 May 1981; second quotation from Chuck Offenburger's column in the *Des Moines Register*, 4 October 1981.

16. *Des Moines Register*, 4 October 1981.

17. *Des Moines Tribune*, 25 August 1981.

18. Linda Hanson, interview by author, Indianola, Iowa, 27 October 2017, and Phylliss Henry, telephone conversation, 10 January 2018.
19. *Sioux City Journal*, 7 September 1981, and Roxanne Conlin, interview by author, Des Moines, Iowa, 4 February 2019.
20. On Roxanne closing in on her goal of visiting all ninety-nine counties, see the *Des Moines Register*, 25 September 1981. On the Iowa Poll, see the *Des Moines Register*, 27 September 1981. Other potential Republican candidates included were Tom Stoner, former chair of the Iowa Republican Party, and Arthur Neu, former lieutenant governor. Among all Iowans, 61 percent wished to see Ray as the Republican nominee, followed by Branstad with 14 percent, Stoner with 6 percent, and Neu with 3 percent. Fifteen percent were undecided. On the Democratic side, 37 percent of Iowans preferred to see Hughes as the Democratic nominee, followed by Harkin with 18 percent, Roxanne with 11 percent, Miller with 9 percent, and Fitzgerald with 6 percent. Eighteen percent were undecided.
21. On the role of Bill Knapp and Ed Campbell encouraging Hughes to run, see William B. Friedricks, *The Real Deal: The Life of Bill Knapp* (Des Moines: Business Publications, 2013), 152–153.
22. *Des Moines Register*, 19, 24, 26, 28 September 1981; *Des Moines Tribune*, 25 September 1981; and *Sioux City Journal*, 12 October 1981.
23. *Des Moines Register*, 14 September 1981, and *Des Moines Tribune*, 26 October 1981.
24. *Des Moines Tribune*, 26 October 1981. See also Roxanne Conlin, interview by author, Des Moines, Iowa, 10 January 2018, and Roxanne Conlin to Caucus Member, n.d., Roxanne Conlin Papers, private collection held by Roxanne Conlin, Des Moines, Iowa; hereafter cited as Roxanne Conlin Papers.
25. Roxanne Conlin to Caucus Member, Roxanne Conlin Papers.
26. Ibid.
27. *Des Moines Register*, 20 November 1981. See also Friedricks, *The Real Deal*, 152–153.
28. Roxanne's quotation from the *Quad-City Times*, 20 November 1981. On her decision to run for lieutenant governor if Hughes could enter

the gubernatorial race, see the *Des Moines Tribune*, 4 December 1981, and Roxanne Conlin, interview, 18 December 2017.

29. Friedricks, *The Real Deal*, 153, and *Des Moines Tribune*, 8 January 1982.

30. *Des Moines Register*, 8 January 1982; Campbell's formal announcement and quotation from the *Sioux City Journal*, 29 January 1982.

31. *Des Moines Register*, 4 February 1982.

32. Ray's press conference and quotation from the *Des Moines Tribune*, 18 February 1982; Branstad's surprise and Cox's quotation from the *Iowa City Press-Citizen*, 18 February 1982; and Branstad's getting into the race from the *Des Moines Register*, 18 February 1982.

33. *Des Moines Tribune*, 1 March 1982.

6. A Run for Governor

1. See William B. Friedricks, *The Real Deal: The Life of Bill Knapp* (Des Moines: Business Publications Corporation Inc., 2013), 153–154.

2. First quotation from Tom Whitney, interview by author, Clive, Iowa, 19 January 2018. Other quotations from the *Des Moines Tribune*, 3 May 1982. See also the *Des Moines Register*, 15 March 1982, and Friedricks, *The Real Deal*, 152–154.

3. Campaign donation amounts from the *Fairfield Ledger*, 27 May 1982; see also Friedricks, *The Real Deal*, 153–154.

4. *Des Moines Register*, 15 March 1982.

5. Ibid., 6 May 1982. On Roxanne's renaming the building, see the *Des Moines Register*, 23 August 1998.

6. Phylliss Henry, telephone conversation with author, 10 January 2018; *Des Moines Tribune*, 12 April 1982; and Roxanne Conlin, interview by author, Des Moines, Iowa, 18 December 2017.

7. On the "It's Our Turn" message, see the *Des Moines Register*, 29 October 1982, and on women's roles in campaigns and grassroots movements, see the *Des Moines Register*, 6 May 1982, and the *New York Times*, 4 February 2018. On Henry's skills in overseeing volunteers, see Laura Ward, telephone conversation with author, 4 January 2018.

8. On LuAnn Olson, see the *Des Moines Register*, 9 June 1982; Roxanne Conlin, interview, 18 December 2017; Tom Whitney, interview; Laura Ward, telephone conversation; and Cathryn Simmons, telephone conversation with author, 8 January 2018.

9. Charlotte Hubbell, interview by author, Des Moines, Iowa, 13 December 2017; Roxanne Conlin, interview, 18 December 2017; and *Des Moines Tribune*, 9 July 1982.

10. Tom Whitney, interview; Roxanne Conlin, interview by author, Des Moines, Iowa, 10 January 2018.

11. Ibid.

12. Laura Ward, telephone conversation.

13. Tom Whitney, interview; Roxanne Conlin, interview, 18 December 2017; David Yepsen, interview by author, West Des Moines, Iowa, 11 December 2017; *Iowa City Press-Citizen*, 19 April 1982; *Des Moines Register*, 9 May 1982; and *Washington Post*, 1 June 1982.

14. Roxanne Conlin, interview, 18 December 2017; Tom Whitney, interview; Jerry Crawford, telephone conversation with author, 18 April 2018; and *Des Moines Register*, 15 March 1982.

15. On his instructions to Chapman, see Tom Whitney, interview. Iowa Poll and second quotation from the *Des Moines Register*, 14 March 1982.

16. *Washington Post*, 1 June 1982; *New York Times*, 7 June 1982; Roxanne Conlin, interview, 18 December 2017; Tom Whitney, interview; and Laura Ward, telephone conversation.

17. *Des Moines Register*, 16 May 1982.

18. Roxanne Conlin, interview, 18 December 2017; Tom Whitney, interview; Phylliss Henry, telephone conversation, 10 January 2018; and Laura Ward, telephone conversation. For Flansburg's column see the *Des Moines Register*, 9 May 1982, and for Roxanne's quotation see the *Washington Post*, 1 June 1982.

19. See the *Des Moines Register*, 9 June 1982; *Iowa City Press-Citizen*, 9 June 1982; *Quad-City Times*, 9 June 1982; and *Sioux City Journal*, 9 June 1982. For more on the primary and the quotation, see the *Des Moines Tribune*, 9 June 1982.

20. *Des Moines Register*, 9 June 1982, and David Yepsen, interview.

21. Roxanne Conlin, interview, 18 December 2017; Tom Whitney, interview; Tom Harkin, correspondence with author, 5 January

2018; *Cedar Rapids Gazette*, 10 June 1982; and *Des Moines Register*, 10, 18, 29 June 1982.

22. *Des Moines Register*, 20 June 1982.

23. Tom Whitney, interview.

24. Roxanne Conlin, interview, 18 December 2017, and *New York Times*, 20 July 1982.

25. Quotation from Roxanne Conlin, interview, 18 December 2017. See also Tom Whitney, interview, and Jerry Crawford, telephone conversation, 18 April 2018.

26. *Des Moines Register*, 2 July 1982, and David Yepsen, interview.

27. Branstad's quotation and Roxanne's explanation from the *Des Moines Register*, 2 July 1982. On Governor Ray, see the *Des Moines Tribune*, 6 July 1982, and Jerry Crawford, telephone conversation, 18 April 2018.

28. Roxanne Conlin, interview, 18 December 2017; Laura Ward, telephone conversation; Charlotte Hubbell, interview; and "Talking Points on Question of Roxanne No State Income Taxes/Net Worth Statement," Conlin's Income Tax folder 1, box 72, Roxanne Barton Conlin Papers, Iowa Women's Archives, University of Iowa Libraries, Iowa City, Iowa; hereafter cited as Roxanne Barton Conlin Papers.

29. *Des Moines Register*, 4 July 1982.

30. Tom Whitney, interview.

31. *Des Moines Register*, 11, 12, 14 July 1982.

32. On the signs and bumper stickers, see Judy Conlin, interview by author, Clive, Iowa, 30 October 2017; Trudy Hurd, interview by author, Des Moines, Iowa, 9 November 2017; Tom Whitney, interview; and *Des Moines Register*, 1 August, 14 October 1982.

33. *Des Moines Register*, 14, 16 July 1982. Ads for the seminar ran in the *Des Moines Register*, 4, 11 July 1982.

34. For the column, see "Letters from Lackey," *Des Moines Register*, 22 July 1982.

35. *Sioux City Journal*, 15 July 1982; *New York Times*, 20 July 1982; and *Des Moines Tribune*, 15 September 1982.

36. *Sioux City Journal*, 31 July 1982. On the "tax flap" phrase, see the *Des Moines Register*, 11 July 1982. Interestingly Bob Case, a political reporter for the *Waterloo Courier*, used the same phrase in an article on Roxanne's tax issue that ran the same day; see the

Waterloo Courier, 11 July 1982. For the Iowa Poll, see the *Des Moines Register*, 1 August 1982.

37. *Des Moines Register*, 12 September 1982, and *Des Moines Tribune*, 13 September 1982.

38. *Des Moines Register*, 12 September 1982.

39. Cathryn Simmons, telephone conversation, and Roxanne Conlin, interview, 18 December 2017.

40. Roxanne Conlin, interviews, 18 December 2017, 10 January 2018; Tom Whitney, interview; and Cathryn Simmons, telephone conversation.

41. Cathryn Simmons, telephone conversation.

42. Ibid., and Tom Whitney, interview.

43. Cathryn Simmons, telephone conversation; Laura Ward, telephone conversation; and Roxanne Conlin, interview, 10 January 2018.

44. "Invest in Iowa Bond Issue," Conlin's Bond Proposal folder 1, Roxanne Barton Conlin Papers; *Iowa City Press-Citizen*, 6 October 1982; *Waterloo Courier*, 19 September, 19 October 1982; *Quad-City Times*, 20 October 1982; Roxanne Conlin, interview, 10 January 2018; and Cathryn Simmons, telephone conversation.

45. *Des Moines Register*, 27 September, 10, 24 October 1982.

46. On advertising, see Cathryn Simmons, telephone conversation. On the last two debates, see the *Des Moines Register*, 12, 13, 30 October 1982. Also see Tom Whitney, interview.

47. Tom Whitney, interview. For the speech, see "Original Draft of Jefferson-Jackson Dinner Speech," Campaign Speeches: Jefferson-Jackson Dinner folder, Roxanne Barton Conlin Papers. For the writing of the speech and the quotation, see Laura Ward, correspondence with author, 18 July 2018, and for coverage of the speech, see the *Des Moines Register*, 17 October 1982.

48. Ibid.

49. Tom Whitney, interview.

50. Ibid.

51. Ibid.; Cathryn Simmons, telephone conversation; and Laura Ward, telephone conversation.

52. Ray's quotation from the *Des Moines Register*, 19 October 1982. On Branstad keeping the issue in the news, see Tom Whitney, interview, and the *Des Moines Register*, 24 October 1982.

53. On newspapers supporting Branstad, see the *Des Moines Register*, 30 October 1982. And see the *Des Moines Register*, 24 October 1982, for its endorsement of Roxanne.
54. *Des Moines Register*, 26, 29 October 1982.
55. For the first quotation and the Iowa Poll, see the *Des Moines Register*, 31 October 1982. See also Roxanne Conlin, interviews, 18 December 2017, 10 January 2018; Tom Whitney, interview; and Cathryn Simmons, telephone conversation.
56. On Crawford watching the returns, see Jerry Crawford, telephone conversation, 18 April 2018; Roxanne Conlin, interview, 18 December 2017; and Tom Whitney, interview. For the election and results, see the *Des Moines Register*, 3 November 1982.
57. *Des Moines Register*, 3, 4 November 1982.
58. On the polling firm's estimates and women's beliefs, see the *Des Moines Register*, 20 August 1984.
59. See Roxanne Conlin, interview, 18 December 2017. Political reporter David Yepsen and adviser Jerry Crawford agreed with Roxanne that the tax issue gave voters who felt uncomfortable about opposing a woman an acceptable reason to vote against her. See David Yepsen, interview, and Jerry Crawford, telephone conversation, 18 April 2018.
60. For Roxanne's comments on *Iowa Press* about her inexperience, see the *Des Moines Register*, 25 October 1982. See also Cathryn Simmons, telephone conversation; Phylliss Henry, telephone conversation, 10 January 2018; Laura Ward, telephone conversation; Tom Whitney, interview; and David Yepsen, interview.
61. David Yepsen, interview. For more on Branstad, see the *Des Moines Register*, 4 November 1982.
62. David Yepsen, interview.

7. Bouncing Back

1. "Devastated" was the word commonly used to describe Roxanne after her election loss. See Carmela Brown, interview by author, Urbandale, Iowa, 17 July 2017; J.B. Conlin, interview by author, Des Moines, Iowa, 2 March 2018; Judy Conlin, interview by author, Clive, Iowa, 30 October 2017; Trudy Hurd, interview by

author, Des Moines, Iowa, 9 November 2017; and Laura Ward, telephone conversation with author, 4 January 2018.

2. On Roxanne breaking down in the car, see Judy Conlin, interview, and on feeling she had let her supporters down, see Roxanne Conlin, interview by author, Des Moines, Iowa, 18 December 2017.

3. Cathryn Simmons, telephone conversation with author, 8 January 2018; quotation from Roxanne Conlin, interview, 18 December 2017.

4. Roxanne Conlin, interview, 18 December 2017.

5. Laura Ward, telephone conversation. For Roxanne at home, see Carmela Brown, interview.

6. Roxanne Conlin, interview, 18 December 2017.

7. Hale Starr, telephone conversation with author, 29 January 2018, and Joanne Fine, telephone conversation with author, 27 February 2018.

8. Ibid.; Roxanne Conlin, interview by author, Des Moines, Iowa, 10 January 2018; Susan Terry Knapp, interview by author, West Des Moines, Iowa, 28 February 2018; and transcript of Elaine Symoniak, interview by Walt Shotwell, n.d., Roxanne Conlin Papers, private collection held by Roxanne Conlin, Des Moines, Iowa; hereafter cited as Roxanne Conlin Papers.

9. Ibid.

10. Quotation from Joanne Fine, telephone conversation. See also Susan Terry Knapp, interview; Hale Starr, telephone conversation; *Des Moines Register*, 21, 28 July 1986, 5 October 1987; Roxanne Conlin, interview, 10 January 2018; and J.B. Conlin, interview, 2 March 2018.

11. *Des Moines Register*, 29 April 1983, 26 April 1984, and Roxanne Conlin, interview by author, Des Moines, Iowa, 27 December 2018.

12. Quotation from Roxanne Conlin, interview, 18 December 2017. See also Eugene Kennedy, "John Glenn's Presidential Countdown," *New York Times Magazine*, 11 October 1981, https://www.nytimes.com/1981/10/11/magazine/john-glenn-s-presidential-countdown.html?pagewanted=all; *Des Moines Register*, 22 April 1983; and *Washington Post*, 7 March 1983.

13. For a thoughtful piece on John Glenn and his presidential run, see Jeff Greenfield, "John Glenn, Hero and Political Cautionary Tale," *Politico Magazine*, 8 December 2016, https://www.politico.com/magazine/story/2016/12/john-glenn-cautionary-tale-214510.

14. Roxanne Conlin, correspondence with author, 2 March 2019.
15. Roxanne Conlin, interview by author, Des Moines, Iowa, 4 February 2019. For specific information on the Legal Defense and Education Fund (renamed Legal Momentum in 2004), its history, and the quotations, see https://www.legalmomentum.org.
16. Hale Starr, telephone conversation. Quotation on ATLA from the *Washington Post*, 2 May 2010.
17. Dwight James, interview by author, Des Moines, Iowa, 12 February 2018; Roxanne Conlin, interview, 10 January 2018; Bill Wickett, telephone conversation with author, 16 March 2018; and *Burlington Hawk Eye*, 16 May 1978.
18. Roxanne Conlin, interview, 18 December 2017.
19. Ibid.; see also the *Iowa City Press-Citizen*, 14 October 1983.
20. Quoted topics of seminars from ATLA's website, https://www.justice.org/who-we-are/mission-history/expanded-history-association-trial-lawyers-america-atla%C2%AEamerican; second quotation from Dwight James, interview.
21. Dwight James, interview.
22. *Des Moines Register*, 5 March 1989, 6 August 1991, and Roxanne Conlin, interview, 4 February 2019.
23. Dwight James, interview.
24. Dennis Ogden, interview by author, West Des Moines, Iowa, 9 March 2018.
25. Roxanne Conlin, interview, 18 December 2017, and Dennis Ogden, interview.
26. *Centerpiece*, December 1985, 457. *Centerpiece* was an ATLA publication; see Roxanne's website, https://www.roxanneconlinlaw.com/Press-Room/Police-Officer-Injured-by-a-Drunk-Driver.pdf. See also the *Des Moines Register*, 5 October 1985; Dennis Ogden, interview; and Roxanne Conlin, interview by author, Des Moines, Iowa, 11 April 2018.
27. *Sioux City Journal*, 23 July 1987, and *Des Moines Register*, 11 February 1984.
28. Dennis Ogden, interview. Quotation from the *Des Moines Register*, 5 March 1989.
29. *Des Moines Register*, 5 March 1989, and Roxanne Conlin, interview, 11 April 2018.

30. Ibid., and *Centerpiece*, December 1985, 457.

31. *Des Moines Register*, 5 October 1985.

32. Roxanne Conlin, interview, 18 December 2017; Dwight James, interview; Dennis Ogden, interview; Linda Hedlund Wickett, telephone conversation with author, 6 March 2018; and *Des Moines Register*, 2 November 1987.

33. *Des Moines Register*, 23 June 1985.

34. *Des Moines Register*, 13 October, 20 November 1985, 30 January 1986. For the quotation, see the *Des Moines Register*, 3 October 1986.

35. Jerold McMillen, "Civil Rights—Maintaining a Sexually Hostile Work Environment through Sexual Harassment Is a Form of Illegal Sex Discrimination under Section 601A(1)(a) of the Iowa Civil Rights Act—*Lynch v. City of Des Moines*, 454 N.W. 2d 827 (Iowa 1990)," *Drake Law Review* 41 (1992), 563–564; *Lynch v. City of Des Moines*, 454 N.W. 2d 827 (Iowa 1990), http://publications. iowa.gov/1651/1/lynchsc.html; and Deborah Lynch Babb, telephone conversation with author, 3 April 2018.

36. Ibid., and *Des Moines Register*, 15 July, 8 December 1988.

37. Deborah Lynch Babb, telephone conversation, 3 April 2018.

38. *Des Moines Register*, 19 July 1988. See also Roxanne Conlin, interview, 18 December 2017, and Deborah Lynch Babb, telephone conversation, 3 April 2018.

39. See the *Des Moines Register*, 19 July 1988, 24 December 1990, and *Lynch v. City of Des Moines*, 454 N.W. 2d. 830 (Iowa 1990). Quotation from Dwight James, interview. See also Roxanne Conlin, correspondence, 2 March 2019.

40. *Des Moines Register*, 8, 10 December 1988.

41. Ibid., 8 December 1988.

42. On her fees, see the *Des Moines Register*, 7 February 1989. Roxanne's quotation from the *Des Moines Register*, 5 March 1989.

43. *Des Moines Register*, 22 July 1989, 20 December 1990.

44. *Des Moines Register*, 19 April, 20 December 1990. For the editorial, see the *Des Moines Register*, 24 December 1990. See also McMillen, "Civil Rights," 572.

45. Deborah Lynch Babb, telephone conversation, 3 April 2018.

46. *Des Moines Register*, 1 June 1988; Jerry Crawford, telephone conversation with author, 18 April 2018; and Roxanne Conlin, interview, 10 January 2018.

47. Ibid.
48. *Des Moines Register*, 4 October 1988.
49. Ibid., 23 May 1991. Capitol Intermediaries later became Sullivan Payne Company.
50. Ibid., and Charles Levenstein and John Wooding, *Work, Health, and Environment: Old Problems, New Solutions* (New York: Guilford Press, 1997), 201–202.
51. *Des Moines Register*, 13 June 1991. For the quotation and more on the case, see the *Des Moines Register*, 27 January 1995.
52. *Des Moines Register*, 23 May 1991.
53. Ibid., 13 June 1991.
54. Ibid., 21 September 1991, 27 January 1995, and Roxanne Conlin, interview, 11 April 2018.
55. See William B. Friedricks, *The Real Deal: The Life of Bill Knapp* (Des Moines: Business Publications Corporation Inc., 2013), 149.
56. *Business Record*, 3–9 December 1984, and *Des Moines Register*, 1 December 1984.
57. *Des Moines Register*, 5 October 1986, 18 June 1987, and Debbie Conlin Newlin, telephone conversation with author, 21 December 2018.
58. Debbie Conlin Newlin, telephone conversation, 21 December 2018; Roxanne Conlin, interview, 18 December 2017; and *Des Moines Register*, 18 January, 29 July 1984, 18 June 1987.
59. Roxanne Conlin, correspondence with author, 25 March 2018; *Des Moines Register*, 5 March 1989; and Debbie Conlin Newlin, telephone conversation, 21 December 2018.
60. Roxanne Conlin, interview, 11 April 2018, and Debbie Conlin Newlin, telephone conversation, 21 December 2018. For more on her smoking and her quotations, see Roxanne Conlin, correspondence, 25 March 2018. The other quotation is from Linda Hedlund Wickett, telephone conversation.
61. Doug Klein, correspondence with author, 28 March 2018.
62. Jackie Conlin, telephone conversations with author, 20 September 2017, 3 April 2018; Roxanne Conlin, interview, 11 April 2018; and J.B. Conlin, interview, 2 March 2018.
63. Ibid.
64. J.B. Conlin, interview, 2 March 2018, and *Iowa City Press-Citizen*, 11 September 1989.

65. J.B. Conlin, interview, 2 March 2018.

66. *Des Moines Register*, 5 March 1989.

67. Roxanne Conlin, interview, 11 April 2018, and Jeffrey White, correspondence with author, 18 April 2018. On the Sumner Simpson Papers, see the *Washington Post*, 12 November 1978, and http://www.law.harvard.edu/publications/evidenceiii/cases/threadg.htm. Raybestos-Manhattan is now Raymark.

68. Roxanne Conlin, interview, 11 April 2018. For Martin's letter, see https://www.ewg.org/research/document-gallery/martin-letter-1966. Bendix is now part of Honeywell.

69. Ibid.

70. Roxanne Conlin, interview, 11 April 2018, and Dwight James, interview.

71. *Des Moines Register*, 25 June 1989, and Roxanne Conlin, interview, 11 April 2018.

72. Bill Wickett, telephone conversation, and Dennis Ogden, interview.

73. Dwight James, interview, and Roxanne Conlin, interview, 11 April 2018.

74. Quotation from the *Quad-City Times*, 7 March 1990. See also the *Quad-City Times*, 14 January, 6 March 1990.

75. Roxanne Conlin, interview, 11 April 2018. For the quotation and more on the case, see the *Des Moines Register*, 28 July 1990.

76. Roxanne Conlin, interview, 11 April 2018, and *Des Moines Register*, 15 September 1990, 18 February 1993.

77. *Des Moines Register*, 8 September 1990.

78. *Waterloo Courier*, 23 November, 30 December 1990, and Roxanne Conlin, interview, 11 April 2018.

79. John Nahra, telephone conversation with author, 20 April 2018.

80. Ibid., and Melanie Ritchey, correspondence with author, 23 April 2018.

81. Ibid.; *Des Moines Register*, 17 November 2002; and Roxanne Conlin, interview, 11 April 2018.

82. Roxanne Conlin, interview, 11 April 2018, and *Des Moines Register*, 6 April, 8 May 1991.

83. Roxanne Conlin, interview, 11 April 2018.

84. Ibid.

85. Ibid., and Roxanne Conlin, correspondence, 25 March 2018. For
more on Jim's health and the quotation, see J.B. Conlin, interview,
2 March 2018.
86. On Phillis Porter's death, see the *Des Moines Register*, 9 November
1991; for the quotation, see the *Des Moines Register*, 30 May 1993.
87. Roxanne Conlin, interview, 11 April 2018, and J.B. Conlin,
interview, 2 March 2018.
88. Roxanne Conlin, interview, 11 April 2018, and Jody Hayes, "West
Des Moines Police Department Case Investigation Report, 92-
2413, 23 June 1992," Roxanne Conlin Papers.
89. Ibid.
90. Ibid. See also Jerry Crawford, telephone conversation, 18 April
2018, and Maggi Moss, telephone conversation with author,
10 April 2018.
91. For the article and the mug shot, see the *Des Moines Register*, 25
June 1992. On Roxanne's reaction, see Roxanne Conlin, interview,
11 April 2018; Roxanne Conlin, correspondence, 25 March 2018;
and J.B. Conlin, interview, 2 March 2018. For the letters to the
editor, see the *Des Moines Register*, 2 July 1992. Overholser offered
an explanation of the decision to run the mug shot but readers did
not buy it, and they again sent the paper letters calling it a mistake;
see the *Des Moines Register*, 2, 9 July 1992.
92. *Des Moines Register*, 14 August 1992; Stan Haugland to Maggi
Moss, 10 November 1992, Roxanne Conlin Papers; and Roxanne
Conlin, interview, 11 April 2018.
93. *Des Moines Register*, 10 September 1993, and *Sioux City Journal*,
20 March 1994.
94. On being recognized as one of the top ten trial lawyers by the
National Law Journal, see the *Des Moines Register*, 5 March 1989;
on being named one of the hundred most influential lawyers in the
country, see "Profiles in Power: The 100 Most Influential Lawyers
in America," *National Law Journal*, 25 March 1991, 12.
95. *Des Moines Register*, 27 October 1992. Actually, Roxanne began
donating her papers to the University of Iowa Libraries in the 1970s
at the request of special collections librarian Robert McCown. He
contacted her in 1972, when she was an assistant attorney general,
explaining that the university was "attempting to collect the personal

papers of prominent Iowans," and he asked her to donate her papers. They visited a couple of times over the next two years, and she initially donated five boxes of her papers in 1975. She continued adding to the collection, and when the Iowa Women's Archives opened in 1992, her papers were appropriately moved to the new entity; see Kären Mason, correspondence with author, 18 July 2018.

96. Car accident story and quotation from the *Des Moines Register*, 5 March 1989. Lipsman's quotation from Roxanne's website, https://www.roxanneconlinlaw.com/.

8. Hear Me Roar

1. Dwight James, interview by author, Des Moines, Iowa, 12 February 2018; Maggi Moss, telephone conversation with author, 10 April 2018; and Paige Fiedler, interview by author, Johnston, Iowa, 10 May 2018.

2. Roxanne Conlin, "Living with Losing," *Trial*, March 1993. This was one of her twelve ATLA presidential columns, collected in Trial: President's Pages, 1992–1993, Roxanne Barton Conlin, Roxanne Conlin Papers, private collection held by Roxanne Conlin, Des Moines, Iowa; hereafter cited as Roxanne Conlin Papers.

3. Judy Conlin, interview by author, Clive, Iowa, 30 October 2017.

4. Roxanne Conlin, correspondence with author, 25 March 2018. See also Jeffrey White, correspondence with author, 18 April 2018.

5. Ibid. On Roxanne's coronation, see Joanne Fine, telephone conversation with author, 27 February 2018.

6. Roxanne Conlin, "Strength in Diversity," *Trial*, August 1992, in Trial: President's Pages, Roxanne Conlin Papers.

7. *Des Moines Register*, 24 May 1993. On Rush Limbaugh, see Roxanne Conlin, correspondence with author, 2 March 2019.

8. Ibid.

9. Roxanne Conlin, interview by author, Des Moines, Iowa, 1 June 2018; Paige Fiedler, interview; and Dawn Stockton Yager, telephone conversation with author, 22 May 2018.

10. Ibid., and *Des Moines Register*, 24 May 1993.

11. Roxanne Conlin, correspondence with author, 4 May 2018; Paige Fiedler, interview; Dawn Stockton Yager, telephone conversation;

and Larry Eisenhauer, telephone conversation with author,
13 June 2018.

12. Ibid. See also Dawn Stockton Yager, telephone conversation.

13. *Falczynski v. Amoco Oil Co.*, 533 N.W. 2d 226 (1995).

14. Ibid.

15. Ibid.; *Falczynski v. Amoco Oil Co.*, 567 N.W. 2d 447 (1997); and
Roxanne Conlin, interview, 1 June 2018.

16. The medical malpractice case Roxanne lost was *Langner v. Simpson*,
533 N.W. 2d 511 (1995). Here the Iowa Supreme Court upheld
the lower court's opinion that Roxanne's client, Kathy Langner,
had filed her claim of medical malpractice, which took place in
the 1980s, against psychiatrist Floyd Simpson, Spencer Municipal
Hospital, counselor Brian Neboda, and Northwest Iowa Mental
Health Center after the statute of limitations had run out. The
court did not accept Roxanne's arguments that the statute of
limitations should be extended because Langner discovered her
injuries only in 1990 or 1991, Simpson and the hospital conspired
to conceal her injuries, and Langner was mentally ill at the time she
was injured. Quotation from Conlin, "Living with Losing."

17. Roxanne Conlin, interview, 1 June 2018.

18. Ibid. See also Tom Duff, interview by author, West Des Moines,
Iowa, 7 June 2018.

19. Melinda Ellwanger, telephone conversation with author, 12 July
2018; Dawn Stockton Yager, telephone conversation; and Tom
Duff, interview.

20. Tom Duff, interview; Melinda Ellwanger, correspondence with
author, 23 May 2018; and Roxanne Conlin, interview, 1 June 2018.

21. Maggi Moss, telephone conversation, and *Des Moines Register*, 16,
26, 28 September 1995.

22. Ibid.; see also the *Des Moines Register*, 6 October 1995. Quotation
from the *Des Moines Register*, 15 October 1995.

23. For the story on media priorities, see the *Des Moines Register*, 30
September 1995, and for Moss and Roxanne's letter, see the *Des
Moines Register*, 11 October 1995. Sadly, puppy mills are still a fact
of life in Iowa. The Humane Society's annual "Horrible Hundred"
list of the worst puppy mills across the country included ten Iowa
breeders in 2018; see the *Des Moines Register*, 18 May 2018.

24. Roxanne Conlin, interview, 1 June 2018, and *Des Moines Register*, 24 May 1996.

25. Ibid., and *Bleimehl v. Eastman Kodak Co.*, 4-93-CV-307-2 (S.D. Iowa Jan. 27, 1997).

26. Roxanne Conlin, interview, 1 June 2018. Along with more than eighty other Iowa municipal agencies, Cerro Gordo County invested in the Iowa Trust Fund. Created in 1989, the fund pooled investments of such entities with the intent of providing greater returns. Unfortunately, money manager Steven Wimer bilked investors out of millions of dollars. He was ultimately convicted of fraud and sent to prison. See the *Dubuque Telegraph Herald*, 31 January 2003, and William B. Friedricks, *In for the Long Haul: The Life of John Ruan* (Ames: Iowa State University Press, 2003), 209–210.

27. On the Gallion case in general, see the *Mason City Globe Gazette*, 20 November, 28 December 1996. The phrase "high age-related salary" is from https://www.roxanneconlinlaw.com/Case-Summaries/Case-Summaries-Employment-Discrimination.shtml. Roxanne's quotation from the *Des Moines Register*, 20 November 1996.

28. *Mason City Globe Gazette*, 28 December 1996; see also Roxanne Conlin, interview, 1 June 2018.

29. See the *Sioux City Journal*, 26 October 1998.

30. *Des Moines Register*, 13, 20 February, 25 April 1998; Roxanne Conlin, interview, 1 June 2018; and Linda Channon Murphy, correspondence with author, 30 May 2018.

31. Ibid. For Channon's quote, see Linda Channon Murphy, correspondence; for Roxanne's quote, see the Associated Press story in the *Minneapolis Star Tribune*, 13 February 1998.

32. Linda Channon Murphy, correspondence, and *Des Moines Register*, 20 February 1998.

33. Ibid., and Roxanne Conlin, interview, 1 June 2018. For more on the trial and the headline, see the *Des Moines Register*, 13 February 1998.

34. *Des Moines Register*, 13 February 1998.

35. Ibid.

36. *Channon v. UPS*, 629 N.W. 2d 835 (Iowa 2001); see also the *Des Moines Register*, 26 September 2001.

37. Linda Channon Murphy, correspondence, and Roxanne Conlin, interview, 1 June 2018.
38. Ibid.
39. *Des Moines Register*, 27 February 1999. See also Roxanne Conlin, interview, 1 June 2018.
40. *Waterloo Courier*, 26 March 1999; *Madison v. IBP, Inc.*, 536 U.S. 919 (2002); Roxanne Conlin, interview, 1 June 2018; and Tom Duff, interview.
41. Roxanne Conlin, interview, 1 June 2018, and Tom Duff, interview.
42. *Vivian v. Madison*, 601 N.W. 2d 872 (Iowa 1999).
43. Ibid. See also Tory Lucas, "Supervisors Individually Liable under the Iowa Civil Rights Act," *Iowa Lawyer*, 1 June 2001, 22–25, and Roxanne Conlin, interview, 1 June 2018.
44. Quotation from the *Des Moines Register*, 5 March 1989.
45. *Des Moines Register*, 29 September 1993.
46. Roxanne Conlin, correspondence, 4 May 2018; Roxanne Conlin, interview, 1 June 2018; and J.B. Conlin, correspondence with author, 21 May 2018.
47. *Des Moines Register*, 29 September, 29 October 1993.
48. First two quotations from the *Des Moines Register*, 19 October 1993; next two quotations from the *Des Moines Register*, 24 October 1993. See also the *Des Moines Register*, 23, 29 October 1993.
49. *Des Moines Register*, 3 November 1993. For Roxanne's reaction, see Roxanne Conlin, correspondence, 4 May 2018.
50. *Des Moines Register*, 10 January 1994.
51. Roxanne Conlin, interview, 1 June 2018, and Jerry Crawford, telephone conversations with author, 18 April, 13 June 2018.
52. Quotation from the *Des Moines Register*, 10 January 1994. See also Roxanne Conlin, interview, 1 June 2018; J.B. Conlin, interview by author, Des Moines, Iowa, 2 March 2018; Sara Quinn Ketcham, telephone conversation with author, 15 June 2017; Trudy Hurd, interview by author, Des Moines, Iowa, 9 November 2017; and "Dream Wedding: After 30 Years of Marriage," *Cityview*, undated clipping, Renewal of Wedding Vows folder, box 2, Roxanne Barton Conlin Papers, Iowa Women's Archives, University of Iowa Libraries, Iowa City, Iowa.
53. Ibid.

54. *Des Moines Register*, 10 January 1994.
55. Doug Klein, correspondence with author, 28 March, 16 June 2018.
56. Ibid.; Debbie Conlin Newlin, telephone conversation with author, 21 December 2018; Roxanne Conlin, interview, 1 June 2018; *Des Moines Register*, 23 March 1987; and J.B. Conlin, telephone conversation with author, 18 June 2018.
57. Debbie Conlin Newlin, telephone conversation, 21 December 2018.
58. Jackie Conlin, telephone conversation with author, 20 September 2017, and correspondence with author, 27 June 2018.
59. Ibid., and J.B. Conlin, telephone conversation, 18 June 2018.
60. Ibid.; Janey Piersall, correspondence with author, 2 July 2018; and *Des Moines Register*, 25 April 1999.
61. Rebecca Barton Hudlow, correspondence with author, 21 June 2018; Regina Barton Finkelstein, telephone conversation with author, 17 May 2017; and Roxanne Conlin, interview, 1 June 2018.
62. Ibid. Quotation from Roxanne Conlin, interview, 1 June 2018. See also obituary, *Minneapolis Star Tribune*, 21 December 1998.
63. Quotation from Rebecca Barton Hudlow, correspondence, 21 June 2018. See also Roxanne Conlin, interviews by author, Des Moines, Iowa, 2 May 2017, 1 June 2018.
64. Rebecca Barton Hudlow, correspondence with author, 24 June 2018.
65. Ibid., and obituary, *Minneapolis Star Tribune*, 30 December 1999. See also Roxanne Conlin, interview, 2 May 2017; J.B. Conlin, telephone conversation, 18 June 2018; and *Des Moines Register*, 19 February 2000.
66. Roxanne Conlin, interview, 1 June 2018.
67. Ibid., and *Des Moines Register*, 29 November 1998.
68. *Des Moines Register*, 13, 14 March 1999, and *Waterloo Courier*, 12 March 1999.
69. For the first quotation, see Roxanne Conlin, interview, 1 June 2018. For the second quotation and more on the issue, see the *Waterloo Courier*, 12 March 1999.
70. Ibid.; see also the *Des Moines Register*, 16 September 1999, and the *Mason City Globe Gazette*, 7 July 1999.
71. *Cityview*, 19 May 1999.
72. Ibid., 7 July 1999, and *Des Moines Register*, 2 July 1999.
73. *Des Moines Register*, 1, 6 October 1999.

74. Ibid., 1 October 1999.
75. Ibid., and for Roxanne's quotation, see Roxanne Conlin, interview, 1 June 2018. See also the *Sioux City Journal*, 11 November 1999. On Jeris's leaving, see the *Des Moines Register*, 30 March, 3 May 2000.
76. Roxanne Conlin, interview, 1 June 2018. On the expansion of Sixty-Third Street, see http://www.iowahighways.org/highways/desmoines.html.
77. *Des Moines Register*, 18 June 1928; John C. Culver and John Hyde, *American Dreamer: A Life of Henry A. Wallace* (New York: W. W. Norton, 2000); Roxanne Conlin, interview, 1 June 2018; and J.B. Conlin, telephone conversation, 18 June 2018.
78. Roxanne Conlin, interview, 1 June 2018; J.B. Conlin, telephone conversation, 18 June 2018; and J.B. Conlin, correspondence with author, 5 May 2018.
79. Ibid.
80. Ibid.
81. Tom Duff, interview.

9. Taking on Icons

1. Roxanne Conlin, correspondence with author, 23 July 2018, and Paige Fiedler, interview by author, Johnston, Iowa, 10 May 2018.
2. J.B. Conlin, correspondence with author, 22 July 2018.
3. Peggy Dupre, correspondence with author, 26 July 2018.
4. Ibid. See also Melinda Ellwanger, telephone conversation with author, 12 July 2018; Tom Duff, interview by author, West Des Moines, Iowa, 7 June 2018; Linda Hedlund Wickett, correspondence with author, 7 August 2018; and Angie Meyer, correspondence with author, 19 September 2018.
5. Ibid., and Roxanne Conlin, interview by author, Des Moines, Iowa, 14 September 2018.
6. For babies in Roxanne's office, see Angie Meyer, correspondence with author, 30 July 2018; Paige Fiedler, interview; Jean Mauss, telephone conversation with author, 13 August 2018; Roxanne Conlin, interview by author, Des Moines, Iowa, 1 June 2018; Melinda Ellwanger, telephone conversation; Roxanne Conlin, "An Essay on Parenthood," https://www.roxanneconlinlaw.com/Articles/

An-Essay-On-Parenthood.shtml; and Elizabeth Goldberg, "Babies on Board," *American Lawyer*, September 2009, 29.

7. Peggy Dupre, correspondence, 26 July 2018; Melinda Ellwanger, telephone conversation; Tom Duff, interview; Linda Hedlund Wickett, correspondence with author, 7 August 2018; Angie Meyer, correspondence, 19 September 2018; and Roxanne Conlin, interview, 14 September 2018. For the quotation, see the *Wall Street Journal*, 2 June 2004.

8. *Los Angeles Times*, 6 November 1999.

9. Roxanne Conlin, interview, 14 September 2018; Melinda Ellwanger, telephone conversation; and Angie Meyer, correspondence, 30 July 2018.

10. *Des Moines Register*, 1 March 2000, and Roxanne Conlin, interview, 14 September 2018.

11. Quotation from the *Des Moines Register*, 1 March 2000. See also the *Des Moines Register*, 2 March 2000.

12. *Des Moines Register*, 13 March 2000.

13. Ibid., 20 March 2000.

14. Jason Hancock, "Can Conlin Break Through?" *Business Record*, 15 October 2006, https://businessrecord.com/Content/NEWS/Archive/Article/Can-Conlin-break-through-/144/751/39446, and *Comes v. Microsoft Corp.*, 646 N.W. 2d 440 (Iowa 2002).

15. Hancock, "Can Conlin Break Through?" See also Andrew Smith, telephone conversation with author, 30 July 2018.

16. *Comes v. Microsoft Corp.*, 646 N.W. 2d 440 (Iowa 2002), and Roxanne Conlin, correspondence with author, 16 July 2018. Roxanne's first quotation from Roxanne Conlin, interview, 14 September 2018. For her second quotation and more on the decision, see the *Des Moines Register*, 13 June 2002.

17. For the decision and Brammer's quotation, see the *Des Moines Register*, 13 June 2002. See also Roxanne Conlin, correspondence, 16 July 2018, and Richard Hagstrom, telephone conversation with author, 8 August 2018.

18. Roxanne Conlin, interview, 14 September 2018, and Richard Hagstrom, telephone conversation.

19. Ibid.

20. Ibid. See also *Comes v. Microsoft Corp.*, 696 N.W. 2d 318 (Iowa 2005).

21. Paige Fiedler, interview, and *Des Moines Register*, 5 November 1997.
22. Quotation and details of the case from *McElroy v. State*, 637 N.W. 2d 488 (Iowa 2001).
23. Paige Fiedler, interview, and Roxanne Conlin, interview, 1 June 2018. For more on the story and the quotation, see the *Des Moines Register*, 6 July 2003.
24. *McElroy v. State*, 703 N.W. 2d 385 (Iowa 2005).
25. Paige Fiedler, interview; Roxanne Conlin, interview, 1 June 2018; *Des Moines Register*, 18 June 1999; and *McElroy v. State*, 637 N.W. 2d 488 (Iowa 2001).
26. Paige Fiedler, interview. For the Iowa Supreme Court reversing the lower court's decision and sending the case back for trial, see *McElroy v. State*, 637 N.W. 2d 488 (Iowa 2001).
27. Paige Fiedler, interview; Roxanne Conlin, interview, 1 June 2018; *Des Moines Register*, 21 June 2003; and *Iowa State Daily*, 3 July 2003.
28. First quotation from the *Des Moines Register*, 6 July 2003. For the Iowa Supreme Court decision and the second quotation, see *McElroy v. State*, 703 N.W. 2d 385 (Iowa 2005).
29. Roxanne Conlin, interview, 1 June 2018; Paige Fiedler, interview; and *McElroy v. State*, 703 N.W. 2d 385 (Iowa 2005).
30. Richard Hagstrom, telephone conversation, and Roxanne Conlin, correspondence, 16 July 2018. Hagstrom had been involved in the class action lawsuit against Microsoft in California and was also part of the Wisconsin case against the company.
31. Roxanne Conlin, correspondence, 16 July 2018, and *Los Angeles Times*, 20 April 2004.
32. *New York Times*, 20 April 2004. For the quotation and more information on the settlement, see http://news.minnesota. publicradio.org/features/2004/04/19_horwichj_microsoftsettles/. See also Richard Hagstrom, telephone conversation; *Minneapolis Star Tribune*, 20 April, 27 May 2004; https://www.zelle.com/ featured-1.html; "Minnesotans Leave Most Microsoft Settlement Money on the Table," *MPR News*, 11 February 2008; and https:// www.mprnews.org/story/2008/02/11/microsoft.
33. Elizabeth Corcoran, "The Price of Peace," *Forbes*, 29 March 2004, https://www.forbes.com/global/2004/0329/034. html#1975c2387ef5; New York Times, 20 April 2004; Richard

Hagstrom, telephone conversation; and https://www.zelle.com/featured-1.html.

34. Roxanne Conlin, interview, 14 September 2018.

35. Roxanne Conlin, correspondence, 16 July 2018; Jean Mauss, telephone conversation; Andrew Smith, telephone conversation; *Des Moines Register*, 30 November 2006; and https://www.zelle.com/featured-1.html.

36. Andrew Smith, telephone conversation, and Melinda Ellwanger, telephone conversation.

37. Andrew Smith, telephone conversation. For background on Vividata, see https://www.vividata.com/company.html.

38. Ibid. See also Roxanne Conlin, correspondence, 16 July 2018; Jean Mauss, telephone conversation; Melinda Ellwanger, telephone conversation; and Brad Beaman, telephone conversation with author, 21 August 2018.

39. Andrew Smith, telephone conversation, and Roxanne Conlin, correspondence, 16 July 2018.

40. Linda Hedlund Wickett, telephone conversation with author, 6 March 2018; Tom Duff, interview; Jean Mauss, telephone conversation; and Brad Beaman, telephone conversation.

41. Jean Mauss, telephone conversation; Brad Beaman, telephone conversation; Melinda Ellwanger, telephone conversation; Andrew Smith, telephone conversation; and Roxanne Conlin, interview, 14 September 2018.

42. Ibid. See also Richard Hagstrom, telephone conversation.

43. *Des Moines Register*, 4, 30 November 2006.

44. On *Time* magazine's recognition, see http://content.time.com/time/covers/0,16641,20051226,00.html; for the quotation, see Adam Liptak, "Millions for Defense," *New York Times*, 4 February 2001.

45. Richard Hagstrom, telephone conversation; Andrew Smith, telephone conversation; and Roxanne Conlin, interview by author, Des Moines, Iowa, 10 January 2018.

46. *Des Moines Register*, 3, 21 November 2006.

47. *Iowa City Press-Citizen*, 14 November 2006; *Des Moines Register*, 22 November 2006; Hale Starr, telephone conversation with author, 29 January 2018; and Roxanne Conlin, interview, 14 September 2018.

48. *Des Moines Register*, 2 December 2006; Andrew Smith, telephone conversation; Jean Mauss, telephone conversation; Melinda Ellwanger, telephone conversation; and Roxanne Conlin, interview, 14 September 2018.

49. *Des Moines Register*, 2 December 2006, and "Jury Selection Starts in Microsoft Antitrust in Iowa," *Redmond Magazine*, 13 November 2006, https://redmondmag.com/Articles/2006/11/13/Jury-Selection-Starts-in-Microsoft-Antitrust-in-Iowa.aspx.

50. *Des Moines Register*, 1, 2 December 2006. Quotation from the *Des Moines Register*, 2 December 2006.

51. *Des Moines Register*, 2 December 2006.

52. Ibid.

53. Ibid., 12 December 2006, and *Waterloo Courier*, 12 December 2006. For more on the opening statement and the quotation, see Hale Starr, telephone conversation. See also Richard Hagstrom, telephone conversation, and Andrew Smith, telephone conversation.

54. First quotation from the *Waterloo Courier*, 12 December 2006; second quotation from the *Des Moines Register*, 12 December 2006.

55. *Des Moines Register*, 5 December 2006, and *Seattle Times*, 4 December 2006.

56. Ibid., 16, 22 December 2006; quotation from Andrew Smith, telephone conversation.

57. Peter Lattman, "Microsoft Settles Iowa Antitrust Class-Action," *Wall Street Journal*, 14 February 2007, https://blogs.wsj.com/law/2007/02/14/microsoft-settles-iowa-antitrust-class-action/, and *Des Moines Register*, 15 February 2007.

58. For the quotation and the story of the settlement meeting, see Jason Hancock, "Nine Weeks After It Started, This Case Is Closed," *Business Record*, 18 February 2007, https://businessrecord.com/Content/News/Archive/Article/Nine-weeks-after-it-started-this-case-is-closed/144/751/43340. See also Eric Lai, "Restaurant Meal Helps Fuel Microsoft's Iowa Settlement Deal," *Computerworld*, 14 February 2007, https://www.computerworld.com/article/2543527/enterprise-applications/restaurant-meal-helped-fuel-microsoft-s-iowa-settlement-deal.html. For general information on the settlement, see the *Des Moines Register*, 15 February 2007, and the *Washington Post*, 15 February 2007.

59. For Wallis's quotation, see Hancock, "Nine Weeks After It Started," and for Mauss' quotation, see Jean Mauss, telephone conversation.

60. *Des Moines Register*, 19, 20 April 2007; Richard Hagstrom, telephone conversation; Roxanne Conlin, interview, 14 September 2018; and https://www.zelle.com/featured-1.html. See also the *Quad-City Times*, 25 January 2010.

61. *Des Moines Register*, 19 April, 1, 9 September 2007.

62. For the average individual claim figure, see the *Quad-City Times*, 25 January 2010. For letters to the editor complaining about the large fee, see the *Des Moines Register*, 15 September 2007. First quotation from the *Des Moines Register*, 1 September 2007; second quotation from the *Des Moines Register*, 9 September 2007.

63. *Des Moines Register*, 29 January, 1 February 2009. For more and the quotation, see "Des Moines City Councilman New Iowa Democratic Party Chair," Radio Iowa, https://www.radioiowa.com/2009/01/31/des-moines-city-councilman-new-iowa-democratic-party-chair/.

64. On Roxanne saying she would not run, see the *Des Moines Register*, 5 October 2009. For Kiernan's meetings with Roxanne and the quotation, see Michael Kiernan, telephone conversation with author, 10 September 2018. See also the *Quad-City Times*, 27 October 2009. Roxanne's quotations are from "Roxanne Conlin Wins U.S. Senate Primary in Iowa," 9 June 2010, YouTube video, https://www.youtube.com/watch?v=VotAdHegK5k.

65. For Krause's candidacy, see the *Des Moines Register*, 29 March 2009, and for Fiegen's announcement, see the *Des Moines Register*, 12, 16 August 2009.

66. For Gartner's quotation, see *Cityview*, 8 October 2009, http://dmcityview.com/2009/10/08/columns/skinny.html. See also the *Des Moines Register*, 16 November 2009. And see "What the 'Gang of Six' Wants from Health Care Bill," NPR, 9 September 2009, https://www.npr.org/templates/story/story.php?storyId=112222617.

67. Lisa Lerer, "Grassley on Death Panels: 'You Have Every Right to Fear,'" *Politico*, 12 August 2009, https://www.politico.com/blogs/politico-now/2009/08/grassley-on-death-panels-you-have-every-right-to-fear-020615.

68. See Judy Conlin, interview by author, Clive, Iowa, 30 October 2017, and Roxanne Conlin, interview, 14 September 2018. For the quotation and more on the family's position, see J.B. Conlin, interview by author, Des Moines, Iowa, 3 October 2017. Crawford's opposition to Roxanne's run from Jerry Crawford, telephone conversation with author, 18 April 2018.

69. *Des Moines Register*, 16 August, 5 October 2009. For more on Kiernan's mystery candidate and the quotation, see the *Quad-City Times*, 29 September 2009.

70. *Des Moines Register*, 22, 23 October 2009.

71. Ibid., 27 October 2009; *Quad-City Times*, 27 October 2009; Roxanne Conlin, interview, 14 September 2018; and *Des Moines Register*, 11 November 2009.

72. See the campaign video, "Roxanne Conlin for Iowa," 9 November 2009, YouTube video, https://www.youtube.com/watch?v=u9onQcsiaRo. See also the *Des Moines Register*, 11 November 2009.

73. *Waterloo Courier*, 10 November 2009.

74. *Des Moines Register*, 13 November 2009. For more on the search, see Roxanne Conlin, interview, 14 September 2018, and Mark Daley, telephone conversation with author, 7 September 2018.

75. *Des Moines Register*, 12 December 2014, and Roxanne Conlin, interview, 14 September 2018.

76. Daley's quotation from Mark Daley, correspondence with author, 14 September 2018; second quotation and information on Lipsman from Roxanne Conlin, interview, 14 September 2018.

77. For the poll, see the *Des Moines Register*, 16 November 2009. Quotation from the *Sioux City Journal*, 29 November 2009.

78. *Des Moines Register*, 23, 27 October 2009. Daley's quotation from Mark Daley, telephone conversation.

79. "Conlin Releases Strong Fundraising Numbers," *Bleeding Heartland Blog*, 15 April 2010, https://www.bleedingheartland.com/2010/04/15/conlin-releases-strong-fundraising-numbers-updated/; *Des Moines Register*, 16 April 2019; and Mark Daley, telephone conversation.

80. Des Moines Register, 9 June 2010.

81. Ibid., 20 August, 3 September, 1, 12 October 2010.

82. First quotation from Roxanne Conlin, interview, 14 September 2018; second quotation from Michael Kiernan, telephone conversation; and third quotation from Mark Daley, telephone conversation.

83. For the Lipsman story, see Roxanne Conlin, interview, 14 September 2018; on Roxanne's contributing $1 million to the campaign, see J.B. Conlin, interview, 3 October 2017, and Mark Daley, telephone conversation. Fund-raising totals from the Center for Responsive Politics, https://www.opensecrets.org/states/cands.php?state=IA&cycle=2010.

84. For the "One Tough Grandma" ad, see https://www.youtube.com/watch?v=Ld9nY_8Z5ho.

85. *Des Moines Register*, 10 May, 7, 10, 28 September, 10 October, 3 November 2010. See also Alexander Burns, "Poll: Grassley below 50," *Politico*, 7 May 2010, https://www.politico.com/story/2010/05/poll-grassley-below-50-036927; Rasmussen Reports, 17 June 2010, http://www.rasmussenreports.com/public_content/politics/elections/election_2010/election_2010_senate elections/iowa/iowa_senate_grassley_r_54_conlin_d_37; and Roxanne Conlin, interview by author, Des Moines, Iowa, 4 February 2019.

86. Roxanne Conlin, interview, 14 September 2018; *Des Moines Register*, 27 October 2010; and *Sioux City Journal*, 27 October 2010. Quotation from the *Des Moines Register*, 31 October 2010.

87. Election results and Roxanne's quotation from the *Des Moines Register*, 3 November 2010. Crawford's quotation from Jerry Crawford, telephone conversation, 18 April 2018.

88. *Des Moines Register*, 23 October 2009.

10. Changing Pace

1. See Jenny McCuen, "Roxanne Conlin vs. Injustice," 50 *Plus Lifestyles*, August 2007, 9.

2. Debbie Conlin Newlin, telephone conversation with author, 21 December 2018; Roxanne Conlin, interview by author, Des Moines, Iowa, 14 September 2018; and J.B. Conlin, telephone conversation with author, 18 June 2018.

3. Debbie Conlin Newlin, telephone conversation, 21 December 2018.

4. Ibid.

5. Ibid.
6. *Des Moines Register,* 20 July 2004.
7. Ibid., and Joe Gardyasz, "Art on Four Wheels," *Business Record,* 4 April 2009, https://businessrecord.com/Content/Default/Archives/Article/Art-on-four-wheels/-3/988/50883. For more on the business and the quotation, see Stacey Horst, "One of the Largest Muscle Car Shops in USA Is Here in Iowa," 20 November 2013, https://www.kcci.com/article/one-of-the-largest-muscle-car-shops-in-usa-is-here-in-iowa/6886073.
8. Quotation from Horst, "One of the Largest Muscle Shops." See also Gardyasz, "Art on Four Wheels," and the *Iowa City Press-Citizen,* 18 April 2008.
9. Jackie Conlin, telephone conversation with author, 3 April 2018.
10. Ibid.
11. Ibid.
12. J.B. Conlin, telephone conversation with author, 28 September 2018. And see James Conlin to All Conlin Properties Employees, 8 September 2006, J.B. Conlin Papers, private collection held by J.B. Conlin, West Des Moines, Iowa; hereafter cited as J.B. Conlin Papers.
13. Ibid.
14. J.B. Conlin, telephone conversation, 28 September 2018.
15. Ibid.
16. Quotation from Roxanne Conlin, interview, 14 September 2018. See also J.B. Conlin, telephone conversation, 28 September 2018.
17. J.B. Conlin, correspondence with author, 25 September 2018.
18. Ibid., and James Conlin to All Conlin Properties Employees, 27 December 2013, J.B. Conlin Papers.
19. Judy Conlin, correspondence with author, 8 October 2018.
20. Ibid.
21. Ibid., and Doug Klein, correspondence with author, 28 March 2018.
22. Roxanne Conlin, interview, 14 September 2018.
23. Debbi Kickham, "Crystal Cruises' Dance Program Is Symbol of a Bygone Era," *Forbes,* 19 June 2018, https://www.forbes.com/sites/debbikickham/2018/06/19/crystal-cruises-dance-program-is-symbol-of-a-bygone-era/#4ab6aad51ef6, and Roxanne Conlin, interview by author, Des Moines, Iowa, 10 January 2018.
24. Rhoda Barton Olsen, correspondence with author, 5 October 2018.

25. On the Polk County Democrats Women's Event, see Tamyra Harrison, *The Women of Polk County Politics: 18 Years of Making Herstory* (Des Moines: Lead and Iron Publishing and Consulting, 2016), 21, 27, 59–60, 73–75, 77–78, and https://www.polkdems.com/women-s-event.

26. Roxanne Conlin, interview, 10 January 2018. See also the *Des Moines Register*, 25 January 2004.

27. See Nicholas Lemann, "The Newcomer: Senator John Edwards Is This Season's Democratic Rising Star," *New Yorker*, 6 May 2002, https://www.newyorker.com/magazine/2002/05/06/the-newcomer.

28. *Des Moines Register*, 30 January 2003.

29. On getting office space in the Griffin Building, see the *Des Moines Register*, 29 March 2003.

30. First quotation from the *Des Moines Register*, 7 June 2003. Second quotation and Roxanne's consideration of running against Grassley in 2004 from the *Des Moines Register*, 25 January 2004.

31. *Baltimore Sun*, 14 January 2004.

32. *Des Moines Register*, 7 July 2004. See also John Skipper, *The Iowa Caucuses: First Tests of Presidential Aspiration, 1972–2008* (Jefferson, N.C.: McFarland and Co., 2010), 126–141.

33. See Skipper, *Iowa Caucuses*, 142–161.

34. *Des Moines Register*, 12 August 2008, and Marc Dorian and Lauren Effron, "John Edwards and the Mistress: A Breakdown of One of America's Most Sensational Scandals," 12 November 2013, https://abcnews.go.com/Politics/john-edwards-mistress-breakdown-americas-sensational-scandals/story?id=20854336.

35. *Des Moines Register*, 20 April 2010.

36. Roxanne Conlin, interview, 14 September 2018; J.B. Conlin, telephone conversation, 28 September 2018; and Michael Beckel, "Chuck Grassley Challenger Roxanne Conlin Gave Big to Democrats, Trial Lawyers," 9 November 2009, https://www.opensecrets.org/news/2009/11/chuck-grassley-challenger-roxa/.

37. Ibid.

38. Roxanne Conlin, interview, 14 September 2018.

39. Paige Fiedler, interview by author, Johnston, Iowa, 10 May 2018.

40. Rox Laird, correspondence with author, 3 January 2018. For more on the story and the quotation, see Mark Bennett to Roxanne Conlin, 3 February 2019, in possession of the author.

41. Quotation from Mark Bennett to Roxanne Conlin, 3 February 2019. See also Roxanne Conlin, interview by author, Des Moines, Iowa, 4 February 2019.

42. Roxanne Conlin, interview, 14 September 2018, and J.B. Conlin, correspondence, 25 September 2018.

43. Ibid.

44. Ibid.

45. Ibid.

46. Ibid.

47. Ibid., and "Community Foundation Connection: Eat Greater Des Moines and the Conlin Family," 20 June 2018, https://www.desmoinesfoundation.org/news-and-events/news/community-foundation-connection-eat-greater-des-moines-and-the-conlin-family.

48. Iowa Coalition Against Domestic Violence press release, "Roxanne Conlin Funds Scholarship Program for Survivors of Domestic Violence," 13 September 2011, in possession of the author; https://www.desmoinesfoundation.org/news-and-events/news/community-foundation-connection-eat-greater-des-moines-and-the-conlin-family; and Roxanne Conlin, interview, 14 September 2018.

49. Iowa Coalition Against Domestic Violence press release, 13 September 2011.

50. Roxanne Conlin, interview, 14 September 2018.

51. Kim Baer, correspondence with author, 28 September 2018, and Roxanne Conlin, interview, 14 September 2018.

52. Roxanne Conlin, interview, 14 September 2018.

53. Ibid. On the snowstorm, see the *Des Moines Register*, 27 February 2013.

54. Roxanne Conlin, interview, 14 September 2018.

55. *Des Moines Register*, 27 February 2013; "Doing Well: Roxanne Conlin Recovering from Mild Stroke," 27 February 2013, WHO-TV, https://whotv.com/2013/02/27/doing-well-roxanne-conlin-recovering-from-mild-stroke/; and Roxanne Conlin, interview, 14 September 2018.

56. Roxanne Conlin, interview, 4 February 2019.

57. Roxanne Conlin, interview, 14 September 2018.

58. See the video, "Toast and Roast of Roxanne Conlin, 2013," Roxanne Conlin Papers, private collection held by Roxanne Conlin,

Des Moines, Iowa; hereafter cited as Roxanne Conlin Papers. Other speakers included Dick Calkins, former dean of Drake Law School; Brian Galligan, the son of late law partner and close friend Michael Galligan, who had passed away the previous year; Gene Meyer, former head of the Iowa Division of Criminal Investigation and president of the Greater Des Moines Partnership; friends Maggi Moss and Loretta Sieman; local Democratic activist Mary Campos; educator and one-time tutor for J.B. Mary Sconiers-Chapman; and judges Arthur Gamble and Joel Novak.

59. Roxanne Conlin, interview, 14 September 2018.
60. Quotation from McCuen, "Conlin vs. Injustice," 9.
61. "Toast and Roast," Roxanne Conlin Papers.

11. Ever the Advocate
1. Becky Kolosik, "Giving a Voice to the Voiceless: Meet Roxanne Conlin," *WOW: Women of Worth*, February–March 2017, 7.
2. Roxanne Conlin, interview by author, Des Moines, Iowa, 4 February 2019.
3. Ibid., and Louise Noun, *More Strong-Minded Women: Iowa Feminists Tell Their Stories* (Ames: Iowa State University Press, 1992), 132–133.
4. *Des Moines Register*, 19 February 2018, and *Quad-City Times*, 24 January 2018.
5. *Clinton Herald*, 31 May 2018, and Roxanne Conlin, interview, 4 February 2019.
6. Roxanne Conlin, interview by author, Des Moines, Iowa, 14 September 2018.
7. *Iowa City Press-Citizen*, 20 October 2015, and Roxanne Conlin, interview, 4 February 2019.
8. Ibid.; *Cedar Rapids Gazette*, 20 October 2015; *Des Moines Register*, 20 October 2015; and Roxanne Conlin, interview, 14 September 2018.
9. Quotation from the *Cedar Rapids Gazette*, 20 October 2015. And see the *Iowa City Press-Citizen*, 20 October 2015.
10. *Cedar Rapids Community School District v. Parr*, 227 N.W. 2d 486 (1975). For changes to the Iowa Civil Rights Act, see *McQuistion v. City of Clinton*, 872 N.W. 2d 817 (Iowa 2015).

11. *Cedar Rapids Gazette*, 25 December 2015.
12. *McQuistion v. City of Clinton*, 872 N.W. 2d 817 (Iowa 2015).
13. Ibid.
14. Dar Danielson, "Iowa Supreme Court Hears Case of Pregnant Clinton Firefighter," 12 March 2015, https://www.radioiowa.com/2015/03/12/iowa-supreme-court-hears-case-of-pregnant-clinton-firefighter/.
15. Ibid. For more on the case and the quotation, see the *Cedar Rapids Gazette*, 25 December 2015. For the U.S. Supreme Court case, see *Young v. United Parcel Service*, 575 U.S. ___ (2015).
16. Roxanne Conlin and Associates, Case Summaries—Employment Discrimination, *McQuistion v. City of Clinton* (2015), https://www.roxanneconlinlaw.com/Case-Summaries/Case-Summaries-Employment-Discrimination.shtml.
17. *Waterloo Courier*, 1 October 2013; https://www.studentaffairs.iastate.edu/iaahf/inductees.php; https://northiowatoday.com/2017/10/17/opinion-lionel-fosters-long-distinguished-list-of-accomplishments-makes-him-top-choice-in-ward-2-council-race/; and Roxanne Conlin, correspondence with author, 14 November 2018.
18. *Mason City Globe Gazette*, 2 April, 10 June, 30 December 2014, and *Des Moines Register*, 4 April, 21 August, 31 December 2014.
19. *Des Moines Register*, 1 September 2012.
20. Ibid., and *Des Moines Register*, 10 October 2012.
21. *Fagen v. Grand View University*, 861 N.W. 2d 825 (Iowa 2015). As the case moved forward, Fagen amended his complaint, adding NPI Security, which provided security to Grand View University, as a defendant, and he settled separately with the students.
22. *Fagen v. Grand View University*, 861 N.W. 2d 825 (Iowa 2015).
23. Ibid., and Roxanne Conlin, interview, 14 September 2018.
24. For more on the story, see the *Des Moines Register*, 19 September 2015.
25. Chris Isidore, "Lawyers Are Lining Up to Take on Volkswagen," 29 September 2015, CNN Business, https://money.cnn.com/2015/09/26/news/companies/volkswagen-emission-scandal-lawsuits/index.html; Richard Hagstrom, telephone conversation with author, 8 August 2018; and Roxanne Conlin, interview, 14 September 2018.
26. Roxanne Conlin, interview, 14 September 2018, and Roxanne Conlin, correspondence, 14 November 2018.

27. Ibid., and Richard Hagstrom, telephone conversation.
28. Sara Randazzo, "Elizabeth Cabraser Tapped to Lead VW Consumer Litigation," *Wall Street Journal*, 22 January 2016, https://blogs. wsj.com/law/2016/01/22/elizabeth-cabraser-tapped-to-lead-vw-consumer-litigation/.
29. Ibid.
30. For the quotation and the settlement, see Alison Frankel, "Why Volkswagen Was Smart to Fold in Emissions Cheating Case," 28 June 2016, https://www.reuters.com/article/volkswagen-emissions-frankel-idUSL1N19K26S. See also the *New York Times*, 27 June 2016, and Roxanne Conlin, correspondence, 14 November 2018.
31. Ibid., and *Los Angeles Times*, 28 June 2016.
32. For Breyer's approval of the settlement, see Camila Domonoske, "Judge Approves VW's $14.7 Billion Settlement over Emissions Scandal," 25 October 2016, https://www.npr.org/sections/thetwo-way/2016/10/25/499301280/judge-approves-vws-14-7-billion-settlement-over-emissions-scandal. Roxanne's quotation from Roxanne Conlin, correspondence, 14 November 2018.
33. Roxanne's quotation from the *Iowa City Press-Citizen*, 25 November 2017. See also Chris Godfrey, correspondence with author, 18 November 2018; *Sioux City Journal*, 4 January 2006; *Cedar Rapids Gazette*, 30 June 2017; and Roxanne Conlin, correspondence, 10 December 2019.
34. *Des Moines Register*, 30 November 2012.
35. Ibid., and Roxanne Conlin, interview, 4 February 2019.
36. Randy Evans, "Taxpayers Have Been Taken for an Expensive Ride," *IowaWatch.org*, 12 September 2018, http://www. iowawatch.org/2018/09/12/evans-taxpayers-have-been-taken-for-an-expensive-ride/.
37. Chris Godfrey, correspondence, 18 November 2018.
38. Quotation from Chris Godfrey, correspondence, 18 November 2018. See also the *Des Moines Register*, 30 November 2012. For more on the lawsuit, see "Terry Branstad, Iowa Governor, Slapped with $1 Million Sexual Discrimination Lawsuit by State Commissioner," *HuffPost*, 13 January 2012, https://www. huffingtonpost.com/2012/01/13/terry-branstad-iowa-governor-sexual-discrimination-lawsuit_n_1205093.html.

39. *Waterloo–Cedar Falls Courier*, 18 January 2012.
40. *Des Moines Register*, 30 November 2012. See also Roxanne Conlin, correspondence, 10 December 2019.
41. Ibid.
42. Ibid., 6 June 2014. See also Roxanne Conlin, correspondence, 14 November 2018.
43. See Michael Gartner's "Civic Skinny" column, "Lawyers, Politicians: Settle the Chris Godfrey Case. And a Bad Weekend for Two Channel 13 Reporters," *Cityview*, 11 June 2014, http://www.dmcityview.com/civic-skinny/2014/06/11/lawyers-politicians-settle-the-chris-godfrey-case-and-a-bad-weekend-for-two-channel-13-reporters/. For Godfrey leaving his job and the quotation, see Ryan Foley, "Iowa Workers' Compensation Commissioner Godfrey Resigning," *Insurance Journal*, 6 August 2014, https://www.insurancejournal.com/news/midwest/2014/08/06/336935.htm.
44. *Des Moines Register*, 7 June 2015.
45. Ibid. Roxanne's quotation from Roxanne Conlin, correspondence, 14 November 2018. In the midst of this litigation, Jim and his real estate partnership sold the Griffin Building in July 2016. Roxanne and Conlin Properties stayed in the downtown structure until the following June, when the law firm and the property management company moved into their new building less than a mile southwest of Roxanne and Jim's home. For information on the sale and move, see the *Des Moines Register*, 30 July 2016, and J.B. Conlin, correspondence with author, 20 November 2018.
46. *Godfrey v. State*, 898 N.W. 2d 844 (Iowa 2017). See also the *Des Moines Register*, 14 September 2016, 30 June 2017.
47. *Des Moines Register*, 7 September 2018. For LaMarca's bill, see Michael Gartner's "Civic Skinny" column, "Sabbaticals: Space Bicycles, a Suicide in 1634 and Mexican Accents. LaMarca Bills Top $1 Million," *Cityview*, December 2018, 13.
48. Chris Godfrey, correspondence, 18 November 2018.
49. Angie Meyer, correspondence with author, 7 August 2019.
50. *Des Moines Register*, 6 June 2019.
51. Ibid.
52. Jean Mauss, correspondence with author, 31 July 2019.
53. Ibid., and Paige Fiedler, correspondence with author, 30 July 2019.

54. Jean Mauss, correspondence, 31 July 2019.
55. For J.B.'s arrest and the first quotation, see the *Des Moines Register*, 11 June 2019. For Roxanne's motion (her third) to move the trial and Paige Fiedler's consideration of a request for a mistrial, see the *Des Moines Register*, 21 June 2019.
56. *Des Moines Register*, 15 June 2019; Paige Fiedler, correspondence, 30 July 2019; and Jean Mauss, correspondence with author, 5 August 2019.
57. See the *Des Moines Register*, 15 June 2019, and https://www. radioiowa.com/2019/06/14/branstad-testifies-in-trial-over-his-treatment-of-state-agency-chief/.
58. See Michael Gartner's "Civic Skinny" column, "A Drama Avoided," *Cityview,* August 2019, 23.
59. *Des Moines Register*, 22 June 2019.
60. Ibid., 16 July 2019.
61. Godfrey's quotation from https://www.kcrg.com/content/news/ Former-gay-state-official-wins-15M-in-discrimination-case-against-Branstad-512752201.html. Roxanne's quotation from https://www. iowapublicradio.org/post/jury-decides-former-gov-terry-branstad-discriminated-against-gay-employee-awards-15-million#stream/0.
62. *Des Moines Register*, 18 July 2019.
63. Ibid., 7 August 2019. On the defense motion to overturn the verdict, see the *Des Moines Register*, 31 July 2019.
64. *Des Moines Register*, 31 July 2019.
65. For McCall's ruling against the motion to overturn the jury verdict, see *Des Moines Register*, 13 November 2019. For the state's decision to appeal the case to the Iowa Supreme Court and quote, see *Des Moines Register*, 23 November 2019.
66. For Crawford's quotation, see *dsm*, November–December 2016, 78. And see Maggi Moss, telephone conversation with author, 10 April 2018.

Conclusion: Nine Lives

1. Roxanne Conlin, interview by author, Des Moines, Iowa, 14 September 2018.

2. Tom Whitney, interview by author, Clive, Iowa, 19 January 2018, and Patti Huston, telephone conversation with author, 20 July 2017.
3. Melinda Ellwanger, telephone conversation with author, 12 July 2018, and Laura Ward, telephone conversation with author, 4 January 2018.
4. Amanda Dorr Meers, telephone conversation with author, 5 December 2017.
5. For a list of past presidents of the Association of Trial Lawyers of America and American Association for Justice, see https://www.justice.org/who-we-are/leadership/past-presidents.
6. For Roxanne's interest in advancing the law and making it more progressive, see Roxanne Conlin, interviews by author, Des Moines, Iowa, 11 April, 1 June 2018, and Melinda Ellwanger, telephone conversation. For the quotation, see Chris Godfrey, correspondence with author, 18 November 2018.
7. On the calls to Roxanne's office, see Roxanne Conlin, interview, 14 September 2018. For the quotation, see Bill Knapp, interview by author, West Des Moines, Iowa, 28 April 2017.
8. For Tom Colvin's quotation, see Peter Lattman, "Law Blog Lawyer of the Day: Roxanne Conlin," *Wall Street Journal*, 15 February 2007, https://blogs.wsj.com/law/2007/02/15/law-blog-lawyer-of-the-day-roxanne-conlin/. Roxanne's office had always held the overflow of foster kittens. This remained the case up until the summer of 2018, when Angie Meyer, Roxanne's administrative assistant, developed allergies to the kittens; see Angie Meyer, correspondence with author, 16 November 2018.
9. For the story about the URLs, see Roxanne Conlin, interview by author, Des Moines, Iowa, 4 February 2019. Quotation from Dick Calkins, *Guilty Beyond a Reasonable Doubt* (Ishpeming, Mich.: BookVenture Publishing, 2018), vii.
10. Louise Noun, *More Strong-Minded Women: Iowa Feminists Tell Their Stories* (Ames: Iowa State University Press, 1992), 118.
11. First quotation from Roxanne Conlin, interview, 4 February 2019; second quotation from Noun, *More Strong-Minded Women*, 118.

INDEX

Throughout this index, the abbreviation RBC will be used to indicate references to Roxanne Barton Conlin. Page numbers appearing in italic type refer to pages that contain photographs.

A

Abortion rights, 96, 105, 123

Abzug, Bella, 58, 60, *116*

Adams, Michael C. C., 12–13

affirmative action, 44, 52

age discrimination, 156–58, 233–34

air pollution, 76

Albrecht, Timothy, 238–39, 241

Alice Barton Scholarship program, 225

American Association for Justice, 222, 230, 249. *See also* Association of Trial Lawyers of America

American dream, 8-9, 16

American Dream Machines, 214

American Republic Insurance Company, 46–47

Amoco, 152–54

Anderson, Alexandria (granddaughter), 137, *208*

Anderson, Colin (grandson), 137, *209*

Anderson, Dale, 130–31

Anderson, Devin (grandson), 137, *209*

Anderson, Kermit, 75, 76, 87

Anderson, Kerry, 137, 166

Anderson, Ted, 105

Anderson Properties, 166

Animal Rescue League of Iowa, 7, 155–56, 177, 223, 250

animal welfare activism of RBC
   financial support for Animal Rescue League, 223
   kitten fostering, 7, 177, 223, 250
   poodle rescue efforts, 31
   puppy mill lawsuit, 155–56, *205*, 292*n*23

antitrust lawsuits, 178–81, 184–91

asbestos lawsuits, 6, 140–44

Association of Trial Lawyers of America (ATLA)

annual conventions, 125, 139–40, 150–52, *203–4*

on asbestos litigation, 139–40

funds donated by RBC, 222

increase in diversity of, 150–51

Minority Caucus, 150

name change to American Association for Justice, 249

RBC as parliamentarian of, 126

RBC as president of, 7, 120, 144, 149–52, *203,* 249

RBC as vice-president of, 144

RBC's early involvement with, 124–26

Women Trial Lawyers Caucus, 150

Avenson, Don, 86, 90

Axne, Cindy, 109

B

Baer, Kim, 225

Ballmer, Steve, 188, 191

Barr, Patty, 18–19

Barton, Alice Bernice (mother)

ancestry, 10

background, 8, 10–11

career, 24–25

death, 168–69, *205*

marriage to Bill Barton, 11

mental health issues, 65, 86

photographs, *111, 113, 116*

scholarship program named for, 225

Barton, Charlotte (aunt), 10

Barton, Charlotte Grant (grandmother), 10, 17

Barton, Marion William "Bill" (father)

alcoholism and domestic violence, 9, 12–13, 21, 23–24, 65

ancestry, 10

arrest, 24

background, 8, 10

career, 14–16, 20, 24–25

on childhood of RBC, 13, 14

death, 168

marriage to Alice Barton, 11

military service, 11–13

photographs, *111, 113*

pilots license, 17

post-military readjustment to civilian life, 12–14

Barton, Ray (grandfather), 10

Barton, Raymond (brother)

Alice Barton Scholarship program, 225

birth, 15

childhood, 23–25

death of parents, 168–69

photographs, *113, 116*

RBC celebrity roast, 227

at wedding of RBC to Jim Conlin, 27

Barton, Rebecca. *See* Hudlow, Rebecca "Becky" Barton (sister)

Barton, Regina. *See* Finkelstein, Regina "Gina" Barton (sister)

Barton, Rhoda. *See* Olsen, Rhoda Barton (sister)

Barton, Rhonda. *See* Richmond, Rhonda Barton (sister)

Bartz, Harvey, 53–54

Baumgarten, Carol, 121

Beaman, Brad, 5, 188

Beaumont, Thomas, 196

Beeman, Joe and Beverly, 142

Belin, David, 91

Beller, Judy, 19

Bendix (manufacturing firm), 140

Bennett, Mark, 223

Berntsen, Rob, 219

Bill and Melinda Gates Foundation, 188–89

Blane, Richard, 75

Bleimehl, Edward, 156–57

Boeyink, Jeffrey, 238–39, 241–42, 245

Boies, David, 188, 236

Bookmeyer, Eric, 234

Boswell, Leonard, 222

Braley, Bruce, 227

Brammer, Bob, 180

Branstad, Terry

    Chris Godfrey, employment discrimination lawsuit, 238–46

    gubernatorial campaign (1982)

        analysis of election win, 110

        announcement of candidacy for, 92

        financial disclosure statement, 101, 102

        on financial disclosure statement of RBC, 100–101, 109

        fundraising, 94

        on Jim Conlin's business ethics, 106

        mistakes during, 105, 108

        newspapers' endorsement of, 107

        polling data on, 6, 89, 97–98, 103, 105, 108

        televised debates, 103, 105–6

    as U.S. ambassador to China, 109

Bremer, Celeste, 143

Breyer, Charles, 236–37

Brinkman, Richard, 38

Brown, Carmela "Cookie," 31–32, 35, 81, 121, 227

Brown, David, *206*

Brown, Doug, 85

Brown, James, 142

Brunk, Frank, 134

Buechele, Arnold, 53–54

bullying, 234–35

Burridge, John, 134–36

Bush, George W., 221

Butts, David, 79–80, *211,* 227

C

Calkins, Dick, 250–51

Campbell, Bonnie, vii–ix, 134

Campbell, Edward "Ed"

    death, viii–ix

    gubernatorial campaign (1982), viii, 81, 91–94, 97–98

    on Hughes running for governor (1982), 89

Capitol Intermediaries, 134–35

Carter, Jimmy, 72, 73–74

Cedar Rapids Community School District v. Parr (1975), 51, 231, 248

Cedar Rapids Gazette on gubernatorial campaign of RBC, 88

Cerro Gordo County, 157–58, 293*n*26

Channon, Linda, 158–61

Chapman, Tom, 97–99

childcare facility licensure, 57

Chisholm, Shirley, 55–56, 58

Christiansen, Carl, Jr., 142–43

Cityview on Chris Godfrey lawsuit, 240, 244

civil rights, 4–5, 36–37. *See also* Iowa Civil Rights Act; Iowa Civil Rights Commission

Civil Rights Act (1964), 45, 47, 51, 162

Civil Rights Act (1991), 158

Clark, Ronald, 127–29

Cleary, Eleanor (aunt), 12

Clinton Community School District, 230

cocaine, 77

Collins-Robson, Mary Jean, 55

Columbia University, 42

Colvin, Tom, 250

Comes, Joe, 178–80

Comes v. Microsoft (2002), 178–81, 184, 186–91

Comito, Frank, 62–63

Community Foundation of Greater Des Moines, 223, 224

Conlin, Courtney Briese (daughter-in-law), *208,* 216–17

Conlin, Debbie. *See* Newlin, Debbie Conlin (stepdaughter)

Conlin, Jackie (daughter)
  alcoholism, 138, 215
  birth, 33
  career, 138, 214–15
  childhood, 64–67
  education, 81, 138
  on hobbies of RBC, 79
  on parents' relationship, 63
  photographs, *115, 117, 208*
  on RBC as U.S. district attorney, 74
  renewal of vows ceremony of parents, 165

Conlin, James Barton "J.B." (son)
  birth, 40
  career, 139, 167, 215–17
  childhood, 64–67
  education, 81, 139, 217
  on father's health issue, 144
  on father's sense of humor, 163
  as general contractor for parents' home, 173–74
  marriage to Courtney Briese, 216
  on parents' relationship, 66
  philanthropy with parents, 224
  photographs, *115, 117, 208*
  on RBC as U.S. district attorney, 74
  on RBC senate run, 196
  renewal of vows ceremony of parents, 165

Conlin, James "Jim" (husband)
  adoption of Doug Klein, 69
  business merger, 136
  career, 30–31, 38, 63–64, 80, 120, 136–37, 163, 216–17
  on career of RBC, 78
  Conlin Company, 80
  Des Moines City Council race (1993), 163–64
  donations to Democratic candidates, 221–22
  education, 31
  financial statement disclosure controversy, 102–3, 107
  Grease Monkey franchise, 122, 166
  health issues, 144–45
  hobbies, 80
  home life, 64–67
  IFA tax credits for apartment complex, 170–72
  marriage to RBC, 4, 26–27
  Mid-Iowa Management Company, 80
  personal home, 172–74
  philanthropy, 222–25
  photographs, *115, 117, 204, 208, 210*
  RBC celebrity roast, 227
  real estate investments, 64, 80, 100–101
  on relationship with RBC, 63
  renewal of vows with RBC, 164–66
  sense of humor, 97, 163
  support for gubernatorial campaign of RBC, 82, 90, 94, 97
  travel and vacations, *210,* 218
Conlin, Judy (sister-in-law)
  Animal Rescue League and, 156
  on career of RBC, 70
  Easter family celebrations with RBC, 218
  frequent contact with RBC and family, 65
  on passion projects of RBC, 150
  photographs, *208*
  RBC celebrity roast, 227
  on RBC's loss of governor race, 119
Conlin, Roxanne Barton (RBC)
  adoption of Doug Klein, 69
  ancestry, 10
  animal welfare activism, 7, 31, 155–56, 177, *205,* 223, 250
  attorney career (*See also* Roxanne Conlin and Associates law firm)
    asbestos lawsuit, 140–44
    as assistant Iowa attorney general, 5, 32, 40, 43–54, 62, *115,* 248–49
    Association of Trial Lawyers of America and, 119–20, 124–26, 139–40, 144, 149–52, *203–4,* 249
    early employment, 5, 32, 38–40

with Galligan and Conlin law firm, 141–44

Inner Circle of Advocates, 7

inspiration for, 4, 10, 247

Iowa Code, gender-neutral rewording of, 57–58, 248–49

with James, Galligan and Conlin law firm, 129–36, 139–41

with James and Galligan law firm, 119, 124–29

mentorship to other attorneys, 155, 161

National Law Journal recognition of, 147, 163

national recognition as potential attorney general, 67–68

retirement, comments on, 228

as U.S. district attorney, viii, 5, 70, 73–76, 84–87, *116*

birth, 11

celebrity roast, 226–28

childhood, 3–4, 9–10, 13–23, *111–13*

children's births, 33, 40

civil rights activism, 4, 36–37, 43–54

death of parents, 168–69, *205*

drunk driving arrest, 145–47, 290*n*91

Easter family celebrations, 217–18

education

elementary and secondary, 16–22, 25

father's influence in, 17–19

law school, 5, 26, 28–30, 32–33, 37–38, *114*

master's degree in public administration, 79

undergraduate, 4, 25–26

feminism, 4–5, 28, 34, 54–55, 95–96, 165–66, 251

grandchildren, 137, 166, 200, *208–9*

Grease Monkey franchise, 122

Gridiron Show performance, 122

gubernatorial campaign (1982), viii, 92–110, 249

advertising, 105

Des Moines Register endorsement of RBC for governor, 107

election loss, 108–10, 119–21

exploratory effort for, 81–92

financial disclosure statement controversy, 100–103, 107, 109, 284*n*59

fundraising, 90, 102, 105–6, 109

Jefferson-Jackson Day dinner speech, 106–7, 109

photographs, *117–18*

polling data on, 6, 86, 89–90, 97–98, 103, 105, 108

televised debates, 103, 105–6

health issues, 144–45, 226–28, 242–43

hobbies, 31–32, 79–80, 121, 139, *211,* 218

in Iowa Women's Hall of Fame, 88

lecturing and speaking engagements, 71–72, 78, 84, 87, *203,* 230

marriage to Jim Conlin, 4, 26–27

personal home, 172–74

philanthropy, 222–28

photographs, *111–18, 203–11*

pilots license, 17, 61

political activism

Carter presidential campaign (1976), 72

Chisholm presidential campaign (1972), 55–56

donations to Democratic candidates, 221–22

early activism, 3–4, 34–37

Edwards presidential campaigns (2004, 2008), 219–21

Equal Rights Amendment and, 71–72

Glenn presidential campaign (1984), 123–24

IFA tax credits for housing project, 170–72

inspiration for, 4

Iowa Commission on the Status of Women, 56–58, 60

Iowa Democratic Party, chair of, 169–70, 174, 247–48

Iowa State Democratic Convention and, 35–36

Iowa Women's Political Caucus, 5, 57–62, 78, 248

Iowa Young Democrats, 35

Kennedy presidential campaign (1960), 4, 34–35

National Women's Political Caucus, 5, 61–62

Polk County Democrats Women's Event, 219

Polk County Young Democrats, 4, 35

real estate investments, 64, 100–101

relevance of life's work, 247–51

renewal of vows with Jim Conlin, 164–66

senate campaign (2010), 194–202, 249

advertising, 200

announcement of candidacy for, 196–97

conceding election, 201

fundraising, 198–200

photographs, *209*

polling data, 198, 200–201

staff, 197–98

sense of humor, viii, 61

seventy-fifth birthday party, *211*

travel and vacations, *208, 210,* 218

women's rights advocacy
as assistant attorney general, 34, 43–51
homemakers rights, 70–71
Iowa Code, rewording of, 57–58, 248–49
Legal Defense and Education Fund of NOW, 124
National Commission on the Observance of International Women's Year, 63, 68, 70–71
sex discrimination law course, teaching, 79
work ethic of, 5, 30, 51, 149
work-life balance, 64–67
Conlin Company, 80
Conlin Company Brokers, 136
Conlin Construction Services, 173
Conlin Family Iowa Charitable Giving Fund, 223
Conlin Properties, 215–17, 224
Conlin Securities Company, 136
conscription to military, 71
Consolidated Packaging Corporation, 76
Constant, John, 190
Cooper and Associates, 90
Cooper Homes, 63
Cotton, Bill, 50
Cox, Jeffrey, 92
Crandon Mill, 76
Crawford, Jerry
as family friend of RBC, 146, 165

on financial disclosure statement of RBC, 284n59
gubernatorial campaign of RBC, 81, 97, 108
Polk County Young Democrats, 35
RBC celebrity roast, 227
on RBC senate run, 196, 201
Critelli, Nick, 193–94
Cullison, Ben, 40, 43
Cullison, Pam, 40
Culver, Chet, 194, 238
Culver, John, 63
Cutler, Lynn, 58–59

D

Dahl, Harry, 39
Daley, Mark, 197–99
Davenport, Jean, 155–56
Davis, Evelyn, 37
Davis, Huebner, Johnson and Burt law firm, 32, 38–39
Dees, Morris, 152
Delahanty, Dolores, 62
Department of Health, Education, and Welfare, 72–73
Department of Justice, 178
Department of State, 63, 68
Des Moines City Council, 163–64
Des Moines Police Department, 47–48, 130–33
Des Moines Register
on drunk driving arrest of RBC, 146, 290n91
endorsement of RBC for governor, 107

on female police officers, 48

on Fitzgerald and gubernatorial campaign, 94

on gubernatorial campaign of RBC, 89, 98–99, 100–103

on job interview discrimination, 73

on Microsoft antitrust case, 180

political cartoons of RBC, 102, *118*

polling data for gubernatorial campaign (1982), 89

on puppy mills, 156

on senate race (2010), 198, 201

on sentencing of Walter Paustian, 75

on sexual harassment in workplace lawsuit, 132–33

on televised debates of RBC, 103

on UPS discrimination case, 160

on Volkswagen emission scandal, 235

Des Moines Tribune

on gubernatorial campaign of RBC, 90–91

on televised debates of RBC, 103

on women's rights advocacy of RBC, 43

Dickinson, Kaylyn and Jeffery, 230

Digital Research, Inc. (DRI)/ Novell, 190–92

disability lawsuits, 230–33

discrimination. *See also* gender discrimination

age and, 156–58, 233–34

in ATLA, 150–51

employees' liability for, 162–63

in employment, 43–45, 152–55, 238–46, 240–41

race and, 44, 51–53, 162–63, 233–34

sexual orientation and, 238–46

Doderer, Minnette, 58

domestic violence, 9, 12–13, 21, 23–24, 65, 225

Donahue Savings Bank, 75

Dorr, Amanda, 75, 248

Drake University, 5, 25–26, 28–30, 32–33, 225

dram shop law, 127–28

Drew, Thomas, 194

drug enforcement, 76–78, 249

Drug Enforcement Administration (DEA), 76, 78

due process rights, 232, 234, 240–41

Duff, Tom, 155, 174, 227

Dunn, Marty, 26

Dupre, Peggy, 154, 177

E

Easley, Jacquie, 227

East, Catherine, 63

Easter holiday celebrations, 217–18

Eastman Kodak, 6, 156–57

Eat Greater Des Moines, 224

Edwards, John, 219–21, 236–37

Ehlers, Beth, 217

Eichmann, Carmen, 141

Eisenhauer, Larry, 152–53

Elbert, David, 80, 84, 103

Ellwanger, Melinda, 155, 227, 248

EMILY's List, 222

Emma Grace (cat), 177

Emmerson, Donna, 154

English as a Second Language (ESL) classes, *210*, 223

Environmental Design Group, 173

Environmental Protection Agency (EPA), 76, 235–37

Equal Employment Opportunity Commission, 159

Equal Opportunity Employment Act (1972), 47

equal protection rights, 232, 234, 241

Equal Rights Amendment (ERA, 1972), 71–72

Equity Brokers Corporation, 136

Ernst, Joni, 109, 110

Espe, Roger, 134–36

Ewing, Pat, 154

F

Fagen, Cameron, 234–35

Falczynski, Danuta, 152–54

Falczynski v. Amoco Oil Co. (1995), 152–54

Farenthold, Frances "Sissy," 58–59, 61

Farley, Lin, 39

Federal Bureau of Investigation (FBI), 76, 78

The Feminine Mystique (Friedan), 34

feminism. *See also* women's rights

Iowa Women's Archives, 148, 290-91*n*95

National Organization of Women and, 54–55

of RBC, 4–5, 28, 34, 54–55, 95–96, 165–66, 251

second-wave feminist movement, 34, 152

sexual harassment awareness and, 39–40

Fennimore, Bruce, 84–85

Fenton, Ray, 156

Ferraro, Geraldine, 123–24

Fiedler, Paige

on generosity of RBC, 222

Iowa State University sexual harassment case, 181–84

as lead counsel in sexual orientation discrimination case, 242–44

photographs, *205, 211*

RBC celebrity roast, 227

teaching RBC to pump gasoline, 176

on work ethic of RBC, 149

Fiegen, Tom, 195, 199

Findley, Brenna, 238–39, 241–42, 245

Fine, Joanne, 121–22, *203*

Finkelstein, Regina "Gina" Barton (sister)

assistance in gubernatorial
campaign of RBC, 86

birth, 15

childhood, 23

cruise with RBC, *208,* 218

death of parents, 168–69

photographs, *113, 208*

summers with RBC and
family, 38, 65, 86

Finkenauer, Abby, 109

firefighter's rule, 127

First Group, 136

First Realty, 136

Fitzgerald, Jerry, 82, 86, 89–90,
92–94, 97–99

Fitzgibbons, John, 74, 75

Fitzpatrick, John, 99, 102, 104

Flagg, George, 163–64

Flansburg, Jim, 98, 106, 107

Flowerree, Ralph, 33

food recovery program, 224

Ford, Gerald, 71

Foster, Lionel, 233–34

Fourteenth Amendment, 50

Friedan, Betty, 28, 34, 54–55, 58

Friestad, Louis, 49, 51

G

Gail, Ricky, 126–29

Galligan, Michael, 76, 124–26,
140–44, *206*

Galligan and Conlin law firm,
141–44

Gallion, Arlene, 157–58

Gamble, Arthur, 159–60

Gammack, Julie, 95, 134

Gartner, Michael, 195, 240, 244

gas pipeline explosion (1978), 76

Gates, Bill, 188–89, 191–92

Gay and Lesbian Victory Fund,
222

Geduldig v. Aiello (1974), 50

Gegner, Norton, 122

gender discrimination
  in ATLA, 150–51
  in education, 5, 29–30
  in employer benefits, 46
  in employment, 5, 32, 45,
  47–48, 130–36
  Equal Opportunity
  Employment Act (1972), 47
  in housing, 57
  Iowa Civil Rights Act and,
  44–45
  in Iowa Code, 57–58
  in job interviews, 73
  in job titles, 48
  in law profession, 39
  in politics, 83, 88, 99, 109
  pregnancy discrimination,
  32–33, 38, 45, 49–51, 231–33
  in private country clubs,
  133–34
  RBC teaching law course on,
  79
  sexual harassment, 39–40,
  124, 130–33, 158–63, 181–84
  in wages, 134–36

gender-neutral language, 57–58,
248–49

gender roles

in Conlin home, 27, 32, 64

education of RBC and, 28–30

in political campaigns, 95

George F. Rutledge and Company, 134

Gerry, Dick, 140

G.I. Bill (1944), 13, 16

Gibbons, Laurie, 214–15

Ginger (cat), 177

Ginsburg, Ruth Bader, 45, 79

Giovannetti, E. J., 39

Girls Leadership Camp, 61

Glanton, Luther, Jr., 24

Glanton, Willie Stevenson, 36–37

Glass, Lynn, 182–84

Glenn, John, 119, 123

Godfrey, Chris, *211,* 238–46, 250

Gordon v. Microsoft (2002), 184–86

Grandstaff, David, 85

Grand View University, 234–35

Grassley, Charles "Chuck," 194–202, 222

Grasso, Ella, 82

Grease Monkey express lube shop, 122, 166

Great Depression, 10

Gridiron Show, 122

Griffin, Edna, 56

Griffin Building, Des Moines, 94, 176–78, 187–88, 194, 220, 310*n*45

Griggs, Leo, 52–53

Groff, Tom, 26, 27, 165

Gronstal, Mike, 227–28

gubernatorial campaign of RBC (1982), viii, 92–110, 249

advertising, 105

Des Moines Register endorsement of RBC for governor, 107

election loss, 108–10, 119–21

exploratory effort for, 81–92

financial disclosure statement controversy, 100–103, 107, 109, 284*n*59

fundraising, 90, 102, 105–6, 109

Jefferson-Jackson Day dinner speech, 106–7, 109

photographs, *117–18*

polling data on, 6, 86, 89–90, 97–98, 103, 105, 108

televised debates, 103, 105–6

H

Habush, Robert, 126

Hacker, Sally, 55

Hagen, Christopher, 75

Hagstrom, Richard "Rick," 181, 184–94, 235–36, 298*n*30

Halberstam, David, 9

Hamilton, Mark, ix

Hansen, Dennis, 173

Hanson, Linda, 5, 61, 62

Hanson, Thomas, 161

Harkin, Tom, 86, 89, 99, 222, 227

Harmon, Boyd, 53–54

Hartman, Patrick, 77

Harty, Frank, 241–42, 245

Harvard University, 42

Hawkins, Lex, 47

Hayes, Jody, 146

Hedberg, Art, 81

Heide, Wilma Scott, 55

Heinen, Linda, 49–51

Henry, Phylliss, 47–49, 85–86, 95

heroin, 77, 249

Hill, Anita, 151–52

Hockenberg, Bud, *206*

homemakers rights, 70–71

Homesteaders Life Insurance Company, 46

Houlihan, Patricia, 147

housing assistance, 224

Hubbell, Charlotte, 95

Hubbell, Fred, 95

Hudlow, Rebecca "Becky" Barton (sister)

    birth, 15

    childhood, 16–17, 23–25

    cruise with RBC, *208,* 218

    death of parents, 168–69

    photographs, *113, 116, 208*

Huebner, Fred, 39

Huebner, Sally, 46–47

Hughes, Harold

    gubernatorial campaign (1982), 86, 89–91

    Iowa Commission on the Status of Women and, 56

    photograph, *118*

    political wins, 35

    support of Ed Campbell for governor, 93–94

Hughes, John, 46, 50

Hume, Dan, 184

Hurd, Trudy, 43, *206*

Huston, Patti, 247

I

IBM, 156–57

ICRC. *See* Iowa Civil Rights Commission

IFA (Iowa Finance Authority), 170–72

IHYC (Iowa Homeless Youth Centers), 224

inheritance laws, 57, 249

Inner Circle of Advocates, 7

Invest in Iowa bond issue, 105

Iowa Beef Processors, 6, 161–62

Iowa Civil Rights Act (1965)

    on employment discrimination, 43–44

    on gender discrimination, 44–45, 51

    on pregnancy discrimination, 49, 51, 231

    on racial discrimination, 44, 52–53, 162

    on sexual harassment in workplace, 131, 133, 162–63, 184

    on sexual orientation discrimination, 241, 245

Iowa Civil Rights Commission (ICRC)

    on age and race discrimination, 51–52, 233–34

    on employment discrimination, 43–45

    on gender discrimination, 46–47

on pregnancy discrimination, 49–50

on sexual harassment in workplace, 131–32, 158–60

statute of limitations, 52, 159, 292n16

Iowa Coalition Against Domestic Violence, 225

Iowa Code, 57–58, 248–49

Iowa Commission on the Status of Women, 56–58, 60, 74, 88

Iowa Democratic Party
    funds donated by RBC, 222
    on gubernatorial campaign of RBC, 102
    Jefferson-Jackson Day dinner fundraiser, 106–7
    RBC as chair of, 169–70, 174, 247–48
    on RBC senate race, 194–95
    RBC's involvement in, 81–82, 85

Iowa Federation of Labor, 96

Iowa Finance Authority (IFA), 170–72

Iowa Homeless Youth Centers (IHYC), 224

Iowa Housing Corporation, 171

Iowa National Guard, 77–78, 249

Iowa Office of the Attorney General
    civil rights complaints to, 43–54
    election for Attorney General (1962), 36
    RBC as assistant state attorney general, 5, 32, 40, 43–54, 62, *115,* 248–49

IOWAREADS, 224

Iowa Realty, 63–64, 167

Iowa Republican Party, 242

Iowa State Democratic Convention, 35–36

Iowa State Education Association, 96

Iowa State University, 7, 76, 84, 181–82

Iowa Supreme Court
    on asbestos lawsuit, 142
    on attorney fee for RBC, 132–33
    civil rights cases, 44
    on dram shop law, 129
    on employee liability for discrimination, 163
    on employment discrimination, 240–41
    on Iowa citizens right to sue state officials, 241
    on medical malpractice, 154, 292n16
    on medical records requests for plaintiffs, 235
    on Microsoft antitrust lawsuit, 180
    on pregnancy discrimination, 50–51, 231, 233
    on racial discrimination, 52–53
    on same-sex marriage, 242
    on sexual harassment in workplace, 160, 183
    on Worth County Board of Supervisors, misuse of funds, 54

Iowa Trust Fund, 293n26

Iowa Women's Archives, 148, 290-91*n*95

Iowa Women's Hall of Fame, 88

Iowa Women's Political Caucus (IWPC), 5, 56–62, 78, 248

Iowa Young Democrats, 35

Iron Workers Local 67 v. Hart (1971), 44–45

Irwin, Jay, 141

J

Jackson, Thomas Penfield, 178

James, Dwight, 124–26, 140–41, 149

James, Galligan and Conlin law firm, 129–36, 139–41

James and Galligan law firm, 119, 124–29

Jamieson et al v. Volkswagen Group of America, Inc. (2015), 236–37

Jefferson-Jackson Day dinner, 106–7, 109

Jeris, Darlene, 170–72

Johns Manville Canada (asbestos supplier), 140, 142–43

Johnson, Kristin, 157–58

Johnson, Lyndon, 35

Johnson, Pauline, 55

Johnson, Shelley, 154

Johnston, Dan, 35

Johnston Community School District, 49–51

Junkins, Lowell, 90

Jurik, Nancy, 29

K

Keene Corporation, 7, 142–43

Kennedy, Edward "Ted," 99–100, 106

Kennedy, John, 4, 34–35, 56

Kepner, Diane, 46

Kerry, John, 220–21

Ketcham, Sara Quinn, 22–23, 27, 165, *206*

Kiernan, Michael, 194–96

King, Mary Lou, 34

Kirk, Maurice, 32–33

Klein, Doug (son)

    adoption by Conlins, 69

    career, 138, 213–14

    childhood, 66–67

    education, 81, 137–38

    marriage to Julie Harned, 166

    photographs, *117, 208*

    renewal of vows ceremony of parents, 165

    support for gubernatorial campaign of RBC, 97

Klein, Gavin (grandson), 166, 200, *208*

Klein, Geneva (granddaughter), 166, 200, *208*

Klein, Janette, 66–67

Klein, Julie Harned (daughter-in-law), 166, *208,* 214

Klein Films, 138

Klosener, Tiffany, 155

Knapp, Susan Terry, 121–22, *203,* 227

Knapp, William "Bill," 63–64, 89, 93–94, 250

Knight, Barron and Thelma, 142
Korean War, 18
Krause, Bob, 195, 199
Kum and Go, 224

L
labor unions, 44, 96, 105, 141, 232
Lackey, Patrick, 102
Lake, Sharon, 45, 50
LaMarca, George, 239, 241
Langner, Kathy, 292n16
Langner v. Simpson (1995), 292n16
Larsen, Pat, 190
Law Enforcement Assistance Administration, 48
Levinson, Larry, 72–73
Liapakis, Pam, 151
Limbaugh, Rush, 151
Lipsman, Paulee, *117,* 148, 197–98, 200, 229
Liptak, Adam, 189
Logemann, Kenneth, 53
Longstaff, Ronald, 162–63
Lynch, Deborah, 130–33
Lynch, Timothy, 130–31

M
Macri, Jan, 40
Madden, Alice Bernice. *See* Barton, Alice Bernice (mother)
Madden, Elizabeth "Bess" (grandmother), 10–11
Madden, William (grandfather), 10

Madison, Gerry, 162
Madison, Sheri Sawyer, 161–62
Mall, Ed, 78
Manville Corporation, 7
Martin, E. A., 140
Martin, John, 77
Martin, Susan, 29
Mason, Kären, 148
Massey Ferguson, 52
Mauss, Jean, 188, 193, 242–43
Maxwell, Michael, 141
May, Joseph, 77–78, 249
McCall, Brad, 240–41, 244, 246
McCall's magazine recognition of RBC, 67–68, 72
McCarthy, Judy, 50
McCormick, Mark, 171
McCown, Robert, 290-91n95
McElroy, Julie, 182–84
McFadden, Monica, 85, 94, 97–98, 123
McGlothlen, Condon, 152
McQuistion, Karen, 231–33
McWhorter, Larry, 87
medical malpractice, 154, 292n16
Microsoft, 7, 178–81, 184–94
Mid-America Pipeline Company, 76
Mid-Iowa Management Company, 80, 136
Miller, Frank, *118*
Miller, Tom, 86, 89, 91, 239
Mills, Bret, 217
minorities. *See* civil rights; discrimination; women's rights

Mondale, Walter, 123–24

Monohon, Linda, 134–36

Monroe, Johnny, 167–68

Montgomery, George, 33

Mooney, Tommy Joe, 20

Moss, Maggi, 146, 149, 155–56, 205, 246

Motley, Ron, 141

Mott, Thomas, 147

Mueller, Robert S., 237

Munn, Roger, 84

Munoz, Robert, 214

Myers, Herbert, 30

N

Nagle, Dave, 83

Nahra, John, 143

National Association for the Advancement of Colored People (NAACP), 4, 36–37

National Bar Association, 203

National Commission on the Observance of International Women's Year, 63, 68, 70–71

National Law Journal on RBC's career, 147, 163

National Organization of Women (NOW)
    Des Moines chapter, establishment of, 54–55
    founding of, 34
    funds donated by RBC, 222
    Legal Defense and Education Fund, 124
    sex discrimination lawsuit, 45
    State by State Guide to Women's Rights, 124

National Women's Political Caucus (NWPC)
    Equal Rights Amendment and, 72
    Iowa chapter of, 5, 57–62, 78, 248
    RBC's involvement in, 78
    RBC's run for president of, 61–62

Nations, Howard, 151

Neboda, Brian, 294n16

Nevins, Greg, 245

Newlin, Connie (stepdaughter-in-law), 95, 208, 213

Newlin, Debbie Conlin (stepdaughter)
    career, 137, 166, 212–13
    childhood, 66–67
    children, 137
    divorce from Kerry Anderson, 166
    education, 81, 137, 166, 213
    Grease Monkey franchise, 122
    marriage to Connie Newlin, 213
    marriage to Kerry Anderson, 137
    photographs, 117, 208
    renewal of vows ceremony of parents, 165
    support for gubernatorial campaign of RBC, 97

Nichols, Wendell, 47–48

Nickerson, Don, 75, 222–23

Nielsen, Christopher, 230

Nielsen, Merlin, 130–31

Nixon, Richard, 56

Noll, Roger, 185, 190

Northwest Iowa Mental Health Center, 294*n*16

Noun, Louise, 55, 56, 58, 148, 251

Novak, Joel, 135–36

NOW. *See* National Organization of Women

NWPC. *See* National Women's Political Caucus

O

Oakley, Brice, 57

Obama, Barack, 221

O'Berry, Toby, 224

Obradovich, Kathie, 196

Odell, Mary Jane, 91

Olsen, Rhoda Barton (sister)
    Alice Barton Scholarship program, 225
    birth, 15
    cruise with RBC, *208,* 218
    photographs, *113, 208*
    on work ethic of RBC, 30

Olson, LuAnn, 95, 105

Olson, Richard, 158–60

One Iowa, 197

Ordway, Gary, 30, 37

Overbaugh, Al, 78

Ovrom, Eliza, 75

Owen, Mike, 107

Owens, Edris "Soapy," 73

Owens, Roger, 73

P

PACs (political action committees), 199, 221–22

Palin, Sarah, 195

Pappas, Bill, 53

Park Cities Pet Sitter, 138, 215

Parr, Joan, 50

Parrish, Alfredo, 147, 222

Paustian, Walter, 75

Pavalon, Gene, 126

Pepper, Ron, 35

Perkins, Janis, 230–31

Phoenix Group, 163, 173

Picker, Jane, 45

Pickrell, Aaron, 219

pipeline explosion (1978), 76

Plymat, Kay, 55

political action committees (PACs), 199, 221–22

Polk County Democratic Party, 35–36

Polk County Democrats Women's Event, 219

Polk County Young Democrats, 4, 35, 247–48

polling data
    on attorney general race (1986), 129–30
    on gender in politics, 98, 109
    on governor race (1982), 6, 86, 89–90, 97–98, 103, 105, 108
    on senate race (2010), 198, 200–201

Porter, Phillis, 145

Powers, Dan, 74

pregnancy discrimination, 32–33, 38, 45, 49–51, 231–33

Pregnancy Discrimination Act (1978), 51

presidential campaigns, RBC's involvement in

    Carter (1976), 72

    Chisholm (1972), 55–56

    Edwards (2004,2008), 219–21

    Glenn (1984), 123–24

    Kennedy (1960), 4, 34–35

Presley, Elvis, 19–20

puppy mills, 155–56, *205, 292n23*

Q

Quad-City Times, on gubernatorial campaign (1982), 107

R

racial discrimination, 44, 52–53, 162–63, 233–34

rape, 57, 198, 229–30, 249

Ray, Dixy Lee, 82

Ray, Robert "Bob"

    Branstad and, 92, 110

    on financial disclosure statement of RBC, 101, 107

    Iowa Commission on the Status of Women, 56

    not seeking re-election (1982), 89–90, 92

    photographs, *207*

    support for IWPC, 59–60

Reagan, Ronald, viii, 70, 81

recession (1970s), 136

Redbook magazine recognition of RBC, 67, 72

Reddy, Helen, 152, *204*

Regency Management and Investment, 136–37, 163, 166

Regenwether, Mark, 232

Reiste, Robert, 88

Reno, Janet, 151

Reynolds, Kim, 109, 110, 239, 241, 246

Richards, Ann, 151

Richmond, Rhonda Barton (sister), 15, *113, 116, 208,* 218

Riley, Phil, 48

Riley Paint, Inc., 190

Rinderknecht, Norman, 144

Roberts, Sylvia, 45

Robinson v. Jacksonville Shipyards (1988), 124

Rose, Jack, 131

Rosenberg, Raymond, 78

Rosenberg, Scott, 188–92

Rosenfield, Dannie, 55

Rowan, Don, 82

Rowe, Audrey, 62

Roxanne and James Conlin Fund, 223

Roxanne Barton Conlin Papers, 148, 290-91n95

Roxanne Conlin and Associates law firm

    age and racial discrimination lawsuits, 156–58, 162–63, 233–34 bullying lawsuit, 234–35

disability discrimination lawsuit, 230–33

employment discrimination lawsuit, 152–55

IFA tax credit procedures, 170–72

Microsoft lawsuit, 178–81, 184–94

office in Griffin Building, 176–78, *207,* 310*n*45

puppy mill lawsuit, 155–56

sexual harassment lawsuits, 158–63, 181–84

sexual orientation discrimination lawsuit, 238–46

staff and clerks, 154–55

starting, 144

third party criminal negligence law, 198, 229–30

Volkswagen emission scandal lawsuit, 235–37

websites, 250

Ruckelshaus, Jill, 58–59

S

Saddoris, Kris, 215–17

same-sex marriage, 213, 242, 244

Scalise, Lawrence "Larry," 36

Scherle, Bill, 75, 77

Schinkle, Anna Marie, 29

Schlafly, Phyllis, 71–72

Selective Service and Training Act (1940), 13

senate campaign of RBC (2010), 194–202, 249

advertising, 200

announcement of candidacy for, 196–97

conceding election, 201

fundraising, 198–200

photographs, *209*

polling data, 198, 200–201

staff, 197–98

7-Eleven Food Stores, 127–28

Sex-Based Discrimination: Texts, Cases, and Materials (Davidson, Ginsburg, & Kay), 79

sexism. *See* gender discrimination; gender roles

sexual abuse, 230

sexual assault, 57, 198, 229–30, 249

sexual harassment, 39–40, 124, 130–33, 158–63, 181–84

sexual orientation discrimination lawsuit, 238–46

Shadduck, Ione, 58

Sherman Antitrust Act (1890), 178

Shirley, JoAnn, 29

Simmons, Cathryn, 103–9, 120

Simpson, Floyd, 292*n*16

Simpson, Sumner, 140

Skeffington's Formal Wear, 190

Smith, Andrew, 6, 186–88, 192

Smith, Mary Louise, 58–60, 62

Smith, William, 87

Somepeoplejustneedtobesued.com, 250

Sovern, Ted, 86

Spencer Municipal Hospital, 294*n*16

Spina, Marilyn, 81

Stanbrough, Gene, 120, 136

Stanbrough Realty, 63

Starr, Hale, 121–22, 124, 189, 191, *203*

State by State Guide to Women's Rights (NOW), 124

stay-at-home mothers and wives, 70–71

Steinem, Gloria, 58

Stiglitz, Joseph, 189

Stockton, Dawn, 153, 155

Streit, Michael, 132–33

Stuart, William, 75

student loan defaults, 75

Suethebadguys.com, 250

Sumner Simpson Papers, 140

Supreme Court. *See* Iowa Supreme Court; United States Supreme Court

Survivors (women's support group), 121–22

survivor's benefits, 57, 249

Swartzwalder, Louise, 55, 62, 71

Symoniak, Elaine, 121–22

T

Tatel, David, 73

Tauke, Tom, 86

third party criminal negligence, 198, 229–30

Thomas, Clarence, 152

Trout, Brent, 234

Tuel, Larry, 171

Tulchin, David, 191

Tully, Rob, 219

Turner, Richard
as Attorney General, 40
discharging employment of RBC, 62
encouragement of RBC's involvement in NWPC, 62
Iowa Civil Rights Commission, RBC as prosecutor for, 43
as U.S. district attorney, 87
on work ethic of RBC, 5, 51

U

United Auto Workers, 105

United Parcel Service (UPS), 7, 158–63, 232–33

United States v. Microsoft (2001), 188

United States Supreme Court
on pregnancy discrimination, 50–51, 232–33
on sexual harassment in workplace, 162

University of Iowa, 7, 139, 148, 217, 230

University of Iowa College of Law, 78–79, 167

University of Iowa Libraries, 292*n*95

V

Van Werden, Larry, 30, 38

Variety – the Children's Charity of Iowa, 225–28

VEISHEA, 84

Vidal, Dagmar, 59

Vietnam War, 35

Villisca Commercial Club, 84

Vilsack, Tom, 169–70, 238

Vivian, Wendy, 162

Volkswagen emission scandal lawsuit, 7, 235–37

Von Stein, Joan, 60

W

Wahlert, Teresa, 238–39, 241

Wakonda Club, Des Moines, 133–34

Wallace, Henry C., 172–73

Waller, Dale, 145–46

Wallis, Rich, 192–93

Ward, Laura, 85, 105, 106–7, 120, 248

Warner, Michael, 152

Watkins, Virginia, 54–55

Weeks, Leona, 45

Weeks v. Southern Bell (1966), 45

Weinburg, Lew, 171

Weitz Construction Company, 44

welfare benefits, 60

Wengert, Patricia, 171

Western Convenience Stores, 127–29

Whitgraf, Cristine, 56

Whitney, Tom
  gubernatorial campaign of RBC, 82, 93–94, 97–101, 104–8
  on meeting RBC, 247
  Polk County Young Democrats, 35

Wickett, Bill, 141

Wickett, Linda, 137, 154, 177

Wiley, Jim, 100

Wilson, Cristine, 56, 58, 85

Wilson, Pamela, 55

Wilson-Sinclair Company, 52–53

Wilson-Sinclair Company v. Griggs (1973), 53

Wimer, Steven, 295n26

Women's Coalition, 72

Women's Law Fund, 45

women's rights. *See also* gender discrimination; National Organization of Women
  abortion rights, 96, 105
  advocacy of RBC as assistant attorney general, 34, 43–51, 130–37
  homemakers rights, 70–71
  Iowa Civil Rights Act and, 44
  Iowa Code, gender-neutral rewording of, 57–58, 248–49
  Iowa Commission on the Status of Women, 56–58, 60, 74, 88
  Iowa Women's Political Caucus (IWPC), 5, 56–61, 78, 248
  National Commission on the Observance of International Women's Year, 63, 68, 70–71
  National Women's Political Caucus (NWPC), 5, 57–62, 72, 78

network of people and
organizations for, 45–46,
54–61

Women's Rights Law Reporter, 45

women's support group, 121–22

Wood, Blair, 54

Woodburn, Chester, 134

World War II, 11–13

Worth County Board of
Supervisors, 53–54

Y

Yepsen, David

on financial disclosure
statement of RBC, 284*n*59

on gubernatorial campaign
(1982), 88, 94, 98–99, 110

on RBC's qualifications for
U.S. district attorney, 74

Young v. United Parcel Service
(2015), 232–33

Youth Shelter Services, 224

Z

Zagnoli, Theresa, 189

Zamora, Heriberto, 52